The Attainment Agenda

The Attainment Agenda

State Policy Leadership in Higher Education

Laura W. Perna and Joni E. Finney

Foreword by Patrick M. Callan

Johns Hopkins University Press
Baltimore

Printed in the United States of America on acid-free paper
9 8 7 6 5 4 3 2 1

Johns Hopkins University Press
2715 North Charles Street
Baltimore, Maryland 21218-4363
www.press.jhu.edu

Library of Congress Cataloging-in-Publication Data

Perna, Laura W.
The attainment agenda : state policy leadership in higher education / Laura W. Perna, Joni E. Finney ; foreword by Patrick M. Callan.
pages cm
Includes bibliographical references and index.
ISBN 978-1-4214-1406-5 (hardcover) — ISBN 978-1-4214-1407-2 (electronic) — ISBN 1-4214-1406-6 (hardcover) — ISBN 1-4214-1407-4 (electronic)
1. Higher education and state—United States—States. 2. Higher education and state—United States—States—Case studies. 3. Education, Higher—United States—States. 4. Education, Higher—United States—States—Case studies. 5. Educational attainment—United States—States. 6. School management and organization—United States—States. I. Finney, Joni E. II. Title.
LC173.P47 2014
378.73—dc23 2013043574

A catalog record for this book is available from the British Library.

Special discounts are available for bulk purchases of this book. For more information, please contact Special Sales at 410-516-6936 or specialsales@press.jhu.edu.

Johns Hopkins University Press uses environmentally friendly book materials, including recycled text paper that is composed of at least 30 percent post-consumer waste, whenever possible.

Contents

Foreword

Patrick M. Callan

The week *The Attainment Agenda* was completed and sent to the publisher, the Organisation for Economic Co-operation and Development (OECD) issued the most recent in its series of reports comparing national education performance. Once again the OECD documented, as it has for most of the past decade, the relatively weak higher education attainment rates of young American adults. The United States ranked twelfth in the proportion of 25- to 34-year-olds who have achieved postsecondary degrees and other credentials. In contrast to the pattern in most nations that perform better, younger Americans—the core of the nation's workforce for the next three to four decades—acquired less education than older workers. This generational gap leaves the United States at a competitive disadvantage in the knowledge-based global economy that increasingly requires education and training beyond high school for employment that supports a middle-class standard of living and that relentlessly punishes undereducated individuals, communities, states, and nations with diminished economic opportunity and reduced standards of living. It is clear that the United States faces educational opportunity and workforce deficits.

If our nation is to be competitive educationally and economically—or to regain international preeminence, as President Barack Obama has advocated—we must improve college participation and attainment under conditions that differ markedly from those of the second half of the twentieth century, when the United States was the global leader. These new circumstances include significant demographic shifts, constrained governmental and private finances, and the opportunities and issues raised by the emergence of digital technologies and online education. The transformation of American higher education required to educate unprecedented numbers of Americans, many from historically unserved and underserved ethnic and economic groups, to higher levels of postsecondary attainment will be profound. The challenge is of at least the magnitude of earlier transformations in the missions and responsibilities of colleges and universities in the late nineteenth and mid-twentieth centuries.

Government initiatives have been central to each of these historic transitions, particularly those that extended college opportunity to new and more heterogeneous populations. In these earlier transformations, including the establishment of land-grant universities in the nineteenth century and research universities and institutions of mass higher education in the decades after World War II, government played a critical role. Effective state and federal policy is no less a necessary condition for the transformation of higher education to serve the needs of American society in the twenty-first century.

In contrast to most of our international economic and educational competitors, higher education policy in the United States is primarily the responsibility of states, not the national government. In the past, the preeminence of the United States in higher education was attributed in part to the diffusion of authority and responsibility for colleges and universities among fifty states and between public and private institutions. While the federal government has a critical role in supporting student financial assistance and research, the responsibility for assuring college opportunity and for addressing the deficits or gaps in college participation and attainment resides principally with states.

These studies of five very different states and the analyses of broader implications offered in this volume bring together two of the core issues of education policy in the second decade of the twenty-first century: the performance of higher education, and the effectiveness of state public policy in influencing performance. This study is particularly important because it captures demographic and economic changes that are reshaping expectations of higher education. Pervasive pressures for change have reopened, for the first time in several generations, fundamental issues: who colleges should serve, how many college graduates the nation and the states need, and who should pay for postsecondary education and training. These rich and insightful state studies describe the policy dynamics of five states as they seek to cope—sometimes coming to grips with, sometimes floundering, and sometimes failing to even raise the most crucial issues—with their responsibilities for higher education.

The central lesson I take from these cases and the analysis provided by Laura Perna and Joni Finney is that state policy is highly consequential to the performance of colleges and universities in meeting societal needs for individual opportunity and national and state prosperity. State policies that focus governmental and institutional efforts on broad public goals, particularly on improving college readiness of high school graduates and higher rates of participation and attainment in postsecondary education, can stimulate improved results in these areas. However, the influence of policy on performance can be negative as well as positive: higher education performance can be undermined by outdated or ill-conceived policies or, not infrequently, by the neglect of important educational, social, and economic issues. In all cases, whether by intention or omission, state policy not only matters but exercises powerful influence on higher education opportunity and attainment.

The case studies discussed in this volume show that, as is true for the nation as a whole, the underperformance of higher education in these states was exacerbated but not caused by the Great Recession and its aftermath. Therefore, economic recovery and return to the *status quo ante* would not in itself assure the improvements needed for opportunity or international competitiveness.

From this research, I also conclude that none of the states studied have established or sustained a policy basis for determining the student share of college costs, although one of the states, Maryland, has made considerable progress. One consequence is that tuition tends to escalate in hard economic times and then to be somewhat mitigated when the economy and state appropriations improve. College affordability has declined as a result. Where statewide plans for higher education do exist, most fail to take into account the likelihood of fluctuations in the economy and state revenues. Such plans set priorities that are not sustainable in recessions, when priorities are most needed. And governance of higher education serves the public interest best when decision making is characterized by checks and balances that allow government, higher education professionals, and market forces their respective roles, maintaining a healthy tension rather than deferring to institutions, government, or the market.

It is now mathematically impossible for the nation and for most states, including those examined in these studies, to achieve an internationally competitive workforce unless historically underserved low-income and ethnic groups enroll and graduate from college in significantly greater numbers. In the past, although American society incurred moral and civic costs for excluding these groups from college opportunity, the American economy was generally prosperous. The twenty-first century economy will extract severe economic penalty for undereducation of significant portions of the population. These state studies make clear for policymakers and for institutions of higher education that the issues of equity, social justice, competitiveness, and educational productivity have converged and can no longer be effectively addressed in isolation.

States, including those studied in this research, as with colleges and universities, may need more fundamental reexamination of their policy and funding frameworks than most have yet undertaken. The case studies describe the crisis of an old—and in its time highly successful—order. Yet neither colleges nor states seem to have confronted the full extent of changes in public policy and educational practice that may be needed to navigate the challenges of the twenty-first century.

The national problem of higher education underperformance must be confronted state by state. These detailed and rigorous state studies describe the various contexts—educational, political, economic, demographic, and historical—in which policy solutions must be sought. Federal policy and philanthropic support can and must contribute to these efforts. The case studies can help both government and foundations to better understand the diversity and complexities of state contexts and, hopefully, increase skepticism of "one size fits all" policy templates.

Finally, this study comes at a time of growing national concern over stagnating social mobility, income inequality, the "hollowing out" of the American middle class, and perceived decline of opportunity. It seems appropriate to ask of each state, of the nation, and of our colleges and universities whether American higher education in our times is an enabler of or an impediment to opportunity and mobility, a countervailing force to social and economic stratification or one of its causes, a party to the implicit social contract that has supported the middle class and middle-class aspirations or a contributor to its unraveling. This volume does not purport to offer answers to these questions, but it certainly provides grist for a critical national debate. Laura Perna and Joni Finney and their colleagues have made an important contribution to our understanding of state higher education policy that has implications beyond the five states they studied. Even more important, this book contributes to the evolving national discourse on the public purposes and responsibilities of states and of institutions of higher education and to the future of educational and economic opportunity in America.

Acknowledgments

This book represents the culmination of a research project that began in fall 2009. As described in chapter 3, we collected and analyzed data for this study from many sources, including a review of existing documents, reports, and legislation; descriptive analyses of existing state and national data sources; and interviews with numerous individuals. We very much appreciate the willingness of these individuals to share information and speak candidly with our team. We value the time and perspectives they shared with us.

The research project benefited from the contributions of many other individuals. Patrick Callan gave us our initial charge: to build on the state-by-state report cards produced by the National Center for Public Policy and Higher Education biennially between 2000 and 2008 (*Measuring Up*) to learn how public policy explains a state's higher education performance. Pat not only reviewed earlier drafts of various versions of documents that ultimately became this manuscript but also assisted with the data collection in Georgia, Illinois, and Washington. We benefited greatly from his insightful reactions and perspectives at many critical junctures in this project.

The conceptualization of the project was also guided by input from our advisory board: Julie Davis Bell, Patrick Kelly, Paul Lingenfelter, Richard Richardson, and Jane Wellman. Other individuals who gave helpful feedback on early drafts of the conceptualization and five state chapters include James Hearn, Rachel Hise, Ross Hodel, Dennis Jones, Harrison Keller, Patrick Kelly, David Longanecker, Aims McGuinness, David Spence, Richard Wagner, and William Zumeta. Through public presentations at the annual meetings of the Association for the Study of Higher Education and the State Higher Education Executive Officers and gatherings sponsored by the Baltimore Education Research Consortium, the Pennsylvania Commission for Community Colleges, Michigan State University, Stanford University, the University of Illinois at Urbana-Champaign, the University of Michigan, and other organizations, we received reactions that productively advanced our work.

We are also grateful to an exceptional team of students who assisted in countless dimensions of this large, complex, multiyear project. From their first day of their doctoral studies, Michael Armijo, Jamey Rorison, and Awilda Rodriguez assisted with many essential tasks, including identifying and organizing our multiple sources of data and constructing descriptive "briefing books" for each state. They also participated in the data collection and analysis for the five state studies. We are grateful for the care and effort they invested in this project.

Others contributed invaluable assistance at other times in this journey. Patrick Kelly helped train our team about the availability and use of sources of state-level data and provided additional technical support. Christopher Miller, Noreen Savelle, and Lori King assisted with many of the logistical details associated with our site visits, and Scott Stimpfel assisted with data verification. Thad Nodine provided editorial assistance on earlier versions of several state studies, and Jennifer Moore assisted with final formatting. Jon Wallace edited earlier versions of our five state reports into one- to five-page "public" documents that we disseminated and posted on the project website.

We received financial support for this project from the National Center for Public Policy and Higher Education (which received its funding from Lumina Foundation and the Bill & Melinda Gates Foundation). Michael, Jamey, and Awilda's involvement in the project was supported in part by the Institute of Education Sciences, U.S. Department of Education, through Grant #R305B090015 to the University of Pennsylvania. The opinions expressed are those of the authors and do not represent the views of funding agencies.

The Attainment Agenda

Chapter 1

Improving Higher Education Attainment of All Students

A National Imperative

Once a world leader, the United States has fallen behind other nations in the educational attainment of its population. Although the percentage of adults age 45 to 54 who hold at least a baccalaureate degree is higher in the United States than in other Organisation for Economic Co-operation and Development (OECD) nations, the United States now ranks below several other nations, including Norway, the Netherlands, Korea, New Zealand, Denmark, and Sweden, in the share of adults age 25 to 34 who hold this credential. While the U.S. invested heavily in the educational attainment of earlier generations, other nations have been investing substantially in their younger populations. Essentially, educational attainment has stalled in the United States, with about 30% of adults in each age cohort holding at least a bachelor's degree. Over this same period, however, educational attainment has been rising dramatically in some other nations. In Korea, for example, 34% of adults age 25 to 34 now hold at least a baccalaureate degree, up from just 17% of adults age 45 to 54.[1]

Given trends in educational attainment and population growth, for 55% of U.S. adults age 25 to 64 to have at least an associate's degree by 2020—the current performance of the best-performing nation—the United States must increase annual degree production by about 8% per year.[2] Yet even an 8% annual increase may be insufficient for the United States to once again lead the world, since this estimate assumes that educational attainment in other countries will not continue to rise.

The Importance of Educational Attainment to Continued Prosperity

Unless educational attainment improves, workers in the United States will lack the educational skills and training required to meet the workforce demands of a global knowledge economy. Nearly all of the 30 fastest growing occupations (in terms of percentage increases) require at least some college, while nearly all of the 30 occupations experiencing the largest declines require no education beyond high school.[3] Drawing on data from the Bureau of Labor of Statistics and research about the continued "upskilling" of current jobs, Anthony Carnevale, Nicole Smith, and Jeffrey Strohl project that 63% of jobs will require education beyond high school in 2018, up from 56% in 1992 and just 28% in 1973.[4] This increase in educational requirements is attributable primarily to an expansion in the skills required for existing occupations, with smaller shares of the increase attributable to the creation of new occupations and growth of occupations that already required postsecondary education. Carnevale and colleagues further project that, at the current rate of degree production, the demand for workers with at least an associate's degree will exceed the supply by 3 million by 2018. Eliminating this deficit will require raising annual degree production by 10%.

A focus on higher education's role in promoting workforce readiness is also necessary because of the need to replace the knowledge and skills of retiring baby boomers, the largest and most educated generation in history.[5] Baby boomers, individuals born between 1946 and 1964, represent nearly 40% of the total population; they began reaching typical retirement age in 2011. The retirement of so many educated workers will likely contribute to labor market shortages, as Anderson and Kennedy assert: "While the statistics vary dramatically (estimates of a labor shortage as early as 2010 range from 800,000 workers to almost 10 million), the inescapable fact remains that the 'baby bust' generation numbers 11 million fewer bodies than the Boomers. Even with productivity gains, technological changes, outsourcing options, and immigration inflows, there simply may not be enough workers to fill available jobs."[6]

Although some argue that the United States suffers from an over-supply of college-educated workers, others counter that the growing wage premium paid to workers who have a college education rather than a high school diploma nullifies this claim.[7] In short, if a college education did not improve workers' productivity, employers would not pay college-educated workers higher wages.[8] The OECD agrees that more, not less, education is required. In its 2012 *Education at a Glance* report, the OECD concludes that recent rapid increases in the educational attainment of most OECD nations have not led to an oversupply of college-educated workers, arguing: "[T]here is little evidence that this expansion has led to an excess supply; on the contrary, most indicators suggest that the expansion of higher education has not kept pace with the demand for those skills. As a result, there is a widening gap in employment prospects among individuals with different levels of education and increasing earnings differentials in most countries."[9]

Clearly, a nation or a state within a nation cannot be prosperous without a highly educated population. The OECD argues that education is critical to ensuring that the workforce has the skills required for national economic growth.[10] Along the same lines, Daron Acemoglu, the Killian Professor of Economics at Massachusetts Institute of Technology, and James Robinson, the David Florence Professor of Government at Harvard University, conclude that a key force differentiating nations that are economically prosperous from nations that are poor is the extent to which a nation promotes the educational attainment of its population. These scholars stress the high price that a nation pays for a poorly educated population. Nations with low levels of educational attainment not only "fail to mobilize their nascent talent" but also fail to realize the economic growth that comes from "encourag[ing] technological innovation, invest[ing] in people, and mobiliz[ing] the talents and skills of a large number of individuals."[11]

Raising our nation's educational attainment is also necessary to counteract the remarkable and growing income inequality that exists in the United States.[12] Many forces contribute to the growth in inequality in this nation, including the decline in public pensions and organized labor, and changes in tax policies. But among the recognized remedies for increasing income inequality is enabling individuals to earn high-quality postsecondary education credentials and degrees that provide meaningful and well-compensated employment.

Even though the United States is one of the world's wealthiest nations, its income inequality is now greater than that of many other nations. Moreover, the magnitude of this inequality has increased in recent years. A number of indicators illustrate the inequality. For instance, at the extreme end of the continuum, nearly one-fifth (18%) of taxable income in 2008, up from 8% in 1980, went to the top 1% of Americans; the top 1% holds an even greater share of the total distribution of wealth in the aftermath of the Great Recession.[13] In 2008 the disposable income of the top 10% of households in the United States was six times greater than the income of the bottom 10% of households. The United States has greater inequality on this measure than all other OECD nations except for Turkey, Israel, Chile, and Mexico (not the group of nations to which the U.S. tends to compare itself).[14] Moreover, attention only to measures of income inequality understates the magnitude of these gaps, given the inequality that exists in many other measures of wealth, including access to affordable health care.[15]

The degree of income inequality, along with stagnation of economic mobility for middle- and low-income Americans, not only makes it difficult for many Americans to pay for postsecondary education but also creates deep political divides.[16] The magnitude of income inequality in the United States also threatens continued economic stability and growth and has potentially negative consequences for our nation's democracy and global influence.[17] If the basic American compact that success comes from working hard and "playing by the rules" is fundamentally broken, it is not hard to imagine the eventual civil unrest that might follow.[18] As Nobel Prize–winning economist Joseph E. Stiglitz succinctly concludes, "Of all the costs imposed on our society by the top 1 percent, perhaps the greatest is this: the erosion of our sense of identity in which fair play, equality of opportunity, and a sense of community are so important."[19]

Reducing Inequality in Higher Education Attainment

The United States cannot achieve the levels of educational attainment required to reach international competitiveness goals or workforce demands without reducing the profound gaps in attainment that persist across groups and improving the educational attainment of Blacks and Hispanics, individuals from low-income families, and individuals living in countless underserved areas within states across the nation, including many inner cities and rural areas. Although research and other reports commonly highlight persisting differences in attainment based on demographic characteristics, our case studies also point to the importance of closing gaps based on geography, since higher educational attainment continues to vary dramatically based on place of residence.

Despite decades of attention from public policymakers, practitioners, and other concerned individuals, college-related outcomes vary widely across groups. For instance, although college enrollment rates have increased for all income groups, the likelihood of earning a college degree continues to rise dramatically with family income. Data from one longitudinal study show that only 11% of adults whose parents had been in the lowest-income quintile earned a college degree, compared with 53% of adults whose parents had been in the top-income quintile.[20] Between 1998 and 2008, college enrollment rates of recent high school graduates trended upward for those in the lowest two quintiles: from 51% to 55% for those in the lowest quintile and from 51% to 57% for those in the second lowest quintile.[21] Yet even with these improvements, the share of recent high school graduates enrolled in college was still 25 percentage points lower for those in the lowest than for those in the highest family income quintile in 2008: 55% versus 80%.[22]

Trends in college enrollment by race/ethnicity show a similar pattern of some progress but remaining gaps. Race/ethnicity is related to, but not perfectly correlated with, income. Average incomes are lower for Blacks and Hispanics than for Whites, but not all Blacks and Hispanics have low incomes and not all Whites have high incomes.[23] Between 1990 and 2010, the share of high school graduates age 18 to 24 who were enrolled in degree-granting institutions rose from 33% to 46% among Blacks, from 29% to 44% among Hispanics, and from 40% to 49% among Whites.[24] Despite these increases, the share of individuals who enrolled in college immediately after graduating from high school continues to be lower among Blacks and Hispanics than among Whites: 62% and 60% versus 71% in 2010.[25] Because of these racial/ethnic differences in college enrollment as well as racial/ethnic group differences in other higher education outcomes, educational attainment also continues to be substantially lower for Blacks and Hispanics than for Whites. In 2009 only 18% of Blacks and 13% of Hispanics age 25 and older held at least a bachelor's degree, compared with 31% of Whites and 49% of Asians.[26]

Demographic trends underscore the necessity of improving attainment—especially among Hispanics, who not only average low levels of educational attainment but also are one of the nation's fastest growing racial/ethnic groups. Non-Whites increased their representation among the total U.S. population by 29% over the past decade, rising from 31% of the total in 2000 to 36% in 2010.[27] Between 2000 and 2010, nearly all (92%) of the nation's population growth was among Hispanics, Blacks, and Asians rather than Whites.[28] Between 2005–6 and 2024–25, the numbers of students attending the nation's public high schools (grades 9 to 12) are projected to increase considerably among Hispanics (by 108%) and Asians (by 74%) and modestly for Blacks (13%) but decline by 11% among Whites.[29] In 2010, racial/ethnic "minority" groups already represented at least 50% of the population—raising questions about the continued appropriateness of the term "minority"—in two of the nation's largest states, California (60%) and Texas (55%), as well as in the District of Columbia (65%), Hawaii (77%), and New Mexico (60%). Non-Whites now represent more than 40% of the population in a number of other states, including Arizona (42%), Florida (42%), Georgia (44%), Maryland (45%), Mississippi (42%), Nevada (46%), New Jersey (41%), and New York (42%).[30]

Clearly, the United States cannot achieve the increases in educational attainment that are required to meet workforce demands and international competitiveness goals without also closing the gaps in educational attainment based on race/ethnicity, family income, and other demographic characteristics, as well as those based on geography. Reducing inequality in higher education outcomes is essential if the nation is to achieve the improvements in educational attainment required for the United States to prosper in a global, knowledge-based society.

Closing these persisting gaps is also important for reasons of efficiency since they cause unacceptable systemic and problematic waste of resources in our educational system. As Acemoglu and Robinson and other observers suggest in their assessment of the forces that contribute to economic prosperity of nations, one source of inefficiency results from the lack of college participation among some capable individuals.[31] When capable individuals do not enroll, neither the individuals nor society realizes the many market and non-market benefits that come from greater levels of educational attainment.

A second source of inefficiency is the high rate of failure at many stages of the educational attainment pathway. Students, families, schools, colleges and universities, the federal and state governments, and many other entities invest considerable financial and non-financial resources into the education of individuals who do not complete their academic programs or move on to maximize their academic potential. About 72% of students who first enrolled in a private non-profit college or university in 2006, 61% of students who first enrolled in a public four-year college or university, 43% of students who first enrolled in a four-year for-profit institution, and 36% of students who first enrolled in a public two-year college completed a certificate or degree within six years.[32] The American Institutes for Research estimated that in just one year, and for only one cohort of students (i.e., those who first enrolled full-time in fall 2002), the current (problematically low) six-year bachelor's degree completion rates were associated with $3.8 billion in lost earnings to individuals, $566 million in lost federal income taxes, and $164 million in lost state income taxes.[33] Individuals and society deserve a better return on their investments.

Clear and Substantial Benefits of Higher Education for Individuals

Persisting gaps in educational attainment across groups are also problematic from the perspective of fairness.[34] Americans have long believed that higher education is an engine of opportunity, providing a mechanism for anyone—regardless of family income, skin color, or place of residence—to attain economic and social prosperity. But variations in educational achievement based on these characteristics translate into differential access to the many benefits that are increasingly bestowed on individuals with postsecondary credentials and degrees. Because of these differences, the countless economic and social benefits that accrue to those with higher levels of education are unequally distributed across the U.S. population.

Among the most visible benefits received by those with a college education is an increase in earnings. For full-time, year-round workers, lifetime earnings (i.e., over a 40-year period) are expected to be about 66% higher for bachelor's degree recipients than for high school graduates.[35] Although earnings continue to be higher for men than for women, earnings increase with educational attainment regardless of gender. In 2009, median annual earnings of year-round, full-time workers were about 60% higher for men and women who had a bachelor's degree ($62,440 and $46,830, respectively) than for men and women who had finished only high school ($39,480 and $29,150, respectively).[36]

Employment rates increase and unemployment rates decline with the level of educational attainment. For instance, for adults age 25 and older in the first quarter of 2010, labor force participation rates were substantially higher for both men and women who had attained at least a bachelor's degree than for those who had completed only high school (82% versus 72% for men; 73% versus 53% for women). Conversely, only 4.6% of those with at least a bachelor's degree were unemployed, compared with 9.7% of those who had completed only high school.[37] Moreover, the benefits of higher educational attainment to employment persist even in an economic downturn. During the Great Recession, individuals age 21 to 24 who had a bachelor's degree experienced fewer job losses, less loss of jobs requiring a college education, and smaller wage declines than individuals age 21 to 24 who held only a high school diploma.[38]

The earnings premium associated with holding a college degree is not only substantial but has also grown over the past few decades.[39] In one quantification of this growth, Massachusetts Institute of Technology economist David Autor estimates that workers with a bachelor's degree earned 95% more per hour than workers with a high school diploma in 2008, a noteworthy increase over the 50% earnings premium in 1980, attributing the growing wage benefit associated with holding a bachelor's degree to both increases in the earnings of workers with college degrees and declines in the earnings of those without.[40]

Experts disagree on whether the observed difference in earnings between those with and those without a college education over- or understates the true magnitude of the gap. Some of the observed difference in earnings based on educational attainment is unquestionably attributable to other differences between individuals, including differences in motivation, ambition, and academic ability.[41] In other words, individuals who earn a college degree would receive higher earnings even without the degree because they have greater self-motivation and other characteristics that are valued by employers. Nonetheless, although "ambition" is difficult to measure, research suggests that the observed earnings premium associated with earning a college degree is reduced but not eliminated after taking into account differences between the characteristics of individuals who do and do not complete college.[42]

Moreover, as other scholars argue, the observed earnings premium for college graduates relative to high school graduates may actually understate the benefits that result from earning a college degree. College graduates realize not only higher wages but also other benefits that improve their financial well-being, including greater likelihood of being employed, a tendency to work more hours per week and per year, and greater likelihood of receiving nonwage benefits, including paid time-off and employer-provided retirement contributions.[43] College graduates also realize many non-market benefits, including improved health, longer life, greater likelihood of lifelong learning, and more informed purchases.[44] The importance of college in conferring these benefits has likely increased as the role of labor unions has declined. Union membership is typically associated with higher wages (especially for unskilled, blue-collar, and less-educated workers), better working conditions, and greater fringe benefits such as paid time off, health insurance, and retirement plans. But both the number and share of employed workers who are members of unions have declined over time. In 2003, union members numbered just 15.8 million (down from a high of 21.0 million in 1979) and 11.5% of all employed workers (down from 28.3% of all employed workers in 1954).[45]

Having some education beyond high school is increasingly required for a middle-class income and upward economic mobility.[46] The likelihood of adult children having family income or total wealth that exceeds that of their parents is higher for those who have completed at least 16 years of schooling than for those who have not. For instance, 42% of adult children with a college degree, but only 21% of those without a college degree, had $100,000 more wealth (defined as total assets less debts) than their parents. Among those who were raised in the bottom quintile of the income distribution, 59% of those with a college degree and only 19% of those without a college degree had at least $100,000 more wealth than their parents.[47]

Moreover, over the past four decades, individuals without a college education have become increasingly concentrated among those with the lowest incomes. More than half (59%) of high school dropouts and a third (35%) of high school graduates were in the lower-income strata in 2007, considerably higher shares than in 1970 (39% and 22%, respectively). Over the same period, those with a bachelor's or graduate degree represented a growing share of those with the highest incomes. In 2007, 48% of individuals with a bachelor's degree and 61% of individuals with a graduate degree were in the upper-income income strata, a greater concentration than in 1970 (37% and 41% respectively).[48]

Higher education is especially important to the upward economic mobility of individuals from the lowest-income families. Analyses of data from the Panel Study of Income Dynamics published by the Brookings Institution show that nearly half of adults who were from the poorest families and did not attain a college education also ended up poor. In contrast, only 16% of college-educated adults from the poorest families ended up as poor as their parents.[49] At the same time, a college degree is virtually required to gain access to the highest-income strata. Only 5% of adult children from the poorest families who did not earn a college degree had incomes in the top quintile, compared with 19% of adults from the poorest families who did earn a college degree.[50]

The Convergence of Individual and Public Benefits

Clearly, individuals who participate in and graduate from college realize many substantial benefits. But too often discussion of such fundamental questions as who should go to college and who should pay for college emphasizes only the individual or private benefits, ignoring the many ways that society also benefits when more individuals enroll in and complete college.

The intertwined nature of the individual and public or societal benefits complicates efforts to cleanly differentiate them. For example, the higher annual earnings, lower rates of unemployment and poverty, and greater likelihood of employer-provided health insurance that college graduates receive are typically framed as benefits to individuals who participate in college.[51] Although these outcomes are certainly desirable for individuals, the benefits extend beyond the individual. Higher individual incomes contribute to a higher tax base and more tax revenues, lower rates of unemployment and poverty translate into less use of social support programs, and greater likelihood of employer-provided health insurance means less reliance on government-supported programs like Medicaid. College-educated individuals also enjoy better health, more job satisfaction, and greater family stability, as well as better educational outcomes for their children, all outcomes that make both the individual participant and society more generally better off.[52]

The many substantial benefits of higher education to individuals—especially the increase in earnings—provide a convenient justification for the growing privatization of higher education costs.[53] The increasing responsibility that students have for paying for college is signaled most dramatically by soaring tuition costs and the growing indebtedness of college students and graduates. Over the past five years (from 2007–8 to 2012–13), average tuition and fees (the "sticker price") for in-state students increased by 24% above the rate of inflation at public two-year colleges, 27% at public four-year colleges and universities, and 13% at private non-profit four-year colleges and universities. These patterns mirror increases that occurred during the prior five-year period (2002–3 to 2007–8), when the sticker price rose by 18% beyond the rate of inflation at public two-year colleges, 31% at public four-year colleges and universities, and 12% at private non-for-profit four-year colleges and universities.[54]

Over the past ten years both the rate of borrowing and the amount of cumulative debt have also increased. For instance, 57% of individuals who received bachelor's degrees from public four-year colleges and universities in 2010–11 had borrowed, up from 52% of bachelor's degree recipients in 2000–1; the average amount borrowed among these graduates was $23,800 in 2010–11, up from $20,100 (in constant 2011 dollars) in 2000–1.[55] Both the rate of borrowing and the amount borrowed have increased regardless of family income. For instance, nearly half (42%) of dependent college students from the lowest family income quartile borrowed an average of $6,200 in 2007–8; by comparison, 36% of dependent college students in the lowest family income quartile borrowed an average of $3,300 in 1995–96.[56]

This shifting of the burden of paying for college costs to students reflects an assumption that students are the primary beneficiaries of higher education, and thus students (and their families) should have primary responsibility for paying the costs. Yet this view ignores the many and substantial public benefits that also result from higher education. Based on his comprehensive review of the market and non-market benefits of higher education that accrue to both individuals and society, education economist Walter McMahon estimated that societal benefits account for about half (52%) of the total benefits of higher education.[57]

The increasing privatization of higher education also ignores the critical societal needs for and benefits of higher education. Throughout our nation's history, the U.S. federal and state governments have recognized the societal benefits through public policies that encourage individual investment in higher education.[58] After World War II, for instance, the federal government provided funding for the "GI Bill," which enabled individuals serving in the armed services to attend college and thereby helped the nation avoid major unemployment of veterans. The federal government enacted and periodically amended the Higher Education Act of 1965, authorizing programs designed to reduce the financial barriers to attendance for students from low-income families and support the transition into and through college for first-generation college students, thus expanding college opportunity for groups that had previously been excluded. State governments encouraged higher education opportunity by creating community colleges and transforming normal schools designed to prepare teachers into comprehensive colleges and universities that offered an array of professional degree programs.

In short, between World War II and until about the mid-1980s, higher education was viewed as a mechanism that benefited both individuals and society. With the GI Bill, the Higher Education Act of 1965 and its 1972 reauthorization, and other government policies (such as the creation of a progressive tax system), inequality in the United States declined.[59]

Beginning in the mid-1980s, however, the orientation of public policy began to change. With the "Reagan revolution," the federal government substantially deregulated the market, scaled-back some public programs, and shifted responsibility for other public programs to states.[60] States, in turn, began to shift more of the responsibility for funding higher education to students and their families. Inequality began to increase as the federal and some state governments reduced social programs designed to level the playing field and reduced the progressivity of the tax system and as structural changes in the economy reduced the demand for unskilled workers and increased the demand for skilled workers.[61]

Just as the expansion of higher education was necessary after World War II, the nation is again at a point when public policy must recognize the convergence of the public and private benefits of higher education. This convergence must be recognized in order to ensure our nation's continued economic prosperity in a global knowledge-based society, meet the growing demand from employers for college-educated workers, and close growing gaps in educational and economic prosperity across groups. These needs all speak to the government's role—as manifest through public policy—in maximizing the benefits of higher education by encouraging greater overall educational attainment and reducing gaps in attainment across groups. The converging of public and private benefits should encourage all those interested in higher education and the associated economic and social prosperity of individuals and our nation to rethink the amount and means of governmental investment and the ways that government-sponsored policies and programs are, and should be, used not only to advance the economic well-being of individual participants but also to meet the societal need for continued economic prosperity. Stiglitz underscores the power of public policy in addressing current societal needs: "Much of the inequality that exists today is a result of governmental policy, both what the government does and what it does not do."[62]

According to 2011 polling data from the Pew Charitable Trusts, Economic Mobility Project, most Americans believe that government should play a role in advancing economic mobility but that it is not effectively assisting those from poor and middle-class families.[63] Most Americans also believe that postsecondary education and training is very important to an individual's future economic prosperity (79%) and that the government should do more to improve college affordability (80%). Suggesting the political challenges associated with identifying the most appropriate path forward, however, Americans believe that the most effective government strategies for improving economic prosperity of individuals include improving college affordability (40%) and enhancing the quality of K–12 education (40%), as well as reducing government spending (48%) and reducing government debt (43%).[64]

The Role of Government in Raising Higher Education Attainment and Closing Gaps

President Obama and the leaders of philanthropic and other policy-oriented organizations have called for improvements so that the United States once again leads the world in the educational attainment of its population. Nonetheless, political support to increase the proportion of the population with some postsecondary education is uneven. Moreover, the federal and state policies that are currently in place were designed for an era of expansion in the U.S. higher education system but not intended to virtually double rates of higher educational attainment.

Federal Higher Education Policies Focus on Research and Student Aid

As Ronald Heck observes, public policies are determined "by the political philosophy associated with governments and the surrounding social and cultural contexts of the settings in which those governments exist." The approach to public policy in the United States is defined by its federalist form of government. Under federalism, powers are distributed between multiple levels of government, with the federal and state governments receiving "their powers from the Constitution" and having "substantial powers and responsibilities." Educational policymaking is influenced by governors, legislatures, and courts at the federal, state, and local government levels, as well as by government administrators, businesses, the media, and the public.[65]

Although the federal government has developed many policies that influence higher education directly and indirectly, one prominent focus has been to appropriate funding to encourage the production of research at U.S. universities. This funding is concentrated in a relatively small number of colleges and universities. In 2009–10, 120 colleges and universities received 58% of the nearly $77.5 billion awarded via federal contracts, grants, and appropriations for federally funded research and development centers.[66] Federal investment in research enhances the nation's production of basic and applied research and improves the ability of public and private universities to compete in research and development. But because federal research dollars may be used only to support research activities, this investment does little to raise the nation's educational attainment. Moreover, the universities that receive these dollars (as a group) enroll far fewer students than other sectors of higher education, particularly public community colleges and public four-year comprehensive institutions.

The primary mechanism that the federal government uses to encourage individual participation in higher education, especially among students from lower- and middle-income families, is its substantial annual investment in student financial assistance. About three-fourths of the total $185.1 billion in student aid received by undergraduates nationwide in 2011–12 was from federal programs (i.e., Federal Pell Grants and other federal grant programs, Federal Work-Study, federal loans, and federal education tax credits).[67] Despite the magnitude of this investment, the federal government's approach to student financial assistance lacks "philosophical coherence" as reflected by the wide array of distinct programmatic goals, lacks "well-considered patterns of policy development," and suffers from the absence of "systematic 'housecleaning' to reduce the policy and program contradictions, inefficiencies, and illogics accumulated in the years since the Great Society era." Only "operational details" of the programs have been altered over time.[68]

Federal loans represent a considerable share of financial aid dollars: 52% of all federal student aid including tax credits and 38% of all undergraduate aid in 2011–12. Although student financial aid and tax credits may ease the burden of paying college costs for those who would attend anyway, student financial aid (especially need-based grants) may also promote the enrollment of students who would not have enrolled without the aid. Research demonstrates that financial aid in the form of grants is positively associated with college enrollment and choice,[69] that the positive effects are larger for grants that are awarded based on financial need than for grants awarded based on non-need criteria,[70] and that the positive effects of grants are larger for students from low-income families than for other students.[71] Research also shows that loans generally are not associated with improvements in college access and completion,[72] but students from low-income families and communities are less willing than other students to use loans to pay college costs.[73]

The Responsibility of States for Improving Educational Attainment

Notwithstanding the federal government's substantial investment in student financial assistance, in the United States individual states have the primary responsibility for developing policies that promote the educational attainment of their populations and close gaps in attainment across groups.[74] Public policies established by the federal government form the context for, and may interact with, the policies that state governments adopt.[75] Interactions between federal and state policies can enhance or undermine efforts to increase educational attainment.

The first major federal-state partnership in higher education was the federal Morrill Land Grant Acts (i.e., the Morrill Act of 1862 and the Morrill Act of 1890). Under these acts, the federal government gave land to eligible states so that states would develop public colleges and universities that advanced education in agriculture and mechanical arts. With the Morrill Acts, "a regularized pattern of state tax support for public universities" began.[76] Today 74 land-grant colleges and universities (18 of which are historically Black colleges and universities) are operating nationwide.[77]

Another notable example of a federal-state policy interaction is the Leveraging Educational Assistance Partnership (LEAP) Program, formerly known as the State Student Incentive Grant (SSIG) program. Originally authorized by the federal government in 1972, this program provided matching funds to states that award grants to students based on their financial need and thus incentivized the establishment of state-sponsored need-based financial aid programs in many states.[78] Nonetheless, the elimination of federal appropriations to LEAP beginning in FY2011 (compared with $63.852 million appropriated in FY 2010) illustrates a weakening of the intergovernmental compact to improve the availability of need-based financial aid.[79] Other than student financial aid, little intergovernmental effort has focused on improving postsecondary educational outcomes.

The federal government has played a more active role in K–12 education, even though states also have primarily responsibility for K–12. The federal No Child Left Behind Act (NCLB), the 2001 reauthorization of the Elementary and Secondary Education Act, is one example of federal and state policy interaction pertaining to K–12 education. Among other provisions, NCLB requires states to annually assess the basic reading and mathematics skills of public school students in select grades. States may develop their own assessments and establish their own standards but must monitor whether schools are making adequate yearly progress and report achievement separately for various subgroups, including economically disadvantaged groups, students with disabilities, students with limited English proficiency, and major racial/ethnic groups. To facilitate comparisons of academic achievement across states, the legislation also requires states that receive federal Title I funds to administer the National Assessment of Educational Progress (NAEP) in reading and mathematics to fourth and eighth graders every two years.[80] Although the high school exams that states implemented in response to NCLB emphasized the need for academic standards, some evidence suggests that they may have resulted in some unintended negative consequences, including focusing the attention of high schools, teachers, parents, and students on meeting standards that are lower than those required for college admission and completion, thus encouraging high school teachers and staff to focus only on students graduating from high school rather than also on succeeding in college.[81] Other positive and negative implications of NCLB have been widely discussed and debated. Although the provisions of NCLB may be altered in the next reauthorization of the Elementary and Secondary Education Act, this intergovernmental work has resulted in greater attention to the measurement of student achievement and differences in achievement across groups.

Reflecting their unique historical and social contexts as well as their particular philosophies toward and priorities for education, states use a range of policies to encourage students to enroll and complete higher education.[82] One dimension of statewide variation pertains to the organization of a state's higher education system. Although much attention has been paid to the rapid rate of growth in the private for-profit sector, in most states the vast majority of students continue to attend public institutions. In fall 2010, 72% of the more than 21 million students enrolled in degree-granting colleges and universities nationwide were attending public rather than private not-for-profit or private for-profit institutions.[83] But, the degree of reliance on public colleges and universities to deliver higher education varies across states and regions. More than 90% of enrollments in several western states (Alaska, Wyoming, New Mexico, and Montana) are in public colleges and universities. In contrast, private not-for-profit institutions play a much greater role in providing higher education opportunity, especially in such northeastern states as the Massachusetts, Rhode Island, New York, and Vermont.[84] In fall 2010 for-profit institutions accounted for at least 15% of total enrollments in Florida, Colorado, Minnesota, West Virginia, Iowa, and Arizona, but less than one percent of total enrollments in Montana and Rhode Island.[85]

The configuration of a state's higher education system influences the types of public policies that are required to promote higher education attainment. For instance, in fall 2010 California, New Mexico, and Wyoming directed more than half of total enrollments into community colleges.[86] A number of states with large populations also have very large numbers of students enrolled in community colleges (e.g., Texas). Community colleges have the advantage of providing higher education at a lower cost to students and taxpayers. But small shares of students transfer from community colleges and earn four-year degrees.[87] Therefore, states with large community college sectors must consider strategies for facilitating student transitions across educational sectors if they are to improve bachelor's degree attainment.

Just as the nature of higher education systems varies across states, so does the level of public subsidy that a state provides for higher education. All states provide financial support to their colleges and universities, but these subsidies vary based on the structure of the state's higher education system; its philosophy about the relative roles of students, colleges, and the state in paying for higher education; and the extent to which it seeks to incentivize enrollment at private colleges and universities. On average, state subsidies covered 71% of education and related expenses at community colleges (i.e., $7,404 per FTE), 54% at public master's institutions (i.e., $6,578 per FTE), and 52% at public research universities (i.e., $8,055 per FTE) in 2007–8.[88] But the share of education and related expenses covered by state subsidies differs dramatically across states. For instance, for public research universities, the state subsidy ranged (in 2007–8) from less than 25% in Colorado, New Hampshire, and Rhode Island, to more than 70% in Alaska, Hawaii, New York, and Wyoming.[89] Total education revenue (defined as state appropriations and net tuition less net tuition used for capital debt service) per FTE also varies. Education revenue per FTE averaged $11,043 nationwide in FY2012, but it ranged from less than $8,300 per FTE in Florida and Washington to more than $16,000 per FTE in Wyoming, Alaska, and Delaware. Total education revenue per FTE over the past five years (from FY2007 to FY2012) declined by an average of 7.9% (in constant dollars) nationwide, but changes over this period varied from about a 25% decline in Idaho and Florida to a more than 15% increase in North Dakota and Illinois.[90]

State higher education systems also diverge in terms of their current levels of educational attainment and the magnitude of improvement in educational attainment required to achieve international competitiveness goals. Such variations might be expected, given differences in the characteristics of higher education systems and state policy approaches as well as differences in numerous dimensions of the broader state demographic, economic, historical, and political context. Even with past and current investments, however, all states except Massachusetts must improve their performance in order for 55% of adults age 25 to 64 to have at least an associate's degree by 2020, the level of educational attainment required for international competitiveness. Table 1 illustrates the variation in required improvements, with several states (e.g., Arkansas, Louisiana, Alaska, Nevada) needing annual increases of more than 12% to reach the level of educational attainment of the best-performing nations. The large and fast-growing states of California, Texas, and Florida all require annual increases in the number of degrees produced that exceed the national average increase of 7.9%.[91]

Fiscal Constraints

Efforts to improve state higher education performance must occur at a time when states are experiencing, and will continue to experience, considerable constraints on and competition for available fiscal resources.[92] Following the economic downturn that began in December 2007, most states suffered sizeable

Table 1 Educational Attainment and Annual Increase in Degree Production Required for 55% of the Population Age 25 to 64 to Hold at Least an Associate Degree by 2020

	% With at Least an Associate Degree (2008)		% Increase Required		% With at Least an Associate Degree (2008)	
	Percent of Adults Age 25 to 64	Rank	Annual Increase	Rank	Age 25 to 34	Age 45 to 64
Nation	**37.9**	–	**7.9**	–	**37.8**	**37.1**
Alabama	31.6	42	10.0	38	31.8	30.7
Alaska	36.3	30	12.8	49	30.5	38.8
Arizona	34.4	38	10.9	44	30.7	36.9
Arkansas	26.5	49	12.3	47	25.9	25.4
California	38.6	21	9.2	34	35.9	40.1
Colorado	45.3	4	3.3	6	41.5	46.7
Connecticut	46.6	2	3.1	5	46.3	45.7
Delaware	37.0	26	8.6	32	36.4	37.2
Florida	36.8	29	8.7	33	35.3	36.9
Georgia	**36.2**	**31**	**10.0**	**39**	**34.0**	**35.7**
Hawaii	42.3	12	6.2	19	40.9	42.8
Idaho	34.8	36	9.8	37	34.1	34.9
Illinois	**40.8**	**15**	**5.4**	**18**	**42.7**	**38.2**
Indiana	33.4	40	8.3	27	36.0	31.0
Iowa	38.8	20	4.4	12	45.9	34.1
Kansas	40.5	16	5.0	15	41.5	39.1
Kentucky	29.2	47	10.7	42	32.2	26.8
Louisiana	27.0	48	12.5	48	28.1	25.9
Maine	36.8	28	8.3	26	36.2	37.4
Maryland	**43.9**	**8**	**5.1**	**16**	**44.6**	**42.6**
Massachusetts	49.6	1	−1.2	1	53.4	47.6
Michigan	35.6	33	8.4	29	35.8	34.2
Minnesota	45.0	6	2.6	4	48.3	40.9
Mississippi	29.3	46	10.8	43	31.7	27.5
Missouri	34.9	34	7.9	24	36.6	33.2
Montana	37.6	25	8.0	25	36.1	36.4
Nebraska	40.5	17	4.5	13	44.1	37.7
Nevada	30.1	45	14.5	50	28.2	32.0
New Hampshire	46.0	3	2.1	3	45.6	44.8
New Jersey	44.6	7	4.3	11	46.0	42.8
New Mexico	33.4	39	10.3	40	28.5	35.7
New York	43.7	9	3.4	7	47.7	40.8
North Carolina	36.9	27	8.5	30	36.0	36.7
North Dakota	45.2	5	1.2	2	49.5	40.9
Ohio	34.9	35	8.3	28	36.4	32.7

Table 1 (continued)

	% With at Least an Associate Degree (2008)		% Increase Required		% With at Least an Associate Degree (2008)	
	Percent of Adults Age 25 to 64	Rank	Annual Increase	Rank	Age 25 to 34	Age 45 to 64
Oklahoma	31.3	43	9.8	36	30.3	31.0
Oregon	38.6	22	8.5	31	36.3	39.3
Pennsylvania	37.9	24	6.2	21	42.8	34.8
Rhode Island	41.4	14	3.9	9	43.4	39.8
South Carolina	34.4	37	9.7	35	34.4	34.0
South Dakota	39.4	19	5.1	17	43.6	36.5
Tennessee	31.3	44	11.1	45	31.3	30.3
Texas	**33.3**	**41**	**11.5**	**46**	**30.7**	**34.2**
Utah	40.2	18	5.0	14	38.2	41.0
Vermont	43.6	10	3.7	8	43.8	43.5
Virginia	43.4	11	4.2	10	42.4	42.7
Washington	**42.0**	**13**	**6.2**	**20**	**39.4**	**42.7**
West Virginia	25.6	50	10.6	41	28.2	23.6
Wisconsin	38.0	23	7.2	22	39.7	35.6
Wyoming	36.0	32	7.6	23	34.3	35.4

Sources: Kelly, "Projected Degree Gap: Percent of 25 to 64 Year Olds with Associate Degrees or Higher"; National Center for Higher Education Management Systems, "ACS Educational Attainment by Degree-Level and Age-Group (American Community Survey)."

declines in revenues. Many states responded to these declines by making policy changes that reduce their ability to achieve improved educational attainment, including reducing state appropriations, increasing tuition, reducing student financial aid awards, and changing the rules for distributing resources (for example, by changing the criteria for receiving state funds or the formula for allocating state funds).

Historically, state revenue shortfalls have generally resulted in disproportionate cuts in appropriations for higher education, given higher education's traditional role as the "balance wheel" in state budgets and the ability of higher education to raise its own revenues through tuition increases.[93] Federal "stimulus" funds appropriated through the American Recovery and Reinvestment Act of 2009 (ARRA) ameliorated the negative impact of this decline on higher education revenues between 2009 and 2011. With ARRA support, total state and local revenue for higher education remained essentially unchanged during that period. However, state and local revenue at public colleges and universities declined in constant dollars even with ARRA support as enrollments increased. State and local support per FTE student in FY 2012 was at its lowest level in 25 years (after adjusting for inflation). Colleges and universities have tended to compensate for the decline in per student revenues by increasing tuition; thus, net tuition revenue per FTE rose in constant dollars by 5% each year between 2009 and 2011, and then by 9.3% between 2011 and 2012.[94]

With the end of ARRA funding, the magnitude of the decline in state revenues during the Great Recession, the slow rebound in state revenues following the official end of the Great Recession, political difficulties associated with raising taxes, and potential negative implications for state budgets of the federal deficit, most states will likely face continued budget challenges into the near future.[95] States will also face continuing constraints on the availability of funds for higher education because of structural budget deficits, defined as the inability of current revenue streams to provide sufficient resources for public services, given trends in the populations to be served. Many of these structural deficits are the result of tax policies that were created to collect revenue from an economy of an earlier era rather than a global, knowledge-based economy. By 2016 the state and local budget deficit as a percent of revenues was expected to average 6% across states but range from a low of 2.1% in Maryland to a high of 10.8% in Texas and 10.9% in Mississippi.[96] Importantly, these projections likely understate the magnitude of the looming state fiscal challenges because they were based on pre-recession data.

Thus, states must identify ways to improve performance in a fiscal context that promises few additional state resources and continued fierce competition (especially from K–12 education and health care programs) for the resources that are available. Corina Eckl, fiscal program director at the National Council of State Legislatures, and Scott Pattison, director of the National Association of Budget Officers, poignantly describe the implications of the constrained fiscal context for higher education:

> With the fiscal situation so dire for states going forward, the higher education funding model is unsustainable. . . . Even with a stronger economy and better fiscal situation for states, the increased demand for funds—for unfunded pension liabilities, health care, corrections, and other parts of the state budget—will make it difficult for recent higher education cuts to be restored. Indeed,

stepping back to view state budgets in a larger context, many state budget experts anticipate "a new normal" of state spending growth that will be much lower than what states were accustomed to in the past.[97]

The Role of States in Raising Educational Attainment

Clearly, renewed attention to the role of state government in improving higher education attainment and reducing gaps in attainment across groups is required. Although the federal government may create policies that complement and incentivize the work of states, state governments have the primary responsibility for addressing the educational needs of their state and population.

With this context as the foundation, this book addresses the following question: How can states use public policy to improve the performance of higher education to maximize the individual and societal benefits, in light of the specific characteristics of their state? These state-specific characteristics include trends in higher education performance and the nature and magnitude of required improvements, the characteristics of the state's higher education system, and the demographic and fiscal context (as described earlier in this chapter) as well as other state-specific contextual characteristics.

We address this question by exploring, in depth, how state policy explains the performance of higher education during the past 15 to 20 years in five states: Georgia, Illinois, Maryland, Texas, and Washington. These states differ in many ways, including their overall educational attainment, disparities in attainment across groups, and the characteristics of their higher education system and governance structures, as well as other demographic, fiscal, and political contextual characteristics. Chapter 3 details the rationale for selecting these five states, compares and contrasts the characteristics of these five states with each other and all U.S. states, and summarizes the procedures that we used to conduct the single and cross-state analyses.

We define higher education performance as the college-related outcomes that lead to improved educational attainment overall and reduced inequality in attainment across groups: academic preparation for college, participation or enrollment in college, completion of college, and affordability of college. These categories include attention to a more complete array of performance indicators than used in some earlier research.[98] They mirror four of the six categories used in the National Center for Public Policy and Higher Education's state-by-state report card, *Measuring Up*. Produced between 2000 and 2008, the biennial report card awarded states grades on each of six dimensions of performance: preparation, participation, affordability, completion, benefits, and learning. The indicators used in *Measuring Up*, the first national effort to systematically examine state-by-state performance, provided clear and easily understood information about different dimensions of performance as well as a mechanism for monitoring gaps in performance across different groups within a state.

Unquestionably, the journey that culminates in postsecondary educational attainment begins early in an individual's life, perhaps at birth. Despite the obvious relevance of many phases of students' formal educational experiences, including early childhood and preschool, elementary, and secondary education as well as higher education, we limit our attention to the high school and college-related segments of the educational pathway. We also consider attainment only up to completion of a baccalaureate degree. This focus not only improves the manageability and tightens the focus of our work but also reflects the present structural approach of policymakers and practitioners to education. In most U.S. states and the federal government, different although related aspects of the educational pathway continue to be treated separately, since early childhood, K–12, and higher education are typically overseen by unconnected governmental agencies, departments, and legislative committees.

Although our data collection protocols and initial conceptualization also included attention to research productivity, we do not include research excellence or productivity in our definition of higher education performance. Certainly, government support for research can create noteworthy direct and indirect benefits, particularly with regard to state and national economic development and productivity as well as quality of life.[99] However, although all states should have some investment in research, the ideal balance between investment in research and graduate study rather than undergraduate education should depend on the educational needs of the state and the characteristics of the economy.[100] Fostering research excellence is a responsibility that is shared by a limited number of research universities, the states in which they are located, and the federal government. When public resources are finite, pursuing research excellence may come at the expense of other statewide goals, particularly statewide efforts to promote the overall educational attainment of its population and to reduce gaps in attainment across group. The Texas case study poignantly illustrates how state efforts to expand research excellence can come at the expense of educating a growing and diverse population. Moreover, limiting state support of research activities may help ensure that resources are not spread across too many institutions, thereby diluting research quality. We exclude research performance from our definition of higher education performance, not because we believe that states should abandon support for research universities, but because investment in research needs to be considered in light of the investments a state must make to improve higher educational attainment. Greater attention to research may create trade-offs for attainment, especially when resources are finite.

In sum, while maintaining the existing quality of research universities is important, we argue that the most pressing societal challenge facing higher education in the United States is to improve the overall educational attainment of the population and reduce gaps in educational attainment across groups. This perspective guides our definition of higher education performance.

No Silver Bullet

Following the release of the *Measuring Up* report cards, many states increased their attention to performance. These biennial report cards allowed states to monitor trends over time in their performance in the graded categories. However, although providing a useful starting point for assessing state performance, *Measuring Up* did not identify the public policies that caused a state to have better or worse performance than other states on particular indicators and did not explain the forces that caused a state's performance to improve or decline over time.

Several recent initiatives focus on the role of states in improving one particular aspect of higher education performance: college completion. These initiatives offer recommendations and resources to states seeking to improve this outcome. For instance, Complete College America, a national initiative sponsored by several foundations, asks states to commit to increasing college completion by: (1) establishing annual state- and institution-specific completion goals; (2) creating and implementing state- and institution-level plans to achieve the goals; and (3) collecting and using data to measure and publicly report progress toward achieving the goals. The National Governors Association specifies that governors who sign on to its Complete to Compete initiative take the following five steps: (1) review data to identify the state's performance at various points in the educational pipeline; (2) assess differences in performance based on race/ethnicity, family income, and geographic region within the state; (3) set targets for improvement on particular performance indicators; (4) consider the ways that current policies and regulations promote or discourage attainment; and (5) link performance to funding decisions.[101]

The "Leaders and Laggards" report issued in 2012 by the Institute for a Competitive Workforce, an affiliate of the U.S. Chamber of Commerce, also defines higher education performance as degree completion. This report grades public higher education in each state on six dimensions: (1) student access and success; (2) efficiency and cost-effectiveness; (3) meeting labor market demand; (4) transparency and accountability; (5) policy environment; and (6) innovation. The report recommends that states promote degree completion by linking some share of state appropriations to degree completion, setting specific targets for graduation rates and other outcomes (e.g., learning or labor market outcomes), and establishing statewide articulation and transfer policies, as well as by improving measures of student learning, increasing efficiency and productivity, promoting transparency by providing more information about higher education performance, and encouraging innovative instructional approaches.[102]

The reports offered by Complete College America, Complete to Compete, and Leaders and Laggards imply the need to understand current levels of performance and existing public policies in order to productively increase completion. Yet none of these reports reveals how public policy and performance are connected, how individual public policies are interrelated, or how public policies effectively improve performance within a state's particular demographic, economic, political, and historical context. Moreover, with their emphasis on college completion, these efforts ignore other critical aspects of the educational attainment process that are fundamental to improving completion. State performance in one area, such as completion, cannot be considered in isolation of other areas. In short, states are unlikely to improve degree completion without also considering how to improve other college-related outcomes, especially college preparation, participation, and affordability.

These initiatives are also unlikely to lead to meaningful improvements in higher education performance because they are focused on providing solutions to "small market failures" without recognizing the root causes.[103] Low levels of attainment and persisting gaps in attainment are not caused by ignorance of effective strategies, but reflect the absence of attention to both the political forces and economic policies that contribute to a state's higher education performance. Thus, as Acemoglu and Robinson recommend, we aim to go beyond identifying superficial solutions by instead focusing on determining the underlying causes of a state's low performance in higher education, recognizing that, although many of the "micro-market failures" may be easy to fix, creating necessary improvements is not possible without a more comprehensive and holistic approach.[104]

Conclusion

To varying degrees, all 50 U.S. states must improve higher education performance in order to ensure the nation's continued economic prosperity in a global knowledge-based society. This improvement is essential to meeting workforce demands as well as increasing equity across groups. Drawing on case studies of five states and building on related prior research, this book offers a comprehensive and holistic framework for understanding how states can use public policy to achieve necessary improvements in higher education performance.

We eschew the current prevailing approach to improving higher education attainment. The nation's preoccupation with improving degree completion, a necessary and worthy goal, cannot be accomplished by identifying discrete "silver bullet" policies or approaches that are focused only on this narrow slice of the educational attainment process and that all states must follow. Focusing on the contribution of particular policies and practices to overall educational attainment and improved equality in attainment across groups will likely improve the efficiency and effectiveness of the resources that are allocated for these purposes, but such efforts are also likely to result only in modest overall improvements in higher education performance.

We argue that creating more substantial improvement requires a holistic and comprehensive approach. At a minimum, state leaders must consider how performance in one area (such as degree completion) is connected to performance in other areas (such as preparation), how particular policies interact to produce expected and unexpected outcomes, and how public policy approaches must be adapted to reflect the context and characteristics of the state. More broadly, such an approach requires greater attention to the role of the state in providing policy leadership and steering of higher education so as to advance a cohesive public agenda for higher education, adopting public policies that not only increase the demand for and supply of higher education but also level the playing field for higher educational opportunity, and considering how its particular contextual characteristics influence not only the relationship between public policy and performance but also the specific public policies that may be realistically adopted.

Chapter 2

Understanding the Relationship between Public Policy and Higher Education Performance

Guiding Perspectives

As in earlier eras, higher education must now play an important role in achieving societal priorities. At this point in our nation's history, renewed attention to the role of state policy in ensuring that higher education is achieving its public purposes is essential. Clearly, states must do more if they are to have the levels of higher education required to meet workforce needs and improve equity in attainment across groups.

Drawing on data collected from case studies of five states, we build on prior studies and other relevant historical literature to propose a comprehensive framework for understanding how state policy may improve overall higher education attainment and close gaps in attainment across groups. The framework that we offer in the final chapter offers a conceptually and theoretically grounded rationale for why public policy should be related to higher education performance within a particular state context. Strong conceptual and theoretical underpinnings are necessary if the findings from our studies of five states are to provide insights into the relationship between public policy and performance in states other than the five we examine or even in our five selected states at other times.

With our five-state studies and a review of prior research and theory, we seek to develop a conceptual model that accounts for the array of potential policies, including policies pertaining to governance, finance, accountability, and transitions, used by states to improve higher education performance. Here performance is the culmination of preparation, participation, completion, and affordability, and is defined as overall higher education attainment and closing gaps in attainment across groups within a particular state context where the context is defined by demographic, economic, political, historical, and other characteristics.

Our goal is broader than identifying a specific policy that will raise higher education attainment or determining the forces that will lead a state to adopt a particular policy. Unlike some other researchers, we do not focus exclusively on the role of system design or governance policy in explaining higher education performance.[1] Research that focuses on a particular public policy, although it does make contributions, does not reflect the fact that higher education attainment is the culmination of a longitudinal, multistage process that begins early in a student's educational career and involves many intermediate outcomes. The most important of these are reflected in the indicators that we use to measure higher education attainment: college preparation, participation, completion, and affordability. The longitudinal and multistage nature of the process means that attention only to the relationship between one public policy and a specific outcome (such as college completion) is unlikely to produce the magnitude of improvement in higher educational attainment that individuals and our nation require.

Our examination of how state public policy explains the performance of higher education is informed by, and builds on, three bodies of prior research. Each of these is described in further detail in the subsequent sections of this chapter. First, our understanding of the relationship between public policy and higher education performance is influenced by the work of Lyman Glenny, Robert Berdahl, Burton Clark, Richard Richardson, and others who examined the responsiveness of state structures to the educational needs of an earlier time. When Glenny, Berdahl, and Clark were writing, state needs and priorities focused primarily on expanding higher education to meet growing demand. Although state needs and priorities as well as other contextual dimensions have changed over the past few decades, the perspectives of these authors provide the foundation for understanding the current state role in ensuring that higher education achieves societal purposes.

Second, our examination is shaped by macroeconomic theories of the role of the public sector that assume that the lever state governments use to increase the demand for and supply of higher education is public policy.[2] The higher education markets that exist today are the product of prior governmental policies related to the structure and design of higher education systems, finance of higher education, movement of students into and through higher education, accountability of higher education, and other issues. Public policy can correct for past inefficient or ineffective state policy decisions as well as persisting "market failure" (described more completely below) and can, consequently, shift higher education systems along a continuum from institutional aspirations toward public purposes in a way that responds to the state context.

The third perspective that informs our examination of the relationship between public policy and performance is the centrality of context. States do not adopt public policy in a vacuum. Moreover, states do not always adopt the same policies at different points in time, and different states adopt different policies to address similar dimensions of higher education performance. The public policies that a state government adopts depend on the state's particular historical, demographic, economic, political, and other state-specific characteristics.

The Role of State Government Structures

Our attention to the role of states in advancing public goals and priorities for higher education builds on a "traditional approach" to understanding the performance of higher education.[3] Robert Berdahl described this relationship in terms of the state's interest in ensuring the accountability of higher education institutions for meeting public purposes and higher education institutions' interest in preserving their own autonomy.[4] Although these two are sometimes viewed as opposite ends of a continuum,[5] Berdahl argued that the preferred structural configuration balances responsiveness to societal needs (accountability) with respect for the "academic ethos" (institutional autonomy). The challenge, Berdahl believed, was to understand how state policies can effectively address public purposes while also recognizing the autonomy necessary to develop robust higher education institutions. Berdahl urged states to find a "suitably sensitive mechanism" for dealing with issues of public priority and not resort to a host of regulations solely for the purpose of compliance. In the ideal state–institutional relationship, states provide leadership for the approval of new graduate programs or new campuses and other issues where the state has a legitimate involvement, but not for substantive matters more closely related to core institutional values, such as curricular content and faculty hiring. Whereas Burton Clark pointed to the "rightful power of the purse" as a justification for "political authority,"[6] Berdahl argued that state involvement in the planning and governance of higher education is appropriate, "[e]ven if the state role in financing higher education were to diminish markedly," given that higher education institutions operate "in a context of state law and state sovereignty."[7]

Lyman Glenny was among the first to articulate the need for a state role in coordinating and governing higher education.[8] Although states established higher education systems between 1900 and 1950, these systems were insufficient to address the expansion of higher education that followed the GI Bill or the call for research spurred by Sputnik and the Cold War.[9] Burton Clark describes the historical roots of the "localized" approach to U.S. higher education coordination: "No national bureau had an important role. Even the departments of education of the separate states, where public responsibility for education became lodged, often had little influence. The private institutions in the nineteenth century became entirely independent of state officials; the leading public institutions had their own boards of control and chartered autonomy."[10]

With the end of World War II, higher education in the United States faced new demands and expectations. States responded to the growing enrollment demand by creating new community colleges (also once known as "junior colleges") and transforming normal schools into comprehensive institutions offering an array of professional programs. With federal financial support, states were also developing one or more research universities to address a growing national research agenda. Observing these trends, Glenny argued that statewide governance structures were required to coordinate the various functions and sectors of higher education for the public good.[11] Glenny was particularly concerned about preserving the teaching missions of higher education institutions and guarding against the overinvestment in research associated with building new research universities as well as the dilution of the quality of research that might result from expanding the missions of comprehensive institutions and spreading limited resources across too many institutions.

Glenny also saw the need for state organizations to serve as a buffer between higher education institutions and a state's elected officials. Such organizations, structured as statewide coordinating boards (in most states), consolidated governing boards (as in Georgia and New York), or subsystems organized by institutional mission (as in California), Glenny argued, would counter political pressure to develop campuses that were not needed or were not located near population centers and would provide the statewide view required when state legislators have limited knowledge of higher education, especially in states with part-time legislatures or without professional staff.

Reflecting these and other rationales, state higher education governance systems changed substantially between 1950 and 1980. The increase in state coordination associated with these changes helped ensure that higher education institutions addressed broad public purposes by managing the growth of higher education, involving private institutions in statewide planning processes, reducing conflict over finite resources, limiting expansion of graduate programs, and providing "oversight of new and emerging institutions."[12] Echoing Glenny's description of the benefits of state-level coordinating structures, Burton Clark described the shift in the United States during the 1960s and 1970s toward greater state coordination of higher education: "Reform has had one main thrust: to bring more administered order into what is the most disorderly of all major advanced systems of higher education. The drift of authority for a quarter-century has been steadily upward, toward a growing web of multicampus administrations, coordinating boards of higher education, state legislative committees and executive orders, regional associations, and a large number of the national government."[13]

Drawing on his examination of higher education systems around the world, Clark offered the "triangle of coordination" (later labeled by others as the "triangle of tensions"[14]) to depict three models: academic oligarchy (or the professional system), state authority, and the market.[15] Especially when compared with other nations, the U.S. higher education system has historically reflected less attention to bureaucractic, political, or professional forms of coordination and relatively greater emphasis on market interaction. Defined broadly as "nongovernmental" and "nonregulated," a market system "facilitates change by means of competition among enterprises and extremely loose coupling that allows enterprises and sectors to move disjointedly in various directions."[16] Although stressing the powerful "adaptive capacity" of the market form of coordination and noting that the characteristics of the U.S. higher education system that limit attempts at greater state coordination, Clark also observed that all forms of coordination have limitations. Particularly important is the potential utility of state coordination "to bring order out of [the] disorder" associated with the market form of coordination.[17]

Building on Clark's triangle of coordination as well as Williams' conceptualization of higher education finance, Richard Richardson and colleagues considered the implications of the ways a state balances the interests of society with the interests of higher education institutions for the performance of the state's higher education system. Using data collected from case studies of seven states and a broader definition of higher education performance than enrollment growth, the authors concluded that a state's higher education performance depends on the interaction between the design of a higher education system (categorized as federal, unified, or segmented) and four state policy roles: providing resources (by subsidizing the cost of higher education), regulating (by setting tuition and fees, restricting use of resources to particular purposes, etc.), advocating for consumers (by providing student financial aid), and steering (by encouraging institutions "to produce outcomes consistent with governmental priorities").[18] Their findings also suggest that the responsiveness of a state higher education system to public priorities is greater in unified and federal systems than in segmented systems, since unified and federal systems allow for the representation of public interests, whereas segmented systems typically focus on institutional interests or interests that are not always aligned with public priorities.[19]

Richardson and colleagues summarized the consequences for higher education performance of state policies that do not adequately balance the interests of higher education institutions and the market:

> States that fail to establish an appropriate role for managing the conflicting pressures of professional values and the market end up with less satisfying outcomes than those that do. Ignoring the market in favor of state-planned systems of public higher education increases costs and limits responsiveness to emerging state needs and priorities. Excessive reliance on state regulation removes institutional incentives for efficiency and quality. Excessive reliance on consumer choice substitutes what people are willing to buy at present for longer term investment strategies. Overzealous market structuring can leave the most expensive tasks to public institutions.[20]

Along the same lines, Richard Richardson and Mario Martinez also point to the roles of system design and other state mechanisms for improving higher education performance.[21] Drawing on the perspectives of Nobel Prize–winning economist Elinor Ostrom and others, Richardson and Martinez focus on identifying the "rules in use" associated with higher education performance, where "rules in use" are defined as the formal (such as statutes and policies) and informal (such as norms and values) mechanisms that intentionally and unintentionally create incentives for institutional and other leaders to engage in particular behaviors.[22]

Acknowledging the roles of the federal government and institutions but focusing on the role of the state, Richardson and Martinez draw on data collected through case studies to identify 23 rules that explain differences in higher education performance in five states (California, New Mexico, New Jersey, New York, and South Dakota).[23] These 23 rules include aspects of system design, including the presence of a state coordinating board, size of the private not-for-profit sector, and absence of self-governing public colleges and universities, as well as the nature of state leadership, defined as the presence of clear goals, priorities, and accountability mechanisms. The 23 rules also include attention to policies explicitly designed to promote "access and achievement," including state need-based student aid, programs to promote enrollment of students from historically underrepresented groups, and initiatives to assess student learning outcomes, as well as fiscal policies pertaining to state appropriations to private colleges and universities, criteria considered in state funding formula, and tuition and fees at community colleges relative to public four-year institutions.[24]

The Role of Public Policy Levers

Although the state case studies led by Richard Richardson underscore the role of system design and governance structures in promoting higher education performance,[25] these studies do not offer a rationale for how or why public policy is related to performance. To address this limitation, our study draws from the economic theory of human capital and macroeconomic theories about the role of the public sector.

According to this perspective, public policy is the lever that governments use to adapt the higher education market to realize improved higher educational attainment. Scholars have defined the higher education market in various ways. For instance, in their examination of the role of system design in explaining higher education performance, Richardson and colleagues defined the market broadly to include both economic dimensions related to the demand for and supply of higher education and "noneconomic" contextual characteristics, including changing demographic characteristics, political support for higher education, and changing technology.[26]

For conceptual clarity, we define the market more narrowly. Consistent with the view of economists, we understand the higher education market, in its purest form, to be made up of buyers (that is, students and their families) and sellers (that is, colleges and universities) that interact with the possibility of exchanging money (represented by tuition and fees) for goods and services (degrees). The higher education market that exists today is the product of decades of intervention by public policymakers. Although the U.S. higher education system is characterized by the general absence of centralized management,[27] throughout our nation's history, federal and state governments have adopted public policies that shape the structure and design of the higher education market, especially with regard to the array of higher education institutions that are available to students in each state, and that influence, both positively and negatively, the investment of individuals in their higher education.

The past, current, and future use of public policy to influence the higher education market is justified by the economic theory of human capital. Initially developed by Nobel Prize–winning economists Theodore Schultz and Gary Becker in the 1960s, human capital theory predicts that investments (such as education and training) that promote the development of an individual's knowledge, talents, and skills raise an individual's productivity; an individual is rewarded for this enhanced productivity through higher earnings.[28]

Human capital theory assumes that individuals, as rational actors, decide to invest in their human capital by enrolling in college and engaging in other college-related behaviors if their calculation of the expected benefits less the costs exceeds the net benefits of alternative actions.[29] The long-term investment benefits of college enrollment include higher earnings, more fulfilling work environments, better health, longer life, more informed purchases, and lower probabilities of unemployment, while the short-term consumption benefits include enjoyment of the learning experience, involvement in extracurricular activities, participation in social and cultural events, and enhancement of social status.[30] The costs of investing in a college education include the direct costs of attendance (tuition, fees, room, board, books, and supplies) less financial aid received, the opportunity costs of foregone earnings and leisure time, and the costs of traveling between home and the institution.[31]

Economists do not assume that individuals (as rational actors) have complete or perfect information about the benefits and costs of all alternatives, only that they use the information that they have.[32] Economists recognize that, when making these benefit-cost calculations, individuals underestimate the private non-market benefits of higher education. The private non-market benefits, including better health for the individual and his/her spouse and children, and longer life, are substantial, representing, according to one estimate, even more than the private earnings benefits.[33] This underestimation—a form of market failure—is one justification for the use of public policy to influence the higher education market.[34] When market failure exists, the only way to "produce an economically efficient solution" is "through public intervention to try to make the markets work better."[35]

A second source of market failure is the fact that investments in higher education generate societal benefits or "positive externalities."[36] When making college enrollment decisions, individuals consider only the benefits that accrue to themselves as individuals. Yet individuals who enroll and complete college do not capture all of the benefits that their behavior produces. Instead, the benefits spill over to nonparticipants and benefit society more generally through enhanced economic growth and productivity, increased tax revenues, a more engaged citizenry, lower crime rates, lower costs of social welfare programs, greater political stability, and so on. An especially important societal benefit of higher education is its advancement of knowledge and technology in all academic fields. Thus, an individual's earnings reflect not only "the direct effects of his or her education" but also "the indirect effect coming from the education of others in the community and their contributions to available knowledge and civic institutions as well as the education of others in future generations."[37]

Because individuals do not consider these public benefits, the level of investment in higher education that occurs in the absence of government intervention is not economically efficient and is less than optimal from the perspective of society.[38] Public policy is the lever governments use to encourage individuals to invest in higher education and thus maximize the societal benefits of higher education. In short, government policy is a tool for "bring[ing] private incentives and social returns into alignment."[39]

Federal and state governments have adopted a number of policies that influence—with varying degrees of effectiveness—investment in higher education. Some public policies influence the supply, including the availability and characteristics of available higher education opportunities. For instance, the supply of higher education may be increased by finance policies that encourage capital improvements and provide tax-related benefits to not-for-profit and some for-profit institutions. Public policies that incentivize colleges and universities to adopt innovative approaches that reduce the costs of delivering higher education may also increase the supply of higher education opportunities. The supply of higher education may be influenced by government rules that influence the design of a state higher education system and restricted by government rules that control entry into the market; these rules may include state licensure requirements that determine the availability of higher education provided by for-profit institutions. Public policies regulating online courses or programs, branch campuses, and transfer between colleges and universities may also influence the supply of higher education that is available to students in a state.

Other policies influence the demand for higher education. For example, the demand for higher education may be increased through policies that improve students' academic readiness for college (e.g., Common Core Standards), reduce the price that students pay for higher education (e.g., federal and state financial aid), encourage families to accumulate the financial resources required to pay college costs (e.g., 529 college savings plans), and reduce structural barriers to student entry (e.g., affirmative action and other anti-discrimination practices).[40]

Reflecting the understandable interest of policymakers and practitioners in ascertaining "what works" in improving higher education attainment, many studies have sought to identify the effects of these and other policies on a discrete set of outcomes for a particular group of students.[41] This line of research has produced important contributions to knowledge, including the notion that financial aid in the form of grants is positively related to the likelihood of enrolling in college, that financial aid has a larger effect on the college enrollment of students from lower-income than of higher-income families,[42] and that need-based grant aid has a larger positive effect on students' college-enrollment than merit-based grant aid.[43] Studies using experimental and quasi-experimental designs to determine whether a particular program innovation *causes* improved outcomes for a particular group of students demonstrate the benefits to college-related outcomes of such actions as providing information about eligibility for financial aid as part of the income-tax preparation process.[44]

Although these and other studies shed light on the effectiveness of many discrete policies and practices for improving specific college-related outcomes, higher education attainment in the United States continues to be both lower than the socially optimal level and unequal across groups.[45] Thus, although government policy is the primary mechanism for achieving societal goals and priorities, attention only to the role of particular public policies in isolation from other policies and other dimensions of the state context is insufficient. Stiglitz drew a similar conclusion from his assessment of the role of government policy in reducing income inequality in the United States: "Even though market forces help shape the degree of inequality, government policies shape those market forces. Much of the inequality that exists today is the result of government policy, both what the government does and does not do."[46]

The Centrality of Context

The third perspective guiding our examination of the relationship between public policy and higher education performance is that state government actions to improve higher education attainment are influenced by the characteristics of its higher education system as well as its historical, demographic, economic, political, and other contextual characteristics. In short, the relationship between public policy and higher education performance cannot be understood without considering the state context.

The centrality of the political context is illustrated by research examining the political forces that explain why a state adopts a particular higher education policy.[47] As one example of this type of study, Erik Ness uses case study analyses to identify the political processes that explain why such states as New Mexico, Tennessee, and West Virginia adopted merit-based student aid programs, whereas another state with some similar characteristics (North Carolina) did not.[48] In another recent example, William Doyle and colleagues used event history analysis to identify the predictors of a state's adopting a prepaid tuition or savings plan. Testing hypotheses developed from the literature on policy privatization and policy diffusion, their analyses show greater likelihood of adopting one or both of these policies in states with more liberal governments, less competitive elections, and less centralized governance structures than in other states.[49] As a third example, Michael McLendon and colleagues used fixed effects regression analyses to show that such political characteristics as legislative professionalism, partisan control of elected offices, number of higher education interest groups, term limits, and gubernatorial strength are related to state appropriations for higher education even after taking into account differences across states in demographic characteristics and characteristics of a state's higher education system.[50]

The need to attend to a state's context is also suggested by previous case studies examining the relationship between public policy and higher education performance. Although acknowledging the role of contextual forces, however, these prior studies contribute limited understanding to the role of state context in influencing higher education performance. For instance, in their case studies of four states (Florida, Georgia, New York, and Oregon), Andrea Venezia and colleagues noted the relevance of the state's history and its political and educational culture but focused on the organizational structures that link K–12 and higher education and the procedures and norms of state governance in their examination of the policies that a state adopts to promote one aspect of performance: the transition of students from K–12 education into higher education.[51]

Other case studies also provide limited understanding of the role of context in understanding the relationship between public policy and higher education performance. In their examination of the relationship between system design and higher education performance in seven states, Richardson and colleagues assert the importance of such contextual characteristics as the strength of the governor and legislature, the constitutional status of the state's higher education institutions, and collective bargaining and other laws determining the relationship between the state and faculty.[52] But they confound the understanding of contextual forces by including contextual characteristics in their definition of the market.

The conceptual model that guides Richardson and Martinez's examination of the relationship between public policy and higher education performance in five states also assumes the centrality of the state context.[53] Their approach assumes that no "rule in use" exists in isolation and that the effects of any one rule depend on the other rules that are also in place, but they conclude by identifying 23 discrete rules that are associated with improved performance. The transferability of these specific rules to other states is not clear, given the many variations that exist across states. As in studies that seek to isolate the effects of a particular policy or program on a discrete college-related outcome, their approach also does not address the extent to which a state's historical, economic, political, and/or cultural context may permit a state to adopt a particular recommended policy. Thus, for example, although Richardson and Martinez concluded that performance on indicators of undergraduate education is higher in states with a coordinating board and that have least 19% of all students enrolled in private not-for-profit colleges and universities, these findings likely have limited utility for states with other higher education structures and system designs. Similarly, although Richardson and Martinez (as well as other research), show the benefits to college enrollment of a state-sponsored need-based student financial aid program, such a policy is unlikely to be adopted and implemented by a state like Georgia that has a substantial historical and political commitment to awarding aid based on criteria other than financial need.

Conclusion

Each of our five state studies offers a detailed description of the role of public policy in explaining recent trends in higher education performance within a particular state context. Illustrating the centrality of the state context, the specific explanations for higher education performance vary across the five states. Despite these variations, however, our cross-case analyses (presented in the final chapter) build on the perspectives identified in this chapter to produce a comprehensive conceptual model for understanding the role of state policy in improving higher education performance that applies to all five states.

Chapter 3

Examining the Relationship between Public Policy and Performance in Five States

What We Did

WITH CONTRIBUTIONS BY AWILDA RODRIGUEZ

How can a state use public policy to improve the performance of higher education to maximize the individual and societal benefits in light of state-specific characteristics of their state? To address this overarching question, we conducted case studies of the relationship between public policy and performance in five states. We constructed each case study to address the following two questions:

1. What is the performance of higher education in the selected states, where performance is measured by indicators of preparation, participation, completion, affordability, and equity across groups in these indicators?
2. What is the role of public policy in explaining changes from the early 1990s until 2010 in higher education performance in the selected states?

The following chapters address these two questions for each of five states. The final chapter identifies the themes that emerged from our cross-state analyses.

Why These Five States

For our examination of the relationship between public policy and higher education performance we selected Georgia, Illinois, Maryland, Texas, and Washington. Although it is impossible for five states to be representative of all 50 U.S. states, collectively these five states include some of the largest and most important states in the nation as well as states that vary along many critical dimensions, including their current and recent records of higher education performance and the public policies in place.

We used a number of criteria to select these states with the goal of including states that are not only home to large numbers of the U.S. population but also represent diversity on multiple dimensions. For instance, the selected states have high, low, improving, and declining higher education performance. The five states all are home to at least one major urban center but vary in the overall size of their populations and are located in different geographic regions. They vary in the racial/ethnic diversity in their current and projected college-going population and include states with differing fiscal resources and constraints. The states have different political cultures, with variations in the relative constitutional powers of the governor and legislature. They also diverge in terms the characteristics of their higher education systems, with variations in the distribution of enrollments across different sectors and the characteristics of their higher education governance structures.

State Higher Education Performance

As in states across the nation, all five of our study states are home to at least some colleges and universities that are performing quite well. Despite the presence of excellent institutions in all U.S. states, however, most have considerable unmet educational need. Our work focuses on understanding how well a state's higher education system is serving its residents rather than considering only individual institutional rankings or other institutional indicators of performance. We define the state system of higher education not as a formal sector or governance structure (such as the University System of Maryland) but as the collection of public and private not-for-profit and for-profit institutions in the state.

Defining the unit of analysis as the state rather than the institution, the five states in our study exhibit a range of past and present higher education performance. Although all five of the selected states must improve the educational attainment of their populations, the degree of improvement required is greater in Georgia and Texas than in Maryland, Illinois, and Washington. In Georgia and Texas, the current educational attainment of the adult population is below the national average. Table 1 (pp. 18–19) shows that the share of adults age 25 to 64 who hold at least an associate degree ranges from a high of 44% in Maryland, 42% in Washington, and 41% in Illinois to just 36% in Georgia and 33% in Texas.[1]

Of even greater concern than the low overall rates of educational attainment is the fact that in several of our study states educational attainment is lower among the younger generation than among the older generation. Nationwide, similar shares of adults age 25 to 34 and adults age 45 to 64 have attained at least an associate's degree: 38% and 37%, respectively. But table 1 shows that a smaller share of younger (age 25 to 34) adults than of older (age 45 to 64) adults has attained at least an associate degree in Georgia (34% versus 36%), Texas (31% versus 34%), and Washington (39% versus 43%). In contrast, educational attainment (as measured as attainment of at least an associate degree) is higher among younger than older adults in Illinois (43% versus 38%) and Maryland (45% and 43%,).[2] The lower level of educational attainment for younger adults is one force contributing to their lower rates of wealth accumulation.[3]

Given these differences across states in current educational attainment, it is not surprising that the improvements in educational attainment required also vary. Among our five study states, the annual percentage increase in degree production that is required for 55% of the population to hold at least an associate degree ranges from a low of 5.1% in Maryland, 5.4% in Illinois, and 6.2% in Washington, to a high of 10.0% in Georgia and 11.5% in Texas.[4] Although the attainment of older adults is higher than that of younger adults in some states, three of our five states (Georgia, Maryland, and Texas) are among the 32 nationwide that cannot reach international competitiveness goals without raising degree attainment among adults.[5]

In addition to selecting both high- and low-performing states, we intentionally selected states in which performance has improved and declined over time. *Measuring Up*, the nation's first higher education state report card, published by the National Center for Public Policy and Higher Education biennially between 2000 and 2008, utilized a number of indicators and sources of data to provide states with grades in various aspects of higher education performance. As described in chapter 1, we focus on indicators of college preparation, participation, completion, and affordability as the primary intermediate outcomes leading to higher education attainment.[6]

Between 2000 and 2008, affordability declined in all five states. All five of our study states (and all 50 states nationwide) received an F in this category of performance in 2008. But table 2 (p. 49) shows variations across the selected states in other aspects of higher education performance. Georgia's performance was low in 2008 relative to top-performing states, particularly with regard to preparation (C+) and participation (D−), but it improved between 2000 and 2008 in terms of preparation (rising from a D+ to C+) and participation (rising from F to

D–). Performance was also low in Texas, particularly with regard to participation (D– in 2008) and completion (C–). Performance in Texas improved between 2000 and 2008 in terms of preparation (rising from C to B) and completion (from D+ to C–) but declined in participation (from D to D–). Washington was a top-performer in terms of completion (improving from B– in 2000 to A– in 2008) but over this period declined on measures of participation (from C– to D). Illinois was a top-performing state in 2000 in terms of preparation, participation, and affordability—earning A's in all three categories—but experienced worrisome declines, earning a B in preparation, C in participation, and F in affordability in 2008. Although performance declined in participation in Maryland (from A to C)—as it also did in three other study states, Maryland's performance was high relative to other states in other indicators, with a B– in completion in both years and improvements in preparation (from B+ to A–).

Variations in Critical Contextual Dimensions

We selected the five studies to include demographically important states where importance is defined as having a large share of the nation's population, at least one major urban center, and racial and ethnic diversity. We also selected states that vary in other contextual dimensions, including the wealth of the population, the availability of resources to invest in higher education, and the projected demand by employers for college-educated workers.

Population Size and Growth

All five of the states selected are important to the future well-being of the nation since they are home to relatively large segments of the nation's total population. In 2010, three of the five ranked in the top 10 in terms of total population size and all five were in the top 20 (see table 3, pp. 50–51). The importance of improving educational attainment in Texas is underscored by the size and rapid growth of its population. With a population of 25.1 million in 2010, Texas is the nation's second largest state. The traditional college-age population in Texas is projected to increase by 52% between 2000 and 2030, the fifth-fastest growth rate in the nation.[7] Illinois is the fifth largest state (with a population of 12.8 million) and Georgia is the ninth largest (with 9.7 million). Washington and Maryland rank thirteenth and nineteenth in terms of their total populations (with 6.7 million and 5.8 million, respectively). Together these five states were home to about one-fifth of the nation's population in 2010.[8]

The five states are regionally dispersed across the United States, with Washington in the West, Illinois in the Midwest, Maryland in the mid-Atlantic, Georgia in the Southeast, and Texas in the South. Each has at least one major urban center: in 2010–11 all five states had at least one "incorporated city or town" with a population size that ranks in the top 40 of U.S. cities nationwide. Texas has three of the nation's 10 largest cities nationwide (Houston, San Antonio, and Dallas) and six of the nation's 100 largest metropolitan areas.[9]

Racial/Ethnic Diversity of the Population

We also selected states so as to ensure substantial racial/ethnic diversity in the college-going population and/or projected growth in the number and diversity of youth. Table 4 (p. 52) shows that the representation of Asians among high school graduates is above the national average in Washington (9% versus 5.4%) but similar to the national average in Georgia (3.5%), Illinois (4.5%), Maryland (5.7%), and Texas (3.9%).

Blacks represent a considerably higher share of high school graduates in two of the five study states than in the population nationwide (14.5% in 2008): Georgia (35.4%) and Maryland (34.8%). The representation of Blacks among high school graduates is higher in Georgia and Maryland than in all other states except Mississippi and Louisiana.[10] Hispanics represent a substantially higher share of high school graduates in Texas (37.5% in 2008) than of the population nationwide (15.1%). The representation of Hispanics among high school graduates is higher in Texas than in all states except New Mexico.[11] Blacks and Hispanics together now represent half (50.9% in 2008) of all high school graduates in Texas, a substantially higher percentage than the national average (29.6%). The racial/ethnic composition of the college-age population in Illinois approximates the composition of the population nationwide, with Blacks and Hispanics representing similar shares of the populations of Illinois and the nation (16.3% versus 14.5% for Blacks, and 13.8% versus 15.1% for Hispanics in 2008). The state of Washington is less racially and ethnically diverse than the other states and the nation overall, with Blacks and Hispanics together representing just 13.7% of high school graduates in 2008.[12]

In several of our study states, the Hispanic population is projected to increase dramatically in the coming years. Washington will experience substantial growth in its Hispanic population as the number of Hispanic high school graduates is projected to increase by 144% between 2008 and 2025. Similarly, the representation of Hispanics among high school graduates is currently smaller in Georgia and Maryland than it is nationwide (5.3% and 6% versus 15.1% in 2008) but is projected to grow substantially in the coming years, with projected increases in the number of Hispanic high school graduates of 272% in Georgia and 245% in Maryland between 2008 and 2025.[13]

Fiscal Resources and Constraints

Another important dimension of context pertains to the state's fiscal resources and constraints. As described in chapter 1, all five of the selected states (and all 50 U.S. states) are expected to face structural budget deficits over the next several years. Donald Boyd at the Center for the Study of States at State University of New York–Albany projected that by 2016 the state and local budget deficit as a percentage of state revenues will average 6.0% for the nation as a whole.[14] Moreover, these estimates likely understate the magnitude of the challenges, since they are based on prerecession data. Maryland is projected to experience somewhat less stress on the availability of state and local revenues (with a 2.1% projected structural budget deficit), while Texas is projected to experience the greatest fiscal stress among our five study states (with a 10.8% structural budget deficit) (see table 5, p. 53).[15]

The five states also vary in terms of the personal wealth of their populations as well as their taxable resources. Of the five study states, Maryland has the greatest potential fiscal capacity to invest in higher education. Table 6 (pp. 54–55) shows that Maryland has both the highest per capita personal income ($51,038 in 2011) and the highest total taxable resources per capita ($61,515 in 2010). As measured by total taxable resources per capita, Illinois ($54,865) and Washington ($54,546) also have relatively more public resources to invest in public services (including higher education), whereas Texas ($51,543) and Georgia ($44,375) have relatively fewer resources.[16]

Also important are differences in revenue sources. Neither Texas nor Washington has a state income tax. In Washington all tax increases must be approved by two-thirds of legislators; tax increases generating revenue greater than the spending limit must also be approved by two-thirds of voters.[17] The five states differ in terms of their willingness to tax themselves for public services. Nationwide, the effective tax rate averages 8.0% and ranges from a high of 12.7% in Alaska to a low of 5.1% in Delaware. Table 6 shows that the effective tax rate in the five states in this study is somewhat below the national average in Texas (6.6%), Georgia (7.0%), Washington (7.3%), Illinois (7.6%), and Maryland (7.9%).[18]

Income and Income Inequality

Of our five study states, Maryland not only has the higher per capita personal income (table 6) but also less income inequality (table 7, pp. 56–57). Table 6 shows that per capita personal income is above the national average in Maryland ($51,038 in 2011, fourth highest in the nation), Washington ($44,294, thirteenth), and Illinois ($44,140, fourteenth) but below the national average in Texas ($39,593, twenty-sixth) and Georgia ($36,104, thirty-ninth).[19]

Maryland not only has relatively high average per capita personal income (table 6) and median family income (table 7), but also has experienced greater than average growth in median family income over the past decade (33% versus 22%) and has below-average income inequality as measured by the ratio of family incomes for the ninetieth and tenth percentiles (10.4 versus 11.8; table 7). In contrast, Georgia had a median family income below the national average in 2010, slower than average growth in median family income between 2000 and 2010 (15% versus 22%), and greater than average income inequality (12 versus 11.8).[20]

Nationwide, income inequality increased between 1990 and 2010 despite increases in median family income (see table 7). Mirroring national trends, income inequality increased over this period in four of the five states studied. In Texas, the degree of income inequality exceeded the national average in 1990 and 2000; income inequality in Texas declined somewhat between 1990 and 2000 (from 11.5 to 11) but then rose between 2000 and 2010 (from 11 to 11.6) to about the same level as 1990.[21]

Demand for Higher Education

Based on their projections of workforce demands, Carnevale and colleagues estimate that by 2018 63% of jobs nationwide will require at least some postsecondary education. Reflecting differences in the mix of businesses and industries in their economies as well as other forces, the extent to which current and future jobs require higher numbers of better-educated workers varies across states.[22] Table 8 (pp. 58–59) shows that the demand for college-educated workers is greater in Washington, Maryland, and Illinois, where more than two-thirds of jobs are projected to require postsecondary education in 2018, than in Georgia and Texas, where 61% and 60% of jobs respectively are expected to require at least some postsecondary education in 2018.[23]

Characteristics of the Higher Education System and Governance Structures

The five states also differ in the structure of their higher education systems, particularly in terms of the relative roles that different sectors play in providing higher education in the state. Table 9 (pp. 60–61) shows that the private sector plays a relatively more important role in the education of students in Illinois than in other states. In Illinois two-thirds of all students were enrolled in public colleges and universities in fall 2010 compared with about 77% of undergraduates in Georgia, 82% in Maryland, 85% in Washington, and 87% in Texas.[24]

The community and technical college sector plays a notable role in each of the states. In four of the five, the share of students enrolled at public two-year colleges is higher than the national average (34% in fall 2010): Texas (46%), Illinois (42%), Washington (42%), and Maryland (39%) (see table 9).[25]

In three of the five states, the share of students enrolled at for-profit institutions is below the national average (10% in fall 2010): Maryland (4%), Washington (4%), and Texas (5%). Comparable shares of students are enrolled in for-profit institutions in Illinois (10%) and Georgia (11%).[26]

The five states have varying coordinating and governing structures for higher education and represent the types of structures that exist nationwide. One of the five states (Georgia) has a consolidated governing board, whereas the other four states have coordinating boards. The coordinating board functions as a cabinet department in Maryland but not in Illinois, Texas, or Washington. Several of the states also have system-level boards, including boards with constitutional authority (Georgia) and state education boards without governance authority per se (Washington). In Texas, the 45 public four-year institutions are governed by 10 governing boards; six of them are responsible for multiple campuses, and four are responsible for single institutions.[27]

Maryland has a coordinating board (the Maryland Higher Education Commission) that oversees the University System of Maryland (composed of 11 of the state's 13 public four-year institutions) and the state's community colleges, as well as Morgan State University, St. Mary's College of Maryland, the state's independent colleges and universities, and private career schools. Two of the state's public four-year institutions, Morgan State University (a Historically Black Institution) and St. Mary's College, are not part of the University System of Maryland but instead have their own governing boards.[28] In Georgia, the state's technical colleges are overseen by a separate board for technical colleges.[29] Illinois has a separate coordinating board for its 48 community colleges (Illinois Community College Board), and Washington has a separate state board for its community and technical colleges. A statewide association represents the state's community colleges in Texas, but the statewide community college association is voluntary in Maryland.

Procedures Used to Generate the State Studies

Using conventional case study methodology, we collected and analyzed multiple sources of data to produce a case study report for each state.[30] Like other researchers, we assume that the influence of public policy on higher education performance cannot be understood simply by reviewing authorizing legislation but instead must be discerned through fieldwork.[31]

We developed the data collection protocols to reflect our understanding of prior research and the assumptions articulated in chapter 2. We used the same approach to collecting data in each of the five states in order to ensure the comparability of our findings and conclusions across the five states.[32] For each state, we first used existing data sets, media reports, and government and other documents to produce a "briefing book" that described trends in the state's higher education performance as well as its demographic, economic, and political context. The briefing book also identified the public policies pertaining to higher education attainment that appeared to be in place within each state.[33] We used the briefing books to generate state-specific hypotheses about the various contextual forces and public policies that may be influencing higher education performance in the state and to adapt, as appropriate, our subsequent data collection efforts.

Our research team spent three to four days in each of the five states conducting interviews and collecting additional documents. These in-person interviews were supplemented by telephone interviews conducted both before and after the site visits.[34] Whereas Richardson and Martinez[35] focused their data collection on eight "action areas" (planning, program review and approval, information, academic preparation, student financial assistance, tuition and operational support, capital support, and economic development initiatives), we focused on understanding the forces that predicted higher education performance as defined as preparation, participation, completion, affordability, and research excellence. The research team adapted the interview protocol for each state to reflect and test our initial state-specific assumptions and emerging hypotheses.

We conducted individual and group interviews with institutional, state, business, and other leaders whom we expected to be knowledgeable about particular dimensions of higher education performance and relevant policies and practices. In each state we spoke with elected officials and staff in the executive and legislative branches of government; staff and leaders of the state's higher education coordinating and governing boards, student financial aid commission, community college association, and private college association; presidents and senior staff at public four-year and public two-year colleges; leaders of K–12 education agencies and P–16/P–20 entities; business and civic leaders; and other knowledgeable individuals (e.g., leaders of higher education policy organizations, faculty studying higher education policy). Table 10 (p. 62) summarizes the numbers of different categories of individuals interviewed in each state. We interviewed between 25 and 48 individuals in each state, for a total of 172 informants.[36]

To analyze the data, the research team first created a case study database to organize the information collected.[37] Multiple members of the research team participated in the coding and analysis of data. We developed a preliminary list of codes using the guiding perspectives outlined in chapter 2, while also allowing additional codes to emerge.[38] Following this process, we worked to better characterize and substantiate overlapping themes, eventually condensing the data into overarching themes.

We used several strategies to ensure the trustworthiness and credibility of the findings and conclusions. To ensure construct validity, the research team collected information from multiple sources. For each state, we asked two to three individuals who were knowledgeable about the state to provide feedback on an initial case study report.[39]

The five state reports form the basis for the cross-case analyses, which identify the five broad tenets that cut across the five states. We determined these five cross-case tenets through an iterative process that involved identifying themes within and across states and considering the emerging themes in light of relevant prior research, prevailing research, and the guiding theoretical and conceptual perspectives described in chapter 2. We received reactions to and feedback about these themes with experts who are knowledgeable about these five states as well as other U.S. states.

We used these findings to refine our understanding of the most appropriate conceptual framework for understanding the relationship between public policy and performance. The conclusions from the cross-case analysis and their implications are presented in the final chapter.

Conclusion

The next five chapters tell the state-specific stories of the relationship between public policy and performance in each of the five states: Georgia, Illinois, Maryland, Texas, and Washington. Consistent with case study research methods and our emphasis on context, each of these case studies is bounded by the time period examined. Since the world is constantly changing, the likelihood that these state reports (or any case study) describe the situation beyond the particular time period examined is limited. Consistent with conventional approaches, our goal was to use case study methodology to explain the forces that contributed to changes in higher education performance between the early 1990s and 2010 in each of the five states and then use the findings from these case study analyses to develop a conceptual model describing how public policy influences higher education performance.

Although the specifics of these case studies may lag behind the current situation, they provide a rich depiction of the complex and interdependent connections between public policy and performance and how these connections are informed by a state's unique history, politics, and demographic, economic, and other characteristics. Understanding the state-specific stories is an essential first step toward identifying the cross-case lessons. Many state reports have been written about "best" state practices without an understanding of how a particular policy or set of policies fit within a state's complex history and culture. Moreover, many policy solutions fail because they do not consider the compatibility of a policy recommendation within the particular state context, including other policies that are in place.

Each of the five chapters that follow begins with an introduction that identifies the state-specific needs for improved educational attainment within the context of the state's workforce demands, demographic changes, and economic constraints. Then we describe the state's current and past performance of higher education in terms of preparation, participation, completion, and affordability. We supplemented the data provided in *Measuring Up* with data that each state collects to generate a complete, current, and comprehensive assessment of higher education performance on these indicators. The third part of each chapter summarizes key characteristics of the higher education system in that state. The fourth component addresses the question "What explains performance?" This section weaves together the many contextual characteristics with current and past state policy decisions to identify the primary explanations for recent trends in the state's higher education performance.

Table 2 Performance of Selected States on *Measuring Up 2000* and *Measuring Up 2008* Performance Categories

	Preparation		Participation		Completion		Affordability	
	2000	2008	2000	2008	2000	2008	2000	2008
Georgia	D+	C+	F	D−	B−	B−	D+	F
Illinois	A	B	A	C	C+	B+	A	F
Maryland	B+	A−	A	C	B−	B−	D	F
Texas	C	B	D	D−	D+	C−	C	F
Washington	C+	C+	C−	D	B−	A−	B−	F

Sources: National Center for Public Policy and Higher Education, *Measuring Up 2000: The National Report Card on Higher Education,* and *Measuring Up 2008: The National Report Card on Higher Education.*

Table 3 Total Population and Projected Population Growth by State

	Total Count, 2010		Projected Growth (18- to 24-Year-Olds), 2000 to 2030	
	Number (in millions)	Rank	Percentage	Rank
Nation	**308.7**	–	**20**	–
Alabama	4.8	23	−6	40
Alaska	0.7	47	54	4
Arizona	6.4	16	91	2
Arkansas	2.9	32	7	22
California	37.3	1	30	13
Colorado	5.0	22	34	11
Connecticut	3.6	29	4	27
Delaware	0.9	45	6	24
Florida	18.8	4	66	3
Georgia	**9.7**	**9**	**40**	**9**
Hawaii	1.4	40	31	12
Idaho	1.6	39	19	17
Illinois	**12.8**	**5**	**1**	**28**
Indiana	6.5	15	1	29
Iowa	3.0	30	−17	47
Kansas	2.9	33	−3	33
Kentucky	4.3	26	0	30
Louisiana	4.5	25	−5	39
Maine	1.3	41	−5	46
Maryland	**5.8**	**19**	**41**	**7**
Massachusetts	6.5	14	5	25
Michigan	9.9	8	−4	35
Minnesota	5.3	21	16	18
Mississippi	3.0	31	−13	43
Missouri	6.0	18	6	23
Montana	1.0	44	−14	44
Nebraska	1.8	38	−3	34
Nevada	2.7	35	92	1
New Hampshire	1.3	42	14	19
New Jersey	8.8	11	10	21
New Mexico	2.1	36	−7	41
New York	19.4	3	−4	36
North Carolina	9.5	10	49	6
North Dakota	0.7	48	−23	48
Ohio	11.5	7	−7	42
Oklahoma	3.8	28	5	26
Oregon	3.8	27	27	15

Table 3 (continued)

	Total Count, 2010		Projected Growth (18- to 24-Year-Olds), 2000 to 2030	
	Number (in millions)	Rank	Percentage	Rank
Pennsylvania	12.7	6	−5	38
Rhode Island	1.1	43	−5	37
South Carolina	4.6	24	12	20
South Dakota	0.8	46	−15	45
Tennessee	6.3	17	23	16
Texas	**25.1**	**2**	**52**	**5**
Utah	2.8	34	29	14
Vermont	0.6	49	−3	32
Virginia	8.0	12	40	8
Washington	**6.7**	**13**	**38**	**10**
West Virginia	1.9	37	−28	50
Wisconsin	5.7	20	−2	31
Wyoming	0.6	50	−24	49

Sources: U.S. Census Bureau, "Table SF1:P5: Hispanic or Latino Origin by Race"; U.S. Census Bureau, "Table B1: The total population by selected age groups."

Table 4 Racial/Ethnic Composition of High School Graduates and Projected Growth in Hispanic High School Graduates, 2008 to 2025

	Racial/Ethnic Composition of 2008 High School Graduates			Racial/Ethnic Composition of 2025 High School Graduates			Percentage Increase in Hispanic H.S. Graduates, 2008 to 2025
	Asian	Black	Hispanic	Asian	Black	Hispanic	
Nation	**5.4%**	**14.5%**	**15.1%**	**8.2%**	**13.9%**	**25.3%**	**80%**
Georgia	3.5	35.4	5.3	7.3	35.4	15.3	272
Illinois	4.5	16.3	13.8	7.5	13.9	22.7	47
Maryland	5.7	34.8	6.0	11.0	33.0	19.8	245
Texas	3.9	13.4	37.5	5.6	9.6	57.9	115
Washington	9.0	4.4	9.3	14.0	5.7	20.7	144

Source: Western Interstate Higher Education Commission, *Knocking at the College Door: Projections of High School Graduates.*

Table 5 Projected State and Local Budget Deficit as a Percent of Revenues, 2016

	Percent	Rank among U.S. states		Percent	Rank among U.S. states
Nation	**6.0**	–	Montana	5.8	26
Alabama	10.6	3	Nebraska	5.8	25
Alaska	5.7	28	Nevada	9.7	4
Arizona	9.5	5	New Hampshire	2.6	45
Arkansas	8.5	12	New Jersey	2.3	48
California	3.8	38	New Mexico	6.7	21
Colorado	8.5	11	New York	5.0	32
Connecticut	2.4	46	North Carolina	8.9	8
Delaware	4.6	36	North Dakota	2.9	43
Florida	8.1	14	Ohio	4.1	37
Georgia	**8.5**	**10**	Oklahoma	6.7	20
Hawaii	6.3	23	Oregon	4.8	34
Idaho	9.1	7	Pennsylvania	5.4	29
Illinois	**5.7**	**27**	Rhode Island	2.7	44
Indiana	6.3	22	South Carolina	8.1	13
Iowa	7.4	17	South Dakota	7.8	16
Kansas	4.7	35	Tennessee	8.7	9
Kentucky	7.2	18	**Texas**	**10.8**	**2**
Louisiana	6.2	24	Utah	9.4	6
Maine	2.2	49	Vermont	2.3	47
Maryland	**2.1**	**50**	Virginia	4.9	33
Massachusetts	3.3	41	**Washington**	**8.0**	**15**
Michigan	3.5	40	West Virginia	5.2	30
Minnesota	5.1	31	Wisconsin	3.0	42
Mississippi	10.9	1	Wyoming	3.5	39
Missouri	6.8	19			

Source: Boyd, *Projected State and Local Budget Surplus as a Percent of Revenues, 2016.*

Table 6 Fiscal Resources of Selected States

	Effective Tax Rate,* 2010		Total Taxable Resources per Capita,† 2010		Per Capita Personal Income, 2011	
	Percent	Indexed to U.S.	Dollars	Indexed to U.S.	Dollars	Rank
Nation	**8.0**	–	**50,974**	–	**41,663**	–
Alabama	7.1	0.88	39,347	0.77	34,650	42
Alaska	12.7	1.57	68,261	1.34	45,529	10
Arizona	7.2	0.90	42,245	0.83	35,875	40
Arkansas	8.3	1.03	39,184	0.77	34,014	44
California	8.6	1.07	53,817	1.06	44,481	12
Colorado	7.5	0.93	54,228	1.06	44,088	15
Connecticut	8.2	1.02	73,312	1.44	56,889	1
Delaware	5.1	0.64	77,296	1.52	41,635	20
Florida	7.6	0.94	46,287	0.91	39,563	27
Georgia	**7.0**	**0.87**	**44,375**	**0.87**	**36,104**	**39**
Hawaii	9.5	1.18	51,107	1.00	43,053	17
Idaho	7.0	0.87	39,484	0.77	33,326	49
Illinois	**7.6**	**0.95**	**54,865**	**1.08**	**44,140**	**14**
Indiana	8.0	0.99	45,110	0.88	35,550	41
Iowa	7.7	0.96	50,592	0.99	40,470	24
Kansas	8.0	0.99	50,110	0.98	40,481	23
Kentucky	7.9	0.98	40,147	0.79	33,667	47
Louisiana	6.6	0.82	53,914	1.06	38,578	28
Maine	10.3	1.29	42,501	0.83	37,973	31
Maryland	**7.9**	**0.98**	**61,515**	**1.21**	**51,038**	**4**
Massachusetts	8.1	1.00	63,417	1.24	53,621	2
Michigan	8.9	1.11	40,414	0.79	36,533	36
Minnesota	8.4	1.04	54,911	1.08	44,672	11
Mississippi	8.4	1.04	36,130	0.71	32,176	50
Missouri	7.0	0.87	45,038	0.88	38,248	29
Montana	7.9	0.98	41,327	0.81	36,573	35
Nebraska	7.5	0.93	53,780	1.06	41,584	22
Nevada	7.2	0.90	51,806	1.02	38,173	30
N. Hampshire	6.7	0.84	56,586	1.11	45,787	8
New Jersey	9.0	1.12	64,658	1.27	53,181	3
New Mexico	7.9	0.98	40,312	0.79	34,575	43
New York	11.0	1.37	63,885	1.25	50,545	5
North Carolina	7.3	0.91	46,772	0.92	36,164	38
North Dakota	9.0	1.13	56,986	1.12	45,747	9
Ohio	8.6	1.07	43,918	0.86	37,791	33
Oklahoma	7.0	0.87	43,446	0.85	37,277	34
Oregon	6.6	0.82	52,115	1.02	37,909	32

Table 6 (continued)

	Effective Tax Rate,* 2010		Total Taxable Resources per Capita,† 2010		Per Capita Personal Income, 2011	
	Percent	Indexed to U.S.	Dollars	Indexed to U.S.	Dollars	Rank
Pennsylvania	8.5	1.05	48,958	0.96	42,478	18
Rhode Island	8.5	1.06	53,560	1.05	43,992	16
S. Carolina	7.4	0.92	38,379	0.75	33,673	46
South Dakota	6.0	0.75	52,843	1.04	41,590	21
Tennessee	6.6	0.82	43,448	0.85	36,533	37
Texas	**6.6**	**0.83**	**51,543**	**1.01**	**39,593**	**26**
Utah	6.6	0.82	45,468	0.89	33,790	45
Vermont	10.3	1.28	45,835	0.90	41,832	19
Virginia	6.6	0.82	58,967	1.16	45,920	7
Washington	**7.3**	**0.91**	**54,546**	**1.07**	**44,294**	**13**
West Virginia	9.2	1.14	37,977	0.75	33,513	48
Wisconsin	9.1	1.13	47,289	0.93	40,073	25
Wyoming	8.7	1.08	70,848	1.39	47,301	6

Sources: For 2010 effective rate and total taxable resources per capita, State Higher Education Executive Officers, *State Higher Education Finance, FY2011;* for 2011 per capita personal income, National Center for Higher Education Management Systems, "Per Capita Personal Income, 2011."

* The effective tax rate is "Actual Tax Revenue per capita divided by Total Taxable Resources per capita, expressed as a percentage" (SHEEO, 65).

† SHEEO labels total taxable resources per capita a measure of "state income and wealth" (10). This number represents "the sum of Gross State Product (in-state production) minus components presumed not taxable by the state plus various components of income derived from out-of-state sources" (65).

Table 7 Family Income and Income Inequality by State, 1990, 2000, 2010 (current dollars)

	Median Family Income			Increase		Ratio 90/10 percentile			
	1990	2000	2010	1990–2000	2000–2010	1990	2000	2010	Rank 2010
Nation	**$32,432**	**$45,097**	**$55,197**	**39%**	**22%**	**10.2**	**10.7**	**11.8**	
Alabama	26,482	37,988	46,504	43	22	11.4	11.9	12.2	5
Alaska	41,885	53,402	68,620	27	28	8.8	8.4	9.2	47
Arizona	29,353	41,301	50,942	41	23	10.0	9.8	11.2	23
Arkansas	23,498	35,352	42,557	50	20	9.4	9.9	11.1	26
California	35,830	47,293	60,764	32	28	10.3	11.9	11.9	9
Colorado	32,200	48,991	59,751	52	22	9.2	9.3	11.3	19
Connecticut	45,499	59,973	75,014	32	25	8.4	10.1	11.6	14
Delaware	30,865	50,939	60,978	65	20	7.6	8.4	9.9	38
Florida	29,592	40,792	49,987	38	23	9.4	10.5	11.0	27
Georgia	**31,682**	**44,789**	**51,423**	**41**	**15**	**10.3**	**11.3**	**12.0**	**6**
Hawaii	41,977	53,412	72,915	27	37	7.8	10.0	9.9	36
Idaho	27,516	39,992	48,998	45	23	7.8	8.5	9.2	46
Illinois	**36,303**	**50,497**	**60,573**	**39**	**20**	**10.1**	**10.3**	**11.3**	**20**
Indiana	32,000	46,000	52,011	44	13	8.2	8.5	10.2	32
Iowa	29,996	43,978	53,842	47	22	7.8	7.4	9.3	44
Kansas	30,977	44,981	54,082	45	20	8.3	8.9	10.0	35
Kentucky	25,287	37,994	45,518	50	20	12.3	11.1	11.9	8
Louisiana	24,998	35,977	47,221	44	31	13.9	13.8	12.7	2
Maine	29,999	41,654	49,147	39	18	8.2	8.5	9.9	37
Maryland	**41,999**	**56,402**	**74,995**	**34**	**33**	**8.3**	**9.3**	**10.4**	**31**
Massachusetts	40,999	55,655	70,794	36	27	10.2	11.2	12.6	3
Michigan	34,361	48,991	53,050	43	8	10.6	9.6	11.7	11
Minnesota	34,098	51,991	62,498	52	20	8.2	8.0	10.1	34
Mississippi	21,990	33,498	41,165	52	23	12.6	13.1	12.2	4
Missouri	29,999	41,992	50,639	40	21	9.7	9.9	10.9	28
Montana	26,244	36,914	47,757	41	29	8.2	10.0	10.1	33
Nebraska	29,313	44,895	53,663	53	20	7.7	7.4	9.3	45
Nevada	31,998	46,102	55,703	44	21	8.1	9.0	9.4	43
New Hampshire	38,974	52,807	68,534	35	30	6.6	7.4	9.0	48
New Jersey	45,398	60,800	76,994	34	27	8.5	10.6	11.2	22
New Mexico	24,878	34,960	44,996	41	29	10.8	11.5	12.0	7
New York	36,000	46,997	59,968	31	28	12.4	14.2	13.6	1
North Carolina	29,516	41,991	48,608	42	16	9.3	9.9	11.5	18
North Dakota	26,997	39,957	53,667	48	34	8.1	8.9	9.8	39
Ohio	32,044	45,722	52,155	43	14	9.7	9.1	11.5	17
Oklahoma	27,049	37,159	46,148	37	24	10.4	9.6	10.8	30
Oregon	29,206	42,879	51,017	47	19	8.5	9.9	11.1	25
Pennsylvania	32,996	44,997	55,900	36	24	9.1	9.8	11.1	24
Rhode Island	36,663	45,983	60,801	25	32	9.5	10.4	11.8	10

Table 7 (continued)

	Median Family Income			Increase		Ratio 90/10 percentile			
	1990	2000	2010	1990–2000	2000–2010	1990	2000	2010	Rank 2010
South Carolina	28,545	39,454	47,276	38	20	9.4	9.9	11.7	12
South Dakota	25,806	38,362	50,812	49	32	9.2	8.7	9.8	40
Tennessee	27,888	39,971	46,746	43	17	10.2	10.0	11.6	13
Texas	**28,500**	**40,991**	**50,819**	**44**	**24**	**11.5**	**11.0**	**11.6**	**15**
Utah	32,397	50,585	60,449	56	19	7.1	7.4	8.3	50
Vermont	30,999	44,095	54,457	42	23	7.9	7.8	9.5	42
Virginia	35,589	49,882	64,999	40	30	8.9	9.9	11.5	16
Washington	**33,989**	**48,200**	**59,456**	**42**	**23**	**8.6**	**9.5**	**10.9**	**29**
West Virginia	22,335	32,691	43,100	46	32	12.1	10.8	11.3	21
Wisconsin	32,690	47,979	55,999	47	17	8.0	7.7	9.6	41
Wyoming	30,118	40,687	58,403	35	44	8.4	9.0	8.6	49

Source: Integrated Public Use Microdata Series Version 5.0 (Machine-readable database).

Note: Family income data are weighted by PERWT

Table 8 Projected Percentage of Jobs Expected to Require at Least Some Postsecondary Education by 2018

	Total % Requiring At Least Some College	Percentage of Jobs Requiring at Least:			
		Some College, No Degree	Associate's Degree	Bachelor's Degree	Master's Degree or Higher
Nation	**63%**	**17%**	**12%**	**24%**	**10%**
Alaska	62	16	15	21	10
Alabama	58	16	14	20	9
Arkansas	54	14	14	19	7
Arizona	64	19	14	22	10
California	67	18	12	26	11
Colorado	70	17	12	30	12
Connecticut	67	16	11	26	15
Delaware	61	16	11	22	11
Florida	63	21	11	22	9
Georgia	**61**	**15**	**12**	**24**	**10**
Hawaii	68	23	11	25	9
Iowa	64	21	13	23	8
Idaho	63	19	15	22	8
Illinois	**67**	**18**	**12**	**25**	**11**
Indiana	58	16	13	20	8
Kansas	66	17	14	25	10
Kentucky	57	16	13	19	9
Louisiana	53	11	14	21	8
Massachusetts	70	16	10	28	16
Maryland	**67**	**14**	**11**	**26**	**16**
Maine	62	19	11	23	9
Michigan	65	19	14	22	10
Minnesota	70	21	13	27	9
Missouri	60	15	13	23	9
Mississippi	57	19	13	18	7
Montana	63	17	13	24	8
North Carolina	63	19	12	23	9
North Dakota	69	24	13	25	7
Nebraska	66	20	14	24	8
New Hampshire	67	19	11	26	11
New Jersey	66	14	10	29	13
New Mexico	61	16	14	20	11
Nevada	58	17	13	20	7
New York	67	20	9	25	14
Ohio	59	16	13	21	9
Oklahoma	59	16	14	21	8
Oregon	67	18	14	24	10

Table 8 (continued)

	Total % Requiring At Least Some College	Percentage of Jobs Requiring at Least:			
		Some College, No Degree	Associate's Degree	Bachelor's Degree	Master's Degree or Higher
Pennsylvania	60	17	10	23	11
Rhode Island	66	19	11	25	11
South Carolina	60	18	12	21	9
South Dakota	63	21	11	23	7
Tennessee	56	14	13	21	9
Texas	**60**	**14**	**13**	**23**	**9**
Utah	68	22	15	23	8
Virginia	66	15	12	26	14
Vermont	66	19	10	25	12
Washington	**70**	**22**	**13**	**25**	**11**
Wisconsin	64	20	12	23	9
West Virginia	53	15	12	17	8
Wyoming	65	24	14	20	7

Source: Carnevale, Smith, and Strohl, *Help Wanted: Projections of Jobs and Education Requirements through 2018*, 121–22.

Table 9 Distribution of Total Enrollments in Degree-Granting Institutions across Sectors, by State, Fall 2010

		Public				
State	Total	Public Total	Four-Year Public	Two-Year Public	Private not-for-profit	For Profit
Nation	**100%**	**72%**	**38%**	**34%**	**18%**	**10%**
Alabama	100	82	52	30	8	11
Alaska	100	96	94	3	2	2
Arizona	100	46	17	29	1	53
Arkansas	100	89	53	35	10	2
California	100	82	24	58	11	8
Colorado	100	72	44	28	9	19
Connecticut	100	64	35	29	34	3
Delaware	100	73	45	28	27	1
Florida	100	70	59	11	14	15
Georgia*	**100**	**77**	**46**	**31**	**13**	**11**
Hawaii	100	77	39	38	18	5
Idaho	100	75	58	17	21	3
Illinois	**100**	**65**	**23**	**42**	**25**	**10**
Indiana	100	74	51	23	19	7
Iowa	100	47	19	28	15	38
Kansas	100	86	47	40	12	2
Kentucky	100	79	42	37	13	8
Louisiana	100	85	55	30	11	4
Maine	100	71	46	24	27	3
Maryland	**100**	**82**	**43**	**39**	**15**	**4**
Massachusetts	100	44	24	21	54	2
Michigan	100	81	43	37	18	2
Minnesota	100	59	30	30	16	25
Mississippi	100	90	43	47	9	2
Missouri	100	58	33	25	35	8
Montana	100	91	70	20	10	0
Nebraska	100	75	40	34	23	3
Nevada	100	87	78	10	3	10
New Hampshire	100	58	39	20	35	7
New Jersey	100	81	40	41	17	2
New Mexico	100	93	39	54	1	7
New York	100	55	30	25	40	4
North Carolina	100	81	38	43	16	3
North Dakota	100	86	74	12	11	3
Ohio	100	74	46	28	20	7
Oklahoma	100	86	54	31	10	5
Oregon	100	83	40	44	13	4
Pennsylvania	100	54	35	19	37	9

Table 9 (continued)

		Public				
State	Total	Public Total	Four-Year Public	Two-Year Public	Private not-for-profit	For Profit
Rhode Island	100	51	30	21	49	0
South Carolina	100	80	40	40	14	7
South Dakota	100	76	65	11	16	8
Tennessee	100	69	41	28	22	9
Texas	**100**	**87**	**41**	**46**	**9**	**5**
Utah	100	71	53	18	24	5
Vermont	100	60	46	15	38	1
Virginia	100	71	37	34	19	10
Washington	**100**	**85**	**44**	**42**	**11**	**4**
West Virginia	100	63	48	15	9	29
Wisconsin	100	78	48	30	17	5
Wyoming	100	95	34	61	0	5

Source: National Center for Education Statistics, *Digest of Education Statistics 2011*, table 224.

* Data for Georgia describe the configuration of higher education in fall 2010.

Table 10 Number of Interviewees per State

	Georgia	Illinois	Maryland	Texas	Washington
Total	36	29	25	34	48
State political leadership*	4	5	4	10	8
State higher education leadership†	18	13	14	9	22
Institutional leadership‡	6	6	4	8	8
K–12 and P–16/P–20 education	4	1	1	1	2
Business, research, philanthropic	1	1	1	2	4
Other participants	3	3	1	4	4

* Includes leaders and senior staff in the executive and legislative branches of government.

† Includes leaders of the state higher education coordinating/governing boards, student financial aid commission, community college association, and private college association.

‡ Includes presidents and senior staff at public four-year and two-year colleges and universities in the state.

Chapter 4

Perpetuating Disparity

The Performance and State Policies of Higher Education in Georgia

WITH CONTRIBUTIONS BY MICHAEL ARMIJO

Over the past decade, the performance of higher education in Georgia has remained below the national average on most key measures of higher education attainment.[1] Although the state has been successful in workforce education (as measured by the completion of short-term certificates at technical colleges) and research, Georgia ranks below most states (thirty-first in the nation) in the percentage of adults (ages 25 and older) who have attained an associate degree or higher.

Georgia must improve the performance of higher education in order to meet changing workforce demands. The state has a long history in agriculture with some manufacturing but is projected to experience substantial growth in highly skilled occupations. Many service-sector corporations such as Delta/Northwestern Airlines and UPS now call Georgia home. Substantially more new jobs created in the state between 2008 and 2018 are expected to require at least some postsecondary education (about 306,000) than are projected to require no more than a high school education (about 160,000), although the proportion requiring more than a high school education is a somewhat lower percentage than the projected national average (61% versus 63%).[2] Given trends in degree production and projected population growth, Georgia will need to increase its annual production of associate and bachelor's degrees by 10% per year in order for 55% of its workforce (ages 25 to 64) to hold at least an associate degree by 2020, the level of attainment of the best-performing nations.[3] Like many other states, Georgia will not be able to reach this goal by increasing the education attainment of young adults only; the state must also approve college participation and degree completion of nontraditional-age students.[4]

Georgia will also not be able to achieve these increases in educational attainment without substantially improving the attainment of the state's sizable Black and fast-growing Hispanic populations. In 2005 only 30% of Blacks and 14% of Hispanics in the state (ages 25 to 34) had attained at least an associate degree, compared to 43% of Whites.[5] The state's population ranks first in the nation in the number of Blacks and tenth in the number of Hispanics.[6] Blacks represented 30% of the state's population in 2010, compared with 12% nationally. Between 2008–9 and 2019–20, the representation of Hispanics is projected to double from 6% to 12%.[7]

Efforts to raise overall attainment and improve equity in attainment across groups must recognize the fiscal resource constraints. The wealth of Georgia's population is relatively low, ranking thirty-eighth in per capita personal income.[8] Georgia's per capita personal income has lagged behind the national average historically (at $35,490 versus $40,584 in 2008), and the gap increased from 1998 to 2008.[9] The state also ranks below the national average ($50,974) in total taxable resources per capita (at $44,375), an indication of its relatively low overall tax capacity. The effective tax rate in Georgia in FY2010 was 7.0%, below the national average of 8.0%.[10]

Over the past decade, state appropriations for higher education in Georgia have declined in constant dollars by 36% from $9,818 per FTE in 2002 to $6,277 per FTE in 2012.[11] In January 2011, Governor Nathan Deal (Republican) proposed a revised budget for fiscal year 2011 that incorporated revenue estimates that were $27.5 million lower than originally projected. For fiscal year 2012, the General Assembly passed a state budget that was 2.3% above the budget for fiscal year 2011, but the budget for higher education was reduced by 8.1% for fiscal year 2012, with a reduction of 9.1% for colleges and universities and a drop of 2.1% for technical colleges.[12] As in other states, constraints on state revenues—particularly for higher education—will likely continue into the near future, given structural budget deficits and other forces.

Adding to Georgia's fiscal challenges, the state's lottery sales, used to support the well-known HOPE Scholarship and Grant Program and other public programs, have not kept pace with previous annual increases. Growth in lottery sales averaged 6.2% annually from 2000 to 2009, and the proceeds to education grew 3% annually over this period. In 2009, however, the proceeds to education increased by only 0.05%.[13] From 2010 to 2011, total ticket sales declined 1.3% and education proceeds declined 4.3%.[14] The state lacks sufficient reserves to fill the gap between education revenues from the lottery and student eligibility levels for HOPE Scholarships and Grants. In his state-of-the-state address in 2011, Governor Deal explained, "Over the past several years, HOPE pays out more than the lottery brings in. In fiscal year 2010, over $150 million of reserve funds were spent. In fiscal year 2011, it is estimated that over $300 million of reserves will be needed if this pattern is not reversed. By fiscal year 2013, all of the reserves will have been expended and HOPE cannot meet its obligations."[15]

Higher Education Performance

Georgia improved modestly between the early 1990s and 2010 on some measures of college preparation, participation, and completion but continues to lag behind the national average on most indicators. Moreover, the state's low overall performance masks even lower outcomes for Black, Hispanic, and low-income residents.

Preparation for Postsecondary Education

Since the mid-1990s, Georgia has trailed the nation in high school graduation rates, whether calculated by using the average freshman graduation rate (62% for Georgia compared with 73% nationwide) or the Cumulative Promotion Index (56% for Georgia compared with 69% nationwide).[16]

The state has made notable improvements in some measures of student achievement in younger grades. The share of eighth grade students scoring at least proficient on national math assessments increased from 13% in the early 1990s to 27% in 2009. During the same period, the share of eighth graders scoring proficient also improved in reading (from 25% to 27%), science (from 21% to 23%), and writing (from 23% to 29%).[17]

The state has also made considerable improvements in Advanced Placement (AP) participation. The share of Georgia high school seniors taking at least one AP exam during high school increased substantially from 2006 to 2010—from 26.6% to 39.2%.[18] A state K–12 education leader we spoke with described AP as "the single best thing that we're doing to get kids better prepared for college."

Participation

Georgia has improved on measures of college participation but still falls below national averages and best-performing states. Following the upward trend nationwide over this period, the proportion of 18- to 24-year-olds enrolling in some type of postsecondary education in Georgia increased from 23% in 1991 to 31% in 2009. Throughout this period, however, Georgia's college participation rates were below the national average (31% versus 36% in 2009).[19] Similarly, the "chance for college" in Georgia, defined as the likelihood that a ninth grader will enroll in college right after high school graduation, rose considerably from 31% in 1998 to 41% in 2008 but remains below the national average (44%), slightly below the average of southern states (42%), and well below the top-performing states (58%).[20]

Completion

Following the same pattern, degree completion rates in Georgia increased somewhat during the past decade but continue to be substantially below the national average and the top-performing states. About 47% of first-time, full-time students who entered college in Georgia in 2002 completed a bachelor's degree within six years, up from 44% for the 1997 cohort but below the national rate of 56% and the rate of top states (65%) for the 2002 cohort.[21] Three-year completion rates for first-time, full-time students who entered public two-year colleges also increased over this period, from 23% in 1998 to 26% in 2008, but remain below the national average (28%) and well below the median of the top five states (41%).[22]

When transfer to other four-year institutions is considered, the six-year graduation rate for first-time, full-time students who entered a four-year institution in Georgia in 2002 (64%) is comparable to the national average (65%).[23] Georgia has the highest baccalaureate degree completion rate in the nation for students who start at a public two-year college or technical college (20% for Georgia compared with a 10% average nationwide).[24]

Georgia has also been relatively successful in terms of workforce education. The state leads the nation in the overall number of certificates and degrees awarded from all colleges and universities per 100 enrolled students.[25] From 1998 to 2008, the number of certificates awarded increased by 144% in Georgia compared with 66% nationwide.[26] During the same period, the number of associate degrees awarded increased by 69% in Georgia compared with 31% nationally.[27]

Affordability

As in other states, higher education is becoming less affordable in Georgia, and students and families are paying an increasing share of the cost. The net price of college (college expenses minus financial aid) represents a growing portion of family income for students in all types of colleges and universities in the state. From the early 1990s to 2007, the net price of college as a share of family income in Georgia increased:

- from 16% to 21% at public two-year colleges,
- from 10% to 15% at public four-year colleges and universities, and
- from 57% to 68% at private four-year colleges and universities.[28]

Between 1999 and 2009, median family income in Georgia measured in constant dollars declined by 7.1%, while tuition rose by 30.4% at public two-year colleges and by 48.9% at public four-year colleges and universities.[29]

Gaps in Performance across Groups

Attention only to measures of preparation, participation, and completion for the population overall masks persistent gaps in these indicators by race/ethnicity and family income in Georgia. In terms of preparation, only 13% of low-income eighth graders, but 27% of all eighth graders, scored at or above proficient on the 2009 national assessment in math.[30] High school graduation rates in the state are considerably higher for Whites than for Blacks and Hispanics (65% versus 48% and 43% in 2007, using the CPI calculation).[31] Failure rates on the Georgia High School Graduation Test are also higher for Blacks and Hispanics than for Whites. In 2009–10, 19% of Blacks and 18% of Hispanics failed the English component of the test, compared with 8% of Whites.[32] The representation of Blacks has increased over time among AP test-takers (from 20.1% in 2005 to 24.0% in 2010) and among those test-takers who achieved a three or higher on at least one AP exam (from 9.4% in 2005 to 11.6% in 2010). But the representation of Blacks on these indicators remains well below their representation among graduating high school seniors in Georgia (34.8% in 2010).[33] With regard to college participation, only 28% of Black and 11% of Hispanic 18- to 24-year-olds were enrolled compared with 39% of Whites.[34]

Bachelor's degree completion rates are low for all groups in Georgia, but they are even lower for Blacks and Hispanics than for Whites. Statewide, 41% of Black students, 44% of Hispanic students, and 48% of White students who entered four-year colleges in Georgia full-time for the first-time in 2002 completed a bachelor's degree within six years.[35] Among Georgia adults ages 25 to 34 in 2005, just 30% of Blacks and 14% of Hispanics had attained at least an associate degree, compared to 43% of Whites.[36]

The Structure of Higher Education in Georgia

In fall 2008, 581,898 students were enrolled in degree-granting institutions in Georgia, an increase of 91% from fall 2000. In fall 2008, the University System of Georgia (USG) enrolled 52% of all college students in the state, and the Technical College System of Georgia (TCSG) accounted for about 26% of all students. Small shares of students are enrolled in the state's private not-for-profit sector (9.5%) and the private for-profit sector (12%).[37]

Created in 1931, the University System of Georgia is constitutionally autonomous. At the time of our visit in February 2010, the University System of Georgia consisted of four research universities, two regional universities, thirteen state universities, eight state colleges, and eight public two-year colleges.[38] In late 2011 and early 2012, however, the system's Board of Regents approved the transformation of six of its eight two-year colleges into state colleges that offer a limited number of baccalaureate degree programs. In 2012, Georgia reported having only two public two-year colleges; today the University System of Georgia lists all the former public two-year colleges as state colleges.[39] Also in 2012, the Board of Regents approved the consolidation of eight public four-year colleges and universities into four such institutions. None of the consolidated institutions included institutions that were formerly two-year colleges or historically black colleges or universities (HBCUs).[40]

Three of the four-year institutions in the University System of Georgia are HBCUs: Albany State University, Fort Valley State University, and Savannah State University. The state also has seven private, not-for-profit four-year HBCUs: Clark Atlanta University, Interdenominational Theological Center, Morehouse College, Morehouse School of Medicine, Morris Brown College, Paine College, and Spelman College.

Created in 1984, the Technical College System of Georgia (TCSG) (formerly the Department of Technical and Adult Education) is the state agency responsible for the state's 26 technical colleges. Although these institutions offer certificate, diploma, and associate degree programs as well as continuing education and economic development programs, most TCSG awards are certificates of less than one year (66% in 2009–10).[41] An additional fifth of TCSG awards were certificates of at least one year but less than two years (17%) or certificates of at least two years but less than four years (6%); only 12% of TCSG awards were associate degrees.[42] The Technical College System merged 13 of its colleges into 7 on July 1, 2009, thereby reducing the total number of technical colleges from 33 to 26.[43] Administrative changes rather than campus closures, these mergers were designed to generate cost savings and other efficiencies.

What Explains the Higher Education Performance in Georgia?

Given its contextual characteristics and the structure of its system of higher education, what accounts for Georgia's success in workforce education; consistent below-average performance in college preparation, participation, and degree completion; and persistent disparities in college-related outcomes by race/ethnicity and family income? Many forces contribute to Georgia's higher education performance, but the following four themes appear paramount: (1) the historical legacy of segregation in higher education; (2) state higher education policies focused on economic development and workforce readiness; (3) the absence of sustained state policies to ensure the preparation and smooth transition of students across educational levels and sectors; and (4) the failure to strategically use available state fiscal policies to improve overall attainment and reduce gaps in attainment across groups.

Historical Legacy of Segregation in Higher Education

Current gaps across racial groups in higher education performance in Georgia cannot be understood without understanding the state's historical legacy of segregation of higher education.

Like Maryland and Texas, Georgia is one of 19 southern and southern-border states that have been subjected to federal desegregation mandates. In 1961, after years of litigation to desegregate public higher education in Georgia, the National Association for the Advancement of Colored People (NAACP) won a landmark case that granted admission to the University of Georgia to two Black students. Shortly thereafter, partly to avoid federal intervention, the University of Georgia and other Georgia public and private institutions began to admit Blacks. In March 1973, the federal Office for Civil Rights (OCR) ordered the Georgia Board of Regents to submit a plan for the complete desegregation of all institutions in the University System. The Board of Regents submitted a series of plans over the course of several years that failed to meet desegregation requirements. In 1983, however, the Board of Regents secured federal approval for its revised plan, and in 1988 the OCR ruled Georgia (and seven other states) to be in compliance with the provisions of Title VI of the Civil Rights Act.[44]

Few state and institutional leaders mentioned race during our interviews. Those who responded to our questions about how the state is seeking to improve the participation and completion rates of Blacks most frequently mentioned the University System of Georgia's African American Male Initiative. Launched in 2002, this initiative is designed to identify enrollment barriers facing Black men and support pilot projects to address these barriers system wide. The University System reported that in 2008 25 programs paid special attention to educational pipeline issues in enrolling Black males. According to the System's annual report for fiscal year 2009, the six-year graduation rate for first-time, full-time Black male freshmen increased from 29% for those who entered in fall 1997 to 37% for those who entered in fall 2002, suggesting the effectiveness of these efforts.[45]

Despite this initiative and the release from oversight by OCR, however, substantial racial/ethnic inequity in higher education enrollment and completion remains in Georgia.[46] For example, two-thirds (66%) of all Black undergraduates and 56% of all Latino undergraduates, but only 49% of White undergraduates, are enrolled in the state's less selective institutions: the private for-profit institutions, the two-year institutions of the University System (that existed at the time of our case study), and the Technical College System. In contrast, 43% of White students, but only 25% of Black students and 37% of Hispanic students, were enrolled at the state's public four-year institutions in 2008–9. Private non-profit institutions enrolled 9% of Black, 8% of White, and 7% of Hispanic undergraduates. The state's three public HBCUs enrolled 14% of all Black undergraduates in the University System (including two- and four-year institutions) and 22.5% of all Black undergraduates in the system's four-year institutions.[47]

State Higher Education Policies Focused on Economic Development and Workforce Readiness

Through such initiatives as the Georgia Research Alliance and the Quick Start program and the scope of the Technical College System of Georgia, Georgia has provided sustained statewide attention to research competitiveness and workforce development. This attention appears to have important societal benefits, particularly in terms of economic development and workforce training. These state policies also encourage enrollment in non-degree-granting workforce training programs at the state's technical colleges, especially for students with lower levels of academic preparation, students from lower-income families, and Black students.

The Georgia Research Alliance

Since 1990, the state has provided funding to support the Georgia Research Alliance, a not-for-profit organization designed to encourage cooperation among business, research universities, and state government and to broaden and strengthen the state's economy. The purpose of the Research Alliance is to attract the world's preeminent scientists to lead programs of research and development at affiliated Georgia public and private research universities with a focus on areas with the most potential for generating new companies and helping established companies grow and create new science and technology jobs.[48]

The Research Alliance receives state support with the goal of attracting private and federal dollars. The Alliance reports that in its first 19 years it has leveraged $525 million in state funding into $2.6 billion of additional federal and private investment.[49] A state policy expert explained, "We try and help drive the state toward higher expenditures in research and development to attract more federal funding. That's really the lifeblood of the academic research enterprise. We attract top talent at universities. We establish endowed chairs, build lots of research laboratories, and build on capability for universities to do cutting-edge research. And that has positioned the state to become more competitive in funding from many of the federal agencies."

Indeed, three of the state's research universities ranked in the top 100 institutions nationwide in federal research and development expenditures in 2008: Emory University ranked twenty-eighth (at $291.1 million); Georgia Institute of Technology ranked thirtieth (at $281.2 million); and the University of Georgia ranked ninety-eighth (at $102.8 million).[50] In 2007, the state ranked twenty-seventh in total research and development expenditures per $1,000 of gross state product.[51] Georgia also has the fourth highest investment in research per full-time faculty in the nation. In 2003, research expenditures averaged $143,755 per full-time faculty member at public research universities in Georgia, compared with $82,977 nationwide.[52]

Quick Start

The Quick Start program is another long-standing entity in Georgia that bridges education, government, and business to support economic and workforce development. Created by education, political, and business leaders in 1967, Quick Start provides customized workforce training free of charge to qualified businesses in Georgia or that are relocating to the state. Overseen by the Technical College System of Georgia, Quick Start promotes collaboration between the state's technical colleges and companies in need of workforce education. Quick Start has been consistently funded as a part of the governor's budget since 2004, with $22 million appropriated in FY2013.[53]

The program delivers a majority of its training projects to small and medium-sized companies, and many of its projects are in targeted manufacturing fields. In fiscal year 2008, 158 of the companies served were small businesses, 43 were medium-sized companies, and 22 were large companies. During the same year, 88% of Quick Start's projects supported Georgia's manufacturers, including many in the automotive, aerospace, and biotechnology industries.[54]

State Policies That Encourage Enrollment in TCSG Workforce Training Programs

The geographic accessibility of the state's technical colleges is one factor that likely promotes enrollment at these institutions. Since the technical colleges are geographically dispersed in convenient locations, TCSG officials told us, most residents live within 30 minutes of a technical college.

Other state policies encourage enrollment in non-degree-granting workforce training programs at the Technical College System of Georgia. Prior to 2011, students who enrolled in these programs typically qualified for the state's HOPE Grant Program, a financial aid program that covered 100% of tuition and some fees.[55] Whereas the state's better-known HOPE Scholarship program requires recipients to satisfy various academic requirements to receive and maintain the aid, the HOPE Grant program has historically had no academic eligibility requirements. In response to lottery shortfalls, however, effective 2011 students are required to maintain a 3.0 average to be eligible for continued financial support from the HOPE Grant.[56]

The pre-2011 eligibility requirements of the HOPE Grant likely contributed to the stratification of enrollment and degree attainment in the state. Lower-achieving students (who are disproportionately low-income students of color) are relatively concentrated in the technical colleges—the institutions with the lowest net price. Reflecting the well-established positive relationship between family income and conventional measures of academic achievement, students from low-income families are disproportionately represented in the technical colleges. In 2008–9, 38% of students in the Technical College System received a

Pell Grant,[57] an indication of their low-income status, compared with only 28% of students at the public four-year institutions in the USG.[58] Blacks represented 42% of undergraduates enrolled in the state's technical colleges in fall 2008 but only 20% of undergraduates enrolled in the state's public four-year institutions.[59]

Absence of Policies to Ensure Adequate Preparation and Smooth Transitions

Since the 1990s, Georgia has made considerable efforts to better link its K–12 schools with colleges and universities. These long-standing efforts have generally resulted in better collaboration across state agencies, but they have depended on gubernatorial leadership and have suffered from the lack of sustained statewide policies—particularly policies linked to finance or accountability—to improve student preparation for and success in college. The transfer of students from two-year to four-year institutions within the University System of Georgia appears to have worked effectively (before the elimination of the two-year institutions), but state and institutional leaders have only recently begun to address the structural barriers that have historically limited the transfer of students from the TCSG into the USG.

Long-standing but Varying Attention to P–16 Coordination but Little Policy Change

Georgia has long been a leader in the P–16 education movement, an effort that seeks to link K–12 and postsecondary systems in order to improve the preparation and smooth transition from high school to college. In Georgia, P–16 efforts began in the early 1990s with the development of 15 regional P–16 councils and one statewide council. These initial efforts were sponsored by the University System of Georgia and supported by then-Governor Zell Miller. A key achievement of the regional councils was to highlight and provide legitimacy for P–16 work within the University System. These regional councils focused primarily on "project-based" work such as improving teacher preparation programs and increasing state standards in K–12 education, particularly in math and science.[60]

Governor Miller then created, via executive order, a statewide Education Coordinating Council (ECC) to replace the initial statewide council (while maintaining the regional councils). Governor Barnes subsequently formalized this structure when he signed into law the A-Plus Education Reform Act of 2000 (House Bill 1187). The ECC developed the Office of Educational Accountability

Report Card, now known as the Georgia Scorecard, and created accountability indicators for the agencies that were council members. The ECC's effectiveness was limited, however, by the contentious relationship between Linda Shrenko, the elected superintendent of the state's K–12 educational system, and then-Governor Barnes.[61]

Governor Barnes left office in January 2003, and Georgia's P–16 efforts remained dormant until 2006, when his successor, Governor Sonny Perdue, created the Alliance of Education Agency Heads to replace the ECC during his second term in office. According to staff for Governor Perdue, through the Alliance "the leaders of our state's education agencies work together to guarantee that Georgia's students receive an excellent education, from pre-K to Ph.D." Members of the Alliance include the governor's education advisor and representatives from the Department of Early Care and Learning, Governor's Office of Student Achievement, Georgia Professional Standards Commission, Georgia Student Finance Commission, and Technical College System of Georgia. In addition, the Alliance has two members with relatively greater autonomy: the chancellor of the University System of Georgia and the chief (elected) state superintendent.

Governor Perdue identified the following five goals for the Alliance: (1) increase high school graduation rates, decrease high school dropout rates, and increase postsecondary enrollment rates; (2) strengthen teacher quality, recruitment, and retention; (3) improve workforce readiness skills; (4) develop strong education leaders; and (5) improve the ACT/SAT score of Georgia students.[62] According to one state K–12 education leader, "The Alliance heads get together every month. Everyone attends. They talk, it's honest."

Under Perdue's leadership, the state's educational agencies (the state Department of Education, University System of Georgia, and Technical College System of Georgia) articulated goals that corresponded to the Alliance's goals. In its strategic plan, the state Department of Education listed the same five goals that the Alliance identified, as well as a sixth: "to make policies that ensure maximum academic and financial accountability."[63] The University System and the Technical College System each included a strategic goal that is loosely aligned with the work of the Alliance. One of the University System's strategic goals is to "strengthen partnerships with other education agencies," and one of the Technical College System's goals is to "guarantee student access and the opportunity for success at all levels."[64]

The Alliance has also contributed to the launch of several statewide college-readiness initiatives. The state has collaborated with the American Diploma Project to replace its tiered high school diploma options with a single diploma, effective for the incoming ninth grade class in 2008, and to develop more rigorous college preparatory requirements. Students now have the option to take academic and career-technical courses including Advanced Placement, dual enrollment, joint enrollment, industry certification, and career pathways. The new requirements are aligned with Georgia Performance Standards (GPS) for math, science, social studies, and English language arts. Beginning with the incoming ninth grade class of 2010–11, all students must pass exams in these four areas by graduation. At the time of our data collection, the state's agencies were working through the Alliance members to establish cut scores on the Georgia High School Graduation Test (GHSGT), an eleventh grade exam. The state planned to create opportunities for students who do not pass the exams to receive additional instructional support and retest in the twelfth grade.

Nonetheless, although bringing together the state's key education leaders, the ability of the state's P–16 entities to create lasting policy changes is limited by several characteristics.[65] As with P–16 structures in other states, the Alliance is an advisory organization only and does not receive dedicated state resources to support its work. As a leader of one of the Alliance's member agencies explained, "Each agency brings its own resources to the Alliance. The one full-time staff for the Alliance is paid by three of the agencies. There is no direct funding."

The state's P–16 efforts also depend on gubernatorial leadership and may not last beyond the term of a given governor. Nathan Deal was inaugurated as Georgia's eighty-second governor in January 2011, and the future of the Alliance under his leadership was initially uncertain. After a brief hiatus, the Alliance has been continued under Governor Deal's leadership. Governor Deal's administration has eliminated or reduced several education initiatives that his predecessor, Governor Perdue, championed. For instance, Governor Perdue created the Governor's Cup Challenge in 2004 to focus attention on student achievement and raise SAT scores in the state and the Graduation Coach program in 2005 to place a "coach" in each of the state's middle and high schools to provide assistance to students at risk of failing to earn a high school diploma. Neither of these programs appears to be a priority under Governor Deal.

Gubernatorial leadership for P–16 education reform is especially important in Georgia because the legislative session is short. The General Assembly meets for only about 40 days per year. The legislature also has limited authority over the state budget since it may only make reductions (not increases) in the governor's proposed budget. A state legislator we spoke with said that "our higher education committee does very little" in developing higher education policy and that the way higher education is organized in Georgia provides the legislature with "less of a role to play" compared with other states.

The success of the state's P–16 entity in creating policy reform has also been limited by characteristics of the membership. The Alliance now has a new state superintendent (elected by voters in November 2010) and a new chancellor of the University System (appointed by the Board of Regents in fall 2011). The governor has indirect influence over the priorities of these leaders, since he appoints the University System's Board of Regents and the State Board of Education, and he approves the budgets of both entities. But a state higher education agency leader summarized the challenges to P–16 policy reform when the state superintendent is elected: "Having the state superintendent elected changes everything. Everyone else reports to the governor, directly or indirectly. The governor can control everyone's agenda, except for the state superintendent, who has her[/his] own agenda."

In summary, over time the locus of P–16 work in the state has shifted from regions to the state and the state has developed a culture of collaboration across state education agencies. This collaborative culture has likely contributed to the development of a single high school diploma and the establishment of cut scores on the Georgia High School Graduation Test. However, the instability of P–16 work under different governors, turnover in leadership among members of the P–16 entity, and the potential conflict between the priorities of the governor and the elected state superintendent of schools have contributed to the absence of sustained state policy that produces meaningful improvements in academic readiness for college.

Data Limitations Associated with Monitoring the Educational Progress of Students

Improving data collection and reporting in P–16 education has been a priority in Georgia under several governors, but persisting limitations in the state's systems for data collection and accountability have likely hampered efforts to create effective policies linking the state's educational sectors. Several leaders we interviewed said that Georgia's state-level agencies are working to collect and report data more effectively but that few agency databases are connected in ways that make them easily accessible in user-friendly formats. One leader of a state higher education agency described the common practice of carrying a flash drive across the street to another agency in order to link data.

Some of the strengths of the state's data and accountability systems can be found in the Education Scoreboard, which was developed by the Governor's Office of Student Achievement (GOSA). The scoreboard reports performance data across the education systems, including indicators for K–12 public schools, the University System of Georgia, and the Technical College System of Georgia. Benchmarks are provided with comparisons of Georgia's performance in relation to averages for southern states, the nation, and with Georgia's previous years. In addition to providing state averages for each system of education, the Education Scoreboard reports performance of individual schools, colleges, and technical colleges.[66] The Georgia Department of Education has also developed a "strategy map" that summarizes progress toward achieving the department's strategic goals.[67] The Technical College System uses a "system scorecard" to monitor and benchmark performance in technical education and adult education. Likewise, the University System of Georgia, according to officials with whom we spoke, provides accountability reports on enrollment, financial aid, faculty, and degree production.

Despite these efforts, the Data Quality Campaign, in its 2010 State Analysis, found that Georgia has not yet taken the following three actions considered as "good practice" in developing effective data and accountability systems: (1) provide timely access to information, (2) promote educator professional development and credentialing, and (3) promote strategies to raise awareness of available data.[68] In its study on higher education accountability, the Education Sector also noted limitations of the state's data systems in the alignment of "state priorities with concrete goals for achievement" and formal linkages between "budgetary decisions" and the "performance of state postsecondary education."[69]

During Governor Perdue's tenure, Georgia sought funding from foundations and from the federal government to improve and link state data systems. The Alliance of Education Agency Heads played a role in building the collaboration needed to submit a successful proposal for the federal Race to the Top program, which awarded $400 million to the state over four years to implement a statewide education reform strategy.[70] That reform effort allotted $32 million to improve data systems, including a data warehouse across the P–20 spectrum and an interagency data sharing agreement that may address weaknesses identified by the Data Quality Campaign.[71]

Structural Barriers to Transfer from the Technical College System to the University System

State and institutional leaders that we spoke with praised the effectiveness of transfer pathways between the public two-year and four-year institutions within the USG. A leader of a state higher education agency said, "Transfer works well here. Seamless transfer is guaranteed if students complete the core curriculum." The University System has defined a core curriculum with 60 credit hours that are fully transferable to other institutions in the system.[72]

Yet student transfer from the Technical College System to the USG has historically been more problematic. Although articulation agreements had been established locally between some individual technical colleges and local four-year institutions, at the time of our review statewide articulation between the technical colleges and USG had not been achieved. The leader of a state higher education agency summarized the challenges in transferring between these two sectors, arguing: "Higher education institutions have to strengthen articulation between USG and the technical colleges so transfer is seamless. . . . The TCSG Board wants transfer to be a possibility and has little patience for lack of articulation. They were demanding agreement on 25 to 44 core courses for transfer. So far, we have agreement with USG on only 5 base courses—and this agreement took three years to work out."

Recognizing these and other transfer challenges, in July 2008 Governor Perdue appointed a working group called "Tough Choices or Tough Times" to "study education policies and practices to make Georgia more globally competitive." Among other suggestions, the working group recommended that Georgia (1) create a comprehensive community college system by merging the technical colleges and the University's System's public two-year colleges, (2) enforce pathways for transfer between institutions of the two systems to ensure the transfer of credits from one system to the other, or (3) remove all duplication of teaching and administrative resources between the systems.[73]

Since our visit, the state has moved to reduce barriers that have historically limited transfer between the two sectors. In March 2012 the USG Regents approved an expansion of general education courses in TCSG that are transferable to USG from 5 to 27 courses.[74] USG also established a Postsecondary Oversight Council to "monitor the implementation of these additional courses for transfer between the two systems."[75] The TCSG has also shifted from its quarter system to the semester system used by the University System.

These policy changes move Georgia in the right direction to strengthen education pathways between workforce education and degree opportunities for state residents. As described earlier, however, all of the eight public two-year colleges have also recently become four-year institutions. The implications of these changes for students transferring from the technical college are not yet clear.

Characteristics of the state's student financial aid programs also create financial barriers for students seeking to transfer between these two public systems. As described earlier in this chapter, Georgia's HOPE Grant is available only to students enrolled in a non-degree program; the HOPE Scholarship is available only to students enrolled in degree programs. But unlike the HOPE Grant (prior to the changes recently enacted in response to the shortfall in lottery revenues), the HOPE Scholarship is limited to students who meet specified academic eligibility criteria. As a result, students who transfer from a non-degree granting program to a degree-granting program do not receive state financial aid unless they meet the HOPE Scholarship's academic eligibility criteria.

Lack of a Clear Plan to Accommodate Enrollment Growth in Degree-Granting Institutions

Further contributing to low levels of degree attainment is the absence of a clear plan for accommodating projected enrollment growth in the state's public degree-granting institutions. Although the USG recognized the need to increase its capacity to serve more students in its strategic plan—expanding capacity in the University System to enroll 100,000 additional students by 2020[76]—neither the USG nor the TCSG has developed a clear plan to accommodate this expected enrollment growth.

Most of the state's projected population growth is in the Atlanta metropolitan area, which grew by 24% between 2000 and 2009, accounting for 68% of the state's growth over that period.[77] In 2010, the Atlanta metro area, with a population of more than 5.2 million, was home to 54% of Georgia's residents. A leader of a state higher education agency described the challenges of managing projected enrollment growth in the Atlanta area: "We are growing very rapidly. For 100,000 [new] students [statewide], 66,000 are going to be in metro Atlanta. Creating capacity is very expensive. We would need to build up, not out. We need to figure out how to build two-year colleges in Atlanta, or attract students to South Georgia, where there is already capacity, through intentional effort. Capacity is cheaper there. But, there are lots of working and place-bound students in Atlanta."

At the time of our visit, the USG was developing plans to accommodate enrollment growth by expanding its eight two-year colleges. Since that time, the missions of these institutions have expanded, enabling all of them to offer a limited number of bachelor's degrees; all of the former public two-year colleges are now classified as a four-year institution.[78]

Failure to Strategically Use Available State Fiscal Policies to Improve Overall Attainment and Reduce Gaps in Attainment across Groups

Georgia has adopted a model of shared responsibility for higher education finance. Under this cost-sharing approach, the state has committed to provide 75% of the costs of student education at the University System of Georgia, with the remaining costs coming from tuition and fees.[79] During the recent recession, however, Georgia's political leaders were unable to maintain stable funding for higher education or restructure the state's higher education systems to achieve cost efficiencies or greater productivity.

From 2004 to 2009, the average state subsidy of higher education declined for all public sectors in Georgia. The greatest decline was for the research universities (a drop of 27.7%), while the smallest average decline was in the University System's two-year colleges (a drop of 1.4%). State funding for the technical colleges declined by 9.6% over this period.[80] As a result, Georgia's model of shared responsibility for higher education finance is being undermined: students are paying a greater portion of the overall share of higher education costs than in the past. The student share of the cost in Georgia now exceeds 25% in every sector: research universities (57%), regional universities (42%), state universities (40%), public HBCUs (38%), state colleges (38%), two-year colleges (33%), and technical colleges (29%).[81]

The following sections illustrate that finance policies and practices in Georgia are not tightly aligned with statewide goals to improve higher education. Some of these policies and practices contribute to stratification of educational attainment for state residents.

Emphasis of State Appropriations on Enrollment

The University System distributes state funds to its institutions based on a formula that is driven by enrollment and credit hours. One challenge with this approach is that the state's enrollment data lag behind real-time enrollment levels by two years, so institutions are compensated for enrollment growth two years after the fact.[82] In his 2010 state-of-the-system address, the chancellor of University System explained, "We have added more than 40,000 students in the last three years, and our funding formula is now 30,000 students behind."[83] Appropriations for the Technical College System also rely on an enrollment-based funding formula.

With the emphasis on enrollment, state financing for the University System and the Technical College System provides no incentives for innovation, cost restructuring, productivity improvements, or degree completion. Some state leaders told us that linking state funding to performance is not likely in the current economic environment of constrained resources. The leader of a public college said, "I think there could be [financial incentives for performance]. The hard part would be [that] the current financial situation makes it difficult. We're looking at another $300 [million] to $400 million in cuts. It's a matter of survival on our campuses right now." An official from the Technical College System explained that "TCSG has made preliminary steps toward performance funding with nominal sums but hasn't done any this fiscal year and probably won't do any next year."

State-Funded Student Financial Aid Based on Academic Criteria

Compared with other states, Georgia invests substantially in student financial aid. In 2009–10, Georgia ranked second in state grant dollars per full-time-equivalent student (at $1,766). The national average was $627 per FTE.[84]

In 1992, Governor Zell Miller established the Georgia HOPE (Helping Outstanding Pupils Educationally) Scholarship Program, which became the largest merit-based financial aid program in the country. To fund the program, the legislature created the Georgia State Lottery through the Lottery for Education Act, which asserted that the purpose of the HOPE program was to supplement and not supplant traditional education sources of funding.[85] The HOPE program also included the HOPE Grant, an initiative designed to support students seeking technical education.[86]

At the time of our data collection in Georgia, students seeking to qualify for a HOPE Scholarship were required to graduate from high school with a 3.0 grade point average and enroll in a degree-granting program. To maintain a HOPE Scholarship, college students were required to have at least a 3.0 grade point average at checkpoints of 30, 60, and 90 credit hours.[87] For those who maintained their eligibility, a HOPE Scholarship paid for in-state tuition, mandatory fees approved by the HOPE program, and a book allowance.

A key concern is that the awarding of financial aid based on academic achievement contributes to the stratification of higher education participation, choice, and completion by family income and race/ethnicity. As a state policy expert told us, "The large low-income population of Georgia doesn't benefit from HOPE, and tuition as a ratio of income [without the HOPE scholarship] makes state schools not very affordable. HOPE is used to appease the middle class." As institutional selectivity increases, the percentage of students receiving HOPE Scholarships increases and the percentage of students receiving Pell Grants declines. For instance, among undergraduates enrolled at a research university in 2008–9, 43% received a HOPE Scholarship and only 20% received a Pell Grant. In contrast, of the students enrolled at the University System's two-year institutions, 11% received a HOPE Scholarship but 38% received a Pell Grant.[88]

Another limitation is that two-thirds of HOPE Scholarship recipients do not maintain eligibility. Of those who entered the University System in fall 2003 with a HOPE Scholarship, only one-third (32%) were able to retain a 3.0 average through the 90-credit-hour checkpoint within six years of enrollment. More than half of students who received a HOPE Scholarship lost it after their first year.[89]

At the same time, the state targets very little financial aid to students with financial need. Georgia's need-based financial aid program, the Leveraging Educational Assistance Partnership (LEAP), is virtually nonexistent, representing less than one percent of Georgia's state total student aid expenditure.[90] In fiscal year 2011–12, Governor Deal and the legislature, in acknowledgement of the increased financial need of students, instituted the Student Access Loan Program to provide low-interest loans (at 1%) for 6,000 of the students with the greatest financial need. Funded at $20 million, the program is supported with lottery revenues and was part of the overhaul of the HOPE Scholarship and Grant Program undertaken by the Deal administration. Students may borrow, after applying for federal and state grant and loan programs, a maximum of $10,000 to attend college.[91]

Tuition Increases Constrained by HOPE Scholarships and Grants

Since its creation in 1993, Georgia has spent over $6 billion on HOPE Scholarships and Grants.[92] One positive consequence of this sizeable investment has been that state policy decisions about tuition levels and student financial aid have been linked. Until 2011–12 (as explained in the next section) HOPE awards funded full tuition and most fees for all recipients, as well as some other expenses, at public institutions. Since the state funds HOPE awards from the Georgia lottery, the state has incentive to keep tuition levels in line with available lottery revenues.

The USG has formal authority to set tuition levels, and its Board of Regents negotiates with individual institutions to set tuition and fees. Since the Technical College System is a state agency, tuition is set in collaboration with state leaders. Tuition levels are consistent across the TCSG, but fees may vary by campus.

The University System works informally with governor to establish tuition. As one state official said, "The governor is always engaged in the conversation, but ultimately he cannot dictate what the tuition increase will be." During our visit to Georgia in 2010, state leaders confirmed that one of the reasons the governor works with the state higher education systems is to ensure that tuition increases are considered in relation to available lottery revenues. A leader of a public college explained that the HOPE program keeps tuition "artificially" low: "HOPE is great, but has unintended consequences. It has kept tuition artificially low to keep revenues from crossing expenditures with the HOPE program. Tuition increases are always checked with Georgia Student Finance Commission to not break HOPE. The governor will look over tuition increases—and the governor appoints the Board [of Regents], so they will comply."

Greater Stratification with Changes to HOPE Scholarships and Grants

Since our visit to Georgia, the HOPE program has been scaled back, largely due to changes in the state's financial resources. In response to declines in lottery revenue, Governor Deal, with legislative support, pushed forward with plans to ration HOPE Scholarships and Grants. In this process, the financial need of students was not a primary consideration.

In 2011, the legislature passed House Bill 326 to modify eligibility requirements for the HOPE Scholarship and Grant. The Zell Miller Scholarship was also created, a new program that pays full tuition for students who graduate from high school with at least a 3.7 grade point average and a score of 1200 on the math and verbal sections of the SAT (or an ACT composite scale score of at least 26). These changes were in effect as of 2011–12.

The HOPE Scholarship is still available to students with at least a 3.0 grade point average in high school, but the amount available now depends on annual lottery revenue. The bill also increased the number of advanced courses that students must take during high school to be eligible for the award.[93] In the past, students who lost their HOPE Scholarship award could regain it be achieving a 3.0 GPA at any of the checkpoints. Additionally, the bill created an academic eligibility requirement for students to maintain the HOPE Grant. HOPE Grant recipients now must maintain a 3.0 grade point average to retain the award. Now students who lose their HOPE Scholarship or Grant have only one opportunity to regain it; if they lose it for a second time, they cannot regain it again regardless of their performance.[94]

The heightened academic eligibility requirements will likely only exacerbate the stratification of higher education enrollment in the state, given the positive relationship between income and academic achievement. Moreover, one of the benefits of the HOPE programs as previously structured was that it sent a simple and clear message to high school students and their families about the affordability of college for those who prepare academically in high school: if students received a 3.0 average by the time they graduated, then their college tuition would be covered by the state.[95] The scaling back of the HOPE program has complicated this signaling, since most qualifying students do not know the amount of their awards until annual lottery revenues are determined.

By reducing the share of tuition covered by the HOPE program, the new changes may also further reduce college affordability in the state. This reduction has effectively removed the incentive for state leaders to keep tuition increases in line with lottery revenues. As a result, the HOPE program may no longer serve as a damper on tuition increases. Requiring students to maintain a 3.0 average to be eligible for continued financial support under the HOPE Grant program may weaken the state's effectiveness in awarding workforce certificates.

Conclusion

Georgia's record of attention through various public policies to economic development and workforce training has produced many benefits. These public policies build on strengths of its research universities and the Technical College System as the Georgia Research Alliance, Quick Start, and other policies expand access to and the affordability of workforce training programs. These long-standing public policies also appear to have made Georgia more competitive in attracting federal research dollars and new business and industry to the state.

But the state has been markedly less successful at producing sustained policies that promote degree attainment, particularly for the state's low-income population, substantial Black population, and small but rapidly growing Hispanic population. Georgia lacks a clear plan to accommodate the projected enrollment growth in the postsecondary system, a need that is increasingly important as the state's young population grows larger and more diverse. One reason that policies have been hard to sustain is a lack of continuity in state higher education leadership. Governors have had shifting policies and priorities, and no other voice or institution at the state level consistently speaks for all of higher education.

Georgia has long been recognized for its partnerships between K–12 and higher education, including efforts to create such state-level working groups as the Alliance of Education Agency Heads. Although improving collaboration among state education agencies, however, these entities have not yet created the P–16 educational policy reform that is required to create lasting improvements in college readiness or completion.

Although stratification by income and race in higher education outcomes is not unique to Georgia, few states have explicit policies that encourage it. Nearly all of Georgia's state-sponsored student financial aid to students in degree-granting programs is awarded on the basis of academic criteria rather than financial need. Historical challenges in transferring from the Technical College System to the University System have compounded the problem. Recent policies may begin to address the structural barriers to transfer, but the expansion of the mission of the public two-year colleges within the USG to offer bachelor's degrees may create other unintended consequences.

To compete economically with other states and nations, Georgia must raise the educational attainment of its population and reduce disparities in attainment across demographic groups. To reach this aim, the state needs to develop finance and other policies that are linked to statewide goals for improved higher education performance.

Chapter 5

A Story of Decline

The Performance and State Policies of Higher Education in Illinois

With contributions by Jamey Rorison

In the mid- and late 1990s, Illinois led the nation in the performance of its higher education system, its ability to set shared goals and priorities for higher education, and its strategic use of resources to achieve its goals and priorities. During the past decade, however, the state has experienced substantial declines in all of these areas.[1]

Workforce trends and international competition suggest that Illinois will need to reverse these trends, since larger numbers of better-educated residents will be required to meet projected workforce demands and reach the level of educational attainment of top-performing countries. According to projections for the decade from 2008 to 2018, about 418,000 new jobs in the state will require at least some postsecondary education, compared with about a third as many (148,000 new jobs) that will need no more than a high school diploma. By 2018, approximately two-thirds of all jobs in Illinois will require at least some postsecondary education or training.[2] Based on trends in degree production and projections of population growth, Illinois must increase its production of associate and bachelor's degrees by 5.4% annually in order for 55% of its workforce (ages 25 to 64) to hold at least an associate degree by 2020.[3]

Demographic trends present challenges to statewide efforts to improve the educational attainment of Illinois residents. The state roughly mirrors the U.S. population in its racial and ethnic mix, with Blacks comprising 14.4% of the state population in 2009 (compared with 12.1% nationally) and Hispanics making up

15.3% (compared with 15.8% nationally).[4] Over the next two decades, the state's Hispanic population is projected to increase dramatically, though at a somewhat lower rate than the national average (28.7% in Illinois versus 37.0% nationwide).[5] Between 2008–9 and 2027–28, the number of high school graduates in Illinois is projected to increase by 17% for Hispanics, while declining by 24% for Whites and 31% for Blacks.[6] Given the extent to which Hispanics in Illinois tend to underperform other population groups in higher education, the growing Hispanic population presents an important area of focus for the state in improving the performance of higher education.[7]

The City of Chicago also represents a key challenge for state efforts to improve higher education performance. As the third-largest metropolitan area in the nation, Chicago has about 22% of the state's total population and is more diverse than the rest of the state.[8] The city's population is about 34% Black and 27% Hispanic.[9] Income levels also tend to be lower in Chicago. Median family income in Chicago was $53,226 in 2009, compared with $62,363 for the state as a whole.[10] To be successful, state efforts to improve higher education performance will likely need to account for the size, income disparity, and racial and ethnic diversity of Chicago. A leader of a regional higher education consortia highlighted the importance of improving performance in Chicago: "Quite frankly, if you're going to make any inroads in the areas that need improvement—the low percentage of 18 to 24 year olds enrolled in college, for example—you've got to go to Chicago to get that to happen. When the whole population of the state is projected to increase only 6 percent in the next 20 years, if you're going to make any advancement as a state, you've got to get it from Chicago."

Although declines in the state's higher education performance began before the recent recession, efforts to increase educational attainment must recognize continued constraints on available state fiscal resources into the near future. General funds appropriated for fiscal year 2011 were 10.7% lower than general funds appropriated in 2009.[11] This drop in appropriations reflects declines in state revenues as well as the loss of federal stimulus funding. Illinois had a projected budget shortfall of $13 billion for fiscal year 2011.[12] This shortfall represents 47% of the state's general fund budget, a substantially larger percentage than any other state; the next largest, Arizona, had a projected shortfall representing 9.7% of its budget.[13]

Reflecting the overall decline in state revenues, the state's budget for higher education in fiscal year 2011 ($2.1 billion) was approximately $100 million lower than for 2010 ($2.2 billion). About $86 million of the reduction was to be borne by universities. Appropriations for community colleges were $14 million lower in fiscal year 2011 compared with 2010.[14] Compounding these state budget cuts, in 2010 the state was unable to provide public universities with appropriated funds in a timely manner. The *Chronicle of Higher Education* reported that as of June 30, 2010 (i.e., the end of the state's fiscal year), Illinois had not yet allocated $464 million of the total amount appropriated to its public universities for the 2010 fiscal year and further noted: "Although the state passed a budget on time, it is still expecting tax revenues to fall some $13-billion short of what is needed to pay its bills for the fiscal year that began July 1, including nearly $5-billion owed to state agencies for the previous budget."[15]

Illinois' fiscal challenges are unlikely to end soon, despite an increase in state income tax that was approved in January 2011. The Economic Recovery and Budget Reform Act, passed by the legislature and signed by Governor Pat Quinn (D), authorized a temporary 66% increase in the state's individual income tax rate (from 3% to 5%) and a temporary 46% increase in its corporate tax rate (from 4.8% to 7%)—provided that the state limits spending growth to 2% per year.[16] Nonetheless, like other states, Illinois is projected to face severe budget cuts as a result of the shortfall between projected revenues from current taxing structures and expenditures for state services over the next few years. Legislative fiscal directors have described the state's fiscal circumstances as "dire."[17]

Current and projected constraints in fiscal resources underscore the importance of establishing shared goals and priorities for higher education, using resources strategically to attain these goals and priorities, and monitoring progress toward their achievement. Progress in each of these areas is required if the state is to reverse recent declines in higher education performance, close gaps in higher education outcomes, and raise educational attainment levels to meet projected workforce needs and international competitiveness demands.

Higher Education Performance

In the late 1990s, Illinois was a top-performing state in preparing students for college, enrolling residents in college, and keeping college affordable. Compared with other states, large percentages of Illinois residents earned a high school diploma or a General Education Development (GED) diploma by age 24, earned high scores on college entrance exams, and enrolled in college immediately after high school. At this time, Illinois led the nation in the shares of young adults (ages 18 to 24) and working-age adults (ages 25 to 44) enrolled in college. Illinois was also a top performer in keeping higher education affordable for families as measured by (1) the share of family income required to attend the state's public two-year and four-year institutions, and (2) the availability of state need-based financial aid.[18]

Since the late 1990s, however, the performance of higher education in Illinois has declined, as described below. The state has experienced declines in measures of college participation and affordability and has substantial variation in higher education outcomes based on geographic region as well as students' race/ethnicity and family income.

Preparation and Participation

Over the past decade, Illinois improved on some measures associated with preparing students for college-level academic work. For example, high school graduation rates increased from 1996–97 to 2006–7,[19] and the percentage of eighth graders scoring at or above proficient levels on the National Assessment of Educational Progress in math increased from 2003 to 2009.[20]

These improvements in preparation did not, however, lead to higher rates of college participation. Over the past decade, Illinois experienced declines in the percentage of high school freshmen enrolling in college within four years (from 48.3% in 1998 to 43.5% in 2008) and the percentage of high school graduates immediately enrolling in college (from 62.7% in 1998 to 57.4% in 2008).[21] Meanwhile, the percentage of young adults (ages 18 to 24) enrolled in college increased somewhat (from 32.8% to 33.2% between 2001 and 2007),[22] but the share of 25- to 49-year-olds dropped from 8.5% to 6.6% over the same period.[23]

Completion

In 1998, Illinois was well below the top-performing states in the percentage of students earning a bachelor's degree within six years (54.5% in Illinois compared with 66.5% in Massachusetts in 1998).[24] From 1998 to 2008, Illinois increased both the percentage of students earning a bachelor's degree within six years (from 54.5% to 58.9%) and the percentage of students earning an associate degree within three years (from 23.8% to 24.5%)[25] However, improvements in the completion rate for bachelor's degrees may be attributable in part to increases in the selectivity of the state's higher education institutions as the state's performance in participation was declining over this same period. Between 2001 and 2009, the distribution of ACT scores for admitted students shifted upward at five of the state's twelve public universities. The largest shift occurred at the University of Illinois at Urbana-Champaign, where ACT scores increased from 23 to 26 at the 25th percentile and from 28 to 31 at the 75th percentile.[26]

Affordability

College affordability has been declining in Illinois. The share of family income required to attend colleges and universities in the state, less financial aid, increased substantially at public two-year institutions (from 19% to 24% between 1999 and 2007) and almost doubled at public four-year universities (from 19% to 35%). The share of family income required to attend private four-year colleges and universities rose from 47% to 69% over the same period.[27] From 1999 to 2009, median family income in Illinois fell by 6.5% in constant dollars, while tuition increased by 100% at public four-year universities and by 38% at public two-year colleges.[28] At the start of the decade, Illinois was the top-performing state in its level of investment in financial aid for low-income students.[29] But state support for need-based grants dropped from $1,036 to $745 per undergraduate full-time-equivalent (FTE) student from 1999–2000 to 2008–9, a decline of 28%.[30]

Gaps in Performance

Statewide indicators mask substantial differences in higher education outcomes within Illinois. The state's strategic plan for higher education, *The Public Agenda for College and Career Success,* characterizes these differences as the "tale of two states of Illinois": "One Illinois is well-educated and prosperous, with virtually unlimited opportunities. The other is vastly underserved educationally and struggling economically, with severely constricted opportunities. Between these two states of Illinois is a 'prosperity gap' that relates directly to large and widening disparities in educational attainment—by race/ethnicity, by income, and by region."[31]

Educational attainment is substantially higher in the Chicago suburbs and some "downstate" counties (for example, McLean and Champaign) than in the south side of Chicago and rural areas of the state.[32] Educational attainment is also substantially lower for Blacks and Hispanics than for Whites, and for low-income than for high-income residents. The Illinois Board of Higher Education (IBHE), in its 2009 *Report to the Governor and General Assembly,* found that "Hispanic, black, and American Indian students remain underrepresented in Illinois colleges and universities, with significant gaps in educational attainment."[33]

These gaps in attainment are consistent across measures of preparation for college, participation in college, and college completion in Illinois. For example, the percentage of young adults (ages 18 to 24) who were enrolled in postsecondary education in 2006 was substantially lower for Hispanics than for Whites (a gap of 20 percentage points) and for Blacks compared with Whites (a gap of 16 percentage points).[34] Blacks who do enroll are overrepresented at for-profit institutions; they constituted 25.4% of students attending for-profit institutions in 2006 but only 15.3% of students attending all institutions in the state.[35] Only 36.1% of Black students and 44.0% of Hispanic students attending four-year colleges and universities graduated within six years in 2009, compared with 65.8% for White students and 69.1% for Asian American students.[36]

The Structure of Higher Education in the State

Illinois has developed an extensive and diverse system of higher education. In fall 2010, the state was home to 181 degree-granting institutions and branches: 9 public four-year universities on 12 campuses, 48 community colleges, 84 private not-for-profit colleges and universities, and 37 for-profit institutions.[37] In addition, 26 out-of-state institutions are approved to offer degree programs in the state.[38] The share of students enrolled in public colleges and universities who attend community colleges is higher in Illinois (63%) than the national average (49%).[39] About one-fourth of all undergraduates enrolled in postsecondary education in Illinois in fall 2010 attended a private not-for-profit institution.[40] State policymakers in the 1960s, facing the need to expand higher education, decided "to use the capacity of private colleges and universities rather than building new four-year institutions—and to create a system of community colleges to accommodate most of the increases in new students at the lower-division level." Richard Richardson called these decisions "important legacies that contribute to the shape of contemporary Illinois higher education."[41]

What Explains the Drop in Higher Education Performance?

Given the state's extensive system of higher education, why did its performance decline? Why is Illinois no longer a recognized national leader in higher education? The drop in higher education performance in Illinois follows a fundamental change in the state's higher education governance. In spring 1995, the state legislature passed a higher education reorganization act that was signed into law by Governor Jim Edgar. Adopted in response to institutional demands for greater autonomy and in order to reduce administrative costs, the new law ended the "system of systems" that had governed Illinois higher education for three decades.[42]

The system of systems can be traced to the Illinois Board of Higher Education's master plan of 1964, which called for four governing boards to represent 12 public universities.[43] This structure was articulated in greater detail in the Board of Higher Education's 1966 *Master Plan for Higher Education in Illinois—Phase II.* Under this vision, the system of systems was designed to retain "the identity, institutions, and purposes" of existing higher education systems while also creating one overall system that can "comprehend the diverse educational needs of the state" and recognize the role that each system plays in "the total statewide development of higher education."[44]

In eliminating the system of systems, the 1995 reorganization act replaced the governing boards of two of the systems with individual local boards at 7 of the state's 12 public universities. The 1995 change in higher education governance provides the context for two themes driving the state's recent decline in higher education performance: (1) the inability to establish shared state goals and priorities for higher education, and (2) the failure to allocate available resources strategically to meet state goals and priorities.

The Inability to Establish Shared Goals and Priorities

In recent years, Illinois state leaders have failed to establish and build consensus around shared statewide goals and priorities for higher education. The state's higher education system is fragmented; state leaders do not come together to make collective strategic decisions for higher education.

The state and institutional leaders we interviewed recognize the importance of improving higher education performance, but they perceive little capacity within Illinois to establish shared goals and priorities for achieving this improvement. This conclusion was articulated by the leader of a public university who told us, "There is almost no identifiable intentional public policy toward Illinois higher education at this moment. We have had 10 years of governors who really haven't cared about higher education policy. We really haven't had anybody in the General Assembly that cares about higher education policy. And quite honestly, we have not had the capacity within the Illinois Board of Higher Education to lead on higher education policy."

As described below, the lack of statewide policy capacity for higher education can be traced to several developments and conditions in the state, including the dissolution of the system of systems, political corruption and inattention to higher education at the state level, the lack of accountability for higher education performance, and challenges in coordinating across education sectors and levels.

Dissolving the System of Systems

Created in 1961, the Illinois Board of Higher Education is charged with coordinating the state's public universities and community colleges, its independent not-for-profit colleges and universities, and its independent for-profit institutions. Before the 1995 reorganization, the state board worked with the leaders of four separate "systems" of higher education: the Board of Governors represented five universities; the Board of Regents represented three universities; the Board of Trustees of Southern Illinois University represented two campuses; and the Board of Trustees at University of Illinois represented two campuses. As articulated in the 1966 IBHE *Master Plan for Higher Education In Illinois—Phase II*, the system of systems was designed to retain "the identity, institutions, and purposes" of existing systems while also creating one new system that recognizes the role that each system plays in "the total statewide development of higher education" and that in its "totality can comprehend the diverse educational needs of the state for the foreseeable future."[45]

Under the system of systems, the Illinois Board of Higher Education referred to itself as "the only state agency broadly representative of both higher education and the public interest."[46] In his study, Richardson noted that the board, operating under the system of systems, was often able to advance a "united front" on higher education issues and encourage university governing boards to align institutional priorities with state priorities. Although not without criticism, a prior case study credited the system of systems with "creating a politically responsive environment (although not one necessarily focused on educational priorities)."[47] The state's system of systems was designed to provide a mechanism for balancing power and resources across the state's diverse set of universities and balancing institutional priorities with state needs. The 1995 reorganization changed this balance, elevating institutional priorities, particularly the priorities of the research universities, and weakening the state coordinating function and reducing its ability to balance institutional priorities with public needs.

Whereas before the 1995 reorganization the state board worked with the leaders of four systems of higher education, it now must coordinate with nine system and university heads, a change that further complicates the state board's efforts to provide leadership. The hybrid structure includes the boards of two university systems (the University of Illinois and Southern Illinois University) and the local boards of seven public universities. The reorganization act did not increase state board's authority to provide a check on the increase in institutional autonomy created through the local boards.[48] A bill proposed at the time of the reorganization would have granted the state board additional responsibilities, including the authority to approve tuition and fees, but this bill was not passed by the Legislature.[49]

An example of the Board of Higher Education's previous success (under the system of systems) in aligning institutional priorities with state goals is the Priorities, Quality, and Productivity (PQP) Initiative. During the early 1990s, PQP was designed to encourage the state's higher education institutions to improve their quality and productivity by shifting resources away from lower-quality programs and services and toward higher-priority programs and services consistent with each institution's mission. The state board worked with institutional leaders to establish measures of productivity in instruction, research, service, and administration and to prioritize programs and services in light of institutional missions. Richardson found that the PQP Initiative, in demonstrating accountability of higher education, improved the state board's "reputation for effectiveness" among the governor, the legislators, and institutional leaders.[50]

The state board is statutorily required to provide system planning, make budget recommendations, approve and review instructional programs, authorize independent and out-of-state institutions, administer federal and state grant programs, and maintain the state's higher education data system. In reality, the Board of Higher Education now focuses primarily on responding to requests from the legislature, generating reports, and performing regulatory responsibilities especially with regard to the state's for-profit institutions. Although the state board was once viewed as powerful and effective, it is now perceived as weak and ineffective. Presidents of the state's universities now bypass the board and go directly to the State Assembly; the board no longer presents the unified front. The leader of a state policy and research institute summarized prevailing practice, stating, "Even in the best of times [the state's universities] are good at making end runs around the state agencies. Now they are pretty much all on their own."

In this new governance arrangement, the state board, after decades of stable and respected leadership, is having difficulty retaining its own leaders, which may further restrict its effectiveness. In the eight years since Keith Sanders left the position of executive director of the state board in 2003, five individuals have held this position. Whereas seven people served as chair of the state board in the

41 years from 1961 to 2002, four people have served as chair in the nine years since 2002.

Political Corruption and Inattention to Higher Education at the State Level

The ability of the state Board of Higher Education to set shared goals and priorities for higher education has also been affected by a lack of commitment to higher education among state political leaders. Illinois is a state that provides its governor with strong "appointive powers" (for example, in relation to budget, organizational, tenure, and veto powers).[51] Some state and institutional leaders who were interviewed for this study described current Governor Pat Quinn as "higher-education friendly," but most interviewees characterized higher education as a low priority for governors over the past decade. A leader of a state policy and research institute told us, "When Blagojevich was governor, he had an anti-higher-education mentality. Everybody's strategy was to keep your head down, don't do anything that will call attention to you because then you'll be in the line of fire. He really set higher education back in a big way."

The charges of corruption associated with recent governors have also limited state government effectiveness. George Homer Ryan (R) served as governor from 1999 to 2003. In 2006, he was convicted on 18 federal counts associated with his administration of the Illinois Secretary of State's Office prior to becoming governor, including racketeering, bribery, extortion, money laundering, and tax fraud. He was sentenced to six years and six months in prison. Rod Blagojevich (D) was elected governor in 2002 and re-elected in 2006. In January 2009, he was impeached by the Illinois Senate after he was charged with racketeering, extortion, and bribery. Lieutenant Governor Pat Quinn took over the governorship in January 2009 after Blagojevich was removed from office. In 2010, Quinn won the democratic primary in a close contest and was elected after narrowly defeating Republican State Senator Bill Brady.[52]

The challenges of setting shared goals and priorities for higher education are compounded by doubts about the caliber of higher education appointments made by these recent governors. In the 1990s, Richardson found that the perceived quality of the members of the Illinois Board of Higher Education enhanced its authority.[53] In contrast, several state leaders interviewed questioned the qualifications of those appointed since the 1990s. A leader of a state policy and research institute explained: "Under prior administrations, the board was typically a pretty high caliber group of individuals. There were a lot of business types, civic-leader type people on it, CEOs, doctors. Usually not much higher education background, but they brought a really great perspective. They were all well-educated and held influential positions. When Rod Blagojevich became governor, he saw the higher education board as a place to reward his political donors."

Questions have also been raised about the qualifications of gubernatorial appointees to the board of the University of Illinois at Urbana-Champaign, the flagship university. With the 1995 reorganization, the board became appointed by the governor rather than elected. Former director of the Illinois Legislative Studies Center at the University of Illinois at Springfield Jack Van der Slik wrote in 2010, "In 1995 the education community anticipated that a variety of distinguished people would accept such appointments, people who would not ever consider running for election to such positions. What was not expected was a lack of serious concern by governors about their appointees. . . . Blagojevich made appointments . . . that placed political donors with dubious scruples about higher education governance into key positions."[54]

Questions about state leadership for higher education are not limited to the governor's office. The Illinois legislature, for its part, has been characterized by many as partisan and lacking consistent and substantive leadership for higher education. At the time of our interviews (spring 2010), Democrats controlled both the House (70 Democrats, 48 Republicans) and Senate (37 Democrats, 22 Republicans).[55] After the November 2010 elections, the Democratic margin was reduced in both chambers (64 Democrats and 54 Republicans in the House; 35 Democrats and 24 Republicans in the Senate). State legislators and other state leaders interviewed for this study questioned the ability of the legislature to establish shared goals and priorities for higher education through its primary policy lever, the budget, particularly in the face of advocacy by the localized boards of higher education. A state senator said, "In years past there had been much better leadership . . . advocating and concerned about educational agenda items . . . as the budget was shaped. Now we have chairs that are very content to go through the motions."

Scandal also taints other state and institutional higher education leaders. In September 2009, B. Joseph White resigned from his position as president of the University of Illinois in response to revelations that "politically connected applicants" were given preference in the admission process.[56]

Political discord also reaches to state administrative functions within higher education. The Illinois Student Assistance Commission and the Illinois Community College Board, both of which officially report to the state Board of Higher

Education, were described to us as acting independently. A leader of one state agency said, "The amount of time we spend trying to just get simple information out of [another state agency]—I mean, there isn't outright warfare—but actually there has been on some levels."

Tension among education agencies and the executive and legislative branches of government is not unique or new to Illinois, but the magnitude of discord in Illinois appears to be limiting the state's ability to improve the performance of higher education. The most recent statewide master plan, *The Public Agenda*, exemplifies the state's inability to establish shared goals and priorities. At the direction of the state legislature (through passage of House Joint Resolution 69 in 2007), the Illinois Board of Higher Education developed a comprehensive 10-year strategic plan for higher education that reflects input from many stakeholders. Although this document thoroughly describes the challenges that must be addressed, it does not specify targets for performance or prioritize its many recommendations. Some state and institutional leaders interviewed for this study were very critical of the plan's limitations in affecting state policy. A leader of a public university said this about the plan: "I think it is as weak as dishwater. I do not think it gives any particular strategic direction. I don't think it's linked with budget allocations. The biggest thing is, I do not think anyone is paying attention except the board itself, as it should. Is the governor paying attention? Is it going to influence budget allocations? Will it drive institutional behavior? Part of the reason is there was not the intellectual visionary capacity within the staff and the [state] board."

Lack of Accountability

Another manifestation of the lack of shared goals for higher education is the absence of incentives for public colleges and universities to improve performance or meet state needs. The state's dire fiscal situation has resulted in the elimination of most grant programs administered by the Illinois Board of Higher Education. Formerly, the board was able to use its grant programs to leverage institutional change that is aligned with state priorities.

Even where the state has identified priorities for higher education, it has not developed incentives for institutions to improve performance. For example, attention to closing gaps in educational attainment across racial/ethnic groups has been mandated by the state legislature and is reflected in state board documents. The board is required by law to present an "Underrepresented Groups Report" to the governor and the legislature annually.[57] The board's report in 2009 provides information on underrepresented groups as required by statute (i.e., regarding racial and ethnic minorities, women, and persons with disabilities) as well as information on disparities by income and region. However, no action or consequences appear to follow from the information in the report.

Appropriations to higher education institutions do not incentivize institutions to improve performance. Appropriations to public universities reflect a base-plus approach, while appropriations to community colleges are based on reimbursable credit hours. Some state leaders we interviewed expressed interest in developing a performance-based funding system. But many doubted that such a system could be implemented, given the current constraints on state revenues and likely opposition from public universities. Institutional opposition in the recent past is reflected in the outcome of HB 4906, the Higher Education Accountability Act. Introduced in January 2010 by Representative Richard Myers (R), HB 4906 would have required the state's public universities to: "develop annual academic, financial, and enrollment plans that outline (i) tuition and fee estimates, (ii) enrollment projections, (iii) how to meet state policy objectives, and (iv) accepting a number of accountability measures, including meeting benchmarks related to accessibility and affordability." The bill also would have required the state board to develop "performance indicators to measure whether public universities in this state are meeting state policy objectives."[58] In March 2010, the bill was re-referred to the Rules Committee. According to a state leader, "The unions and the institutions killed it. They argued that it was an unfunded mandate, even though all the information that was being requested already is supplied by the universities."

The state board has experienced challenges in using available data to identify and achieve state priorities. In 2010, Education Sector noted that the strength of the state's data system is in "gathering information on a wide breadth of performance measures."[59] Of particular note, the state board funds and supports the use of innovative reports—called High School Feedback Reports—that each public university provides annually to high school guidance counselors and principals across the state. The report provides information on academic grades during freshman year in various subjects, showing the degree of success of that high school's graduates at the university. In addition, the state has begun working to establish the Illinois Longitudinal Data System (ILDS), a comprehensive data system designed to track students longitudinally from prekindergarten and K–12 education through postsecondary education and into the workforce.

Despite these recent efforts, the state does not have a good track record in using the information it has gathered. Education Sector reported that the state's data systems need improvement in using information for governance, strategic planning, and funding purposes and in providing transparency and information to parents and students.[60] The 2009–10 Data Quality Campaign (DQC) found that Illinois had taken only four of ten key state actions necessary for establishing a culture of effective data use.[61]

Ongoing Challenges in Supporting Student Transitions

Establishing shared state goals and priorities is particularly important to improving student transitions across educational sectors and levels. The Illinois Articulation Initiative (IAI) was established in 1993 to facilitate the transfer of general education courses for students attending any of the 100 participating institutions. The success of this initiative is suggested by the above-average rate of degree completion for Illinois students who start at a community college: 25.6% of students beginning at a two-year institution in Illinois in fall 2002 graduated with an associate's degree, compared with 21.2% nationwide; and 14.9% graduated from a four-year institution, compared with 12.1% nationwide.[62] Several state and institutional leaders we interviewed said that the initiative has facilitated transfer and articulation, with one state leader asserting: "We have a strong articulation in the community college system because of what we call the Illinois Articulation Initiative, where courses transfer across the state."

Nonetheless, state and institutional leaders have also emphasized the need for continued improvement. In 2010, the state board reported that "students face significant challenges in achieving a seamless transition from one sector to the other."[63] A 2006 evaluation offers ten recommendations for improving the Illinois Articulation Initiative, with particular attention to the General Education Core Curriculum and options for students who have not completed the core curriculum.[64]

In terms of aligning K–12 and higher education, the state now requires high school students to pass the Prairie State Achievement Examination (PSAE) in order to receive a regular high school diploma. Performance on the test is used to assess Adequate Yearly Progress (AYP) at the school, district, and state levels, but this assessment is not aligned with college readiness standards. Under the auspices of the American Diploma Project, Common Core Standards, and International Benchmarking projects, state leaders are now working to align high school and college curricula, but the state does not yet have end-of-course assessments. The state had hoped to use federal funding from the Race to the Top competition to develop these exams, but its application was unsuccessful.

In 2007, the state legislature passed a bill to establish a P–20 Council to work with the governor, legislature, and education agencies to promote coordinated infrastructures among educational sectors and support the alignment of K–12 and postsecondary curricula and assessments, among other functions to improve student transitions and success. In 2008, then-Governor Blagojevich signed the bill (Illinois Public Act 95-0626) authorizing the establishment of the P–20 Council but did not make any appointments during his term. Appointments were finally made by Governor Quinn in 2010. The P–20 Council follows an earlier effort, called the Joint Education Community, to encourage cooperation across the state's education agencies. The P–20 Council receives no state funding, and, according to many observers we interviewed, it lacks a focused agenda.

The Failure to Allocate Available Fiscal Resources Strategically

As with many states, Illinois faces substantial fiscal challenges in supporting its key functions, including the financing of higher education. Fiscal constraints created by the recent economic downturn magnify the importance of using available resources strategically to meet the state's overall policy goals. Yet even before the recent economic downturn, Illinois was experiencing challenges in allocating available resources to achieve statewide goals and priorities for higher education. Over the past decade, Illinois has shifted away from funding need-based student financial aid and reduced support for students in the independent sector. The state has neither developed a planned statewide approach to tuition increases nor aligned state appropriations with state priorities for higher education.

A Policy Shift Away from Need-Based Student Financial Aid

One of the most salient changes in Illinois in recent years is the decline in its long-standing success in providing state-funded need-based financial aid to students. Despite a history of substantial investment, the state's appropriations for need-based aid have not kept pace with recent increases in inflation, tuition and fees, or demand.

The primary source of state-funded financial aid for students attending colleges and universities in Illinois is the Monetary Award Program (MAP), which represented 91% of the expenditures for student aid by the Illinois Student Assistance Commission (ISAC) in fiscal year 2010.[65] The program has been targeted toward students with financial need. In fiscal year 2008, for example, the mean taxable income of recipients was $23,558, and 44% of recipients had an expected family contribution of zero.[66] Nearly half (47.8%) of recipients in fiscal year 2008 had a family income below $20,000; just 7.5% had a family income above $60,000.[67] In comparison with other states, Illinois has allocated high amounts to need-based aid. In 2008–9, the state ranked sixth in need-based undergraduate grant aid per undergraduate FTE student ($746 in Illinois compared with $476 for the national average). Illinois was also fourteenth that year in total undergraduate grant aid per undergraduate FTE student ($783 in Illinois compared with $660 nationally). In 2008–9, total state grant expenditures represented 14% of state fiscal support for higher education operating expenses in Illinois, the twelfth-highest share in the nation.[68]

Despite these favorable comparisons with other states, Illinois has lost ground in keeping college affordable for its families and students. State appropriations for the Monetary Award Program have lagged behind increases in tuition and inflation in recent years. The maximum award covered 100% of average tuition and fees at public community colleges and four-year universities in fiscal year 2002, but by fiscal year 2010 the maximum award covered 66% at community colleges and 48% at public universities.[69]

In July 2009, in response to state budget shortfalls, the General Assembly reduced funding for MAP by approximately $200 million, essentially eliminating funding for spring 2010 awards. In response to efforts by college and university leaders, student demonstrations, "an organized offense" coordinated by the Illinois Student Assistance Commission and support from Governor Quinn, the legislature restored this funding in October 2009.[70] Yet MAP funds continue to be insufficient to provide aid to eligible students. The Student Assistance Commission has responded to funding shortfalls by dispersing aid on a first-come, first-served basis. In fiscal year 2010, about 130,000 eligible applicants did not receive a MAP grant because they applied after the available funding was exhausted.[71] The practice of dispersing aid on a first-come, first-served basis affects community college students disproportionately, since many community college students apply shortly before the start of the academic term; about 71% of the more than 143,000 eligible applicants denied MAP funds for fiscal year 2011 were attending public two-year colleges.[72] The Illinois Student Assistance Commission estimates that approximately 150,000 eligible applicants will be denied MAP funds by end of fiscal year 2011.[73]

The Illinois Board of Higher Education has identified a set of options to improve the efficient and effective use of MAP funds, but at the time of our data collection there was no consensus on how to proceed on them.[74] Implementing at least some of these options will require the state board to garner support from other state higher education agencies. One proposed option was to modify the MAP eligibility requirements to encourage low-income students to become better prepared academically for college (i.e., to modify MAP to resemble Indiana's 21st Century Scholars program). According to the state board, this modification would be designed to "leverage financial aid for low-income students to encourage completion of a rigorous high school curriculum."[75] This change has not garnered widespread support. A leader of a state higher education agency expressed the political challenges of getting agreement on this proposal:

> [One state agency], for whatever reason, and it still is totally a mystery to me, hated it, and it ripped apart every analysis. They poisoned the well. It was unbelievable, and I've never seen anything like it. So here we have three agencies that are—I mean, it wears me down. We had a 105,000% cooperation from the city of Chicago. The Business Roundtable and Boeing were like "absolutely." But yet the agency that would have to administer it, because statutorily they have the MAP funds, said, "It's a ruse, you're just giving away money."

In his state-of-the-state address for 2010, Governor Quinn emphasized his commitment to identifying a dedicated funding source for the Monetary Award Program. Consistent with this commitment, the Illinois Student Assistance Commission proposed supplementing state funding for MAP by issuing revenue bonds for community college MAP recipients that would be repaid through taxes paid by these recipients.[76] This proposal has received mixed responses; the Illinois Community College Board and key legislators have publicly stated their dissatisfaction with it.

Declining Support for Students in the Independent Sector

State financial aid and other grant programs have historically been used in Illinois to support enrollment at the state's private colleges and universities and to encourage these institutions to participate in statewide master planning. Yet some state programs that have previously provided incentives for enrollment in private institutions have been cut due to budget shortfalls. Currently, the primary state policy lever for encouraging enrollment at private institutions in the state is the Monetary Award Program. Students attending some of the state's for-profit institutions (for example, the DeVry University of Technology) are also eligible for MAP grants.

State and institutional leaders we interviewed described MAP as a cost-effective approach for expanding the capacity of the state's higher education system. Nonetheless, the shares of MAP dollars and awards received by students attending the state's private not-for-profit colleges and universities have declined over the past decades. Students at these institutions received 69% of all MAP dollars in fiscal year 1980, 58% in 1990, 46% in 2000, and 40% in 2009.[77] Moreover, the Illinois Board of Higher Education has proposed that "limiting MAP to public institutions" could help to "target MAP funds more effectively to achieve student access and success goals."[78]

Lack of a Planned Statewide Approach to Tuition

When the state legislature dissolved the system of systems, it also ceded control of tuition to the institutions of higher education. Individual public universities now have the power to set their own tuition without the involvement of the governor, the legislature, or the Illinois Board of Higher Education. A state senator we interviewed implied the benefits of the system of systems to the balancing of state and institutional priorities when he compared tuition setting and budget requests under the system of systems (when Jim Edgar was governor) with the process today: "Under a different governor, Jim Edgar, IBHE was empowered to be more of a moderator or prioritizer of capital construction and tuition setting. Universities had to go through IBHE to make the case. This is not the situation with the past or present governor. Universities come in to make their own case for every issue. IBHE is a reference point, but not a door that universities need to pass through."

The local board of each community college also sets tuition at its institution. But in contrast to the public universities, tuition increases at community colleges tend to occur within the parameters set by the Illinois Community College Board and by the preferences of voters who elect the board members at each local institution.

As reported earlier, tuition at two- and four-year public colleges and universities has grown substantially over the past decade, while family income has dropped. Tuition increases are covering an increasing share of the costs of postsecondary education across all types of public institutions, meaning that a larger share of the burden of paying for higher education has been shifted onto students and their families. From 2003 to 2009, the share of average education and related expenses per FTE student that was covered by tuition increased from 43% to 53% at public research universities, from 35% to 48% at public master's institutions, and from 27% to 32% at community colleges.[79]

In an effort to stabilize tuition levels at public four-year institutions for students who are already enrolled, Governor Blagojevich signed legislation in 2003 establishing the Truth in Tuition Policy. Effective beginning in 2004–5, the policy freezes tuition levels (but not fees) for undergraduate students at public four-year institutions at the time they first enroll. State and institutional leaders we interviewed pointed to the negative unintended consequences of this policy, with one leader stating that it "puts four years of tuition increases in every single year."

During our data collection, some state legislators expressed great frustration about the rate of tuition increases at public universities and the lack of transparency about the forces contributing to these increases. In April 2010, the state senate created a subcommittee to examine the procedures for setting tuition. The legislature also authorized the Board of Higher Education to conduct a study of affordability.

Some state leaders we interviewed acknowledged the need to develop ways to link decisions about appropriations, tuition, and financial aid so that the state can implement strategies that are better aligned to meet statewide goals. One of the nine options that the Illinois Board of Higher Education identified to use MAP funds more effectively to improve student success is "developing a shared-responsibility model akin to Oregon's financial aid program."[80] As a leader of a state higher education agency said, however, Illinois has not achieved this linkage:

> On a statewide basis, IBHE is really trying to get all of us higher ed folks and the people in the legislature to try to think about tuition and financial aid and appropriations for schools all in a more unified way. Because now they really are decided in a very separate, very disparate process. . . . It's not even always the same legislative committee that will consider university budgets and consider the budget for student financial aid. . . . There's no explicit structure that allows them to make any connections among all of those things.

State Appropriations Not Aligned with State Priorities

In recent years, state appropriations for higher education have not been aligned with state goals for higher education. Perhaps reflecting the relatively high share of students in Illinois who are enrolled in private colleges and universities, in 2009 the share of state expenditures allocated to public higher education in Illinois (6.1%) was lower than the national average (9.8%).[81]

At public community colleges in Illinois, state appropriations have been based largely on cost per credit hour, with little attention to developing incentives for improved performance or cost-restructuring based on other measures. Funding for community colleges comes from three sources: local property taxes, state grants, and tuition. About a third of community college revenue is expected to come from each of these three sources, but state appropriations are currently insufficient to achieve this distribution. Property taxes are set locally, with the maximum rate set by the state. The state also provides equalization funds to account for differences in property tax revenue for community colleges in different parts of the state. In recent years, however, the equalization grants have been inadequate to bring all community colleges to the statewide average.

The state has also been unable to maintain financial support for the research functions of higher education. In fiscal year 2008, Illinois eliminated funding for the State Matching Grant Program, which offered matching grants for public and private colleges and universities competing for federal and corporate research grants. The Illinois Board of Higher Education reported that the state's appropriation of $9.5 million for this program in fiscal year 2007 resulted in $111.6 million in grants from the federal government and other sources.[82] An external evaluation of the program for fiscal year 2000 concluded that it "is a very worthwhile strategy for increasing federal and corporate research funds."[83] Nonetheless, for the first time since the program was established in 1998, the state appropriated no funds to it in fiscal year 2008.

Illinois has also been unable to allocate resources to expand pilot programs designed to improve student success rates. These pilot programs, which if scaled statewide might be able to improve higher education performance, include the following:

- The College and Career Readiness Pilot Act of 2007 is designed to reduce remediation by establishing partnerships between high schools and community colleges. The pilot sites have five key goals: assess college readiness, lower the need for remedial coursework, align curricula of high schools and community colleges, provide academic support and enrichment to high school seniors, and develop a local evaluation process.[84]
- The Baccalaureate Completion Grants program seeks to improve bachelor's degree completion rates by making awards to partnerships of

two- and four-year colleges and universities. These competitive grants support "baccalaureate completion programs at off-campus sites such as community colleges, high schools, community centers, and online."[85] However, some state leaders we interviewed suggested that the program has deterred but not eliminated the interest of community colleges in offering bachelor's degrees.

- The MAP 2+2 program is designed to maximize eligibility for Monetary Award Program grants for students who are dually admitted to a community college and a public university. Under the program, students attending a community college during their first two years receive MAP eligibility as if they were to attend a public university all four years. By reducing loan debt, the program facilitates transfer for financially needy students. Although the Board of Higher Education has identified MAP 2+2 as an option for more efficient use and targeting of MAP funds, the program currently serves small numbers of students and requires individual four-year and two-year institutions to negotiate their own transfer arrangements.

In an effort to secure scarce public resources for higher education, improve the alignment of funding with state goals and priorities, and demonstrate accountability, the Illinois Board of Higher Education recently modified its approach to requesting appropriations from the legislature. In fiscal year 2009, the state board adopted an "investment approach" that links its budget requests to goals and levels of performance identified in *The Public Agenda* (the state's master plan for higher education). Historically, colleges and universities have submitted budget requests to the state board, which in turn has submitted these requests to the governor and the legislature. The state board has traditionally established "general rules" to guide budget requests (for example, with attention to salary increases and tuition and fee increases). The state board has also produced analyses of institutional costs.[86]

Beginning in fiscal year 2009, the Illinois Board of Higher Education no longer produces "a single recommendation" but instead proposes "a range of investment options consisting of investment levels, or 'steps.'" The fiscal year 2011 budget request also organizes budget recommendations in terms of the goals specified in *The Public Agenda*. The stated goal of this approach is "to present well-reasoned options to policymakers that can be accommodated at various levels of funding, given other state priorities and available resources."[87] As a leader of a state higher education agency explained, the board's "investment levels" seek to make the case for how higher education would use additional funding:

> The way the legislature works in the last ten years or more is the leaders get together at the end of the session and say, here is what the budget is, and they all vote on it. . . . IBHE used to get a number from the governor's budget office: "Here's what you can ask for." . . . To get around that without directly defying the governor and the budget office, IBHE adopted this investment approach, and therefore IBHE is not actually saying that it should actually have a 6% increase, but it's going to put that out there because we really could use it, and here's how we would use it, and here's what you'll get.

Nonetheless, the state board's new budget approach does not appear to have been effective in holding the line on state cuts to higher education.

Recent state budget shortfalls and declines in revenues (described earlier) reduce the availability of public funding for higher education, which has profound effects on those seeking to improve higher education performance. A leader of a state higher education agency summarized legislators' current challenges in governing within a severely constrained state budget: "They are really frustrated. They can't give institutions what they want. They can't give financial aid what it needs. And not only is it true with higher education, but it's true with every single service that the state supports. You can sense the genuine frustration among many legislators that the problem is so enormous, so intractable, that they've almost thrown their hands and said, 'We can't do anything.'"

Even if state revenues were to rebound substantially, it is unclear whether the improved fiscal environment would translate into additional funding for higher education. Regardless, increasing state funding for higher education, while necessary, is likely not sufficient to solve the problems of reduced higher education performance. The state must also improve its ability to establish shared goals and priorities and to use available fiscal resources to achieve them.

Conclusion

Workforce trends and international competition suggest that Illinois will need larger numbers of better-educated workers over the coming decades. At the same time, demographic trends, combined with drops in higher education performance, appear to be creating a "prosperity gap" in educational attainment in the state by race/ethnicity, income, and region. The state is also facing substantial fiscal shortfalls, but it is important to note that the decline in higher education performance began before the recent budget challenges; increased funding is necessary but not insufficient to improve performance.

The magnitude of these challenges underscores the importance of developing policy leadership capacity for higher education in Illinois, identifying and gaining consensus on statewide goals and priorities, and determining how to use available fiscal resources to improve higher education's performance. The state has begun, since the main data gathering for this study was completed, to take some steps toward examining and improving the finance structure of higher education.[88] Under Senate Joint Resolution 88, the state created a Higher Education Finance Study Commission made up of representatives from the state legislature, businesses, K–12 schools, and higher education. The commission was designed to "evaluate higher education budgeting practices in Illinois, consider fresh ideas and new approaches from other states, and develop recommendations to the IBHE, the Governor, and the General Assembly to more closely align the financing of colleges and universities to goals of the *Illinois Public Agenda for College and Career Success*."[89]

In its final report released in December 2010, the commission concluded that "higher education finance in Illinois does not promote the four goals of educational attainment, college affordability, workforce modernization, or economic development." The commission recommended that the state "implement a new finance and budgeting design based on institutional performance in achieving the goals of the *Illinois Public Agenda for College and Career Success*." The commission also recommended that that state "reform the Monetary Award Program (MAP) to promote increased access and success for low-income students." Finally, the commission recommended that the Illinois Board of Higher Education work with the state's public higher education institutions to "identify economies and efficiencies and report to the General Assembly with recommendations on streamlining and cost-saving measures."[90]

In spring 2011, the legislature followed up on these recommendations by passing and sending to the governor for signature HB 1503, a bill (now Public Act 97-320) that requires the state Board of Higher Education to include in its budget recommendations, beginning in fiscal year 2013, allocations to community colleges and public universities based on "performance in achieving state goals related to student success and certificate and degree completion."[91] To develop performance metrics, the Board of Higher Education is to create a steering committee that includes representatives from the Office of the Governor, General

Assembly, public colleges and universities, state agencies, business and industry, and statewide organizations representing faculty and staff.

While these are promising steps, it remains to be seen whether state leaders, working within a constrained fiscal environment and with the legacy of political corruption, can build consensus on statewide goals and priorities for higher education and use existing resources strategically to improve performance in reaching those goals. If this can be done, Illinois may have an opportunity, despite the recent erosion in higher education performance and challenges to political leadership, to recover its status as a national leader in higher education.

Chapter 6

Much Accomplished, Much at Stake

The Performance and State Policies of Higher Education in Maryland

With contributions by Jamey Rorison

Maryland leads the nation in the educational attainment of its population.[1] In 2008, 43.9% of adults in Maryland (ages 25 and older) held at least an associate degree, compared with 37.9% of adults nationwide.[2] Even with this relatively high performance, Maryland aspires to even greater attainment.[3] A leader of a state higher education agency we interviewed explained that Maryland seeks to compete globally, not nationally, stating: "Our governor has made it clear that we are not measuring ourselves against the southern states or against any other state, quite frankly. Our goal as a state is to be among the most competitive countries in the world."

Based on trends in degree production and projected population growth, Maryland needs to increase its annual production of associate and bachelor's degrees by 5.1% per year in order for 55% of its workforce (ages 25 to 64) to hold at least an associate degree by 2020.[4] Raising attainment rates among students of traditional college age (i.e., about 18 to 24) will not be sufficient to reach the state's goal for international competitiveness; Maryland must also improve educational outcomes for nontraditional-age students.[5]

The state must also improve its higher education performance if it is to meet projected workforce demands. Between 2008 and 2018, considerably more new jobs in the state are projected to require postsecondary education (213,000) rather than a high school education (107,000). About 67% of all jobs in Maryland are expected to require at least some postsecondary education or training by 2018, a higher percentage than the national average (63%) and among the highest percentages nationwide. Maryland ranks eleventh in the nation in the percentage of jobs requiring at least a bachelor's degree.[6] The state's higher education performance must also improve to respond to other changes in the state economy and workforce such as the Base Realignment and Closure process.[7]

To reach the required levels of educational attainment, Maryland must reduce gaps in educational performance across demographic groups. Educational attainment is considerably lower for native-born Marylanders than for residents who move to the state. According to one report, 35% of native-born Marylanders had at least a bachelor's degree in 2009, compared with 43% of Maryland residents who were from another state or country.[8] In other words, three out of four Maryland residents with a bachelor's degree or higher were born in another state.[9]

The importance of improving educational attainment of Blacks and Hispanics in the state is underscored by demographic trends. As noted by the University System of Maryland (USM), "The fastest growing segments of Maryland's population are those groups traditionally less likely to pursue and complete postsecondary education."[10] Blacks represent a considerably higher share of the population of Maryland than of the nation as a whole (28.7% compared with 12.1%).[11] Hispanics represent a smaller share of Maryland's population (7.2% in 2009) than the U.S. population overall (15.8%),[12] but (as illustrated in chapter 3) most of the state's projected growth in high school will be among Hispanics.[13]

Degree attainment rates must be improved among the state's Black and Hispanic populations if Maryland is to meet its statewide goals. From 1990 to 2005, the share of 25- to 64-year-olds in Maryland who had attained at least an associate degree increased among Blacks (rising from 22.5% to 26.8%) but declined among Hispanics (falling from 31.6% to 25.9%). Over the same period, the share of Whites with at least an associate degree also increased (from 38.2% to 48.4%), leaving a gap of 21 percentage points between Whites and Blacks in 2005 and a gap of 22 percentage points between Whites and Hispanics.[14]

Improving the state's higher education performance will also require better performance in the City of Baltimore. As the nation's twentieth-largest metropolitan area,[15] Baltimore is home to 10.8% of the state's population.[16] Yet only 29.5% of adults in Baltimore have completed at least an associate degree, compared with 41.5% statewide.[17] The city's population has a higher percentage of Blacks (63.1%) than does the state as a whole (28.5%).[18] Income levels are lower in Baltimore, with a median household income of $22,911 in 2009, compared with $34,236 statewide.[19]

As described in chapter 3, Maryland is a relatively wealthy state. Yet despite having higher median personal and family income than many other states, Maryland's efforts to increase educational attainment and reduce gaps in education among groups must also recognize the likelihood of restrained fiscal resources for the foreseeable future. From fiscal years 2005 to 2008, Maryland increased its general fund support for higher education by 34%, a higher rate than the national average (23%).[20] In the wake of the Great Recession, however, Maryland has experienced revenue shortfalls. General fund revenues declined by 5% in fiscal year 2009, and by an additional 2.4% in 2010.[21] For 2011–12, the General Assembly reduced state funding for four-year colleges and universities only slightly (to $1.1 billion, reflecting health insurance and pension benefit savings), increased funding for community colleges by 5.7% (to $314 million), and maintained funding for independent colleges and universities (at $38.4 million).[22] Responding to constraints imposed by structural budget deficits and other forces (as described in earlier chapters), Governor O'Malley articulated the need to accomplish more with fewer fiscal resources: "The ongoing financial crisis has called upon us to re-imagine what a government can do well, and to redesign better ways to serve and protect the people of Maryland as we move forward."[23]

Higher Education Performance

In many respects, Maryland is a national leader in the performance of higher education. The state performs relatively well on some indicators of college preparation, participation, and completion as well as on measures of college student transfer. Despite this level of achievement and the state's improvement on some indicators over the past decade, most indicators of preparation, participation, and completion continue to be lower for the state's Blacks and Hispanics than for Whites. The relatively low rates of performance on measures of preparation and participation as well as the gaps in achievement among groups are surprising, given the state's wealth and high levels of overall educational attainment.

Preparation for Postsecondary Education

In 2011, 2012, and 2013, *Education Week* ranked Maryland's public school system first in the nation. Nonetheless, other indicators suggest the need to improve students' academic readiness for college, especially among Black and Hispanic youth. The University System of Maryland reports: "More than most of our competitor states (i.e., those states Maryland competes against most closely for businesses and jobs, including PA, NY, NJ, VA, NC, MA, CA, WA, and OH), Maryland struggles with issues related to the success of its 'academic pipeline,' the steady progression of students moving from ninth grade into high school and then directly on to college and a baccalaureate degree."[24]

Maryland lags behind top-performing states on measures of academic preparation for college. Over the decade, Maryland's high school graduation rate (as measured by the Cumulative Promotion Index) increased only slightly, from 74.5% in 1996–97 to 76.8% in 2007–8. The 2007–8 rate was sixteenth highest in the nation, above the national average (71.7%) and the average of most southern states (67.8%) but lower than the median of the top five states (81.4%).[25]

In recent years the performance of Maryland's middle school students has improved on some measures of academic preparation. The percentage of the state's eighth graders scoring at or above proficient on the national assessment in math increased from 30% in 2003 to 40% in 2009 and from 31% to 36% in reading over the same period. Yet although Maryland outperforms the national average and median of the southern states, it continues to trail the top states.[26] Maryland, however, ranks first among all states in the proportion of students that earn a three or higher on at least one Advanced Placement exam.

Participation

Participation in higher education in Maryland improved over the past decade, but it continues to be lower than in top-performing states. The share of 18- to 24-year-olds enrolled in college rose from 28% in 1991 to 32% in 2007. This performance in 2007 is well below the top states (44%) but comparable to the national average (34%) and the median of southern states (32%).[27] Following the same pattern, the college-going rate of high school graduates in Maryland, at 62.9% in 2008, is below the median of the top five states (74.2%), but is comparable to the national average (63.3%). The chance for college by age 19 in Maryland increased from 39% in 2000 to 45.8% in 2008, but it remains lower than the top states (58.2% in 2008).[28]

Completion

Bachelor's degree completion rates for students who enter public colleges and universities in Maryland have improved in recent years and are well above the national average. In 2009, about 64.1% of first-time, full-time students in Maryland completed a bachelor's degree within six years of enrolling, up from 59.8% in 1997. This completion rate for Maryland (64.1% in 2009) is substantially higher than the national average (56%) and the average for southern states (51%).[29]

When transfer to other four-year institutions is also taken into account, Maryland is the top state: 76% of first-time, full-time students complete a bachelor's degree within six years, compared with 65% nationally.[30]

In contrast, the state's associate degree completion rate (21.8% in 2009) is lower than the national average (29%) and the average for southern states (25%). Maryland's performance on this measure has improved over the past decade, however, since just 12.8% of first-time full-time students in Maryland completed an associate degree within three years of enrolling in 1997. Moreover, Maryland performs better than the national average in the completion of bachelor's degrees among students who first enroll in community colleges. About 15% of students beginning at a two-year college in Maryland in fall 2002 graduated from a four-year institution within six years, a rate higher than the national average (12%) but below the top states (20%). Following a similar pattern, the share of students beginning at a two-year college in Maryland in fall 2002 who graduated with an associate degree within six years (21%) is comparable to the national average (21%), but lower than the best-performing states (45%).[31]

Affordability

As in other states, higher education in Maryland has become less affordable for students and their families. The net price of college (college expenses minus financial aid) represents a growing portion of family income at Maryland's community colleges, public four-year colleges and universities, and private institutions. From the early 1990s to 2007, the net price of college as a share of median family income in Maryland increased from:

- 22% to 23% at public community colleges,
- 19% to 25% at public four-year colleges and universities, and
- 55% to 68% at private four-year colleges and universities.[32]

Median family income in Maryland, measured in constant dollars, was relatively flat over the past decade, rising just 0.2% from 1999 to 2009. By contrast, tuition rose by 24.9% at public four-year universities and 6.4% at public two-year colleges (in constant dollars).[33]

Gaps in Performance

Statewide performance in college preparation, participation, and completion in Maryland masks not only the lower achievement in Baltimore (described in the introduction to this chapter) but also the lower performance of the state's Blacks and Hispanics and those with lower family incomes. In terms of college preparation, much smaller percentages of Blacks (15%) and Hispanics (26%) than of Whites (56%) and Asian Americans (76%) scored at least proficient on the eighth-grade national assessment in math in 2009. Only 17% of low-income Maryland students (that is, those eligible for the federal free and reduced-price lunch program) scored at or above proficient on the eighth-grade math assessment, compared with 50% of students who were not eligible for this program.[34] In 2007, high school graduation rates (calculated using the Cumulative Promotion Index) were substantially lower for Blacks (62%) and Hispanics (65%) than for Whites (82%).[35]

With regard to college participation, only 32% of Blacks and 25% of Hispanics ages 18 and 24 were enrolled in 2006, compared with 42% of Whites.[36] Degree completion rates in Maryland are also lower for Blacks. In 2008, only 42.6% of Blacks in Maryland completed a bachelor's degree within six years, compared with 70.8% of Hispanics and 73.8% of Whites.[37]

The Structure of Higher Education in Maryland

Maryland's system of higher education is composed of 13 public four-year colleges and universities, 16 public community colleges, 22 private nonprofit four-year institutions, and 10 for-profit institutions.[38] In fall 2010, about 82% of the students who were enrolled in degree-granting institutions in Maryland were attending a public rather than a private nonprofit (17%) or private for-profit (1%) institution. Community colleges accounted for 39% of total undergraduate enrollment in fall 2010, similar to the national share (38%).[39]

Since its creation by the state legislature in 1988, the Maryland Higher Education Commission has been responsible for "the planning, supervision, and coordination of Maryland's postsecondary education system."[40] The commission's director serves as secretary of higher education and is a member of the Governor's Executive Council.

The state's 16 community colleges were once coordinated by a separate statewide board but are now under the oversight of the commission.[41] Each college is operated locally, except for Baltimore City Community College, which was taken over by the state in 1991 and is now considered a state agency. Each community college has a distinct and exclusive service area, with one college per county in the state's more populated areas and one college for multiple counties in the state's rural areas. The Maryland Association of Community Colleges, a voluntary nonprofit organization, was created in 1992 to advance the collective goals and priorities of these institutions.

Also in 1988, the University System of Maryland (USM) was created to improve the coordination of higher education. According to a leader of a state higher education agency, "Governor Schaefer simply wanted a structure that was easier for him to deal with and to manage—not 13 or 14 boards or trustees bugging him about higher education."

Eleven of the state's 13 public four-year colleges and universities are within the USM. Morgan State University and St. Mary's College of Maryland are public but stand-alone institutions. The University System includes the University of Maryland University College (UMUC), a regionally accredited institution that offers both online and face-to-face classes in 170 locations in 26 nations. In 2009, about one-third of UMUC's 86,417 students were Maryland residents.[42] Observers have described UMUC as "a nationally recognized model for developing and delivering distance learning."[43]

Four of the state's public four-year institutions are Historically Black Institutions (HBIs): Morgan State University, Bowie State University, Coppin State University, and the University of Maryland Eastern Shore (UMES). The latter three institutions are part of the University System of Maryland.

The state also offers eight Regional Higher Education Centers. Although the legislature formally adopted a statutory process for establishing regional centers in 2000, three of the centers have been operating since the 1990s: Southern Maryland Higher Education Center (1994); Technology Center in Harford County (1995); and Waldorf Center for Higher Education (1997). The regional centers were created to promote access to baccalaureate and graduate degree programs in underserved areas of the state and to address workforce needs.[44] Most centers are collaborations between community colleges and four-year universities. The University System of Maryland has administrative oversight for two centers, and the Maryland Higher Education Commission has responsibility for the remaining six. Student enrollments are credited to the individual colleges and universities that lease space from the regional centers, but the Maryland Higher Education Commission collects enrollment data for students enrolled in 2+2 undergraduate programs and graduate programs.[45] From FY 2006 to FY 2012, full-time-equivalent (FTE) enrollments at regional centers increased by 72%, from 3,541 to 6,099. Two of the regional centers (Shady Grove and Arundel

Mills) account for nearly two-thirds of total enrollments at the centers (40% and 20%, respectively).[46]

Created in 1971, the Maryland Independent College and University Association represents 17 of the state's private nonprofit four-year colleges and universities. The Maryland Higher Education Commission oversees the state's for-profit institutions.

What Explains the Higher Education Performance in Maryland?

Given the characteristics of the state context and higher education system, what accounts for recent patterns of higher education performance? More specifically, what accounts for Maryland's relatively high bachelor's degree completion rates but relatively low levels of college preparation and participation, especially when considered in light of the state's high overall levels of educational attainment and wealth as well as its persistent gaps in performance based on race/ethnicity, income, and region? Our analyses reveal that many factors contribute to Maryland's outcomes, but four themes appear to be predominant: (1) stable and respected political and higher education leadership; (2) a record of collaboration across and within educational sectors but few policies that ensure college readiness; (3) continued challenges in resolving a history of racism and segregation; and (4) strategic use of fiscal resources to achieve state goals and priorities.

Stable and Respected Political and Higher Education Leadership

Maryland has a highly educated population that generally understands, values, and promotes the benefits of higher education. Perhaps in reflection of this longstanding characteristic, Maryland's key stakeholders have developed a strong history of clearly articulating statewide goals and priorities for higher education.[47]

This legacy for higher education has been informed by a stable political leadership. For instance, William Donald Schaefer, governor from 1987 to 1995, directed the creation of the University System of Maryland; and Parris Glendening, governor from 1995 to 2003, once served as a professor of government and politics at the University of Maryland, College Park. Since 2007, Martin O'Malley, a former mayor of Baltimore, has served as governor.

The Maryland legislature also has a history of steady leadership and many leaders who have had direct experience with education. For instance, Thomas "Mike" Miller Jr. has been a legislator since 1971 and senate president since 1987.

The chair of the Senate Education, Health, and Environmental Affairs Committee, Joan Carter Conway, has served in the legislature since 1997. The chair of the Senate Education Subcommittee, Paul Pinsky, has served in the legislature since 1994 and is a former teacher and former president of the Prince George's County Educators' Association. The Speaker of the House of Delegates, Michael Busch, has served in the legislature since 1987 and is a former teacher. The current chair of the Appropriations Committee, Norman H. Conway, has served in the legislature since 1987 and is a former teacher, principal, and Title I program coordinator.

The University System of Maryland has also had stable and well-regarded leadership. Since its establishment in 1988, the University System has had only three chancellors. John Toll served the first two years, from 1988 to 1989; Donald Langenberg served the next twelve, from 1990 to 2002; and William "Brit" Kirwan has served as chancellor since 2002. Kirwan came to this position with nearly 40 years of experience as a faculty member and university president. His national reputation for expertise in higher education issues is signaled by the numerous national panels that he chairs and awards he has received.

Building on this history of stable and informed leadership, elected officials and higher education leaders have generally been able to work together to articulate and advance statewide goals and priorities. Nonetheless, relationships among state leaders are not without tensions. In some ways, the Maryland Higher Education Commission plays more of a supporting than a leadership role in higher education in the state, particularly relative to the roles played by the governor, the legislature, and the University System of Maryland. In addition, many elected and institutional leaders have disagreed about the best ways to move forward in bringing the state into compliance with the 1964 Civil Rights Act (as discussed later in this chapter). Nonetheless, the state benefits from a shared sense of civic-mindedness, a long-standing record of political support for educational goals, and a history of collaboration and cooperation.

Record of Collaboration across and within Educational Sectors but Few Policies that Ensure College Readiness

Maryland has several long-standing initiatives designed to improve students' academic readiness for college. These efforts demonstrate cooperation across education sectors but have resulted in few policies designed to ensure college readiness. The Southern Regional Education Board (SREB), after completing a review of college readiness efforts in several states, concluded that, although Maryland has led the nation for several years in many aspects of education, "much work remains in establishing a comprehensive, statewide college-readiness initiative." The report urged the governor and state legislators to "take command" of the state's P–20 College Success efforts.[48] The report also suggested that the state work to improve college readiness by enacting legislation, as many other states have done.[49]

P–20 Entities but Few P–20 Educational Policies

For more than 15 years, Maryland has had a prekindergarten-to-college structure in place to promote cooperation across education sectors. In 1995, the Maryland Partnership for Teaching and Learning, PreK–16, was established by the University System of Maryland with the state Department of Education and the state Higher Education Commission. In 2002, the three agencies formalized the PreK–16 group through a memorandum of understanding. The chairmanship rotated among the three institution heads. Through an executive order in 2007, Governor O'Malley renamed the group the P–20 Leadership Council of Maryland and expanded membership by adding two additional state agencies: the Department of Labor, Licensing, and Regulation, and the Department of Business and Economic Development. The state legislature subsequently endorsed these changes and added legislative members to the council.

The governor's endorsement of this initiative was further signaled by his decision to serve as chair of the council. The president of one public four-year university pointed to the governor's involvement, stating, "When this governor came in, he decided he wanted to chair it himself, which gave it even more exposure. He comes to a lot of the meetings, sometimes stays, sometimes just comes in, does his piece."

Although the state has had a cross-sector group in place since 1995, its accomplishments appear to focus on the current council's third goal, to "strengthen communication and collaborative decision-making among" the participating agencies. The council's other two goals are to align "high school expectations with college admission requirements" and to "improve the quantity and quality of teacher candidates."[50]

Despite the existence of the P–20 council, the state needs to make more substantial progress in aligning its high school exams with measures of college readiness. At the urging of the chairs of the legislative budget committees, the P–20 council appointed a College Success Task Force to recommend greater alignment and coordination between the K–12 and higher education segments. Maryland's High School Assessment Program requires students to pass end-of-course exams to graduate from a public high school. The High School Assessments were recommended by the Governor's Commission on School Performance in 1992 and first administered in 2001. Passage of the exams became a high school graduation requirement beginning with the graduating class of 2009, replacing the Maryland Functional Tests.[51] Students can take the High School Assessments multiple times, starting as early as seventh grade, but they typically take them in the ninth or tenth grade. The four areas of assessment are English language arts, algebra/data analysis, biology, and government.

The Governor's P–20 Leadership Council and some of our interviewees noted the need to more closely align the High School Assessments with college readiness indicators.[52] A policy advisor to an elected state leader told us that the exam "has no predictive value for college success and in fact is ranked at a tenth-grade level. So those tests definitely have to go by the wayside and will be replaced with the kind of common core assessment."

Others suggested that implementing the recommendations made by the P–20 Leadership Council requires overcoming financial, political, and administrative challenges. A leader of a state higher education agency summarized these challenges: "The P–20 council has looked at many of the major issues you would expect. I think that funding may be a part of the challenge. It's putting the dollars and the legislative muscle and policy behind some of these things once they're studied, once they're put into a report, and then identify people who are responsible for staying on them."

Maryland is one of 24 states now participating in the PARCC (Partnership for Assessment of Readiness for College and Careers) Consortium. The PARCC Consortium, which is funded through a $186 million grant from the U.S. Department of Education, is designed to "develop a common set of K–12 assessments in English and math anchored in what it takes to be ready for college and careers."[53] The state appears to be deferring efforts to further address college readiness until the consortium completes its work. As a leader of a state K–12 education department explained, "As assessments are developed through PARCC, I would expect that there would be some work linking the course exams. We don't know what exams are going to be developed. That's 2014–15. I do not anticipate that in Maryland we'll be doing any development of exams between now and then. Because we signed on to PARCC, that's really the direction we're headed."

Articulation and Transfer

Maryland has worked across educational sectors to promote articulation and transfer of course credits, but progress has been limited. As in most other states, the receiving institution generally determines whether to grant credit for courses taken at a community college.

One recent state-level effort to facilitate transfer of credit and promote associate degree completion is the development of articulated programs that transfer credits as a group rather than as individual courses. The first such program, established in 2001, was the associate of arts in teaching (AAT) in elementary education and elementary special education; it has since become a model for agreements in other teaching areas, including English, Spanish, mathematics, physics, and chemistry. The AAT is formally defined not in legislation but in the Code of Maryland Regulations.[54] In 2010–11 the state implemented a statewide articulation agreement for the associate of science in engineering (ASE). Like the AAT, students may "transfer the ASE degree in a block, rather than on a course-by-course basis, into a Maryland four-year engineering program to which they have been accepted." These degrees do not guarantee admission into a particular program at a given four-year college or university, but they do promote transfer of degrees in total "without further review by Maryland public and private four-year institutions."[55]

The AAT and ASE are defined by student learning and performance outcomes rather than by a common numbering system across colleges or by requirements for colleges to teach the same course. A leader of a state higher education agency told us,

> A college can organize or arrange content in any way that fits its mission, logic, [or] faculty expertise, as long as all the outcomes are accounted for. MHEC requires that any community college applying for approval of an AAT (and now ASE, engineering), demonstrate through a "cross-walk" chart where in the program a given outcome is mastered. . . . So, for example, John Dewey's active learning theory could be covered in a course on History of Ed or Philosophy of Ed, or Foundations of Ed, or whatever. If that is a required knowledge area outcome, the college applying for the degree has to demonstrate where and when it is taught in the program.

In addition to promoting transfer, the AAT program, according to the state Higher Education Commission in 2007, "has enhanced the role of two-year institutions as a provider of future classroom teachers." However, the program's early impact has been relatively small in terms of numbers of students served: "In the four years in which the AAT program has produced graduates, its numbers have surged from 8 to 170."[56]

In another effort to facilitate transfer, state law enables any student at a Maryland public institution who has at least a 2.0 grade point average and has earned an associate degree or at least 56 credits to be admitted to any University System of Maryland institution of his or her choice, on a space-available basis.[57] The policy does not guarantee admission to "limited enrollment/selective admissions" programs; admission to these programs may have additional requirements, including a minimum grade point average and completion of particular courses. An institutional leader we spoke with praised the policy but suggested that there are some potential challenges: "The policy has worked well until now, but we are feeling some pressure because I think the campus feels that it's turning away better-prepared students even from some community colleges that don't have quite yet 56 credits. And so it's something we're actually looking at, [whether] we need to move it [the grade-point-average requirement] up to 2.2 or 2.5, but right now that's what the policy is."

Another challenge with the current law is that transfer is guaranteed to students who earn at least 56 credits, which is several credits short of the number required for an associate degree. This provision may contribute to the state's relatively low rates of associate degree completion.

Prior to the creation of its P–20 entity and AAT program, education sectors in the state were collaborating to develop statewide General Education and Transfer regulations. In fall 1993, chief academic officers from the public two-year colleges met with representatives from the University System to develop a core package of general education courses that would be transferrable across public colleges and universities in the state while also providing incentives to students to complete as much of their associate degree coursework as possible at the community college level. During this process, the colleges and universities played a stronger leadership role than the Maryland Higher Education Commission.

Also in 1993, the University System developed an online "articulation system," called ARTSYS, which is designed to help students determine which courses will transfer from particular community colleges to particular public and selected private four-year colleges and universities in the state. A president of a four-year university explained its value: "You can literally go on this thing and, say, 'I'm graduating from Baltimore County Community College and I think I'd like to major in accounting. Here are the courses I've taken. Here's my major. Boom, what do I need?' And it just spits it out. You can do that for every campus in the state—two-year/four-year, four-year/four-year. That's been a huge help."

Despite Maryland's history of developing policies and practices to promote transfer, the state has not succeeded in preventing the loss of credits for students who have completed an associate degree and who transfer to a four-year institution in the state. About 60% of 2008 community college graduates who transferred to a four-year institution reported that they did not receive credit for all community college courses in which they had earned at least a "C." Common reasons that students reported for these losses of credit were that the four-year institution did not offer comparable courses (46%) and that "the student had earned more than 60 credits at the community college" (44%).[58]

Availability and Use of Data

A key factor that influences the ability of education sectors to work together to improve student outcomes is the availability and use of data. One of the most effective uses of the state's data system appears to be the Student Outcome and Achievement Report (SOAR), which measures the performance of the state's high school graduates and community college transfers at public four-year colleges and universities. The state Higher Education Commission created and distributed the first SOAR report in 1990 (before the state's first P–20 Council was established) to respond to the General Assembly's 1988 mandate to "improve information to high schools and local school systems concerning the performance of their graduates at the college level."[59] A state leader told us, "The SOAR report is a way of testing the product and what the high schools have done. That's turned out to be a well-regarded report."

Nonetheless, the state continues to maintain separate data systems for K–12 education and higher education. Improvements in data linkages across the sectors are needed to promote further collaboration around efforts to improve student performance. According to a scorecard developed by Education Sector, Maryland's efforts to gather accountability information about student outcomes and institutional practices are "in progress." The scorecard concludes that the state "does a very good job of presenting up-to-date information longitudinally" but "provides limited statewide information through the state's strategic planning process."[60]

Linking data systems so as to track the educational progress of students from pre-K–12 through postsecondary education is part of the fourth goal of the state

Higher Education Commission's strategic plan.[61] A final report by the statewide Commission to Develop the Maryland Model for Funding Higher Education (known, in short, as the Funding Commission) also recognizes the need to link student-level data across educational sectors—including K–12 education, the Higher Education Commission, the University System, the Maryland Association of Community Colleges (MACC), and the Maryland Independent College and University Association (MICUA). The report identifies several procedural and financial challenges related to accomplishing this goal.[62]

The state legislature, in seeking to improve its application for funding from the federal Race to the Top program, passed Senate Bill 275 in 2010, specifying that the state would establish, by December 31, 2014, a "fully operational" longitudinal data system that spans pre-K through employment and that includes both public and private educational institutions. The state's proposal was successful in earning Race to the Top funding. As a leader of an organization representing higher education institutions said, the state is now seeking to link its existing data systems:

> [The legislature] established a governing board to develop that system. What we have agreed to in Maryland is that the longitudinal data system that's put together as a result of the Race to the Top is going to build on all these systems we already have: the system of the Higher Education Commission, so that we don't have to change all our reporting requirements; the system we already have at K–12 education, which is already very comprehensive; and the system at the Labor Department. So the idea is that we're going to have a meeting of all these systems, and we've just [got] to make sure they talk to each other.

Continued Challenges in Resolving the State's History of Racism and Segregation

Higher education performance in Maryland is also influenced by the state's legacy of racism and segregation and its past and current efforts to address this history. As a leader of one public university explained: "I think it's important to make certain that whatever performance discussions that are written, at least about Maryland, take place within the context of its history. Maryland is a place where Thurgood Marshall couldn't go to school. And so we're still wrestling with that. It's still under OCR [Office for Civil Rights] oversight, one of the states that have not been released yet."

Like Georgia and Texas, Maryland is one of 19 southern and southern-border states that, prior to the 1954 Supreme Court decision on *Brown v. Board of Education*, operated a higher education system that was racially segregated. Since 1969, the state and the federal Office for Civil Rights (under the U.S. Department of Education) have engaged in periodic negotiations to bring the state into compliance with Title VI of the 1964 Civil Rights Act. The 2000 Partnership Agreement committed the state to nine goals, including improving the retention and graduation rates of Black students; expanding 2+2 partnerships and articulation; and avoiding "unnecessary program duplication and expansion of missions and program uniqueness and institutional identity at HBCUs."[63] In its most recent report to the Office for Civil Rights in June 2006, the state documented its progress toward attaining the nine commitments.[64]

The state's ninth commitment under the Partnership Agreement is "to enhance the HBIs [Historically Black Institutions] so they become 'comparable and competitive with the TWIs [traditionally white institutions].'" In its 2006 report, the state argued that it has met this commitment "by providing the additional funding specified and completing the capital projects listed in the Agreement" as well as by supporting additional projects to further enhance campus environments and facilities.[65] According to a state legislator, the state "has made concerted efforts to increase FTE funding"—that is, funding per full-time-equivalent (FTE) student—at the four public HBIs. The University System allocates funds to the three HBIs that are under its purview, while Morgan State University receives a direct appropriation from the legislature. The state's 2006 report noted that state general fund appropriations to the HBIs grew by 7% from fiscal years 2001 and 2006, compared to a 1.8% increase in general fund appropriations to the state's public colleges and universities overall. Since 2007, actual state appropriations to HBIs exceeded the appropriations that would have been expected, given the share of full-time equivalent students enrolled annually, based on state appropriations to public four-year institutions in the state.[66] The state has provided funding for operating and capital expenses at HBIs through the HBI Enhancement Grant, another product of the desegregation discussions.

The statewide Funding Commission, working through a subcommittee focused on Maryland's HBIs, noted differences in the needs and missions of HBIs and TWIs, stating that, "unlike TWIs, HBIs have a dual mission to provide regular collegiate programs and to provide strong developmental education for students, mostly from low-income families."[67] Emphasizing the importance of improving bachelor's degree completion rates at HBIs, the panel recommended that the state-funded Access and Success Program be replaced with a new program. Established in response to an earlier OCR review, the Access and Success Program had provided annual funding to the HBIs since 2001. The panel concluded that Access and Success Grants had provided funding for support services at HBIs but lacked "common or specific criteria and appropriate goals and accountability."[68]

Other issues are also influenced by oversight from the Office for Civil Rights. In recent years, Morgan State University and the institutions under the University System have disagreed about program duplication issues. The HBI subcommittee of the Funding Commission noted the "confusion and concern about current funding levels" created by "the lack of state-level coordination between institutional missions, new program approvals, and available funding."[69]

State efforts to limit program duplication have created some concern that traditionally White public four-year institutions are unable to offer programs that would meet changing student and employer demand and improve institutional competitiveness. These leaders perceive greater limits on new programs at TWIs when those programs might be perceived as competing with current offerings at Morgan State University. A leader of a statewide higher education organization told us, "I think it's been very hard for the citizens of the state. For example, UMBC [University of Maryland, Baltimore County] has a bunch of engineering courses. But they can't offer electrical engineering, despite the request of citizens who need it, because Morgan State has objected." Another institutional leader summarized the tensions, stating, "The new program review process is subjected to too much politics and not about the workforce development needs in the state."

Some of the underlying conflict around program duplication is related to institutional aspirations for growth. A leader of a state higher education agency articulated the challenges associated with managing institutional aspirations in the context of OCR oversight: "Everybody wants to grow. Towson wants to grow; Morgan wants to grow; Bowie wants to grow; Salisbury wants to grow. And so we do have to look at that in terms of resources and where are we going to get the resources, in terms of the Office for Civil Rights and those issues, [and] in terms of access and geography."

Maryland not only has not yet been released from oversight by the Office for Civil Rights, but at the time of our data collection it was also facing a lawsuit on the desegregation of its higher education system. In November 2005, the state Higher Education Commission approved a new joint Master of Business Administration (MBA) program between the University of Baltimore and Towson University. This approval was granted despite the objections of Morgan State

University, which claimed that the new program would unnecessarily duplicate its MBA program and lead to further segregation in Baltimore-area universities. Under Maryland statute, program approval decisions by the commission are final and are not subject to further review. Prompted by the MBA decision, the House and Senate passed legislation (HB 1634 and SB 998) in 2006 to authorize "judicial review in the circuit court of a decision by the Maryland Higher Education Commission regarding the duplication of academic programs."[70] This legislation was vetoed by Governor Ehrlich. In 2007 and 2009, legislation was introduced to require the commission either to reconsider its 2005 decision or to determine whether an unnecessary duplication of programs exists, if requested by an HBI. This legislation failed to pass both houses. In 2010, legislation similar to the 2006 bill also failed. This MBA decision is one of the plaintiffs' complaints.[71] A leader of a state higher education summarized the negative implications of the lawsuit: "There's no advantage to your state being criticized publicly for still operating a dual system of higher education. There's no advantage to having a case like this go to trial and running the risk of losing in the state and then you've got to come back and identify remedies. So it's unfortunate that it has gotten this far."

Strategic Use of Fiscal Resources to Address State Goals and Priorities

In recent years, Maryland's higher education leaders have set a goal of improving the affordability of higher education and made concerted efforts to strategically use available fiscal resources to achieve this goal. Through the Tuition Affordability Act of 2006, the governor and the legislature created the Commission to Develop the Maryland Model for Funding Higher Education, commonly known as either the Funding Commission, or the Bohanan Commission.[72] The higher education funding model proposed by the 27-member commission is designed "to link state support to institutions of higher education, tuition, and levels of institutional and state financial aid to serve student access and the needs of the state."[73] The commission's final report, released in December 2008, provided recommendations for the state's funding model, HBIs, other aspects of higher education funding (e.g., student aid programs and regional centers), capital needs of higher education, efficiency in higher education, workforce development, and "future progress."[74]

The "overarching recommendation" of the Higher Education Commission's 2009 strategic plan is to "implement the higher education funding model for Maryland" proposed in the Funding Commission's final report. To implement the key recommendations from the report, Delegate Bohanan and others introduced legislation in 2009. Although this initial bill did not pass the House, Bohanan and colleagues introduced a subsequent bill that was signed into law (House Bill 470 and Senate Bill 283) in May 2010.[75]

Maryland's overall approach to higher education finance has several strengths. State leaders are taking action to improve college affordability by linking appropriations and tuition. The state is also linking increases in tuition to growth in median family income and using investment funds to reduce volatility in appropriations and stabilize tuition increases. The state's unique historical approach to linking appropriations across sectors encourages higher education institutions in Maryland to speak to the legislature with one voice. Two limitations in Maryland's financial approach are (1) a relatively low state investment in a large number of student financial aid programs, and (2) few fiscal incentives for institutions to achieve statewide goals and priorities.

Linking Appropriations and Tuition

Although tuition levels at Maryland colleges and universities continue to exceed the national average, the state is making efforts to use appropriations to make tuition stable and predictable for students and families. Addressing college affordability by limiting tuition increases is consistent with the Funding Commission's recommended approach to balance quality, affordability, and access in higher education: "*high* state funding of higher education institutions, *moderate* tuition levels, *high* state need-based financial aid, and accountability."[76]

In an effort to moderate tuition levels, in 2006–7 the state passed legislation freezing undergraduate resident tuition at the four-year public institutions within the University System of Maryland as well as at Morgan State University. Since then the governor and the legislature have worked indirectly through the appropriations process to freeze tuition or limit tuition increases. A state legislator told us:

> When Martin O'Malley was elected governor in 2007, he chose to give us the money to not do a tuition increase. So he bought down that tuition increase. He said, "Look, you want to do a 4% tuition increase, that's $18 million. I'm going to put an additional $18 million in your budget with the agreement, not statutorily required, just an agreement that you do your best to freeze tuition." And we did that. And so that became then the second year of the tuition freeze. That happened again for a third year and then for a fourth year. And then last

> year when we submitted our budget increase, we put in an increase for a 5% tuition increase. . . . While the Governor could not buy down the entire tuition increase of 5%, he bought down two points of it. We then said, "Okay," and we agreed to do a 3% tuition increase for in-state undergraduate tuition.

State and institutional leaders praised these efforts to negotiate with the institutions to improve college affordability. An institutional leader stated, "When I talk to most of my colleagues [in other states], there's kind of a love-hate relationship [with the governor] and they're, in some ways, at war. And that really doesn't exist in Maryland. His [the governor's] number one [campaign theme] is how he's worked with the system to hold tuition."

Community colleges were not included in the tuition freeze. Nonetheless, a president of a community college said, "We were certainly asked, to the extent that we could, not to increase tuition or if we had to increase tuition, to not do it in such a way that it would impact access. Many community colleges have chosen not to increase tuition over the past two years."

Although in-state undergraduate tuition in Maryland continues to be substantially higher than in most other states, the extent to which tuition in Maryland exceeds the national average has declined in recent years.[77] The Funding Commission recommended that, moving forward, in-state tuition and fees at the state's public two-year and four-year institutions be set "at or below the fiftieth percentile of comparable institutions in . . . competitor states."[78]

Using State Investment Funds to Reduce Volatility in Appropriations and Stabilize Tuition Increases

A second strength of the state's recent approach to higher education finance is the establishment and use of the Higher Education Investment Fund (HEIF). In 2008, the governor and the legislature created the fund to support "strategic investments in higher education, essentially to build the capacity of USM's institutions to meet the educational requirements of the twenty-first century" and to provide a cushion when state revenues decline.[79] Legislation permanently authorizing the Higher Education Investment Fund was signed into law in May 2010.[80]

The Investment Fund is financed by an increase in the state corporate income tax. The Funding Commission identified three uses of the fund: "to supplement general fund appropriations to the public four-year institutions, to fund capital projects for the public four-year institutions, and to fund workforce development initiatives administered by MHEC."[81] A state legislator told us that the Investment Fund "is designed to provide the sort of the rainy day fund, or the cushion, if you will, for higher education. We increased the corporate income tax in the state. And that additional revenue is designed in principle to be there to provide a backstop when state revenues fall, general fund revenues fall. . . . And in robust years, rather than accept a 15% increase, we might only provide half of that as an increase to the institution and bankroll the rest for sort of leaner times."

Drawing from another recommendation of the Funding Commission, the state has designated a portion of the Investment Fund for a Tuition Stabilization Trust Account. The Trust Account is to be used to "supplement general fund appropriations" to the state's public four-year colleges and universities with the goal of "stabilizing tuition costs of resident undergraduate students."[82] The authorizing legislation, signed in May 2010, limits increases in-state undergraduate tuition and fees at public colleges and universities to no more than "the increase in the three-year rolling average of the state's median family income."[83]

Linking State Appropriations for All Higher Education Sectors

The state's historic and unique practice of linking appropriations for the various higher education sectors is another strength of its approach to higher education finance. As required by state law, state funding for the public four-year colleges and universities drives appropriations for community colleges and eligible private nonprofit four-year colleges and universities. State appropriations for Morgan State University, St. Mary's College of Maryland, and Baltimore County Community College are determined separately.[84]

The linking of funding across sectors is consistent with the Funding Commission's recommendations. The legislature has periodically approved modifications to the allocation for the various sectors:

> State appropriations per FTES (full-time-equivalent student) for the prior fiscal year at the degree-granting public four-year institutions except UMB, UMUC, and UB is multiplied by a factor currently codified in state law. For the community colleges, the factor was enhanced in 2006 legislation that phases in a 5 percentage point increase over six years; in fiscal [year] 2010 the factor is 27 percent, increasing to 30 percent in fiscal 2013 for the locally operated community colleges. Baltimore City Community College's formula is also increasing 5 percentage points to 71 percent in 2013. Eligible private institutions receive 16 percent of the state appropriation per FTES under current law.[85]

Appropriations to individual institutions in the University System are determined by the governor and the USM Board of Regents.

The responsibility for funding the community colleges in Maryland is expected to be shared, with one-third coming from the state, one-third from the county in which the college is located, and one-third from the student.[86] The state share is determined by the John A. Cade formula, which was approved by the legislature in 1996. Due to cost containment in fiscal year 2011, this formula currently provides to the Maryland Association of Community Colleges about 20 cents for every dollar appropriated to the USM public four-year institutions.

Eligible private colleges and universities, through the Joseph A. Sellinger program, receive state appropriations that are linked to appropriations for the public four-year institutions. This program, in effect, uses state resources to expand the state's higher education capacity. Established in 1973 and named for a former president of what is now Loyola University Maryland, the Sellinger program is designed to "provide modest public support for private higher education to preserve and strengthen a dual system of higher education."[87] The program provides unrestricted operating funds, but funds must be used for nonsectarian purposes. The private colleges and universities that receive these funds are sensitive to the political need to demonstrate to the legislature the public benefits that result from these appropriations. A leader of one of the beneficiary private colleges said, "To defend the program, we [that is, the receiving private institutions] collectively demonstrate that most of the funds are used for student aid." Consistent with this assertion, the Maryland Independent College and University Association promotes the role of member institutions in advancing college access and degree production in the state. On its website, the association claims that 84% of Sellinger funds received by member institutions are allocated to institutional financial aid for Maryland residents.[88]

State appropriations to Maryland institutions are not only linked across sectors but also benchmarked, through "funding guidelines," to the funding levels of peer institutions in other states. A leader of a public university explained this as follows:

> The state said, "You are to be funded at the level of your peers," and they established the peers. The peers for UMCP to be compared against and funded at the level in facilities and operating are UCLA; Berkeley; Michigan; North Carolina; and Illinois. They set up a process called funding guidelines, where

> they look at the revenue. They develop a number for funding per student. They look at what proportion of that is funded by tuition. The rest becomes the obligation of the state. And they measure their performance by how much they provide to attain that goal.

In its final report, the Funding Commission recommended that the state continue with this approach, including the benchmarking of state appropriations to peer institutions, "defined as institutions of similar size, academic program makeup, and demographics, and provides a funding target that recognizes through a factoring system the diverse characteristics of institutions."[89] The Funding Commission also recommended the following additional funding guidelines: "Maryland should set the goal for the per-student investment in the state's four-year traditionally white institutions (TWIs) to match the 75th percentile and in the public Historically Black Institutions (HBIs) to at least the 80th percentile of a set of comparable peer institutions in the 9 states ('competitor states') with which Maryland principally competes to attract employers."[90]

The Funding Commission estimates that fully adopting its recommended higher education funding model would cost $758.3 million per year, or an additional $85 million per year (net of inflation) over the next 10 years.[91] Most of this cost ($666 million) is associated with raising state appropriations to institutions to the level of peers and competitors; $196 million of the $666 million represents an increase over the current funding guidelines. The remainder represents the annual cost of the Tuition Stabilization Trust Account ($15 million), the cost of providing need-based aid per full-time-equivalent student at the level of peers in competitor states ($70 million); and the cost of supplemental funds to the state's HBIs for undergraduate education ($7.4 million).

One benefit of linking appropriations across sectors in the state is that it encourages higher education to speak with a single voice in terms of state funding requests. The Maryland Independent College and University Association asserts that, by linking appropriations for the state's private colleges and universities to enrollment at selected public four-year institutions, the formula "encourages cooperation and collaboration among Maryland's segments of higher education."[92] A state legislator described the strengths of this approach: "I think it does not force governors or legislatures to choose between segments of higher education. I also think it, in some degree, helps keep some stability. You may have from time to time governors that are pro-community college, or a very pro-four-year governor, and legislators also. It discourages them from picking and choosing between segments of higher education."

Relatively Low Investment in a Large Number of State Student Financial Aid Programs

The recommendations of the Funding Commission also emphasize the importance of "*high* [levels of] state need-based financial aid."[93] As with the funding guidelines recommendations, the commission recommends that state funding for need-based aid per student be set at the 75th percentile of its competitor states.[94]

Historically, the state has invested relatively small amounts in its need-based aid. From fiscal year 2005 to 2009, state investment in need-based aid more than doubled, increasing from $42 million to $85 million.[95] Yet Maryland still ranked only nineteenth in terms of state need-based undergraduate grant dollars per FTE student in fiscal year 2009, down from fourteenth in fiscal year 2005.[96] The availability of state aid in Maryland continues to be lower than the national average as measured by the estimated number of state financial aid awards per FTE student (.245 versus .298).[97] The state also ranks below the median in the share of tuition covered by need-based financial aid. The maximum award for the state's largest need-based program (The Delegate Howard P. Rawlings Educational Assistance Grant) has been $3,000 since the program was established in 1991.[98] The Guaranteed Access Grant, a program more narrowly targeted toward the state's lowest-income students, provides larger awards but leaves many recipients at both two- and four-year institutions with "unmet need, even after taking out student loans."[99]

Moreover, the state operates a large number of discrete state aid programs—22 in 2008.[100] These include merit-based aid programs (for example, the Distinguished Scholars Program), workforce shortage grants, a grant program for part-time students, aid for armed services personnel, and legislative scholarships. The Funding Commission, noting that merit aid awards have been $3,000 since 1989 and arguing that these awards help retain "highly talented students," recommended "increasing the Distinguished Scholar Award to $6,000 and doubling the number of such scholarships to 700 awards." The commission also recommended increasing the minimum grade point average required to retain the award from 3.0 to 3.3.[101]

A leader of an organization representing colleges and universities statewide described the challenges the state has experienced in prior efforts to eliminate or consolidate aid programs: "The problem with financial aid programs is you have champions in the legislature that do not want to let go of these programs. Even when we managed to close a few, the next year they pass legislation and we end up with some. Often they're named after people, and you just can't get rid of those. It's a collage of programs."

To help students navigate the complexity of state aid programs, the Funding Commission recommended creating "a single application for students seeking state financial assistance."[102] At the time of our visit, the Higher Education Commission's website identified separate applications for each grant and scholarship program.

Few Fiscal Incentives for Institutions to Meet Shared Statewide Goals and Priorities

While the state has worked with institutions to limit tuition increases, Maryland's approach to higher education finance does not include explicit incentives that encourage higher education institutions to achieve other aspects of higher education performance. Although the state's approach to financing higher education has some benefits, its appropriations formula continues to be driven solely by enrollment growth.

As required by the state Department of Budget and Management, the University System and other budget units annually prepare a Managing for Results Accountability Report. This report documents actual and projected performance on various measures designed to assess progress toward four goals specified in state statute: "(1) create and maintain a well-educated citizenry; (2) promote economic development; (3) increase access for economically disadvantaged and minority students; and (4) achieve and sustain national eminence in providing quality education, research, and public service."[103] Maryland sometimes links small amounts of funding to these kinds of higher education performance outcomes but does not have a formal performance-based funding system in place. An institutional leader suggested that most in higher education prefer the status quo, with funding incentives connected to enrollment rather than performance: "We are not very interested in incentive funding. The incentives have been to grow enrollment. I mean that's just generally [true] across the nation."

As part of its deliberations, the Funding Commission considered establishing an Opportunity Fund that would "provide special [public] financial resources for projects that meet important state or institutional goals" and that would "be pursued by institutions that have demonstrated a high capacity to excel." The Opportunity Fund would have allocated only a small amount of resources for this purpose—"up to 1 percent of the state funds for higher education or up to about $15 million in FY 2009."[104] Nonetheless, the proposed fund was not included in the Funding Commission's final report.

Conclusion

Helped by its ability to attract well-educated residents from other states, the overall level of educational attainment in Maryland is high. Nonetheless, Maryland must improve its performance on college preparation and participation if the state is to achieve its own goals for international competitiveness and workforce development. Reaching these goals is unlikely unless the state can improve the educational success of its relatively large Black population and its small but growing Hispanic population. In addition, the state needs to improve educational outcomes in Baltimore and resolve disagreements about how best to use its HBIs and traditionally White institutions to best serve the state's residents and to secure release from oversight by the federal Office for Civil Rights.

Maryland has a well-developed plan for financing higher education that is supported by major stakeholders and that is being implemented consistently—albeit incrementally, due to economic conditions. In a June 2013 follow-up, we learned that the "rainy day" public endowment for higher education that is funded by a new corporate income tax is still in place. Although revenues are growing slowly, a state leader confirmed that "the concept is ingrained" and funds are expected to increase over time so as to reduce the volatility of state funding for higher education. Maryland has also taken important steps to slow the erosion of college affordability for students and families. The governor, legislators, and college and university presidents have worked together to freeze tuition for four years. Maryland has also adopted a tuition stabilization fund to help ensure that tuition is below the 50th percentile of peer institutions. The notion of tying tuition increases to increases in family income also continues to be part of the plan, although family income, on average, has not increased in recent years. In the short term, the state has continued to "buy out" tuition increases with state appropriations to mitigate the impact on students and families.

These accomplishments have the potential to make tuition more predictable and affordable for Maryland residents. Nonetheless, current fiscal constraints may challenge the state's ability to fully implement the recommendations of its statewide Funding Commission. Moreover, the state's fiscal approach provides funding based on enrollment, without providing strong performance incentives that could encourage institutions to improve academic preparation and college completion—objectives that are becoming increasingly important, given the diversity of the state population.

As the economy improves and the state budget recovers, Maryland will have the opportunity to invest new dollars more strategically toward its goals. State leaders have already created a strong foundation of working together on behalf of state residents to support higher education. Can they also work together to leverage necessary improvements?

Chapter 7

Hard Choices Ahead

The Performance and State Policies of Higher Education in Texas

WITH CONTRIBUTIONS BY AWILDA RODRIGUEZ

Over the past decade, Texas has made considerable improvement in several areas of higher education performance, including preparing students for college, increasing college participation, and raising college completion rates.[1] Despite these gains, however, the state continues to perform below the national average on key measures of these outcomes and ranks among the bottom quarter of states (39th) in the percentage of adults (ages 25 and older) who have attained at least an associate degree.[2] To raise the educational attainment of its population, Texas must make additional progress.

Workforce trends and competition from other nations underscore the importance of continuing to improve higher education performance in the state. By 2018, about 56% of all jobs in Texas will require at least some postsecondary education or training. Although this percentage is somewhat lower than the projected national average (63%), more and more jobs in the state are requiring a college education. Between 2008 and 2018, about 1.3 million new jobs in Texas are projected to require at least some postsecondary education, whereas about 915,000 new jobs are expected to require no more than a high school education.[3] Based on trends in degree production and population growth, Texas will need to increase its production of associate and bachelor's degrees by 11.5% per year in order for 55% of its workforce (ages 25 to 64) to hold at least an associate degree by 2020, which is the level of attainment of the best-performing nations.[4] Like many other states, Texas will not be able to reach this goal by increasing the educational attainment of young adults only; the state must also improve educational outcomes for nontraditional students.[5]

State leaders recognize that raising attainment in Texas will require a reduction in gaps in educational performance among racial and ethnic groups.[6] Yet despite improvements over the past decade, the level of educational attainment in Texas continues to be substantially lower for Hispanics and Blacks than for Whites. In 2005, only 15.6% of Hispanics (ages 25 to 64) and 26.6% of Blacks had attained at least an associate degree, compared with 43.1% of Whites.[7]

Reducing educational gaps across population groups is especially critical, given that half the state population is now made up of "minority" groups. Hispanics are the state's largest and fastest growing racial/ethnic group. Hispanics represented 37% of the state population in 2009, compared with only 16% nationally.[8] Nearly one-third of Texans speak English as a second language;[9] furthermore, Texas is home to a large number of undocumented immigrants.[10]

Efforts to further increase educational attainment in Texas must also recognize the likelihood of constrained fiscal resources for the foreseeable future. Over the past decade, total funding for higher education in Texas increased in current dollars from $14.065 billion in FY2001 to $22.729 billion in FY2011.[11] From 2000 to 2010, educational appropriations per full-time student in Texas increased by 30% in current dollars, from $6,822 to $8,897.[12] As with other states, however, Texas has since experienced revenue shortfalls that restrict the availability of state funding for higher education. For instance, the governor's proposed biennial budget for higher education included reductions of 13.7% in 2011–12 and 2.1% in 2012–13.[13] Like other states, Texas is likely to face further constraints on state revenues into the near future. Per capita personal income in Texas is somewhat lower than the national average, with the gap increasing slightly over the past decade. In 2008, per capita personal income in Texas was 98% of the U.S. average.[14] Texas is also one of a small number of states without a state income tax.

Higher Education Performance

Texas has made considerable progress over the past decade in improving higher education performance. Even with these gains, however, the state's performance remains below the national average on measures of college preparation, participation, and completion. Moreover, as identified in *Accelerated Plan for Closing the Gaps by 2015*, the state's update to its 2000 strategic plan, *Closing the Gaps*, indicators of preparation, participation, and completion continue to be lower for the state's Hispanics and Blacks than for Whites.

Preparation

Despite recent improvements, Texas' performance in preparing students for college remains below the national average on many measures. Over the past decade, high school graduation rates in Texas rose from 60.1% in 1997–98 to 66.6% in 2007–8, as calculated by *Education Week* using the Cumulative Promotion Index (CPI).[15] The class of 2008 graduation rate in Texas was comparable to the average for states in the Southern Regional Education Board (SREB) (67.8%), but below the national average (71.7%) and the top states (81.4%). Using an alternative method of calculating dropout rates, Texas reports that, out of 314,079 students in its grade 9 cohort in 2006, 84.3% graduated in the class of 2010—a three percentage point gain from the prior cohort.[16]

Texas has also improved on some indicators of K–12 student achievement prior to high school. From 2003 to 2009, the percentage of the state's eighth graders that scored at or above proficient on the national assessment in math increased from 25% to 36% and remained virtually unchanged in reading (rising from 26% to 27%). In 2009, the share of eighth graders scoring at or above proficient on the math exam (36%) was slightly above the national average (34%) and well above SREB states (28%), but it was below the median of the top-performing states (42%). During the same year, the percentage of eighth graders scoring at or above proficient on reading (27%) was comparable to SREB states (27%) but below the national average (32%) and the top states (42%).[17]

Participation

Texas has also improved on measures of college participation for young residents. From 2000 to 2008, the chance for college by age 19 increased from 32.5% to 37.1%, largely due to improvements in high school graduation rates over this period.[18] Despite this progress, however, the chance for college in Texas in 2008 was below the national average (44%), the median for SREB states (43%), and the median of the top-performing states (58%).[19] The percentage of 18- to 24-year-olds enrolled in college in Texas has shifted upward over time, rising from 27.6% in 1991 to 31.6% in 2009, but remains below the national average (36%), the SREB states (34%), and the top states (42%).[20]

The college participation of older adults has declined in Texas. Only 5.5% of 25 to 49 year olds without a bachelor's degree were enrolled in some type of postsecondary education in 2009, down from 7.3% in 1991. The enrollment rate in 2009 (5.5%) was lower than the national average (7.0%), the SREB states (6.0%), and the best-performing states (9.0%).[21]

Completion

As with college preparation and participation, Texas has improved on several indicators of college completion but remains below the national average on these measures. The 2010 *Closing the Gaps Progress Report* concluded that the state is "on target" with regard to increasing the number of certificates and degrees awarded. From 1999 to 2009, the percentage of first-time, full-time students in Texas who completed a bachelor's degree within six years of enrolling in college rose from 45% to 49%. However, this completion rate for Texas (49% in 2009) is considerably lower than the national average (56%).[22] Similarly, the percentage of Texas students who completed an associate degree within three years of enrolling increased from 17% in 1999 to 25.4% in 2009. Despite this improvement, Texas' rate in 2009 (25%) was slightly above the SREB states (26%) but lower than the national average (29%) and the top states (48.1%).[23] With regard to transfer, the share of Texas students who began at a two-year institution in fall 2002 and graduated with a bachelor's degree within six years is comparable to the national average (12%) but lower than the top-performing states (20%).[24]

Affordability

As in other states, students and families in Texas are paying an increasing share of the cost of higher education. The net price of college (that is, college expenses minus financial aid) represents a growing portion of family income at the state's community colleges, public four-year colleges and universities, and private four-year institutions. From the early 1990s to 2007, the net price of college as a share of family income in Texas increased from 15% to 21% at public community colleges, 18% to 26% at public four-year colleges and universities, and 42% to 67% at private four-year colleges and universities.[25] Median family income in Texas measured in constant dollars declined by 1.5% from 1999 to 2009, but during the same period tuition increased by 31.3% at public two-year colleges and by 86.5% at public four-year colleges and universities (in constant dollars).[26]

Gaps in Performance across Groups

Aggregate measures of performance in college preparation, participation, and completion mask substantial differences based on race/ethnicity and family income. For instance, high school graduation rates in Texas for the class of 2008 were substantially lower for Blacks (59%) and Hispanics (58%) than for Whites (76%).[27] Smaller shares of Black (17%) and Hispanic (25%) than of White (54%) and Asian (67%) eighth graders scored at or above proficient on the national assessment in math in 2009.[28] According to college readiness indicators identified by the Texas Education Agency:

- In 2008–9, 29.4% of White students were enrolled in advanced courses or dual enrollment courses, compared with 20.8% of Hispanics and 18.1% of Blacks.
- Among eleventh and twelfth graders, 25.1% of White students took at least one Advanced Placement (AP) or International Baccalaureate (IB) exam in 2009, compared with 17.3% of Hispanics and 12.9% of Blacks. A substantially larger share of Whites (61.7%) scored at least a three on the AP exam or four on the IB exam than of Hispanics (37.5%) and Blacks (25.5%).
- About 70% of White students were proficient in the English Language Arts Texas Assessment of Knowledge and Skills (TAKS) in 2010, compared with only 52% of Hispanics and 51% of Blacks. A similar pattern is apparent in math, with 78% of White students identified as proficient, compared with just 58% of Hispanics and 49% of Blacks.[29]

Although college participation has improved across racial/ethnic groups in Texas, gaps remain. The percentage of Hispanic public high school graduates who enrolled in college directly after high school increased from 38.4% in 2000 to 49.8% in 2009, while the share of Black high school graduates who entered college directly after high school rose from 38.7% to 46.4%. Yet for public high school students who graduated in 2009, college enrollment rates continued to be lower for Blacks (46.4%) and Hispanics (49.8%) than for Whites (53.3%).[30] *Closing the Gaps Progress Report 2010* concluded that the state's progress on college enrollment rates (i.e., the percentage of the adult population enrolled in higher education) has been above the targets that were set for Blacks and for Whites but has not yet reached the targets for Hispanics. In 2000, about 3.7% of Hispanics and 4.6% of Blacks were enrolled in college. By 2009, these rates increased to 4.4% for Hispanics and 6.5% for Blacks.[31] In 2009, Hispanic enrollment had reached only 87.1% of the 2010 target, whereas Black enrollment exceeded the 2010 target (112.1%).

College completion rates in Texas are also lower for Hispanics and Blacks than for Whites. In 2009, about 29% of Blacks and 37% of Hispanics completed a bachelor's degree within six years, compared with 57% of Whites.[32]

Texas also faces disparities in college-related outcomes by family income. In terms of student performance on the eighth-grade national math assessment in Texas, about a quarter (23%) of students eligible for the federal free and reduced-price lunch program scored at or above proficient in 2009, compared with about half (51%) of students who were not eligible for this program.[33] Among high school graduates in fiscal year 2007, only half (51%) of those who received free or reduced-price lunch met the Texas Success Initiative (TSI) standards in math, reading, and writing, compared with almost three-quarters (72%) of those who did not qualify for free or reduced price lunch. Only 41% of 2008 high school graduates who received free or reduced price lunch enrolled in college, compared with 53% who did not qualify for this federal program.[34]

The Structure of Higher Education in the State

The system of higher education in Texas comprises 45 public four-year colleges and universities, 63 public two-year colleges, 57 private not-for-profit four-year institutions, and 87 for-profit institutions.[35] About 1.54 million students were enrolled in degree-granting institutions in Texas in fall 2010, an increase of 48.6% from fall 2000.[36] In fall 2010, the vast majority (87%) of students enrolled in degree-granting institutions in Texas attended public colleges and universities, and small shares attended private not-for-profit (9%) and for-profit (5%) institutions.[37]

Community colleges account for the majority (55%) of public enrollments in Texas, a larger share than the national average (48%).[38] Enrollments at community colleges have been increasing at a higher rate than at public universities in Texas since the mid-1960s. From 2000 to 2005, fall enrollments increased by 26% at public two-year colleges, compared with 17% at public universities. From 2005 to 2020, enrollments are projected to increase by 19% at public two-year colleges, a higher projected rate of increase than for public universities (13%).[39]

Public and private institutions in the state are coordinated by the Texas Higher Education Coordinating Board (THECB).[40] The state's 45 public four-year institutions are governed by 10 governing boards. Members of each governing board are appointed by the governor and confirmed by the senate. Six of the 10 governing boards are responsible for multiple campuses, and four are responsible for single institutions. The Board of Regents of the Texas State Technical College System, created in 1965, oversees four technical colleges. The public higher education system also includes 50 community college districts with more than 70 campuses. Each community college district has its own (locally elected) board of trustees. There is no statewide board for community colleges.[41]

What Explains Performance in Higher Education in Texas?

Given the context and structure of Texas higher education, what accounts for its recent patterns of performance? More specifically, what accounts for the state's progress in preparation, participation, and completion, but also its persistent performance below national averages in most areas of higher education and its continuing performance gaps across groups? Although several factors contribute to these outcomes, four themes appear to be predominant: (1) challenges associated with regional differences; (2) shared but potentially conflicting goals and priorities; (3) opportunities created by college readiness strategies; and (4) failure to strategically allocate state fiscal resources.

Challenges Associated with Regional Differences

Texas' large size and distinct geographical differences create challenges for achieving statewide goals. Texas is home to six of the nation's 100 largest metropolitan areas, while also possessing vast tracts of rural land.[42] Five large regions are perceived to be critical to increasing postsecondary degree attainment because of "their large and growing at-risk population, their relatively low educational attainment, and emerging favorable conditions for reform in higher education." Four of these regions (the Metroplex, the Gulf Coast, Central Texas, and South Texas) account for 81% of the state's total population, 83% of the state's Hispanic population, 76% of all students who have not completed a postsecondary credential, and 95% of expected growth in the student population. Virtually all students enrolled in two-year or four-year institutions in the Upper Rio Grande are attending low-performing institutions, where low-performing is defined as a graduation rate below the state average.[43]

The five regions collectively enroll 83.4% of the students in four-year institutions and 84.9% of the students in two-year colleges in the state. These five regions vary in many ways, including the percentage of Hispanics in the student-age population, median household income, rate of participation in developmental education, rate of postsecondary completion, and the characteristics of their economies.[44] As a result, the challenges facing higher education vary across these regions. The gap in college enrollment between Whites and Hispanics is greatest at the colleges and universities in Central Texas, which is home to the state's public flagship institutions. High school graduation rates are particularly low in the Gulf Coast. In the Metroplex, Blacks and Whites perform considerably better than Hispanics on indicators of high school graduation and college enrollment. Nearly all colleges and universities in South Texas (21 of 22) are minority serving. El Paso has relatively high rates of high school graduation and college enrollment and small gaps in performance between Whites, Blacks, and Hispanics but low rates of college completion for all groups.[45]

The future of Texas clearly hinges on its success in addressing the needs of students living in these regions. Yet the state faces significant challenges in identifying a statewide approach to improving higher education performance, given regional differences as well as a state culture that values local control. One state policy expert said, "We're all proud to be Texans, but we're very different people, and people in the Valley are very different than people in East Texas, and people in East Texas are very different than people in the Metroplex, and people in Metroplex are very different than people in West Texas. . . . And so it's harder to get a statewide agreement on a lot of these things."

Efforts to create a statewide policy agenda in a large geographic state with multiple urban centers and diverse regions are further challenged by the weak role that the state constitution assigns to the governor. A state leader explained: "We have a so-called weak governor system, and so there is no real entity within the state that I believe does things in the best interest of the state as an entity. . . . We're treating Texas as though it were a loose confederation of small counties. I think *that* more than anything has given rise to the public higher education system that we have here now." Compared with other states, the governor in Texas has relatively little formal institutional power, particularly with regard to the appointment and removal of officials for major state offices, control over the budget, and the ability of the legislature to change the governor's budget.[46]

Whereas the governor in Texas is constitutionally weak, the office of lieutenant governor is strong. Elected separately from the governor, the lieutenant governor is part of both the executive and legislative branches and serves as the president of the state senate. The Texas constitution gives the lieutenant governor the right to debate and vote on all issues and to cast the deciding vote in the case of a senate tie. Like the speaker of the house, the lieutenant governor is required to sign all bills and resolutions.[47]

Some state leaders perceive the lieutenant governor as particularly important to advancing statewide rather than regional interests for higher education. According to a business leader, "Because individual legislators are so focused on their districts in Texas, you have to have someone who looks out for the state. That person is mostly the lieutenant governor."

The lieutenant governor's power has limits, however. Moreover, although the lieutenant governor has structural power, some observers perceive the current governor to be politically stronger than the current lieutenant governor. A state policy expert told us, "The office gives the Texas lieutenant governor more structural power than you see in other states. The most famous Texas lieutenant governors have exercised and increased their power not only through the way they run the senate (committee appointments, legislative agenda, power of recognition, etcetera) but also by placing allies in jobs throughout state government—a strategy the current governor used more effectively than the current lieutenant governor."

Shared but Potentially Conflicting Statewide Goals and Priorities for Higher Education

In October 2000, the Texas Higher Education Coordinating Board adopted *Closing the Gaps*, a strategic plan for higher education that calls for eliminating educational gaps not only in terms of "student participation" and "success" but also in terms of "excellence" and "research." More specifically, the 2000 plan called for the state, by 2015, to increase college enrollment in public and independent institutions by 500,000 students, raise the number of certificates and degrees awarded by 50%, elevate the national rankings of programs and services at the state's colleges and universities, and increase by 50% federal science and engineering research funding to state colleges and universities.[48] In 2010 the coordinating board raised the original student-related *Closing the Gaps* targets to reflect demographic shifts in the state. Participation goals were increased from 500,000 students to 630,000, and the target number of certificates and degrees was raised from 163,000 to 210,000, a 120% increase from undergraduate degree production in 2000.[49]

In its 2010 annual progress report, the coordinating board noted that, although progress had been made in some areas, "other targets seemed even farther out of reach than the year before." In response to these findings, the coordinating board developed "an accelerated action plan" to address four areas where progress was slower than expected: "African American male and Hispanic participation; Hispanic and African American success (degrees and awards); technology (STEM field) degrees and awards; and teacher certifications."[50]

State leaders generally agree on the goals identified in *Closing the Gaps*, and business and education coalitions in the state have helped to foster this agreement. The state has also developed mechanisms for monitoring progress toward achieving the state goals. However, the state is simultaneously focusing available resources on achieving the excellence and research goals, and this is at the potential expense of educational attainment goals, given finite fiscal resources.

Support from Business and Education Coalitions for Improving Educational Attainment

The state's business leaders have a history of advocating for the advancement of education-related initiatives. A state higher education policy expert we spoke with emphasized the need for educated workers, described the challenges of operating in any community that has "an illiterate workforce," and suggested that higher education is crucial to the future of the business climate in Texas. A leader of a state higher education agency described the role of the business sector in influencing state policy generally, and higher education policy specifically, stating, "The business community in Texas is enormously influential in setting every aspect of state policy and . . . is enormously interested in higher education."

Created in 1922, the Texas Association of Business has long advocated for improved educational attainment. With a membership base of more than 140,000 employers and 200 local chambers of commerce, the association has emphasized the importance of improving the educational preparation of the workforce "to keep pace with the demands of employers" and "have a rich supply of workers on hand to fill jobs."[51] Formed in 1994, the Governor's Business Council, a nonpartisan, nonprofit organization has also supported the development of an educated workforce. The council originally focused primarily on K–12 education, but many leaders we spoke with described a shift toward higher education. According to one business leader, "We began to try to engage the legislature, the coordinating board, and our political leadership in a dialogue about the challenge we saw facing higher education in Texas. That effort has been ongoing since the 2007 legislative session, 2009 [session], and we're now getting ourselves ready for 2011."

Renamed the Texas Business Leadership Council, the council supports the development of "a K–16 system-wide vision for the state and support[s] comprehensive studies and programs that elevate our curriculum and methods of teaching." The council is limited to 100 members and includes "leaders of small, medium, and large" for-profit and nonprofit organizations.[52] A business leader described the composition and influence of the council:

> [Members] include some of the largest companies in the state. It also has a geographical distribution and some ethnic and gender considerations as well to fill out the membership. . . . Because of who our members are, it gives us relatively good access. Even though we call ourselves the Governor's Business Council, we don't have a formal relationship with the governor. We were started under a Democratic governor, and then since then we've had two Republican governors and we've had good relationships with all three.

The council has been particularly interested in developing measures of student learning at all education levels. It has recommended that these measures identify "college and workplace readiness" and be reported "against globally competitive benchmarks." The council has also advocated for improved data collection and reporting and has provided recommendations on the types of data the state should report, including "the cost of attendance, productivity measures, allocations of time and funds to classroom instruction, research and other programs, and information on the stewardship and maintenance of institutional assets."[53]

Monitoring Progress toward Goal Attainment

The state collects and reports on measures of performance in five areas: participation, success, excellence, research, and institutional effectiveness and efficiencies. The state reports key accountability measures, contextual and explanatory measures, institutional explanations and descriptions, and out-of-state peer comparisons.[54] *Closing the Gaps* identifies interim benchmarks for the state and requires the coordinating board to report annually the state's progress toward reaching benchmarks, intermediate targets for 2005 and 2010, and overall goals.

The state's ability to monitor progress on the goals identified in *Closing the Gaps* is facilitated by its success in making higher education data available. According to the national Data Quality Campaign, Texas has implemented 8 out of 10 data "essential" elements for improving practice and state policy in education and is thus ahead of other states in this area.[55] In its national evaluation of state accountability systems, Education Sector gave Texas a "best practice" rating for monitoring educational outcomes and institutional practices and an "in progress" rating for the state's alignment between K–12 and higher education systems. Texas also received a "best practice" rating for its efforts in governance and strategic planning.[56]

With state and federal funding, in 2011 the Texas Higher Education Coordinating Board produced its first "Texas Public Higher Education Almanac" in collaboration with "private philanthropy groups working with the state to improve higher education" to provide greater transparency and accountability in higher education. The Almanac, which includes national, state and institutional measures, responds to a 2004 directive from Governor Perry and is to be used in conjunction with the *Closing the Gaps* indicators.[57]

At the time of our data collection, Texas was also developing a robust data system called the Texas P–16 Public Education Information Resource. The system, which spans K–12 and higher education (including for-profit higher education institutions), is managed by the Texas Education Agency and the Texas Higher Education Coordinating Board.[58] State leaders told us that they expected full integration of the K–12 and higher education data systems within the calendar year, and as of June 2013, this information resource was up and running.

Potential Tradeoffs of Multiple Goals When Resources Are Finite

In addition to increasing enrollment and degree completion, especially for Hispanic and Black students, *Closing the Gaps* also describes the state's aspirations to improve the competitiveness of its public research universities both in terms of "excellence," as measured by national rankings and program recognition, and "in academic research and innovation," through greater emphasis on "the research roles of UT–Austin, Texas A&M–College Station, and the research-oriented Medical Centers."[59] The 2010 *Closing the Gaps Progress Report* concludes that the state is "well below target" (i.e., at least 10% below the state target) in terms of national rankings and "somewhat below target" (between 2% to 9% below the state target) with regard to federal expenditures for research and development (R&D) in science and engineering.

Some observers note the absence of a nationally ranked public research university in the state's major economic centers. According to a leader of a state philanthropic organization, "A weakness [of higher education in Texas] is that the alignment between top-tier institutions, nationally competitive institutions, and the urban areas of the state is weak. The three largest urban areas of the state—Dallas–Fort Worth, greater Houston, and San Antonio—none of them has a nationally competitive institution, except Houston, which has Rice, but it's a small place. None of them has a national institution in the state-supported arena." Nonetheless, the state's ambitious goals for seven emerging research universities, supported through the redirection of some public endowments for this purpose, may compete with the state's goal of achieving substantially higher levels of educational attainment when fiscal resources are constrained. The seven "emerging research universities" are Texas Tech University, the University of Houston, the University of North Texas, UT-Arlington, UT-Dallas, UT–El Paso, and UT–San Antonio.

Public Endowments to Support Research / Emerging Research Universities

The state has established secure sources of funding for four-year public institutions through public endowments—a feature unique to Texas—through the Permanent University Fund (PUF) and other funds. Established in the Texas Constitution of 1876 through the appropriation of land grants, the PUF provides support to 21 institutions of the University of Texas and Texas A&M systems, including the health related institutions of both systems and the Texas A&M land grant research and service agencies.[60]

Estimates from December 2008 indicate that the fund holds approximately $8.8 billion in investments as well as two million acres of land. Each year, 5% of the fund's value is transferred to the Available University Fund (AUF), which distributes the money. Two-thirds of the proceeds are for the University of Texas System and one-third for the Texas A&M System. The AUF is used for three primary purposes: "(1) to pay interest and principal due on PUF bonds that are issued to provide construction dollars at 21 institutions of the UT and A&M systems; (2) to provide support for a wide range of programs intended to develop excellence at the University of Texas at Austin, Texas A&M University at College Station, and Prairie View University; and (3) to provide for the expenses of the two respective System Administrations."[61] Revenues from the AUF may be used for instruction, student services, scholarships, and capital improvement.[62]

Through amendments to the Texas Constitution that were passed in 1984 and 1993, the legislature appropriates additional funding to academic institutions, health-related institutions, and Texas State College System institutions that do not receive support from the Permanent University Fund. This appropriation is known as the Higher Education Assistance Fund (HEAF) and is used for many of the same purposes as the PUF: "The institutions can acquire land; construct, repair, and rehabilitate buildings; and purchase capital equipment and library materials with HEAF funds. From 1986 through 1995, the legislature appropriated $100 million in HEAF funds each year. The annual appropriation increased to $175 million each year beginning in 1996. Beginning [in] FY 2008, the annual appropriation increased to $262.5 million each fiscal year."[63]

Revenues for the Higher Education Fund (HEF), a dedicated endowment fund for the benefit of non-PUF institutions, come from legislative appropriations: "Each year between 1996 and 2001, the HEF endowment [has] received annual appropriations of $50 million. Starting in FY 2002, the $50 million appropriated to the HEF endowment was reduced by the amount of interest earned by the HEF, and a corresponding amount was transferred to the Texas Excellence Fund for the benefit of HEAF-eligible institutions. The $50 million annual appropriation to the HEF Endowment was discontinued in FY 2004."[64]

In 2009, the legislature passed HB 51 to repurpose this endowment as the National Research University Fund (NRUF). The new fund is designed to provide funding to "emerging research universities that meet critical benchmarks for achieving national research university criteria, such as certain levels of endowments, certain numbers of Ph.D. degrees awarded, etc."[65] This reallocation of the endowment provided substantial encouragement to Texas' vision of transforming several existing universities into prestigious research universities. On the day that voters approved Proposition 4, which enacted several provisions of HB 51 as a constitutional amendment, former Lieutenant Governor Bill Hobby said, "Tonight's passage of Proposition 4 sends this important message: Texans understand that more nationally recognized research universities will help retain Texas-grown talent, recruit top researchers who will generate billions of dollars in economic growth and create more high paying, permanent jobs."[66] In passing HB 51, the legislature sought to enhance the research capacity, prestige, and performance of the state's public universities, a goal that is articulated in the *Closing the Gaps* strategic plan.

Texas has also created the Research University Development Fund (RUDF), which provides funds "to research universities and emerging research universities for the recruitment and retention of highly qualified faculty and the enhancement of research productivity at those universities." The amount of state funding is "based on the average amount of total research funds expended by each institution annually during the three most recent state fiscal years."[67]

The state further encourages the expansion of research productivity and faculty recruitment at emerging public research institutions through the Texas Research Incentive Program (TRIP). This program provides state grants to match private gifts designed to achieve these goals, with state matches ranging from 50% for gifts between \$100,000 and \$1 million, 75% for gifts ranging from \$1 million to \$2 million, and 100% for gifts ranging from \$2 million to \$10 million.[68]

In addition to potentially diverting finite fiscal resources away from the state's educational attainment goals, these funds may also be too small to make meaningful improvements in research and excellence at so many universities. Some leaders we spoke with said that the impact of these funding programs and incentives is diluted by providing support to too many institutions, rather than concentrating resources more strategically on a smaller number of universities. The leader of a public research university said, "In Texas, in characteristic fashion, this last session, there was this HB 51 bill that put money into emerging research universities, but instead of focusing on one or two, they spread it out across seven different institutions. . . . We love to do that. We take too little money, and we spread it across too many places."

The Governor's Business Council also cautions the state against creating too many research-intensive universities, recommending instead:

> (1) Texas should enhance the independence of the two major research universities, UT-Austin and Texas A&M–College Station, from state and system constraints in order to increase their ability to focus on world-class research and graduate education, and limit undergraduate enrollment; (2) Universities desiring to reach the status of a research university should do so only with strong regional support and significant private sector backing. Regional investment funds could be used to help develop research capacity in line with the area's long-term economic development priorities.[69]

Opportunities Created by College Readiness Strategies

Texas has been recognized as a national leader in its efforts to link K–12 and higher education. A policy expert that we spoke with asserted that the college readiness agenda "is where the state has done most of the work" and has "put in the complete set of policies needed to join [higher education] with K–12 on a statewide college readiness initiative." Texas has been less effective, however, in developing statewide strategies to support transfer between two- and four-year colleges and universities. Recent efforts to allow some community colleges to offer applied baccalaureate degrees show promise but are limited in scope.

Linkages between K–12 and Higher Education

Especially when compared with other states, Texas has made great strides over the past decade toward ensuring that all students graduate from high school academically ready for college-level coursework. In 2001, the legislature established the "recommended" or "college-preparatory" high school program as the default curriculum in public schools beginning with the freshman class of 2004–5 (HB 1144).[70] The recommended program includes the courses typically required to enroll in the state's public colleges and universities. Students may only "opt out" of the recommended program if the student, the parent (or guardian), and a school counselor or administrator agree in writing. In 2010–11 19.9% of students opted out and thus graduated with the minimum rather than the recommended high school requirements.[71]

As another step toward aligning high school and college readiness standards, the legislature in 2006 required the Texas Higher Education Coordinating Board and the Texas Education Agency to "appoint vertical teams in the disciplines of English / language arts, science, social sciences, and mathematics."[72] These teams were charged with establishing the standards for college readiness, defined as the level of preparation a student must attain in English language arts and mathematics courses to enroll and succeed, without remediation, in an entry-level general education course for credit in that same content area for a baccalaureate degree or associate degree program (House Bill 3, §39.024).[73]

As part of this process, representatives from K–12 schools and higher education have collaborated to develop end-of-course (EOC) exams that build toward the college readiness standards. In 2007, Senate Bill 1031 was enacted, which called for the development of "end-of course" assessment instruments for secondary-level courses in algebra I, algebra II, geometry, chemistry, physics, English I, English II, English III, world geography, world history, and United States history.[74] Although state and institutional leaders as well as the Southern Regional Education Board believe that Texas has made greater progress than other states in aligning K–12 and postsecondary curricular standards, additional time is required to see the effects of these efforts.

As suggested by the enactment of these college readiness initiatives into statute, the legislature has been a primary driver of K–16 policy reform in Texas. The senate currently has separate committees for K–12 and higher education, but in the past these committees were combined. A state senator told us that having a single committee handling both K–12 and higher education issues helped legislators make progress in linking them: "The one place in Texas, and perhaps the only place in Texas where both systems were talked about by the same policymakers, was in this committee, because the House committees were separated. We have two different commissioners [of K–12 and higher education]. So everything was operating differently except for this committee [that] had them both together. . . . I want to be very careful not say that it can't be done separately, but merely just say that when it was joined here, it gave a unique ability of the chairman to really focus on those two."

The state also has a P–16 Council, but this entity has been less influential in creating statewide college readiness policies. Leaders of the Texas Education Agency, Texas Higher Education Coordinating Board, and State Board for Educator Certification began the state's P–16 effort in 1998 as an informal network called the Public Education / Higher Education Coordinating Group. Building on this informal effort, the legislature created the P–16 Council in 2003 (Texas Education Code §61.076) with the goal of "ensuring that long-range plans and educational programs for the state complement the functioning of the entire system of public education, extending from early childhood education through postgraduate study." In 2005, the legislature specified that the P–16 Council include representatives from the Texas Education Agency, Texas Higher Education Coordinating Board, Texas Workforce Commission, and Texas Department of Assistive and Rehabilitative Services (HB 2808). In 2007, the council co-chairs used their statutory authority to appoint three additional members to represent education professionals, agencies, business or other members of the community.[75]

Although the P–16 Council provides visibility to cross-sector issues in Texas, it has no formal authority of its own. According to the Texas Higher Education Coordinating Board, the P–16 Council "meets quarterly to provide leadership on P–16 college readiness issues and support the development of regional P–16 councils."[76] But state leaders we spoke with believed that it was the legislature, through the Higher Education Coordinating Board, that took the lead in linking K–12 and higher education to develop college readiness standards.

Other State Initiatives to Promote College Readiness

Texas has also developed and funded other initiatives, such as dual credit courses and early college high schools, which are designed to improve student transitions from high school to college. From fall 1999 to fall 2009, the number of students in Texas participating in dual credit increased 765% to 91,303 students. Over this period, the participation of Hispanics in dual credit programs increased considerably, rising from 23% of all program participants in fall 2001 to 39% in fall 2009. Despite this growth, however, Hispanics, representing nearly 47% of all high school students in Texas, remain underrepresented in these programs.[77]

Texas allows both school districts and colleges to receive funding for students who are enrolled in dual credit courses. According to the Texas Higher Education Coordinating Board, "Decisions about who pays tuition, fees and other costs for dual credit are made at the local level and thus vary from district to district. . . . In practice, surveys conducted by coordinating board staff indicate that most community colleges waive all or part of the cost [for students], while relatively few universities offer waivers."[78]

The state also provides funding to support early college high schools (ECHS). Targeting students "least likely to attend college," the ECHS is designed to provide students with the opportunity to earn 60 college credits in addition to their high school diploma at no cost. In fall 2010, approximately 10,000 students were enrolled at 44 early college high schools and 5 Texas science, technology, engineering, and math (T-STEM) early college high schools.[79]

Texas has also worked to redesign remedial education in order to prepare students for college credit-bearing work and college completion. In 2006, the legislature charged the Texas Higher Education Coordinating Board with establishing and expanding "redesigned developmental and entry-level academic courses" in order "to improve student learning, especially in the large, introductory-level courses, while at the same time reduce instructional costs through a variety of savings mechanisms."[80] The Course Redesign Project potentially has a direct effect on Texas public community colleges, since they enroll the majority of entering college students. Since the state's course redesign efforts are fairly recent, no data are yet available to judge their efficacy.

Few Large-Scale State Policies Promote Transfer across Institutions

Texas has policies that facilitate student transfer across higher education institutions, including transfer from two- to four-year colleges and universities, but it lacks a statewide policy that guarantees the transfer of credits. The approaches being used to improve transfer and completion rates, such as transfer agreements negotiated between individual institutions, remain local rather than statewide. Negotiating transfer agreements by institution is especially challenging in a state as large and diverse as Texas. According to the Southern Regional Education Board, Texas falls short of guaranteeing that "students who earn an associate degree at a two-year college will receive from 60–64 hours of credit when they transfer to a four-year college in the state if they keep the same major."[81]

In an effort to facilitate student transfer from public community colleges to four-year colleges and universities, the Texas Higher Education Coordinating Board established a common course-numbering system in 1993 and the legislature passed a transfer-of-credit law in 1997. State institutions have also worked together to develop lower-division curricula that transfer in a block, such as the associate of arts in teaching (AAT) degree.[82] In 2000, *Closing the Gaps* identified the AAT degree as important to the state's college goal to "recruit, prepare and retain additional well-qualified educators for elementary and secondary schools."[83] As of 2008, 39 community college districts had partnered with four-year institutions to offer an AAT degree. Texas public universities that offer educator certification programs are required to accept all coursework for the AAT degrees from Texas public community colleges.[84] To date only small numbers of AAT degrees have been awarded (e.g., 2,058 in 2010).[85] The Texas Higher Education Coordinating Board is also working to "improve articulation in STEM fields for students who start at two-year institutions and want to transfer to four-year institutions" through grant funding from Lumina Foundation.[86]

Texas is also seeking to improve transfer and degree productivity through the establishment of the applied baccalaureate degree. These degrees are particularly useful for working adults because they "usually involve large transfers of credit, often in the form of an applied associate degree that includes career and technical education courses."[87] Community college baccalaureate degrees in applied science and applied technology were authorized in 2003 (Texas Education Code §130.0012) as pilot programs at three community colleges (Brazosport College, Midland College, and South Texas College). These institutions have received funding based on a formula similar to that used for public four-year institutions.

According to the coordinating board, a total of 1,376 applied baccalaureate degrees (including all such programs at two- and four-year institutions) were awarded between 1989 and 2008, a small overall impact.[88] In a 2009 evaluation of the pilot programs, the coordinating board recommended only judicious expansion of the program in cases with well-documented need. The evaluation also noted that the programs "address very few of the anticipated high-growth occupations in Texas."[89] Although small in number and facilitating transfer without loss of academic credit, applied baccalaureate programs raise questions about mission expansion for the community college sector.

Failure to Strategically Allocate State Fiscal Resources

The budgeting process for higher education in Texas has some strengths, but there are several mismatches between the state's use of fiscal resources and its priorities for raising educational attainment. The state's formula-driven process for higher education budgeting and appropriations has minimized political disputes among institutions and sectors of higher education. However, because the process is enrollment-based and adjusted only incrementally, it limits the state's ability to adapt to new challenges and educational priorities. Meanwhile, tuition deregulation at public four-year institutions has resulted in substantial tuition increases despite legislative oversight. The state's investment in student financial aid is insufficient to meet students' financial need, and financial aid dollars increasingly come from students through set-asides from tuition increases. Texas also lacks coherent policies for meeting the fiscal needs of community and technical colleges, institutions that enroll more than half of all students who seek higher education in the state and that disproportionately serve students from low-income families and racial/ethnic minority groups.

Emphasis of Higher Education Appropriations on Enrollment

The appropriations process for higher education in Texas is formula-driven. The state has a biennial budget process that begins with the governing board of each institution presenting a detailed current operating budget.[90] Then, according to the leader of a state agency, there are "staff-level hearings—legislative and governor's staff meeting with each of the institutions on their budget requests. The coordinating board also submits a proposal as a part of that. The appropriations decisions [for community colleges and four-year institutions] are made separately, but I think there's generally an effort to try to treat them the same."

The complex formula that is used as the basis for higher education funding is driven by enrollment and the cost of instruction in various fields and levels of study. State leaders we spoke with said that the approach helps to depoliticize the process but does not necessarily create equity across institutions. A leader of a public research university said, "Most of the money comes from the formula. And it was an attempt to depoliticize work in the legislature. . . . So they came up with what they thought was a neutral formula. Well, they aren't neutral formulae. It's hard to implement policy through these formulae. . . . I think a lot of people think it's not very effective except at de-politicizing individual budgets."

Moreover, some state and institutional leaders noted unintended consequences associated with the funding formula, including a lag in funding for enrollment growth, incentives for enrollment rather than degree completion, and incentives for enrollment in master's and doctoral programs, which bring higher funding levels than undergraduate programs. In addition, the formula-based process is adjusted only incrementally, limiting the state's ability to adapt to new challenges and educational priorities. Some leaders also believe that the funding formula obscures differences in cost structures across institutional types. A leader of a public research university said, "I think the funding mechanisms for higher education in Texas are reasonable and good except for the research universities. The formulas are not functional for research universities. The average cost is good for institutions that don't have the cost associated with recruitment, retention of talent, and programmatic costs involved with tier-one research levels."

Consideration of Performance-Based Funding

In his February 2011 state-of-the-state address, Governor Perry indicated an interest in allocating funding for public colleges and universities based on performance. In fact, the state has been considering various approaches to this type of funding over the past several years. In 2003, the legislature specified: "As a condition of tuition deregulation, each university shall make satisfactory progress towards the goals provided in its master plan for higher education and *Closing the Gaps,* and the state's plan for higher education. HB 3015 and section 54.0515 require each university to meet acceptable performance criteria, including measures such as graduation rates, retention rates, enrollment growth, educational quality, efforts to increase diversity, opportunities for financial aid, and affordability."[91]

In 2007, the legislature established the Higher Education Performance Incentive Initiative. For fiscal year 2009, the legislature appropriated $100 million for this initiative, and the coordinating board awarded $80 million to public colleges and universities based on increases in degrees awarded, with special weights given to at-risk students and critical fields (such as nursing and STEM). The remaining $20 million was used to fund scholarships for students graduating in the top 10% of their high school class.[92] These funds represent a small share of the $9.98 billion appropriated (from all funds) to higher education in FY 2009.[93]

State leaders we spoke with said that the implementation of the Higher Education Performance Incentive Initiative has focused on fairly narrow measures of performance. They also indicated, however, that the authorizing legislation passed by the 82nd Legislature (2011) provides the framework for expanding the incentives to a broader range of state priorities identified in *Closing the Gaps.*

In support of performance funding, the Governor's Business Council has recommended using state funding to provide incentives for community colleges to achieve performance goals, particularly with regard to developing stronger connections with K–12 education, improving articulation and transfer, and improving degree completion. The council has suggested that the existing state funding formula "is essentially a cost-reimbursement model; it does not incentivize performance—graduating more students, becoming more successful in competing for research, [or] better responding to regional needs."[94]

The legislature is expected to consider allocating some portion of funding to higher education institutions based on the achievement of performance milestones during the 83rd (2013) legislative session. A leader of a community college explained, "The commissioner is positively disposed towards implementing a model that would give credit for achieving certain milestones in performance. There is an issue there in terms of where the funds come from to do that. Should it be an incentive program, which is the way it's done in Ohio and Washington, or should it come out of our base aid, which is what the commissioner has been proposing here? So that's got to be sorted out. But that would be a fairly important enhancement of the performance side of things."

In the 82nd legislative session, the coordinating board was directed, in consultation with institutions of higher education, to devise a funding formula that incorporates undergraduate student success measures. This incentive funding would be in addition to base funding but no more than 10% of total general revenue appropriations for undergraduate education. The coordinating board was also directed to compare the effect of incorporating the success measures into the base funding formula versus providing a separate formula. The recommendations were to be delivered by September 30, 2011, to the Joint Oversight Committee on Higher Education Governance, Transparency, and Excellence for consideration during the 83rd legislative session.

Unaligned Tuition and Aid Policies

The legislature has recognized the importance of providing affordable options for higher education to the large number of undocumented students attending high school in the state. Through legislation passed in 2001 (HB 1403) and later amended in 2005 (SB 1528), undocumented students who meet several conditions concerning their length of residence in Texas are eligible for in-state tuition rates at public colleges and universities.[95]

Nonetheless, the portion of the costs of higher education in Texas paid by students and families has increased in recent years. From 2003 to 2008, the share of average education and related expenses per FTE student that was covered by tuition increased across every sector.[96] Over the same period, the share of average education and related expenses per FTE student that was covered by state and other subsidies declined.[97]

Through legislation passed by the legislature (HB 3015), Texas public four-year colleges and universities gained the authority to set their own tuition rates as of spring 2004. As explained by the Texas Higher Education Coordinating Board, "Prior to 2003, the Texas Legislature had the regulatory authority to set tuition rates and generally mandated the same statutory and designated tuition rate be charged across the state. . . . [Now] there is no upper limit on the amount of designated tuition that a university may charge and the amounts may vary by program, course level, and academic period."[98]

One rationale for deregulating tuition was to address challenges of having a biennial legislature set tuition. A state policy expert told us that, prior to tuition deregulation, there was "rigid, fixed tuition set by the state legislature, which meets once every other year for four and a half months." After tuition was deregulated, however, tuition rates increased substantially. From fall 2003 to fall 2009, the average total academic charges increased by 72% for a student at a public university taking 15 semester credit hours (SCHs).[99] Texas was once a low-tuition state, but tuition and fees are now characterized as "high" at the University of Texas at Austin, "moderate" at the state's public comprehensive universities, and "low" at the state's community colleges.[100]

Some institutional leaders noted that tuition deregulation has helped public universities compensate for the state's relatively low level of appropriations to higher education. A leader at a public research university acknowledged the negative implications for college affordability but stated, "In fairness it has been important for the institution because Texas is historically a low-tax, low-service state. . . . We regulated tuition but [hadn't been] great on the state-support side. So [tuition deregulation] brought things into balance a little more for the state institutions. But [tuition deregulation] is not great on the affordability front, of course."

Even with tuition deregulation, informal pressure from the legislature has controlled tuition increases at least somewhat. The governor may also indirectly exert pressure to limit tuition increases through his appointments to institutional boards. A leader of a different public research university explained:

> [T]he legislature gave the authority to the Board of Regents to set tuition, but the political pressure around keeping tuition low has effectively kept it capped for us. We were capped at 4.95% in the first two years after the tuition-setting policy was changed. That was a decision by the Board of Regents because of political pressures from the state that mandated that it not go any higher than that. And then, this last round, the state didn't pass a law but they made it clear that the state would not want any more than a 3.95% increase so our regents capped it at 3.95 again and the threat is that, if we go above what the state is actually suggesting, that they'll just take the authority away from the regents and recapture the authority—and that is a threat. So effectively, while tuition-setting authority is given to the Board of Regents, the political pressures are so significant, and our regents are appointed by the governor, so it really effectively makes it a very difficult circumstance to manage the university in terms of tuition revenues that we need.

Nonetheless, some leaders suggested that as tuition has increased, Texas has not been guided by state policy regarding the relationship between tuition levels and the availability of student financial aid. According to a leader of a state philanthropic organization, "There's no rationally thought-out concept of what we're charging students, what we're going to do about financial aid, and so forth. For a long time this state had essentially free higher education, and we moved away from it. They just haven't evolved a thoughtful policy about what it is they're trying to deal with."

When the legislature deregulated tuition (HB 3015), it sought to provide more financial aid to students but shifted responsibility for providing that aid to colleges and universities. In HB 3015, the legislature mandated that institutions "set aside at least 15% of the amount of undergraduate and graduate designated tuition charged . . . to be used to provide financial assistance for financially needy undergraduate or graduate students. . . . HB 3015 also required institutions to set aside 5% of the undergraduate amount of designated tuition charged in excess of $46 per semester credit hour to fund the Be-On-Time (BOT) Loan Program."[101] As a result of these set-asides from tuition increases, students have assumed more responsibility for funding financial aid. From 2001 to 2009, the total amount of institutional aid provided to students at public four-year institutions increased by 154% (in 2009 dollars).[102]

Low State Investment in Student Financial Aid

Historically, Texas has been characterized not only as a low-tuition state but also as a low-aid state—that is, the state's investment in student financial aid has been low in comparison with other states. Although some state leaders characterized the policy linkages between tuition and financial aid as "weak," Texas has substantially increased its investment in need-based student financial aid over the past decade.

From 1999 to 2009, the estimated need-based undergraduate grant funding per FTE undergraduate student increased by 159% (in constant dollars)—from $199 in 1999–2000 to $515 in 2008–9.[103] But the average financial aid award per FTE student in Texas ($121 in FY 2009) remains substantially below the national average ($520 in 2009), and the number of state financial aid awards in Texas (242 per 1,000 FTE students) is lower than the national average (298 per 1,000 FTE students).[104] Net tuition in Texas, at $4,158, is comparable to the national average ($4,106).[105]

The Towards Excellence, Access and Success (TEXAS) Grant is the state's largest financial aid program, both in the number of recipients and in total funds awarded. Established by the legislature and implemented in 1999, the TEXAS Grant is awarded to students based on financial need and academic criteria. Recipients must have completed the recommended high school program. Beyond their first year in college, they must meet their institution's requirements for academic progress, and beyond their second year, they must have a cumulative grade point average (GPA) of 2.5 on a scale to 4.0; complete at least 24 semester credit hours per year; and complete at least 75% of the semester credit hours they attempt per year. About 80% of TEXAS Grant recipients had family incomes in the lowest two quintiles in FY 2009. In 2008, 53% of TEXAS Grant recipients were Hispanic, 16% were Black, 24% were White, and 7% were Asian American.[106]

In a report to the coordinating board, the Higher Education Insight Associates attributed some of the state's recent improvements in college preparation, participation, and completion to the TEXAS Grant program.[107] Their analyses indicate that even though the populations of students receiving the TEXAS Grant have low rates of college completion historically (including high proportions of student who are from low-income families, are racial/ethnic minorities, or are first-generation college students), their six-year bachelor's degree completion rates are comparable with those of students who do not receive financial aid and higher than those of students who receive other forms of financial aid.

Funding for the TEXAS Grant has increased, but available funding is insufficient to provide grants to all eligible students. According to the Texas Higher Education Coordinating Board, "at current funding levels [FY 2008], only 51% of eligible students receive a TEXAS Grant."[108] A policy report to the coordinating board concluded that a "perfect storm" had occurred to limit availability of TEXAS Grant funds: "Increased awareness of the need for and availability of higher education by previously under-represented populations, and increased numbers of students graduating with the recommended high school program combined to expand the demand for TEXAS Grants. Concurrently, tuition and fee charges increased substantially while state appropriations for financial aid increased at a much slower rate. The TEXAS Grant, that began as a promise and guarantee, became an unfulfilled competition for limited dollars."[109]

The Governor's Business Council has recommended increasing funding for the TEXAS Grant and adding a new component to target middle-school students, stating: "According to the Texas Higher Education Coordinating Board, full funding would allow more than 60,000 eligible students to receive a TEXAS Grant. . . . In addition, the legislature should establish a new component of the TEXAS Grant program that would target students at the middle-school level and provide for students and families to enter into a 'learning contract.' Students would agree to take the prescribed courses, stay in school, etc., and schools would provide support services (counseling, etc.) that are known to be essential for at-risk students to succeed."[110]

In response to funding shortfalls, the legislature passed Senate Bill 28, which modified the grant program to give priority to financially needy students who are better prepared for higher education. The changes take effect beginning in the 2013–14 academic year. According to the bill summary, the legislation gives "highest priority to students who graduated from a public or accredited private school in Texas, who on or after May 1, 2013, have completed the recommended high school program or its equivalent, and who have attained certain measures of academic success relating to test scores, class rank, grade point average, high school course credits, or college credit hours earned in dual-credit courses."[111]

To encourage degree completion, the legislature in 2003 established the Be-On-Time Loan. This program forgives loans for students attending community colleges, public four-year institutions, or private four-year institutions who graduate "on time" with a grade average of B or higher.[112] Students who do not meet these requirements must repay a zero-interest loan. The Be-On-Time Program was reduced by $28 million dollars (a 29% decrease) in the most recent legislative session. The program currently comprises 12.7% of the 2012–13 budget for financial aid.[113]

The state offers a small amount of financial aid to students who are attending community colleges (through the Texas Educational Opportunity Grant) and private colleges and universities (through the Tuition Equalization Grant). Established by the legislature in 1999, the Texas Educational Opportunity Grant is available to students who continue in college and who meet continuing eligibility requirements. Students may receive awards for up to 75 semester credit hours for four years, or until they receive an associate degree, whichever comes first.[114] Although the legislature has increased funding for the Texas Educational Opportunity Grant, available funding resulted in awards to fewer than 5% of eligible students in 2010–11.[115]

Established by the legislature in 1973, the Tuition Equalization Grant (TEG) is awarded to financially needy students attending private not-for-profit colleges and universities. The state provides relatively little financial aid for students who are financially independent. In fiscal year 2007, independent students received only 10% of TEXAS Grants and 39% of Tuition Equalization Grants. About 6 out of 10 of community college students (61%) receiving Texas Educational Opportunity Grants were independent.[116]

Challenges of Funding Policies for Community Colleges

The state has failed to keep up with growth in instructional costs and enrollment at community colleges. Community colleges determine their own tuition and fee increases, and tuition is more expensive for students outside of a college's designated tax district, even though these students may live within the college's service area. These tuition differentials, along with the declining purchasing power of student financial aid, raise serious questions about the ability of this sector to provide educational opportunity to Texas' most vulnerable populations.

Community colleges rely on local tax revenue, tuition and fees, and state appropriations to fund their institutions. State appropriations for community colleges are based on student enrollment at the institution (contact hours) and median costs of 26 academic and technical programs across the 50 community college districts in the state. A leader of a community college system explained, "There are three essential elements of funding for community colleges. One is tuition and fees, of course. Two is local taxes. And three is state reimbursement for instruction. We are unique from four-year systems in that community colleges by state law are expected to have a local tax levied to support their maintenance and operations costs. There are three legs of the stool for funding." According to the state education code, community colleges must use state funds "exclusively for the purpose of paying salaries of instructional and administrative forces . . . and the purchase of supplies and materials for instructional purposes."[117]

The importance of local taxes to the overall budget for community colleges has increased as the share of administrative and instructional expenses covered by state support has declined, falling from 61% in fiscal year 1985 to 28% in 2007.[118] From 1998–99 to 2008–9, average total contact hours at the community colleges increased by 30%, while state appropriations increased by 27.7%. As a result, formula-funding appropriations per contact hour declined by 23% in real dollars over this period.[119]

Declines in state appropriations have encouraged the state's community colleges to maximize the share of their "service area" that agrees to be taxed to support community colleges. The legislature established the 50 community college service areas in 1995 (via Senate Bill 390) and allocated the majority of counties to these service areas. However, many community colleges have portions of their service areas lying outside their taxing district. In these cases, residents of surrounding areas can vote to be annexed into a community college taxing district.[120] Residents within a taxing district pay lower "in-district" tuition at a community college within their district. All others pay higher out-of-district tuition. On average, a semester credit hour for spring 2011 is 50% higher at the out-of-district rate than the in-district rate ($99 vs. $66).[121] A leader of a community college system told us,

> There are 50 community colleges in Texas. And so the state is divided into 50 areas that are called service areas. We serve all or parts of [a number of] counties. By law you have two primary designations of residents that you serve. You have in-district taxpayers, who get a much lower tuition rate. . . . We set that [tuition rate]; the state does not. We've worked very hard over the years to bring in a number of districts that are taxing themselves. And in return for that tax support, that helps us expand. They must vote themselves in. That's a huge process. But that is how we've dealt with this continued decline from 60% state support to 23%. We have five more communities that will be pursuing elections in November.

The tax base of communities in the 50 community college districts varies widely. But state funding for community colleges does not address equity issues across districts. Instead, variations in the tax base and tax rates across the state result in disparities across community colleges in the availability of revenue from local taxes. According to the Texas Higher Education Coordinating Board, "Some institutions have a significant tax base to generate funding that complements the revenue generated through state appropriations. However, other institutions find themselves in areas with decreasing tax bases and resulting fiscal constraints. Increasing the available funding from local taxes is a complex political process. Some institutions have reached the maximum authorized tax rate and must have a local election to increase it. Others have a very limited tax base and cannot generate significant amounts of revenue even with a tax rate increase."[122]

The state has not developed policies to assist community colleges in expanding their taxing districts. A leader of a community college system explained the challenges this policy vacuum creates for providing postsecondary educational opportunity to the local community:

> The state has no policy that says, if community colleges are pulling the heaviest load, and if well over half of all people entering higher education are coming to community colleges, and if the fastest-growing populations are Hispanics and Blacks, and the economically disadvantaged, and if they come 8 out of 10 to a community college, the state has no policies that say, we'll help you make this "green area" [the taxed district within the service area] bigger. There's nothing that requires communities once they hit a certain size to come into the district to help the community colleges to continue to be the primary trainer and retrainer of the local workforce.

This lack of state policy for addressing the fiscal needs of community colleges challenges state efforts to substantially improve educational attainment, given that these institutions enroll large numbers of the state's population and disproportionately enroll students from low-income families and racial/ethnic minority groups.

Conclusion

Texas has some of the nation's largest metropolitan areas, and its border regions are growing rapidly. Five of the regions in Texas account for most of the state's population growth. Fully utilizing the capacity of community colleges and public four-year institutions located throughout these regions is of utmost importance for Texas to achieve its goals for increasing educational attainment. Reducing educational gaps across population groups is also critical, given that half the state population is now comprised of "minority" groups. Despite improvements over the past decade, educational attainment in Texas continues to be substantially lower for Hispanics and Blacks than for Whites. Hispanics are the state's largest and fastest-growing racial/ethnic group.

Texas is a large and diverse state. Yet through its strategic plan *Closing the Gaps*, the state has successfully garnered broad public support—among elected officials, higher education leaders, and business leaders—for its statewide goals for higher education. Texas uses statewide data systems to monitor progress toward these goals and to report the outcomes publicly. In addition, the state has established regular processes for adjusting and updating the statewide goals. Over the past decade, the state has made progress on its goals, but more work lies ahead.

In seeking to increase educational attainment across population groups and throughout the state, Texas has developed promising policies to improve college readiness, including end-of-course assessments that lead to college readiness standards, dual-enrollment programs, and early college high schools. Continuing efforts to improve college readiness as well as promote the transfer of students from two- to four-year institutions are required.

Finance is a critical policy tool for promoting educational attainment, but Texas' finance policies for higher education are not well designed to achieve this goal. State appropriations, tuition, and financial aid policy are not well coordinated. The current funding formula helps to depoliticize the budget and appropriations process, but it does not encourage alignment of the budgets of colleges and universities with the state's policy goals. The state is considering options related to performance funding, but these policies have not yet been implemented. Tuition deregulation at public four-year institutions has resulted in substantial tuition increases. Meanwhile, state investments in student financial aid have not kept pace with the growing financial need. Set-asides from tuition revenues for institutional financial aid have only increased the responsibility of students in paying for college. Failure to improve college affordability may temper the benefits to college participation and completion of the state's efforts to improve college readiness.

Given Texas' size, governance structure for higher education, and regional diversity, the state's community colleges are particularly important to achieving statewide goals for increased educational attainment. Yet state funding for instructional expenses has decreased dramatically over the last decade. Locally elected community college boards have sought to increase revenue by expanding their tax districts to provide lower tuition for in-district students, but this strategy is challenging to implement in districts serving large numbers of low-income students. State policy development with regard to community college finance should be a priority for Texas.

Equally striking is the state's need to reconsider its policies for increasing the research capacity and prestige of higher education institutions in the state. The state's ambitious goals for its seven emerging research universities and the redirection of some public endowments for this purpose suggest little consideration of the potential policy tradeoffs in the context of finite fiscal resources. With budget constraints likely for at least the next few years, the state's failure to set priorities among competing policy goals—that is, increased research capacity or increased undergraduate access and success—may undermine the state's ability to achieve either goal.

Texas has made progress in several areas of higher education performance over the past decade, but more work is required to close gaps in attainment across groups and raise overall attainment to the level required to meet employers' needs. The state may be able to consolidate and advance these gains by developing policies for higher education finance that are better aligned with state goals and priorities.

Chapter 8

State Policy Leadership Vacuum

The Performance and State Policies of Higher Education in Washington

WITH CONTRIBUTIONS BY MICHAEL ARMIJO AND JAMEY RORISON

Washington has one of the highest levels of education attainment in the nation.[1] It ranks thirteenth among all U.S. states, with 42% of adults age 25 and older in Washington having attained an associate degree or more in 2008.[2]

Nonetheless, for the state of Washington, measuring attainment at the associate degree level is insufficient. As suggested by its top ranking on the State New Economy Index, Washington's economic prosperity depends on the availability of workers who have earned at least a bachelor's degree. Sponsored by the Ewing Marion Kauffman Foundation and the Information Technology and Innovation Foundation, the State New Economy Index "measures the extent to which state economies are knowledge-based, globalized, entrepreneurial, IT-driven and innovation-based."[3]

The number of new jobs projected by 2018 that will require at least some postsecondary education is higher in the state of Washington than in nearly every other state. Many more new jobs in the state (259,000 between 2008 and 2018) will require workers to have at least some postsecondary education than will require no more than a high school education (107,000).[4] By 2018, 70% of all jobs in Washington are projected to require workers to have at least some postsecondary education or training, a higher percentage than the national average (63%).[5] The state projects job reductions in logging, manufacturing, and some other traditional industries but job increases in other industries, including business services, computer-related industries, and health care.[6] A state policy expert we interviewed characterized the state economy as one of the most technology-intensive in the nation.

To meet the demands of employers and reach the level of educational attainment of top-performing states and countries, Washington must improve both associate and baccalaureate degree production in higher education. To date, the state has relied on its ability to attract well-educated residents from other states and countries to fully meet these demands.

In its *2008 Strategic Master Plan for Higher Education*, the Washington Higher Education Coordinating Board identified as its primary goal the need to increase educational attainment, particularly among younger residents.[7] Based on trends in degree production and projections of population growth, Washington must increase its annual production of associate and bachelor's degrees by 6.2% each year in order for 55% of its workforce (ages 25 to 64) to hold at least an associate degree by 2020, which is the level of attainment of the best-performing nations.[8]

To reach the required levels of educational attainment, the state must reduce gaps in higher education outcomes that persist across demographic groups. As noted in the *2008 Strategic Master Plan for Higher Education*, the state is home to increasing numbers of "people who have not fared well" in the state's educational system, including "the poor, people of color, and immigrants."[9] The state's high overall attainment masks the lower attainment of Hispanics and Blacks compared with Whites. In Washington, 17% of Hispanics and 34% of Blacks age 25 to 64 had earned at least an associate degree in 2005, compared to 44% of Whites and 54.8% of Asians.[10]

Efforts to increase educational attainment will need to recognize and account for constraints on available fiscal resources. As described in chapter 3, Washington is a relatively wealthy state. Wealth is concentrated in the Seattle/Tacoma metro areas, whereas the poorer counties tend to be in the southwestern and eastern parts of the state. Despite its relatively high median personal and family income, state residents appear to have little appetite for increasing taxes.[11] Washington is one of the few states in the nation without an income tax. In November 2010, voters defeated Ballot Initiative Measure 1098, which would have imposed an income tax on the state's most affluent residents and dedicated the revenues to education and health services. Washington's ability to raise revenues or increase expenditures for public services is also limited by Initiative 601, which was approved by voters in 1993 and modified in 2005.[12] Initiative 601 mandates an annual expenditure limit across the major state funding accounts, including the general fund, and "requires the governor's budget to be consistent with the expenditure limit."[13] Through a combination of revenue and expenditure restrictions, Initiative 601 constrains state spending during periods when the economy is booming, which in turn limits the state's ability to catch up from previous recessionary cuts and to keep pace with "caseload growth" in such areas as Medicaid, K–12 education, and higher education.[14]

As in other states, Washington has experienced state revenue shortfalls over the past several years that further constrain the availability of public funding for higher education. Following reductions to higher education by the legislature in the 2009–11 operating budget and the 2011 supplemental budget, the biennial budget for 2011–13 reduces appropriations to the state's public higher education institutions by 24% over 2007–9 and assumes a 20% increase in tuition revenue.[15] These appropriations could be reduced even further since, in November 2011, the state announced that revenues through June 2013 would be lower than projected, resulting in a $1.4 billion shortfall for the 2011–13 biennium.[16] Like other states, Washington will likely face continued budget constraints into the future as a result of projected structural deficits and other restrictions on revenues for higher education.

Higher Education Performance

Washington leads the nation in the percentage of students in four-year colleges and universities who graduate within six years of enrolling. However, the state's production of bachelor's degrees per capita is below the national average. Washington's performance also lags behind the national average in preparing students for college. The performance of the state's small but growing Hispanic population, when compared with Whites, is considerably lower on most indicators of college preparation, participation, and completion.

Preparation for Postsecondary Education

Despite some recent improvement, Washington continues to fall below national averages on many measures of academic preparation for postsecondary education. Washington's high school graduation rate of 67.9% in 2007, as calculated using the Cumulative Promotion Index (CPI), was the 16th lowest in the nation—lower than the median of most western states (72.6%) and well below the top-performing states (81.0%).[17] The state's *2008 Strategic Master Plan for Higher Education* points to "low levels of [secondary] educational attainment" as an important challenge to raising educational attainment generally, noting that one-fourth of adults in Washington between the ages of 18 and 24 lack a high school diploma; one-third of adults between the ages of 18 and 64 have attained only a high school diploma; and nearly half of Latinos ages 25 and older lack a high school diploma.[18]

Participation

Compared with other states, Washington performs poorly in the proportions of young and working-age adults enrolled in higher education. The state's *2008 Strategic Master Plan for Higher Education* reports a leaky educational "pipeline" for students on the way to completion of at least an associate degree; only 40 out of every 100 students who start ninth grade enter college on time.[19] Between 1991 and 2008 the percentage of 18- to 24-year-olds enrolled in college remained virtually unchanged in Washington, fluctuating between 28% and 30%, but increased nationwide from 29% to 36%.[20] In addition, 6% of 25- to 49-year-olds without a bachelor's degree were enrolled in postsecondary education in 2007, down from 7.8% in 1991. This enrollment rate is lower than the median of the five top-performing states (8.9%) but higher than the national average (5.6%) and comparable with other western states (6.0%).[21]

Completion

Washington is one of the top-ranked states in the nation in the share of students graduating from public four-year institutions within six years of enrolling. In 2008, about 65% of first-time full-time students completed a bachelor's degree within six years, substantially higher than the national average (56%) and the average for western states (48%). The state's performance on this measure increased from 61% in 1997.[22]

Despite this strong performance, however, Washington trails most other states in the total number of bachelor's degrees produced per capita. In 2007–8, Washington produced 22.4 bachelor's degrees per 1,000 residents ages 20 to 34—fewer than the national average (25.7).[23]

Washington performs better than the national average but below top-performing states in supporting student transfer from two-year to four-year institutions. Reframed from the perspective of community colleges, however, only 15% of students beginning at a two-year institution in fall 2002 graduated from a four-year institution within six years—more than the national average (12%) but fewer than the top-performing states (20%). Following a similar pattern, the share of students beginning at two-year institutions in fall 2002 who graduated with an associate degree within six years is higher than the national average (32% versus 21%), but lower than the top states (45%).[24]

Affordability

As in other states, attending college in Washington has become less affordable for students and their families in recent decades. The net price of college (college expenses less financial aid) represents a growing portion of family income at Washington's community colleges, its public four-year colleges and universities, and its private institutions. From the early 1990s to 2007, the net price of college as a share of median family income increased from 20% to 25% at public community colleges, from 22% to 31% at public four-year colleges and universities, and from 55% to 72% at private four-year colleges and universities.[25] From 1999 to 2009, median family income in Washington declined in constant dollars by 1.9%. During the same period, tuition increased in constant dollars by 42.4% at public two-year colleges and by 39.5% at public four-year colleges and universities.[26]

Gaps in Performance

Statewide performance in college preparation, participation, and completion in Washington masks substantial differences based on race/ethnicity and family income. High school graduation rates, as calculated using the CPI, were substantially lower in 2007 for Hispanics (55%) as compared with Whites (72%).[27] Smaller shares of Blacks and Hispanics than of Whites met state standards, as measured by scores on all portions of the 2008–9 Washington Assessment of Student Learning (WASL) and the new High School Proficiency Exam in 2009–10. Over the past decade, the difference in performance on state reading assessments between White and Hispanic tenth-graders narrowed from a 30.2 percentage point gap in 1999–2000 to a 13.8 percentage point gap in 2008–9. During the same period, however, the White-Hispanic gap did not narrow in math, with a 27.5 percentage point gap in 1999–2000 and a 27.9 percentage point gap in 2008–9.[28] In terms of performance by family income, 20% of Washington students eligible for the federal free and reduced price lunch program scored at or above proficient on the eighth grade national assessment in math in 2010, compared with 51% of students whose family income level exceeded the limits for this program.[29]

College participation rates in the state are also lower for Hispanics than for students from other racial/ethnic groups. Among public high school graduates in

2008, only 45% of Hispanics (45%) enrolled in college within a year of graduation, compared with 60% of Blacks, 64% of Whites (64%) and 71% of Asian Americans.[30]

College completion rates are also substantially lower for Hispanics than for Whites. In 2008, 52% of Hispanics completed a bachelor's degree within six years, compared with 66% of Whites.[31] Among full-time students who are seeking degrees at the state's community and technical colleges, only about half of Hispanics (49%) and Blacks (48%) were "making substantial progress" toward their degrees compared with about two-thirds of Whites (63%) and Asian-Americans (65%). Substantial progress is defined as "graduating or earning some credit in four or more quarters over a two-year period."[32]

The Structure of Higher Education in Washington

Although Washington was home to 23 private not-for-profit four-year institutions and 19 for-profit institutions in fall 2010,[33] most students are enrolled in a public college or university. About 85% of students enrolled in degree-granting institutions were attending a public rather than a private not-for-profit (12%) or private for-profit (3%) institution.[34]

Community colleges account for 64% of public enrollments in Washington, a substantially higher percentage than the national average (48%).[35] The State Board for Community and Technical Colleges (SBCTC) provides leadership for the state's 34 community and technical colleges. In 1991, the legislature shifted responsibility for technical colleges and adult basic education from the K–12 system to this state board. The state and institutional leaders we spoke with noted the benefits of this structural change, with one leader stating that this restructuring intentionally put "all of postsecondary workforce education in the same place." Some described this change as increasing "attention and resources" for adult basic education and allowing statewide actions "as a system to advance state policy initiatives that were really about making education and training available to more people."

What Explains the Higher Education Performance in Washington?

Given this structure, what accounts for recent patterns of higher education performance in Washington? More specifically, what accounts for the state's relatively low levels of college preparation and high rates of bachelor's degree completion for those who enroll, but low total production of bachelor's degrees?[36] Although other forces also play a role, three themes drive these outcomes: (1) lack of political commitment to implementing a statewide plan for higher education, (2) insufficient strategies to support student readiness for and participation in bachelor's degree programs, and (3) failure to strategically use available fiscal resources to achieve statewide goals and priorities.

Lack of Political Commitment to Implementing a Statewide Plan for Higher Education

Over the past several years, state policymakers and college and university leaders in Washington have repeatedly articulated the need to improve college preparation and raise degree production. In its January 2011 final report, the governor's Higher Education Funding Task Force called for the state's six public universities to increase bachelor's degree production, especially in science, technology, engineering, and math (STEM). More specifically, the task force called for producing 6,000 more bachelor's degrees annually by 2018, with one-third of those degrees coming from STEM fields.[37] The state has produced several other plans that document the need to improve educational attainment and that describe the magnitude of the improvement required. Unlike in most other states, Washington's legislature has approved these plans. However, the state has had difficulty gaining traction on statewide initiatives based on these planning efforts. At the time of our data collection, the state was attempting to change higher education governance by eliminating the Higher Education Coordinating Board, the entity in the state charged with state policy leadership. It is too early to identify the effects of this change on higher education performance.

State Planning Efforts but Minimal Changes in State Policies

Washington Learns was an important planning effort that laid the foundation for education policy discussions in the state. Created by the state legislature in 2005 (through SB 5441), the Washington Learns Steering Committee and its advisory committees studied the state's education system, structure, and funding before issuing a comprehensive set of recommendations in November 2006. Governor Christine Gregoire (D), who was inaugurated in 2005, co-chaired the steering committee and submitted the final report. Contributing to the planning effort were advisory committees focusing on early learning, K–12 education, and higher education.

The overall statewide goal, as identified in *Washington Learns*, is "to raise educational attainment in Washington through a world-class, learner-focused, seamless education system in order to compete globally and thrive locally."[38] In 2006, the legislature took action on six of the seven recommendations presented in the interim report:

1. Established a new cabinet-level Department of Early Learning,
2. Created a new program to provide academic support to high school students in math,
3. Provided funding to make available to all high school students programs that provide information about college and careers,
4. Established a program to provide grants for pre-apprenticeship career pathway programs,
5. Provided funding to continue the Transitions Mathematics Project, and
6. Provided funding to support development of the longitudinal student data system.[39]

The legislature discussed but did not take action on the report's recommendation to "provide high school students the opportunity to assess college readiness during the 10th or 11th grade."[40] Of the report's recommendations, this one may have had the most potential to improve coordination between K–12 schools and higher education.

One of the five major initiatives in the Washington Learns final report focuses on increasing opportunities for college and workforce training. Several of the strategies outlined in the "quality and accountability" initiative also pertain to higher education, including creating a P–20 Council, benchmarking performance and funding to the Global Challenge States (the nation's top-performing states on the New Economy Index), establishing a state tuition policy for higher education, improving accountability through performance agreements in the state budget for colleges and universities, and establishing a ten-year plan for colleges and universities to increase enrollment capacity to "accommodate high school graduates and adults, with an emphasis on increased degree production in high-demand fields."[41]

Nonetheless, despite its efforts to include some strategies to improve higher education, Washington Learns appears to have had minimal impact on higher education in the state, with the exception of laying a strong foundation for the state's *2008 Strategic Master Plan for Higher Education in Washington*. According to a state legislator, "Higher ed could have been addressed more out of Washington

Learns, but I think that became an early foundation piece for the master plan. I think those conversations helped because the master plan came right along after that."

Produced by the Washington Higher Education Coordinating Board (HECB), the *2008 Strategic Master Plan* builds on *Washington Learns* and on planning documents from the State Board for Community and Technical Colleges and the Workforce Training and Education Coordinating Board. Per state law, HECB is required to develop "a strategic master plan for higher education every 10 years and update the plan every four years."[42]

The primary statewide goal identified in the *2008 Strategic Master Plan* is "to increase the total number of degrees and certificates produced annually," so that Washington continues to lead other Global Challenge States (GCS) in the production of associate degrees and certificates but "would move from sixth to third among the GCS in terms of bachelor's degrees awarded and from last to fifth in advanced degrees awarded."[43] The master plan calls for three broad efforts to achieve its vision by 2018: (1) increase enrollment and success in postsecondary education, (2) use education and research resources to advance economic growth and innovation, and (3) create "a new system of incentives and accountability that rewards higher education institutions that help achieve the goals" identified in the plan.[44] The plan also specifies that increasing educational attainment will require: greater funding to expand enrollment capacity at colleges and universities, additional strategic planning to improve the distribution of enrollment across sectors, and other strategies to increase student access and success.

A few state and institutional leaders we spoke with criticized the *2008 Strategic Master Plan* as lacking rigor, innovation, and solutions, as well as including unrealistic goals and having limited impact. In the words of the leader of one of the state's business organizations, "It is safe to say the state legislators and governor have understood it [the master plan], and it has been kind of constant in the policy reports that have been produced, yet the state has not made much headway on it and certainly isn't making any at this time."

Governor Gregoire identified education as a top priority during her term in office, but the state and institutional leaders we interviewed gave mixed reviews to her efforts to develop and implement higher education policy, including her efforts to follow up on the recommendations of the master plan. Some acknowledged that the governor had played an important role in using her "bully pulpit" to garner support for the master plan and for Washington Learns. But many also described her inability to influence the legislature or advance a statewide rather than an institutional or sector-based policy agenda for higher education.

Current fiscal restrictions may have limited efforts to achieve the master plan's goals, including its objective to increase bachelor's degree attainment. As a staff member to the state senate noted, "In many ways, the economy overwhelmed them [HECB] because the [master] plan has big goals within ten years—increasing production by 20,000 students a year, things like that. Even in the best of times [these goals are] quasi-attainable. The legislators did buy in, but I am not sure if they realized what that would really take."

Ineffective Structures and Strategies for Advancing Statewide Goals and Priorities

Even before the current fiscal downturn, state policy efforts often reflected institutional and sector-based needs rather than a shared, statewide perspective on the goals and priorities for higher education. An emphasis on institutional over statewide priorities may be attributable in part to the absence of effective mechanisms for fostering collaboration or coordination across public and private, two-year and four-year sectors as well as across institutions within the public four-year sector. As one longtime state policy observer described, "When Washington Learns was operating, the governor pejoratively used the term *silos*. She talked about education as a field full of separate silos. It was a good metaphor because that is how it is. You have the four-year publics, the four-year privates, the community colleges, and they all have their little fiefdoms." Another state policy expert told us that each of the public four-year institutions emphasizes its own needs rather than pursuing a common agenda.

Governor Gregoire sought to create structural changes to facilitate collaboration and cooperation across education agencies but has had limited success. As recommended in *Washington Learns,* Governor Gregoire created, via executive order in May 2007, a P–20 Council. The council's charge was to "hold state government accountable and measure progress toward ten long-term goals for a world-class education system" that were developed by Washington Learns.[45] The P–20 Council had 11 members, with representatives from the offices of the Governor, Superintendent of Public Instruction, Department of Early Learning, State Board of Education, Professional Educator Standards Board, HECB, Workforce Training and Education Coordinating Board, State Board for Community and Technical Colleges, Council of Presidents, Independent Colleges of Washington, and tribal education programs. Nonetheless, according to a state policy expert, the P–20 Council was very short-lived and met only a few times.

The concept of a single entity focused on improving performance and alignment across all systems of K–12 and higher education is assumed to be a central role of the state Department of Education that the governor proposed in January 2011. This new entity would have combined existing state early learning, K–12 education, and higher education agencies into one cabinet-level Department of Education, with the vision of creating "a seamless" and "student-centered" education system. This proposal came midway through the governor's second term and reached beyond the recommendations of Washington Learns and other previous state policy discussions. The goals of the governor's proposed consolidation were to

1. Focus on students and student learning,
2. Promote coordinated, innovative, flexible, student-centered services,
3. Eliminate duplication and provide more efficient administration,
4. Provide clear lines of authority and responsibility to increase accountability, and
5. Provide a "one-stop education shop" for the public.[46]

The governor's proposal, which would require legislative approval, was described as "sure to be controversial" in news reports at the time.[47] In particular, the proposed elimination of the elected state superintendent's position in favor of an appointed post generated immediate political opposition as soon as the proposal was announced. The legislature did not approve this reorganization in its 2011 session, and the governor did not advance it again in future sessions.

Meanwhile, the state leaders we spoke with expressed dissatisfaction with the existing governance frameworks for the state's public four-year colleges and universities, largely due to their inability to generate shared action toward statewide policy goals. State and institutional leaders consistently characterized the public four-year sector as "politically weak," unresponsive to the state's budget problems, and lacking coordination. The state's public four-year colleges and universities are decentralized, each with its own board that is appointed by the governor and approved by the state senate. The Council of Presidents, a voluntary association established in 1968 by the presidents of these institutions, was designed to provide a forum for presidents and senior administrators "to convene, share views, debate issues of common interest, and where possible, achieve consensus on issues affecting higher education."[48] But achieving consensus among the presidents of these institutions has been difficult. A state policy expert suggested that the council's narrow focus on the public four-year sector has limited its impact on state policy: "The Council of Presidents can't really see beyond the traditional four-year institution vista. I'm sure that's a gross overstatement, but they can't even begin to speak for higher education. They have very little to do with workforce training in the state, and they have nothing to do with private colleges and universities."

State and institutional leaders also told us that the Washington Higher Education Coordinating Board has played a limited role in promoting the attainment of statewide goals for higher education. The coordinating board was created by the state legislature in 1985, but predecessor boards had existed since 1970. The board was charged with providing "strategic planning, coordination, monitoring, and policy analysis for higher education in Washington,"[49] as well as with representing "the broad public interest above the interests of the individual colleges and universities."[50] The board also has administered the state student financial aid programs. State leaders generally praised the board for its management of student financial aid but criticized its efforts in developing statewide policies for higher education. One leader summarized this view, saying there is "a lot of satisfaction with how student financial aid is operated, but a lot of dissatisfaction with the board's ability to act in that policy role."

Likely reflecting this discontent with the board's effectiveness, the legislature in spring 2011 abolished the Higher Education Coordinating Board, effective July 1, 2012. The board was to be replaced by two new entities: the Office of Student Financial Assistance, and the Council on Higher Education.[51] The "purpose and functions of the Council for Higher Education" were to be determined by a higher education steering committee that is made up of representatives from the governor, legislature, higher education institutions, and the public.[52] The law creating this change acknowledges the broad role of the Higher Education Coordinating Board in the past, but it emphasizes the importance of "prioritizing scarce resources" and creating an entity devoted strictly to administering student financial aid so as to provide "the highest level of service" in this area.[53] The law authorizing these changes also indicates the legislature's perception that the coordinating board is ineffective in its policy functions and delegates the board's public policy responsibilities to the colleges and universities, as the law states:

> The legislature further intends to eliminate many of the policy and planning functions of the higher education coordinating board and rededicate those re-

> sources to the higher education institutions that provide the core, front-line services associated with instruction and research. Given the unprecedented budget crises the state is facing, the state must take the opportunity to build on the recommendations of the board and use the dollars where they can make the most direct impact.[54]

In contrast to the dissatisfaction regarding the Higher Education Coordinating Board, we found that state, institutional, and business leaders uniformly characterized the state's community college system as effective and politically strong. Although officially coordinated by the Higher Education Coordinating Board, the State Board for Community and Technical Colleges (SBCTC) has had its own budget and agenda-setting authority. It has also defined and pursued its own legislative agenda. Some described the community colleges as being more "flexible" and "adaptive to the education consumer" and to employers, compared with the public four-year institutions. A state policy expert summarized these views, praising the state's community colleges as being "very well led, very smart about using their geographic impact, the fact that they are spread in everybody's legislative district. They are perceived as responsive to different players, they do their legislative relations very well, and they produce a good product. They are one of the best community college systems in the country and they act on it."

Coordinating the state's 34 community and technical colleges is certainly not without challenge. Nonetheless, the leaders we spoke with emphasized the high level of collaboration and consensus among the community colleges and their statewide board. As a leader of a community college said, "We collaborate certainly with the state office pretty directly in terms of setting the legislative agenda. . . . That is really a presidential interest and trustee sort of prerogative. Somehow in some magic negotiations between the trustees and the presidents and the state board staff, they hammer out kind of a state legislative agenda that we all kind of can agree on."

With the governor's call for a new Department of Education and the elimination of the Higher Education Coordinating Board in 2012, it remains to be seen how the State Board for Community and Technical Colleges will work with the four-year colleges to increase baccalaureate degree production, one of the state's priorities for higher education.

Insufficient Strategies to Support Student Readiness for and Participation in Bachelor's Degree Programs

State and institutional leaders we interviewed repeatedly described a disconnect in the state between the high rate of student enrollment in community colleges and the low rate of bachelor's degree production per capita. Among the contributors to this disconnect are insufficient academic preparation to enroll in four-year institutions, a mismatch between the distribution of the population and the location of public four-year colleges and universities, and disincentives for four-year institutions to enroll transfer students. Community colleges have received authority to offer bachelor's degrees in applied technical fields, but the numbers of degrees awarded through these programs have been very small and raise questions about mission creep.

Insufficient Academic Preparation to Enroll in Four-Year Institutions

The state operates several programs that are perceived by many to improve students' academic readiness for college. For traditional-age students, Running Start, the largest dual enrollment program in the state, enables high school students to simultaneously earn college and high school credits. Through the program, high school juniors and seniors can enroll in designated courses offered at one of the state's 34 community or technical colleges or at Central Washington University, Eastern Washington University, Washington State University, or Northwest Indian College. In 2009–10, 3% of the associate degrees and certificates awarded by the state's community and technical colleges were received by high school students participating in Running Start. Although some state policy experts question these estimates, a progress report published by the State Board for Community and Technical Colleges claims notable financial benefits of the program: "With 12,459 FTES [full-time-equivalent student] enrollments in 2009–10, Running Start resulted in a savings of about $41.3 million for parents and students and about $53.2 million for taxpayers. The savings represent the tuition and state support costs of 12,459 FTE students attending a higher education institution for one year."[55]

The effectiveness of Running Start in improving academic readiness for college may be limited, however, by the underrepresentation of racial/ethnic minorities and lower-income students. Students of color represent 22% of Running Start students but 35% of students enrolled in programs funded by both state funding and funding from external organizations. Moreover, participants are largely from "middle-class to high-income families, with approximately 15% of Running Start students receiving waivers from fees, indicating low income."[56]

Whereas Running Start focuses on preparing more high school students for college, the Integrated Basic Education and Skills Training (I-BEST) program, is a national model for promoting educational attainment among adult learners. The program pairs instructors of English as a second language (ESL) or adult basic education with professional-technical instructors "to concurrently provide students with literacy education and workforce skills." In a 2005 report, the Washington State Board for Community and Technical Colleges quantified the benefits of the program: "I-BEST students earned five times more college credits on average and were 15 times more likely to complete workforce training than were traditional ESL students during the same amount of time."[57]

Available at all 34 community and technical colleges, the I-BEST program is designed to provide an educational pathway for students, beginning with a high school diploma and continuing to at least a certificate. A leader at the State Board for Community and Technical Colleges explained,

> Everything they learn builds also towards a two-year degree, which articulates to the four-year degree. That was the other change in mindset we've had as a system: no more terminal or dead-end courses. Everything we teach has to have a pathway and articulate to the next credentials or the next step. Anyone who gets a high school diploma or GED has to have enough then to build on to the two-year. The certificates all have got to go to the two year. . . . The standard we are at right now is that nobody should leave us without getting at least one year's worth of college credits and a certificate of some kind. . . . But we view that as the floor rather than the goal; that's the minimum you get people to.

Despite the potential benefits of these two long-standing programs, the state has made slower progress in systemically improving college readiness for all students by aligning high school graduation requirements with college entrance requirements. *Washington Learns* called for the State Board of Education to "amend high school graduation requirements to include a minimum of three years of math" by December 2007 and for the Higher Education Coordinating Board to "amend minimum college admissions standards to require three years of math, including math in the senior year, or demonstrated competence in math skills through algebra II" by September 2007.[58] However, a leader in the state department of education described on-going challenges to accomplishing this goal: "The [high school] graduation standard has not been very strong. It's getting better and better and better, but you used to be able to take, in math for example, you only needed two years of math. Well, this year's group of freshmen now needs three. They could take pre-algebra and general math forever and that would get them out of high school."

High school graduation requirements remained below the minimum requirements for enrolling in a state public four-year institution through 2011. State statutes require the Higher Education Coordinating Board to "establish minimum college admissions standards" for entrance into public four-year colleges and universities.[59] As of summer 2010, the requirement was for at least 15 credits in high school, including four credits in English, three credits in math, two credits in laboratory-based science, three credits in social science, one credit in art, two credits in foreign language, and one credit in a senior year math-based quantitative course.[60] In November 2010, the Washington State Board of Education recognized that the state's high school graduation requirements were not aligned with minimum college admissions requirements, were lower than those of other states, and were the same as those required of the state's high school graduates in 1985. In response, the state board adopted "a new set of career and college-ready graduation requirements" that is aligned with the minimum four-year public college admission requirements. The requirements will take effect for the graduating class of 2016.[61] Nonetheless, while ensuring that students have taken the minimum courses required for admission to public four-year institutions in the state, these new requirements do not ensure that students are prepared to meet the academic expectations of higher education.

The state has only recently revised its mechanisms for assessing academic preparation. In spring 2010, the state replaced the Washington Assessment of Student Learning (WASL) with two tests: the Measurements of Student Progress (MSP) for students in third through eighth grade and the High School Proficiency Exam (HSPE) for high school students. Students must now pass the HSPE (or state-approved equivalent) to graduate from high school. The state has also recently developed and is now implementing standard end-of-course exams to assess course-specific knowledge and skills. In spring 2011, end-of-course exams replaced the math portion of the HSPE. Students in grades 7–12 began taking end-of-course biology exams in spring 2012.

Mismatch between the Distribution of the Population and the Location of Public Four-Year Colleges and Universities

A second challenge that contributes to relatively low rates of bachelor's degree production in Washington involves the lack of alignment between the distribution of the population and the location of the public four-year colleges and universities. The state's public comprehensive institutions are designed to serve particular regions, but there are only four of these institutions. One of the state's two research universities (Washington State University) is in a relatively isolated area. In contrast, the state's population is not only dispersed over large sparsely populated areas of the states but also condensed in areas without sufficient access to four-year institutions. The Higher Education Coordinating Board describes this challenge as follows: "While Washington has an abundance of natural resources, the impact of mountains and waterways and the limited access to highways in some areas make it difficult for portions of the population to go to college. Low population density over large tracts of land also makes it difficult to provide opportunities for people to go to college. Conversely, rapid population growth in some areas where we have minimal higher education presence also poses challenges."[62]

In its *Regional Analysis Report 2011*, the Higher Education Coordinating Board documents the positive relationship between the availability of higher education institutions and college participation rates. The report also suggests the importance of geographic proximity to college participation, stating, "Students tend to enroll in colleges and universities that are nearby. Not surprisingly, UW, WSU, and TESC [The Evergreen State College] have the most geographically diverse attendance patterns, but the branch campuses and regional institutions tend to draw more heavily from the counties in or close to where they are located."[63]

Given the distribution of public four-year colleges and universities, the state's 34 community and technical colleges are the primary point of access to college for many Washington residents. These institutions are dispersed throughout the state and offer opportunities to enroll via distance education. The state appropriated about $1.1 million to the community and technical colleges in fiscal year 2010 and again in 2011 "to enhance online distance learning and open courseware technology." The state required that the funds be allocated "based solely upon criteria of maximizing the value of instruction and reducing costs of textbooks and other instructional materials for the greatest number of students in higher education, regardless of the type of institution those students attend."[64]

Consequently, the state has a high rate of community college enrollment but continues to face challenges increasing its low rate of bachelor's degree production. Washington has attempted to expand regional access to four-year degree programs by creating branch campuses of the research universities. Together, the state's two public research universities have five branch campuses: two for the University of Washington and three for Washington State University.

Established with support from the coordinating board and the legislature in the early 1990s, the branch campuses' effectiveness for achieving state goals and priorities is limited for several reasons. One challenge is the affiliation of branch campuses with the state's public research universities rather than with the less-expensive comprehensive institutions. As in other states, Washington's public research universities offer baccalaureate and graduate programs, including doctoral and professional degrees, while its comprehensive institutions offer programs leading to bachelor's and master's degrees. A policy scholar described the irony of assigning the branch campuses to the state's research universities, explaining that the branches "were not designed to look much like research university campuses. Rather, the branches were very specifically designed to meet the identified access needs of their regions without many other 'frills.' "[65] A state policy expert observes the negative implications of branch campuses for the cost of higher education: "[Washington does not] have a cheap system because they have grown in their most expensive sector. It was, I think, foolish on their part. When they built additional capacity, they built it in Washington State University and in the University of Washington rather than in their state colleges, and they allowed all of their state colleges to become comprehensive universities. And so they have a relatively expensive model on which to work."

Branch campuses have also had a limited effect on bachelor's degree production. In a concession to the state's community colleges and private colleges and universities, enrollment at the branch campuses was initially restricted to upper-division students.[66] In 2006, however, the branch campuses were permitted to enroll freshmen.[67] In addition to the initial restriction of branch campuses to upper-division coursework, the impact of branch campuses has been further restricted by inadequate funding and lack of diverse programming. A leader in the state higher education coordinating board told us, "We've got a research institutional branch campus structure that's anemically under-developed. We've got branch campuses around the state that took a very long time to build enrollments, way below initial expectations. They've been around for 20 years and they are still bumping up around 2,000 or so FTES [full-time-equivalent students] per institution when, back when they were created, it was expected they'd be between 6,000 and 10,000 by this time."

Another strategy the state has used to expand access to bachelor's degree programs is "university centers." Yet this approach has also had limited impact. Washington now has ten university centers that provide baccalaureate degree programs and that are "operated jointly by two- and four-year institutions or on a stand-alone basis."[68] A former leader of the state higher education coordinating board explained: "In the last two decades the state has almost formalized the 2 + 2 approach where four-year institutions—mostly the so-called regional institutions—it's mostly been Central and Eastern—but they have partnered with community colleges and jointly built buildings on the college campus. You have 500 to 1,000 FTES getting baccalaureate degrees through a four-year institution but located on a community college campus. We call those university centers."

Although the rate of growth in bachelor's degrees awarded is greater at the branch campuses and university centers than overall for the state, the actual numbers of degrees awarded by branch campuses and university centers are still relatively small. From 2000–2001 to 2005–6, the number of bachelor's degrees awarded from all institutions in the state increased by 15%. The number of bachelor's degrees awarded over this period grew by 69% at the centers and 41% at the branch campuses, compared with increases of only 10% at the main campuses of the research universities and 8% at the comprehensive institutions.[69]

Even with the faster rate of growth at the centers and branch campuses, however, the main campuses of the research universities continue to produce about half of all bachelor's degrees awarded by public colleges and universities in the state (48% in 2005–6). In 2005–6, about one-third (35%) of bachelor's degrees were awarded by comprehensive colleges; only 10% were awarded by the branches and 7% by the centers.[70] Moreover, enrollment at the branch campuses continues to be below capacity. The 1990 Strategic Plan for higher education asserted that the five branch campuses had capacity to enroll 12,700 upper-division and 4,300 graduate students, or 17,000 total students.[71] But, although enrollments have been increasing over time, only 9,133 students were enrolled at the branch campuses in 2010–11.[72]

Transfer to Four-Year Institutions Promoted by Articulation Policies but Disincentives for Four-Year Institutions to Enroll Transfer Students

As the Higher Education Coordinating Board notes, transfer is critical to improving bachelor's degree attainment, given the state's relatively high reliance on community and technical colleges as the point of entry into the higher education system.[73] About one-third (n=113,358) of all students enrolled in community and technical colleges in 2009–10 reported that they expected to transfer. Considerably fewer students actually transfer, although the number of students transferring from two-year programs to four-year colleges and universities has been increasing. From 2005–6 to 2009–10, the number of transfers from community and technical colleges to four-year institutions increased 12% (from 14,719 to 16,438 students). In 2009–10, about twice as many students transferred from community and technical colleges to public four-year institutions (10,563) compared with private four-year institutions (5,875). But the rate of growth over this period was greater at private institutions (led by the University of Phoenix) than public four-year institutions (36.9% versus 1.3%). The share of students who graduated from a public four-year institution within three years of transferring has been increasing over time, rising from 63% in 2001–2 to 72% in 2009–10.[74]

As authorized by state statute, the Higher Education Coordinating Board has established several policies designed to facilitate the transfer of credits from two-year to four-year institutions. The Policy on Intercollege Transfer and Articulation among Washington Public Colleges and Universities, established by the Higher Education Coordinating Board in response to legislation passed in 1983, specifies that community college students who complete an approved associate degree program enter public and participating private four-year institutions in the state with junior-year status and lower-division and general education requirements met.[75] In 2009–10, 13,074 students completed the Direct Transfer Agreement, 169 students completed a local transfer agreement, and 730 students completed the Associate in Science-Transfer program. By comparison, only 8,064 completed an associate degree in applied science (a "workforce" degree) and 51 completed an applied bachelor's degree.[76] Students who complete one of 19 Major Related Pathways within the Direct Transfer Agreement tend to complete bachelor's degrees with few excess credits but, in 2009–10 only 1,514 completed one of these specialized programs.[77]

In addition to relatively few students completing a Major Related Pathway, another aspect of the transfer process also has limitations: the capacity of four-year colleges and universities to accept transfer students. Increases in enrollment at community colleges are perceived by some state and institutional leaders to increase pressure on public and private four-year institutions to accept more transfer students. The representation of students who have transferred from state community colleges varies considerably across public four-year universities, and this variation has been approved by the Higher Education Coordinating Board as part of a proportionality agreement adopted in 1994. This agreement requires each public four-year institution "to admit a certain percentage of community college transfer students as a proportion of its newly enrolled students, based on its 1992–93 transfer levels."[78] In its *2011 Transfer Report*, the coordinating board concludes that all public four-year institutions meet their transfer goals, which vary from 27% to 32% of new enrollments at most institutions but range to 52% at the University of Washington, Bothell, and 72% at the University of Washington, Tacoma. Data in other reports suggest a different range of variation, with one report showing community college transfers among new enrollments at 13% at the University of Washington, Seattle; 46% at Washington State Tri-Cities; 47% at Washington State University, Vancouver; and 52% at the University of Washington, Tacoma.[79] The University of Washington, Seattle, reports allocating 30% of new undergraduate admission slots each year to students who have transferred from Washington community colleges and/or have completed at least 40 transfer credits at a Washington community college through the Running Start program.[80] A state policy expert said that the University of Washington is often criticized for no longer accepting all transfer applications, something it had done in the past.

Leaders of both two-year and four-year institutions expressed concern about the implications of continued growth in the number of transfer students for the capacity and funding of four-year colleges and universities. The University of Washington, Seattle, reports giving priority to student transfers from state community colleges who have earned academic associate degrees or 90 transferable credits,[81] but some state leaders point to the lack of upper-division capacity as limiting bachelor's degree production in the state. In addition, the devolution of tuition responsibility to public four-year colleges and universities (described later in this chapter) may provide an incentive for institutions to admit more out-of-state students, since these students pay higher tuition; this strategy may reduce the number of slots available to transfer students. As the leader one public university said, "We are trying to figure out how we work with the universities to expand capacity at the upper-division level. That is the pinch point in our state: upper division capacity, not freshman capacity."

Expansion of Community College Missions to Award Bachelor's Degrees in Applied Science

In an effort to expand access to bachelor's degree programs, the state has allowed community colleges to award bachelor's degrees in applied science. The legislature initially established applied baccalaureate programs on a pilot basis in 2005 and then removed the pilot status in 2010. A state policy expert said that this initiative was designed to expand educational opportunities to students who are not located near four-year institutions, meet employer demands more effectively, and respond to a lack of interest by the state's research universities to offer such programming. At the time of our data collection, applied baccalaureate degrees were being offered by 7 of the state's 34 community and technical colleges in a small number of technical fields, including interior design, behavioral science, applied management, hospitality management, radiation and imaging sciences, nursing, and applied design.

Allowing community colleges to award applied bachelor's degrees may expand the state's capacity to deliver upper-division curricular programming. For example, applied bachelor's degree programs may provide access to bachelor's degrees for otherwise underserved populations. A leader in the state board for community and technical colleges explained:

> We are trying to grow that technical-degree-to-bachelor's-degree pathway, because we believe it serves a different population than the typical 18-year-old coming out of high school who can afford to sit out of the labor force for four to six years and earn a bachelor's degree. Our workforce-education students by and large can't afford to do that. It isn't that they are more or less smart than anyone else. They cannot wait to get job skills, so they need to go out and get a job to feed their families. From our perspective, if you are really thinking about a continuum of postsecondary education achievement, then we have to provide multiple pathways for people across various kinds of circumstances or we are never going to hit that educational attainment goal.

Another community college leader said that offering applied bachelor's degrees at community colleges may also help the state meet unmet market demands:

> The specific example for us is we have a very strong respiratory therapy program. Great faculty, great innovators, they do really super stuff. We know that the respiratory therapy community as a profession is trying to move to a bach-

elor's degree, sort of like the nurses, there's an RN pathway; they want to ramp it up. We have the capacity to do that. We have a great program, they want to do that, and it meets an industry need. How can we turn our back on that?

Yet permitting community colleges to award applied bachelor's degrees may also bring another set of problems. In particular, allowing public community colleges to award applied bachelor's degrees may distort the mission of these institutions over time. A state policy expert said, "For these four-year degrees, students pay higher tuition, the colleges employ a different category of faculty—all the things that would lead to a distortion in the mission. The community and technical colleges are a good system, they really are, but they are not going to be good at doing this."

In addition, the demand for these programs so far does not appear to have reached the claims of market need. Community colleges have awarded small numbers of applied bachelor's degrees to date: 35 in 2008–9 and 51 in 2009–10.[82] Since many community and technical colleges have indicated interest, however, the number of awards may increase as these programs gain traction.

Efforts—but Challenges—to Strategically Using Available Fiscal Resources

In recent years, Washington's financing of higher education has had several strengths, especially relative to other states. First, the state's productivity in degree and certificate completion among those who start college is one of the best in the nation. Reflecting in part its proportionately large two-year sector, Washington also ranked third-lowest in terms of total funding from all sources (that is, tuition, fees, and state and local appropriations) per degree or certificate in 2006–7.[83]

Second, decisions about state funding for higher education and tuition have historically been more closely linked in Washington than in other states. For example, *Washington Learns* recommended that the "legislature establish a minimum system-wide goal to have all colleges and universities reach at least the 60th percentile of total per-student funding at comparable institutions in the Global Challenge States within ten years." With the goal of integrating state appropriations and tuition "to provide predictable and stable funding," the governor's Higher Education Funding Task Force likewise recommended in its January 2011 report that appropriations and tuition be linked to achieve the 60th percentile benchmark.[84] More specifically, the task force recommended that, "if state funding rises to the aspirational funding level or above, tuition may be frozen or even reduced if the state provides more support" and "the universities would increase enrollment to meet or exceed the degree production goals."[85] At the time of our writing, however, it does not appear that this recommendation has been adopted.

Nonetheless, as a result of these kinds of efforts, Washington has performed better than most states in maintaining a balance between the state and student share of higher education costs over the past decade. Through 2008 (prior to the recent economic downturn), Washington maintained the state's share of expenses for higher education. The share of average education and related expenses per full-time-equivalent student that was covered by state subsidies remained virtually unchanged from 2003 to 2008 at public research universities (decreasing from 62% to 61%) and public master's institutions (decreasing from 55% to 54%). The share that was covered by the state increased at community colleges from 71% to 75%.[86]

However, efforts to continue to link state funding and tuition have been challenged by the economic downturn in the state. One state policy expert pointed to these challenges, stating, "They [Washington] have done a very nice job on the financial aid side. Their finance policies overall are some of the most intentional in the West and are closer to being in sync than many other states but the current times are testing that."

Looking over a longer period that extends beyond 2008, state appropriations per FTE student decreased from 2000 to 2011 by 23% at the public research universities (in constant 2009 dollars) and by 20% at the public comprehensive institutions, but increased by 4% at community and technical colleges.[87] Unlike most other states but reflecting the distribution of enrollment across sectors, Washington's budget allocates greater total funding to the state's community and technical colleges than to the state's public four-year institutions. As described by a leader of one four-year public college, this distribution reflects a state commitment to protecting access:

> We give more funding to the community college sector than we do the public baccalaureate sector, and I think we are one of the only states in the nation that does that. It was really a shift that took place that has been going on for a long time, but really pronounced the past few years. Our sector [of public four-year institutions] was about $320 million more than the community colleges [in the 2007–9 operating budget approved May 2007], and now they get

> about $60 million more [in the 2011 supplemental budget approved December 2010], so there was nearly a $400 million shift. It happens every time there is an economic downturn. We try to protect the community colleges for access, worker retraining, and that sort of thing at our expense. The higher education pie doesn't grow any, it just gets shifted.[88]

In addition to the devolution of tuition-setting authority to the public four-year institutions, the state has also experienced challenges maintaining its strong historical commitment to providing need-based financial aid. The state has recently developed and begun to implement a performance-based funding system for its community and technical colleges but does not yet use funding to encourage improved performance among the public four-year institutions.

Devolution of Tuition-Setting Authority

Over the past several years, the state legislature has raised, and then eliminated, the ceiling on annual tuition increases for resident undergraduates.[89] For resident undergraduates, *Washington Learns* recommended that "the 2007 legislature set a cap on annual tuition increases of no more than 7%, . . . the historical average in Washington and . . . the annual increase assumed by the Guaranteed Education Tuition (GET) program."[90]

In response to recent declines in state appropriations, the state's research universities have advocated for greater tuition-setting authority. A leader of a public four-year college described the rationale for this position: "You cannot have it both ways from the state. The state can't cut the budget by 33% and ask us to continue to get people out of here on time without letting us raise tuition. I think part of the argument in allowing us to raise tuition 14% the last two years was that it was a lot better for students to be able to get the classes they need and move through the system in four years and pay a little more tuition."

At least some legislators recognize that the public often holds the legislature accountable for tuition increases. One state representative we interviewed told us,

> The public calls me. They don't call the institution. When higher education sits there and says, "We need a 14% increase because we can't afford to pay our bills," which is what happened two years ago, well that's a 100% increase in the cost for a four-year degree. Those people who have been saving, who struggle . . . well they just got shafted because of what? We can't financially manage the politics in our cost structure. Is that the public's problem? I'm their

representative. That's not their problem. So why are they getting screwed on this? Higher education needs to fix its problem first, and then we can negotiate something that makes more sense.

In a partial response to the recession and related higher education budget cuts, for the 2009–10 and 2010–11 academic years the legislature agreed that the governing boards of each of the state's public four-year institutions may raise tuition for resident undergraduates by up to 14% per year. Similarly, the State Board for Community and Technical Colleges was authorized to increase tuition by up to 7% per year for resident undergraduates and up to 14% per year for resident undergraduates enrolled in upper-division, applied baccalaureate programs.[91]

State and institutional leaders have also been debating whether to differentiate tuition and tuition-setting authority by institution. The governor's proposed budget for 2011–13 authorized greater tuition increases for public research universities than for comprehensive universities and for community and technical colleges. The senate's proposed budget authorized annual tuition increases of up to 16% at the University of Washington, Washington State University, and Western Washington University.[92] In January 2011, the governor's Higher Education Funding Task Force recommended that universities gain further authority to set tuition and that tuition rates be "linked to the level of state support and to the tuition charged by each institution's peer colleges."[93]

The Higher Education Coordinating Board also recommended that tuition rates be differentiated across four-year institutions but that resident undergraduate tuition rates continue to be determined by the legislature rather than delegated to institutions. Because of the latter recommendation, the coordinating board, as succinctly characterized by one state representative, "was not popular with our four-year institutions."

Despite the coordinating board's recommendation, in May 2011 the legislature passed and the governor signed legislation (HB 1795) granting authority for setting undergraduate tuition to each of the state's four-year colleges and universities through 2014–15, and with limits through 2018–19. In an effort to counter recent increases in nonresident and international student enrollments, the new law mandates that the University of Washington "enroll at least the same number of resident freshman undergraduate students each academic year as enrolled in 2009–10."[94]

Historical Commitment to Need-Based Student Financial Aid

Washington has attempted to improve college affordability for students by mandating that public four-year institutions allocate a portion of their tuition and fee revenues (above the amount the state appropriates for student aid) to need-based institutional financial aid. Per long-standing state law (RCW 28B.15.820), public baccalaureate institutions must allocate 3.5% of tuition and fees to institutional financial aid to financially needy students. In passing HB 1795 in May 2011, the legislature not only gave public four-year institutions tuition-setting authority but also raised the requirement for institutional financial aid to 5% of tuition and fees for institutions that increase tuition beyond the amount assumed in the operating budget and 4% of tuition and fees for all other public four-year institutions.[95] This increase is intended to help financially needy students compensate for the expected increases in tuition.

In recent years, Washington has been a national leader with regard to the availability of need-based state financial aid. Since 2005–6, Washington has ranked in the top five states nationally in the estimated need-based undergraduate grant dollars provided per FTE student. Total state grant expenditures as a percentage of state fiscal support for higher education increased from 11.3% in 2006–7 to 11.6% in 2007–8, to 12.3% in 2008–9, and to 15.2% in 2009–10. In 2009–10, Washington ranked twelfth nationally on this indicator, up from fourteenth in 2007–8 and 2008–9.[96]

Ninety-five percent of all available state financial aid in Washington is allocated to undergraduates based on financial need.[97] The largest state aid program, the State Need Grant, is available for undergraduates attending public two- and four-year colleges and universities, as well as accredited private-for-profit and not-for-profit institutions whose income is 70 percent or less of median family income.[98] According to the Higher Education Coordinating Board, "In 2009, state aid disbursements totaled more than $231 million annually to more than 77,000 students. Nearly all of this aid is need-based, directed to students whose families earn 30 percent less than the state's median household income of $75,000. For a family of four, this means an annual income of no more than $54,500. About 77,400 students attending 82 colleges and universities received state assistance last year through these programs."[99]

By awarding financial aid to students attending private institutions, the state is lowering the net price of attending these institutions and potentially expanding the capacity of the state's higher education system. Private colleges and universities awarded 27% of all bachelor's degrees produced in the state in 2008–9.[100] The maximum State Need Grant award at public research universities and private not-for-profit four-year institutions was $6,876 in 2009–10. At public four-year comprehensive institutions, the maximum State Need Grant award was $5,030 in 2009–10. At community and technical colleges as well as at private for-profit institutions, the maximum award was $2,690.[101]

In recent years, the state has increased the availability of resources for nontraditional students. Through the Less-than-Halftime State Need Grant, the legislature increased eligibility for the State Need Grant to part-time students. The program began as a pilot in 2005, was extended in 2007, and moved beyond pilot status in March 2011.[102] These efforts build on the recommendation from *Washington Learns* that eligibility for the State Need Grant program be extended "to low-income working adults who are only able to take one college class per term."

Unlike most states, Washington also allocates state financial aid dollars to a need-based State Work-Study Program. About 12% of available state aid is allocated to this program and any financially needy student is eligible.[103] A state policy expert characterized the State Work-Study Program as "probably the best in the country," as it "allows students to have jobs in nonprofit and for-profit ventures."

In response to state revenue shortfalls, the governor proposed a 2010 supplemental budget that included substantial reductions in the State Need Grant and Work-Study programs. In the end, the state fully funded the State Need Grant and restored funding for Work Study to 70% of its prior level.[104] Nonetheless, in recent years, available state aid has been insufficient to meet the demand from all eligible students. The Washington State Budget and Policy Center estimates that, because of budget cuts to higher education in 2009–10, "22,000 students who qualified for financial aid were unable to obtain assistance."[105]

Recognizing the importance of student financial assistance for low-income students and the realities of state revenue constraints, the state has proposed additional and alternatively funded student aid programs. For example, *Washington Learns* recommended establishing a new Washington Learns Scholarship Program to be targeted to low-income students and students whose parents have not earned a bachelor's degree. Beginning in the seventh and eighth grades, students would be informed of their potential eligibility for the aid and would begin receiving support services.

In addition, the governor's Higher Education Funding Task Force recommended creating the Washington Pledge Scholarships as a strategy for promoting bachelor's degree completion among low- and middle-income students. In its January 2011 report, the task force proposed to fund the program through individual and business donations, with the latter incentivized via a new tax credit. The governor's task force summarized the goal as follows:

> Our goal is to create over the next decade a $1 billion endowment for Washington Pledge Scholarships, funded by new, voluntary individual and business donations and incentivized by federal and state tax provisions. By establishing this as a private nonprofit fund, the state can guarantee these funds will always be used for one purpose and one purpose only—ensuring that the gates of our community colleges and public universities remain open to students of all economic backgrounds.[106]

In June 2011, the Boeing Company and Microsoft Corporation each pledged $25 million over five years to support the program.[107] At the time of our data collection, a state policy expert was skeptical about the state's ability to reach its $1 billion goal. Nonetheless, without a state income tax, Washington has fewer options for raising revenue than other states.

Use of State Funding to Incentivize Improved Institutional Performance

In its Student Achievement Initiative, Washington has recently developed a system for linking performance to funding for the state's public two-year institutions. Developed internally by the community and technical colleges, this performance funding system likely contributes to the credibility and political leverage of this sector. Designed to promote accountability and provide financial incentives to improve performance, the Student Achievement Initiative awards "points" in four areas: college readiness of adult basic education students and developmental education students; first-year college success; completion of math requirements; and completion of associate degrees, certificates, and apprenticeships. Each area is measured by academic indicators that research has shown to build "momentum" toward degree and program completion.[108] Financial rewards for colleges are based on annual improvements in overall performance, and colleges are rewarded with supplements to their base funding. The system developed the initiative in 2006, used 2007–8 as a "Learning Year," and first distributed funds based on performance in 2008–9.[109] Nonetheless, although the goal is to increase the incentives over time, total funds allocated based on performance have been very small to date—less than 1% of the system's total budget.[110]

The state has made steps toward implementing performance funding for the public four-year institutions, but these mechanisms are not currently in place. During the 1990s, the state "experimented with a performance funding factor" that allocated a certain percentage of institutional appropriations based on performance, but "this initiative ended after several years."[111] According to a state policy expert we interviewed, the initiative was in operation for only one year. In 2006, *Washington Learns* recommended,

> Beginning in January 2007, the governor's budget will describe specific, measurable results expected of colleges and universities in exchange for the institutional funding proposed. The state budget will include expectations for improvements in outcomes, such as the percentage of students from low- and middle-income families admitted to and retained in programs; the number of degrees produced in specific high-demand programs; the percentage of students who finish their program or degree on-time; and the average number of hours per week that buildings will be in use.

Efforts to implement performance funding for the public four-year institutions have been stalled by the recent fiscal challenges. In 2008, the legislature adopted "a performance agreement process for legislators, the governor's office, and the baccalaureate institutions to negotiate a six-year plan outlining what results will be achieved and the resources expected to achieve them." A committee was formed in 2008 and began its work, but "when the budget outlook for the state changed dramatically, the process was halted."[112]

Building on the National Governors Association's (NGA) Complete to Compete initiative that the governor led when she was chair of the NGA (2010–11), Governor Gregoire requested state legislation to create a new Baccalaureate Performance Incentive Program. Like the Student Achievement Initiative for the state's community colleges, this proposed program would provide incentives for four-year colleges and universities to demonstrate improved "student outcomes and student progress."[113] Legislation designed to implement the recommendations pertaining to performance and accountability from the higher education funding task force was introduced in February 2011 in the regular legislative session. It was reintroduced in the April 2011 special session but was not advanced (SHB 1666; SSB 5717). Legislation signed by the governor in May 2011 (HB 1795) advances a "performance reporting" system whereby the state's colleges and universities are required to annually report data on the metrics specified by Complete to Compete as well as measures of "graduate and professional degrees; science, technology, engineering, and mathematics [STEM] participation; student debt load; and disaggregation of measures based on various student demographics."[114]

Developing an effective system for incentivizing improved performance requires the availability and use of relevant data. The state has made progress in terms of tracking and using data to inform decision making, but more progress is required. While also identifying areas for improvement, the Education Sector concluded that Washington's higher education accountability system fares well in "aligning state priorities with concrete goals for achievement and formally linking budgetary decisions to the performance of state postsecondary institutions."[115] According to the 2009–10 Data Quality Campaign (DQC) survey, Washington had taken some actions needed to establish a strong "culture around how data are used to inform their decisions to improve system and student performance,"[116] but it must do more to "build state data repositories; provide timely role-based access to data; create progress reports with student-level data for educators, students, and parents to make individual decisions; create reports using longitudinal statistics to guide change at system level; implement policies to ensure educators know how to use data appropriately; and raise awareness to ensure all key stakeholders know how to access and use data."[117] At the time of our data collection, the Education Data and Research Center, which is housed in the Office of Financial Management in the Governor's Budget Office, was working to link databases that enable longitudinal tracking of students across successive educational levels, from early learning through higher education and into the workforce.

Washington is one of 29 states in the Smarter Balanced Assessment Consortium (SBAC), a collaboration established in December 2009 and awarded a Race to the Top assessment grant from the U.S. Department of Education in September 2010. A primary goal of SBAC is to "develop a student assessment system aligned to a common core of academic content standards."[118] Washington is also participating in a project led by the Western Interstate Commission on Higher Education (WICHE) that is designed to create a multistate data exchange that permits the tracking of students in four contiguous states through the education system and into the workforce.

Conclusion

Washington's system of public postsecondary education has some strengths, including a well-coordinated and well-respected community college system that has provided access to higher education for many state residents and workforce readiness for adult learners. Bachelor's degree completion rates are high for those fortunate enough to gain access to the state's public four-year institutions, but too few high school students attend four-year degree-granting institutions. The state has developed initiatives to increase access to public four-year colleges and universities, including university centers and branch campuses, and has allowed community and technical colleges to award applied baccalaureate degrees. These efforts, however, produce relatively few bachelor's degrees. As a result, the state lags behind other states in bachelor's degree production and depends heavily on imported talent.

The state has developed and received legislative approval for a number of plans for improving the performance of higher education. Although these plans provide a solid foundation, greater progress is required to ensure college readiness for all state residents and increase bachelor's degree production. The state has made limited progress in implementing a shared statewide public agenda for higher education. While its public four-year sector is perceived to be "politically weak" and uncoordinated, the legislature's decision to grant tuition-setting authority to these institutions reflects a broader state trend toward giving these institutions increasing responsibility for policy and leadership.

In the context of fiscal constraints, the state's historical efforts to link appropriations and tuition and use state financial aid to meet students' financial need are under challenge. The elimination of the Higher Education Coordinating Board and likely future reliance on public four-year institutions to drive policy may further limit the state's capacity to pursue a public agenda that is greater than the interests of individual campuses. The likelihood of continued fiscal challenges, projected demographic changes, and the need to meet projected workforce demands underscore the importance of state policy leadership for improving the state's higher education performance. Whether the state can implement a statewide plan for higher education that links statewide goals to resources regardless of whether the economy is contracting or expanding is yet to be seen.

Chapter 9

Lessons Learned

Conclusions and Implications

The importance of understanding how to improve higher education performance has never been greater, since educational attainment is increasingly required for the economic and social well-being not only of individuals but also of society. As Joseph Stiglitz argues, greater educational attainment will contribute "to a more efficient and dynamic economy."[1]

Despite the well-defined need for higher levels of educational attainment, all five of our selected states—like all U.S. states—must increase attainment if they are to be economically prosperous into the future. The magnitude and types of improvements that are required differ, as Georgia, for instance, must improve transfer between its technical colleges and its public colleges and universities and Washington must increase its production of bachelor's degrees. The direction of recent trends in higher education performance also varies across states, as higher education performance is low but improving in Texas and relatively high but declining in Illinois. These variations notwithstanding, however, current levels of higher education attainment in all states are below socially optimal levels. Moreover, the in-migration of college-educated workers (especially in Maryland and Washington) masks the degree of improvement in higher education attainment (especially with regard to college preparation) that is required for the native population.

Like other U.S. states, all five of our selected states must also do more to close the many gaps in higher educational attainment. Our analyses point to the importance of eliminating differences based not only on race/ethnicity and family income—characteristics that scholars typically highlight when assessing inequality—but also other characteristics including place of residence. As has been established in other research using other sources of data, higher education outcomes in the five states studied are consistently lower for Blacks and Hispanics than for Whites, and lower for those from lower-income than from higher-income families. Our state analyses also reveal variations in attainment based on age, with three of our five states (Georgia, Texas, and Washington) showing lower levels of educational attainment for younger adults (those age 25 to 34) than older adults (those age 45 to 64).[2] States must also consider variations in higher education outcomes based on geography. Our analyses show that higher educational attainment is especially low in the urban centers of Atlanta, Baltimore, and Chicago and in the rural areas of Washington, and that it varies considerably across the many large regions of Texas.

In short, despite the presence of numerous government policies, the opportunity to enroll in and complete college continues to vary dramatically across and within states. As described in chapter 1, states are unlikely to realize the overall levels of higher educational attainment that are required to meet projected workforce needs without closing these gaps. Progress is also essential if we as a society are to reduce continuing inequality in other indicators of individual and societal economic and social well-being. Across nations, policies that improve high school and college completion promote income equality, whereas policies that improve equity in educational attainment foster equity in employment outcomes and increase productivity.[3]

The five preceding chapters paint detailed pictures of the forces that explain the patterns of higher education performance within each state during the time period examined. It is tempting to conclude from these portraits that the forces that influence higher education attainment are highly idiosyncratic and are determined only by state-specific contextual characteristics, including the unique demographic, economic, political, historical, and cultural context and the particular configuration of a state's higher education system and structures.

Nonetheless, although providing vivid illustrations of the need to consider the state-specific context, our cross-case analyses also reveal the essential role that state policy can and must play in improving higher education performance. To raise higher educational attainment to the level required to meet workforce demands and improve equity across groups, state policy must intentionally address the current societal needs for higher education in ways that recognize the state's particular and evolving context.

This final chapter first describes the conceptual model that emerges from our analyses. The model draws from the findings from the state studies and builds on the guiding perspectives discussed in chapter 2. While each state chapter provides a rich picture of how public policy explains higher education performance within the multiple dimensions of a state's specific context, the emergent conceptual model explains the relationship between state public policy and higher education performance across states.

Despite their essential role, higher education policies are certainly not the only public policies that may be contributing to overall attainment or gaps in attainment within a state. Other state policies, including state approaches to taxation (which affect the availability of state revenues to support education expenses), early childhood education, and economic development undoubtedly also play a role. As discussed earlier in this volume, federal policies like No Child Left Behind and Race to the Top may also influence higher education attainment, both directly by promoting college preparation, and indirectly through their interaction with state policy. Other federal policies, including the LEAP program, the expansion over time of federal subsidized and unsubsidized loans, the level of funding for the Federal Pell Grant, and the availability of federal tax credits and tax incentives for college saving, may influence college affordability. Moreover, a number of intermediate organizations and initiatives are also seeking to improve higher education attainment not only in the five study states but also in other states across the nation. Such organizations include nonprofit organizations like Complete College America, Lumina Foundation, and the Bill and Melinda Gates Foundation.

Nonetheless, while we acknowledge that "any complex social phenomenon . . . likely has a multiple of causes," we share Acemoglu and Robinson's goal of offering "a simple theory." Following the example of Acemoglu and Robinson, our conceptual model does not "explain everything" but instead "provides a useful and empirically well-grounded explanation" for how public policy is related to higher education performance.[4] The understandings reflected in this model may not only be applicable to our five states but may also be transferable to other states. This conceptual model may also be used to identify potentially fruitful strategies for improving overall higher educational attainment and closing gaps in attainment across groups both within the five study states and more broadly.

Conceptual Model for Understanding How Public Policy Can Improve Higher Education Performance

The first tenet of our conceptual model (fig. 1) is that the relationship between public policy and higher education performance cannot be understood without considering the context, as defined by a state's historical, demographic, economic, political, and other state-specific characteristics. It is within the state-specific context that public policy has previously influenced, and will continue to influence into the future, both overall higher education attainment and equity in higher education attainment across groups.

The second tenet of our conceptual model stresses the centrality, within the state context, of state policy leadership and steering for improving the performance of higher education. A state's success in raising overall higher education attainment and closing gaps in attainment across groups depends on how and to what extent a state advances a cohesive public agenda that reflects the state's particular higher education needs and relevant contextual characteristics, including the structure of its higher education system and the mission and goals of its higher education institutions. This tenet shows the continued applicability but necessary extension and refinement of the foundational ideas developed by Berdahl, Glenny, Clark, and Richardson (as described in chapter 2) for understanding the role of the state in advancing public priorities.

Consistent with human capital theory and macroeconomic theories of the public sector (also described in chapter 2), the third tenet of the conceptual model is that states use various public policies to promote both the demand for and supply of higher education. The specific policies that a state adopts are determined by the nature of state policy leadership and steering of higher education as well as by characteristics of the broader state context. These policies fall into one of three categories: policies that reflect the strategic use of available fiscal resources to ensure the affordability of college for students, families, and taxpayers; policies that promote the preparation and movement of students across educational sectors and levels without loss of academic progress or credit; and policies that optimize the availability of higher education opportunities for state residents. The fourth tenet of the conceptual model is that, to promote both overall higher education attainment *and* equity in attainment across groups, public policies must be oriented toward equalizing opportunity for higher education.

And finally, as reflected by the feedback loop in figure 1, the fifth tenet is that improving higher education is not a one-time-only task. Instead, improving higher

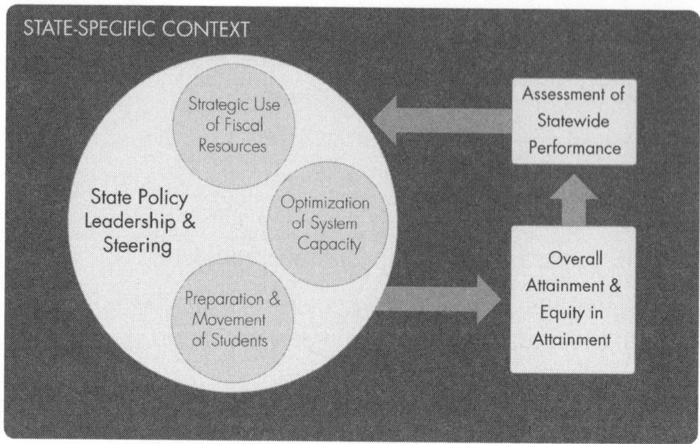

Figure 1. Conceptual Model for Understanding How State Public Policy Influences Higher Education Performance

education performance is an ongoing, adaptable process that requires regularly assessing progress toward achieving performance goals and adjusting public policies to correct for deficiencies and to recognize ongoing changes in the state context.

1. The Relationship between State Policy and Higher Education Performance Cannot Be Understood without Attention to the State Context

The state context is at the foundation for understanding the relationship between public policy and higher education performance (fig. 1). The state studies demonstrate that this relationship cannot be understood without considering multiple aspects of context. Among the most important dimensions that emerged from our analyses are characteristics of a state's demographic, economic, political, and historical context.

Some contextual characteristics influence the types of required improvements in higher education performance. For instance, rapid growth in the Hispanic population has challenged Texas and Georgia, and to lesser degrees Illinois and Maryland, not only to serve more students but also to better serve a population that has not previously been well served by the state or the nation more generally. Improving higher education outcomes for Hispanics is especially important to the current and future economic and social well-being of Texas, where Hispanics now represent 38% of public high school graduates.[5] In Georgia and Maryland, improving the attainment of Blacks is essential, since Blacks now represent more than a third of public high school graduates in these states.

States also differ in the availability of resources to fund public services. Texas and Washington have no state income tax, and in November 2010 Washington voters rejected an attempt to establish an income tax for its wealthiest residents, a tax that would have dedicated revenues to education and health services. Suggesting a different orientation, Maryland recently increased its corporate income tax in order to generate revenues for a new fund designed to reduce the volatility in state appropriations and tuition.

All five of our study states were facing notable constraints on the availability of state fiscal resources for higher education at the time of our data collection, and all five will likely face continued challenges into the near future. But both the relative wealth of states and the magnitude of fiscal resource restrictions vary. In Texas, the oil and gas economy slowed the impact on higher education of the most recent economic stagnation relative to other states. With its proximity to Washington, D.C., and its above average educational attainment, Maryland has remained a hub for national research and related economic growth even during the Great Recession. In contrast, at the time of our data collection, Illinois was experiencing acute limitations on the availability of state revenues; the magnitude of budget constraints seemed to overshadow all other policy concerns and paralyze state policy leadership.

Our findings also reveal that the relationship between public policy and higher education performance cannot be understood without also considering the distribution of political power between a state's governor and its legislature. In Georgia a strong gubernatorial system, coupled with a constitutionally weak legislature that meets only about 40 days per year, all but ensures that local needs are lower on the state's agenda than the priorities of the governor. In contrast, Texas has a constitutionally weak governor but a strong legislature, a pattern that appears to have contributed to the performance of higher education both positively (by facilitating regional support for the state's master plan for higher education, *Closing the Gaps*) and negatively (by permitting unequal funding across the state's community colleges). The state's valuing of local control allows Texas localities (which vary in demographics, educational needs, and other characteristics) to determine whether they will join a community college's service area. Consequently, the statewide goal of "closing the gaps" may be undermined by the decisions of local groups and not advanced through concerted state action.

The historical context, including a state's legacy of segregation and racial discrimination, may also influence the relationship between public policy and performance. Our data revealed differences in the manifestation of segregation and racial discrimination, and the connections of segregation and racial discrimination to higher education performance, in Georgia, Maryland, and Texas, even though all three states are among the 19 southern and southern-border states that are or have been subject to federal mandates to desegregate their higher education systems.[6] Reasons for these differences should be explored in future research. The U.S. Department of Education's Office for Civil Rights (OCR) has released Georgia from oversight but continues to monitor Texas and Maryland. In Maryland, continuing challenges related to the desegregation of the state's higher education system have implications for how the state optimizes higher education opportunities for all residents, particularly its large Black population. Demonstrating the ways that federal policy may interact with state policy, Maryland has responded to federal desegregation mandates by allocating state funding to its historically Black institutions (HBIs) and engaging in other efforts designed to enhance these institutions. Nonetheless, despite these efforts, the state has not yet resolved disagreements between one of the state's HBIs (Morgan State University) and the University System of Maryland related to program duplication and institutional growth aspirations.

2. State Policy Leadership and Steering Are Required to Improve Higher Education Performance

Building on and extending the work of Berdahl, Glenny, Clark, Richardson and others, our case studies suggest the benefits to higher education performance that come with state policy leadership, especially leadership that emphasizes steering roles. Although other policy roles (e.g., providing resources, regulating, advocating for consumers) unquestionably have value, the steering role focuses on encouraging higher education institutions to act in ways that advance societal goals and priorities.[7] In the absence of state policy leadership and steering, colleges and universities respond to other incentives and act (rationally) to advance their own priorities, such as enhancing their own prestige. Consequently, states miss the opportunity to ensure that the collective contribution of higher education to the state's economic and social well-being is greater than the sum of the parts. Other scholars, although not focusing on higher education per se, also stress that governmental efforts to intentionally advance societal goals and purposes are essential to achieving national economic prosperity and income equality within a nation.[8]

A comparison of tuition-setting policies illustrates variations across the five states in the balancing of state and institutional interests. The devolution of tuition-setting authority in Illinois (following the dissolution of the system of systems) and in Washington (following declines in state appropriations) shows a weakening of the state-coordinating role; the result is an emphasis on institutional interests (greater revenues) over statewide goals and priorities (affordability). In Washington, this shift toward institutional interests is tempered by the legislature's requirement that the state's public four-year institutions allocate a portion of tuition and fee revenues to need-based institutional financial aid. In Texas, the legislature also deregulated tuition in 2003, but, suggesting some level of state policy leadership on this issue, has since negotiated tuition levels with the public four-year institutions after several years of steep increases.

In Georgia, the University System of Georgia's Board of Regents has official tuition-setting authority, but the governor has historically provided informal input. In the past, because the state-funded HOPE Scholarship and Grant programs have covered full tuition, the state has had an incentive to control program expenditures (by keeping tuition low). This continued connection may be in jeopardy, however, because the state has recently reduced the share of tuition covered by the HOPE program in response to shortfalls in lottery revenues.

Exhibiting greater policy leadership and steering capacity, Maryland's governor and legislature have worked with public four-year colleges and universities in recent years to first freeze and then limit tuition increases. Building on its historical record of gubernatorial and legislative support for and direct personal connections to higher education, the state has also adopted and begun to implement a comprehensive financing plan for higher education that includes stabilizing state appropriations from year to year, linking tuition increases to family income, increasing need-based financial aid, and improving efficiency and productivity in Maryland's public institutions.

One question raised by our analysis is the relative contributions of system design and leadership to advancing statewide goals and priorities for higher education. Some researchers have concluded that the importance of leadership to performance depends on the system design. For example, in their earlier case study, Richardson and colleagues found that higher education performance in Georgia depends on the leadership of the chancellor of the University System of Georgia, given the constitutional status of the state's unified system; that is, strong leadership keeps institutional interests in check. But they conclude that although leadership is important to higher education performance, it will be ineffective without a system design that encourages some degree of statewide coordination: "Certainly leadership matters, but even good leaders should not be expected to achieve consistent results in the presence of a system design that inhibits institutional collaboration and system synergy. Leadership can make a system perform better or worse than its structural design, but it cannot compensate for badly designed systems or mismatched policy environments."[9]

Richardson and Martinez also imply the role of leadership in their assessment of the forces that contribute to a state's capacity to change the "rules in use" and improve higher education performance. Drawing from the work of others, they define capacity in terms of a state's ability to set meaningful priorities for higher education within the state, gather and use data to encourage accountability of higher education, promote alignment and cooperation across higher education sectors as well as between higher education and other entities (e.g., K–12 education, employers), and address conflict in ways that are consistent with a state's goals and available resources. The authors identify variations across their five study states in both the capacity to change rules (with more capacity in New Jersey and less in New Mexico) and location of rule changes (at the state level in New Jersey, New York, and South Dakota and at the segment or institution level in California and New Mexico).[10]

Our findings suggest that, regardless of system design, state policy leadership and steering influence higher education performance. Like the research by Richardson and colleagues, our state studies indicate that, in order to improve performance, leaders must understand deficiencies and the need to improve performance to meet current and changing state requirements and must articulate a clear statewide agenda for the state's higher education system. Even when it is seemingly divergent from the goals and priorities of individual higher education institutions, this agenda must be broadly supported and provide a blueprint for identifying and implementing policies that achieve statewide goals and priorities.

The Illinois state study exemplifies the challenges for higher education performance that come with the absence of a cohesive public agenda for higher education that is shared and supported by state, institutional, and business leaders. Among the state policy leadership challenges in Illinois is the failure of the master plan to identify priorities for state action. Although detailing the many areas of higher education that must be improved, the Illinois master plan provides little guidance for identifying which of the many recommendations, strategies, and action steps are most important or which should be adopted if resource constraints limit the actions that are possible. In the absence of a shared agenda that identifies clear priorities, it is not surprising that the state has implemented few of the recommended strategies or action steps and that it has been unable to bring to scale pilot projects designed to improve student outcomes, even when these pilot programs have a demonstrated record of success.

In contrast, aided by a record of stable and respected political and higher education leadership (that is, aspects of the state's political and higher education context), state and institutional leaders in Maryland have a shared understanding of the importance of public policy and institutional practice for improving college affordability in the state. With this shared statewide agenda, Maryland has moved to implement policies that promise to improve college affordability in the state.

While illustrating the benefits of policy leadership to higher education performance, our analyses also raise questions about the forms of statewide organization that will most effectively promote state policy leadership and steering. From their case study analyses, Richardson and Martinez note the challenges that states without "an effective interface agency" experience in improving higher education performance. They conclude that some form of "coordinating entity with appropriate authority" is required "to set reasonable boundaries within which universities with their own governing boards are encouraged to balance institutional or segmental priorities against those of other stakeholders."[11]

Along the same lines, our state studies also show the importance of having some mechanism that promotes state policy leadership and steering. In Illinois, the state's abandonment of its system of systems in the mid-1990s, a shift from a federal to a segmented system, was followed by a decline in many measures of higher education performance. The system of systems served to balance power across the state's higher education institutions; power was not concentrated in one system or sector (such as the state's research universities). At the same time, the Board of Higher Education provided a steering and leadership function, balancing statewide priorities with the goals and interests of higher education institutions.[12] Under this configuration of state coordination, Illinois led the nation on most measures in *Measuring Up 2000*, the state report card on higher education performance.[13]

The state's abandonment of the system of systems, coupled with the political context of corruption, changed this balance of power. New systems emerged that increased the power of the state's two major research universities. With political corruption came skepticism of the qualifications and caliber of gubernatorial appointments to higher education boards. The influence of the Board of Higher Education declined, and with discord and distrust among various state agencies, no clear voice advocated for the public interest in higher education. Recreating an environment that once again recognizes the role of the state in improving higher education attainment, while also providing institutions with the autonomy and incentives to innovate, is the major challenge Illinois must address to improve its higher education performance.

The Washington study also reveals the benefits to higher education performance of some type of coordinating entity. The state's community and technical college system, although not a governing board, is politically strong and works with the state's community and technical colleges to address statewide issues. In contrast, the public four-year institutions in Washington generally operate relatively independently, without the statewide policy leadership provided for the two-year institutions. Washington's Higher Education Coordinating Board historically played a weak role in advancing a statewide agenda for the state's public four-year institutions. At the same time, the public four-year institutions, particularly the University of Washington and Washington State University, have enjoyed relatively greater freedom and influence with the legislature. The power of the research universities is exemplified by the state's decision to expand branch campuses of research universities rather than other sectors of higher education, a costly and ineffective approach to addressing the state's need to expand enrollment capacity. The Higher Education Coordinating Board supported this policy because it was wary of taking on the powerful research universities (given the legislature's support of these institutions). The legislature's decision to dissolve and reconfigure the Higher Education Coordinating Board further suggests both a lack of confidence in the coordinating board's policy functions and a view that public policy functions should be devolved to the state's public four-year institutions. The emphasis of state policy making on addressing institutional and sector-based priorities contributes to Washington's low baccalaureate degree production and its resulting need to import college graduates from other states to meet employment needs.

In Texas we found a great deal of consensus among state leaders for the goals identified in its master plan for higher education, despite the state's large size, diverse regions, and culture of valuing local control and respecting regional distinctions. This finding may be attributable to the effectiveness of coordinating board members in counteracting "some of higher education's parochial interests" and articulating the role of higher education in meeting statewide goals and priorities, a conclusion Richardson and colleagues drew in their earlier case study of Texas.[14] This consensus, supported by political and business leaders, has likely contributed to the state's recent improvements in measures of higher education performance.

Further progress, however, will likely depend on the coordinating board's ability to resolve an emerging conflict between two goals for higher education: expand the state's seven emerging research universities and close gaps in higher education attainment across groups. Addressing both priorities may be impossible when resources are finite. Allocating resources to encourage improved research capacity, prestige, and performance may reduce the availability of resources to promote overall educational attainment and close gaps in attainment across groups. Other research also raises flags about Texas' attention to enhancing research productivity. For instance, in their five-state study, Richardson and Martinez found that California and New Mexico, "states with autonomous research universities operating in the absence of effective state coordination tend to pursue research prominence as a priority," "spend more tax dollars on their higher education systems, and perform less well on undergraduate indicators" of performance.[15]

In Georgia, the Georgia Research Alliance, started with state funding and private investment, represents an effective mechanism for balancing statewide and institutional priorities for research. This entity has contributed to the growth in research dollars at the state's public and private research universities without over-expanding the research enterprise. The Alliance works with and across its member institutions to develop competitive research programs. Initiated by the state, the Alliance is now an independent not-for-profit entity with presidents of private corporations and public universities as well as representatives of state government serving on its board. The state's high production of certificates is another outcome of statewide policy leadership designed to address a statewide need. Through its QuickStart program, Georgia has improved the education and preparation of its workforce by enabling technical colleges to provide customized workforce training at businesses at no charge. The state also promotes enrollment of students in workforce training programs at technical colleges through its HOPE Grant.

At the same time, more problematic dimensions of Georgia's higher education performance are attributable to the absence of an effective mechanism for advancing statewide goals. Structural barriers have restricted transfer between institutions in the University System of Georgia and the state's technical institutions and consequently limited attainment for degree-seeking students. Also suggesting insufficient attention to statewide steering and leadership, the strategic plans developed by the University System of Georgia and the Technical College System call for enrollment growth but do not articulate how this growth will be met.

Thus, although suggesting the importance of state policy leadership and steering, the cross-case analyses raise questions about the ability of current statewide structures to provide the policy leadership and steering that are required to meet current societal needs and priorities. Disagreement about the ideal form of statewide organization of higher education for advancing societal goals is not new, as demonstrated in Michael McLendon's historical review of these structures. Proposals to reform higher education governance structures were especially common in the 1980s and 1990s.[16]

Although our study does not resolve this debate, our findings do indicate that the state coordinating organizations established during an earlier era may not be the best structures for achieving current societal needs: increasing higher educational attainment and closing gaps across groups in attainment. Fifty years ago public and institutional agendas were more closely aligned than they are now. Today colleges and universities have their own capacity for growing and determining market needs; they are mature organizations.[17] Some public institutions—especially public flagship universities—now have substantial endowment funds to meet operational expenditures and many (as in Texas and Washington) are politically powerful. The status and prestige of these institutions tends to dominate public discourse, often at the expense of the access and teaching missions of other institutions. Governors tend to appoint well-connected business and political leaders to the boards of public research universities, whereas the appointments to coordinating boards tend to be less visible and politically weak.

In the current context, existing structures may be unable to advance a public agenda for higher education and promote public discussion about future policy options and necessary trade-offs. Of the five states studied, only Maryland appears to currently have the policy leadership needed to encourage the development and implementation of a statewide investment strategy for higher education. In all five states, existing higher education structures provide inadequate linkages across educational sectors to ensure the academic preparation and smooth transition of students across educational sectors and levels or the availability of data that fully inform decision making. The fragmented and decentralized nature of educational policy at the state level contributes to the absence of a public agenda that would both strengthen education and better serve public purposes.

3. Improving Performance Requires Adopting Policies That Increase the Demand for and Supply of Higher Education

As described more completely in chapter 2, public policy is the mechanism that governments use to increase the demand for and supply of higher education in their state. Our cross-state analyses point to three categories of public policies that shift the demand and supply curves to improve higher education attainment:

1. Policies that strategically use available fiscal resources to ensure the affordability of college for students, families, and taxpayers;
2. Policies that promote the preparation and movement of students across educational sectors and levels without loss of academic progress or credit; and
3. Policies that optimize the availability of higher education opportunities for state residents.

Rather than identify any "silver bullet," our analyses point to the value of creating a cohesive statewide approach to improving higher education performance. Any policy that is adopted must be adapted so as to meet the specific characteristics of the state context, including the characteristics of the state's higher education system and the other public policies that are also in place.

We discuss each of these three policy categories in further detail after describing the fourth tenet of the model: the need for policies that level the playing field for higher education opportunity. In addition to identifying the collection of policies that will improve overall higher education policies within a particular state context, policymakers must also consider the extent to which policies will close gaps in attainment across groups within the state. To achieve international competitiveness goals and meet projected workforce needs, the United States must develop all of its talent. Moreover, closing gaps in attainment across groups requires a broader definition of equity, one that is not restricted only to race/ethnicity and family income but that also considers geography and other attributes that systematically disenfranchise various groups.

4. Improving Equity in Higher Education Attainment Requires Policies That Level the Playing Field for Educational Opportunity

The fourth tenet of our conceptual model is that, to improve not only overall attainment but also equity in attainment, the public policies that a state adopts and implements to increase the demand for and supply of higher education must address the barriers that limit opportunity for various groups. Some of these barriers may be attributable to a state's historical legacy of segregation and racial discrimination, as described in the Maryland, Georgia, and Texas chapters. Other barriers have other causes and have implications for equality of opportunity based not only on race/ethnicity but also on family income, age, geographic location and other characteristics.

A state's failure to level the playing field for higher education has disproportionate negative implications for the attainment of groups that now have the lowest educational attainment—including those from low-income families, Blacks and Hispanics, and individuals living in particular geographic locations within a state. Stiglitz observes the negative consequences for income inequality when a government fails to reduce inequity across groups in educational opportunities: "If certain minorities are disproportionately poor, and if the government provides poor education and health care to the poor, then members of the minority will suffer disproportionately from poor education and health."[18] Public policies that promote equity in higher education attainment are critically important, given the persisting gaps in attainment across groups, the changing demographic characteristics of the population, and the increasing demand for college-educated workers.

For instance, strategically allocating available fiscal resources (the first category of policies for raising overall higher education attainment) is required to close gaps in attainment, since research consistently demonstrates that increases in the price of attending college (via increases in tuition and/or decreases in financial aid) have a greater negative affect on the enrollment of students from lower-income than on higher-income families.[19] Promoting the preparation and movement of students across educational levels without loss of progress is also essential, since data and research consistently confirm the importance of academic readiness to college-related outcomes and document the lower academic readiness of groups with the lowest levels of attainment.[20] Optimizing the availability of postsecondary educational choices is most important for groups of students who are least mobile and least knowledgeable about higher education, including individuals who are disproportionately from low-income families and racial/ethnic minority groups. Without ensuring college affordability, academic readiness, and accessible higher education opportunities, a state will not only fail to achieve the required overall levels of higher education attainment but also perpetuate inequity in higher education attainment.

The five study states have made varying progress in closing gaps across groups in higher education outcomes in recent years. For example, Texas has narrowed racial/ethnic group gaps, but gaps persist in Georgia. None of the states in our study are likely to eliminate gaps in attainment across racial/ethnic or other dimensions with the higher education policies that are currently in place.

Using public policy to level the playing field for higher education opportunity is warranted because of society's interest in fairness.[21] Despite the number of colleges and universities in the United States, higher education outcomes continue to be stratified based on family income and race/ethnicity as well as place of residence. Higher education attainment continues to vary across groups because of differences in the primary predictors of college enrollment and completion, including the adequacy of academic preparation and readiness for college, the availability of financial resources to pay for college, and the possession of the knowledge and information required to enroll in and navigate college and financial aid processes. But the extent to which individuals have the opportunity to become adequately academically prepared to enroll and complete college, possess the financial resources required to pay college, and be knowledgeable about college requirements and expectations continues to depend on forces that are often beyond their control, including the educational resources that are available in the community in which they live and the high school they attend as well as other characteristics of the local, state, and regional contexts in which they are embedded.[22]

As McMahon succinctly argues, "Seeking more equal educational opportunity or more equal access does not imply equalizing the outcomes. . . . Equality of educational opportunity is far short of that and a goal that remains to be achieved."[23] For instance, compared with their peers from lower-income families, high school students from higher-income families are more likely, by definition, to have the financial resources to personally pay the costs of attending higher education and, given the reliance of many school districts on revenues from local taxpayers, tend to attend better-resourced schools that provide better academic preparation for college.[24] High school students who are the first in their families to attend college not only lack complete information about the private non-market benefits of higher education but are also less likely than other students to possess accurate and complete knowledge and understanding about academic and other eligibility requirements, procedures for gaining admission and securing financial aid, and the benefits of higher education.[25]

The extent to which improving equity in higher education based on race/

ethnicity, income, geography, and other dimensions relevant to particular states is a shared statewide goal and priority varies across the five states in our study. In Maryland, state and institutional leaders consistently articulated the shared goal of improving the affordability of higher education, implying recognition of the financial barriers that limit attainment for individuals from low-income families. In interviews with our research team in Texas, state, business, and institutional leaders unfailingly discussed the importance to the state's future economic prosperity of closing gaps in higher education attainment across racial/ethnic groups, given the state's increasingly diverse population. Texas has made noteworthy progress in achieving the goals for reducing gaps across groups in participation and degree completion that are outlined in its master plan, *Closing the Gaps*, even though challenges remain (as with the funding of community colleges, discussed below).

In Illinois, a state where the racial/ethnic distribution of the population mirrors that of the nation, the master plan for higher education frames the state's higher education attainment "problem" as the "tale of two states." The plan describes the large and expanding "prosperity gap" and attributes this gap to differences in educational attainment by race/ethnicity and family income, as well as geographic region.[26] Although clearly describing the need to close gaps in higher education attainment, however, the master plan has not been embraced by political, state, or institutional leaders beyond the Board of Higher Education.

The explicit attention in Texas and Illinois to closing gaps in higher education attainment is in sharp contrast to what we found in Georgia. While some acknowledged the need to improve attainment in Atlanta, the state and institutional leaders we interviewed were reluctant to discuss racial/ethnic group gaps in higher education outcomes in the state, a state in which Blacks represent more than a third of public high school graduates.[27]

Policies That Reflect the Strategic Use of Available Fiscal Resources to Ensure the Affordability of College for Students, Families, and Taxpayers

Higher education certainly requires a reliable, sustained base of public resources to promote overall attainment and equity in attainment as well as to ensure quality. At the time of our data collection, all five states were experiencing the consequences of the Great Recession, including constraints on the availability of state funding for higher education and other public services. The level and other characteristics of funding in some states (including Illinois' delay in remitting to the public colleges and universities funds that the state had appropriated) in recent years have been unacceptably problematic.

Although public investment is critical, several other dimensions of the funding of higher education must also be stressed. First, the higher education attainment problems in the five study states began before the start of the most recent economic downturn. Second, volatility of state revenues for higher education will likely continue into the future, mirroring swings in the economy. In addition, because of structural budget deficits, all states will continue to face constraints on available fiscal resources into the near future. In short, most states will have to accomplish more with fewer public resources. This reality underscores the need to use available fiscal resources strategically in order to raise overall higher education attainment and improve equity across groups.

Our five states reveal the ways that higher education finance policies, to varying degrees, intentionally and unintentionally perpetuate and exacerbate differences in attainment across groups. Awarding state financial aid based on financial need is one approach to leveling the playing field for higher education opportunity because it recognizes differences in the financial resources that individuals have to pay the costs of attending college. Nonetheless, even with a need-based aid policy, negative consequences for the stratification of higher education attainment may still arise. For example, Illinois responded to shortfalls in the availability of funding for its need-based grant program by dispersing grants on a first-come, first-served basis. This response had a disproportionately negative effect on the availability of grants for community college students, since they tended to apply after available aid was dispersed.

In Washington, another state with a long-standing substantial commitment to providing state-funded need-based grant aid, available funds have also been insufficient in recent years to meet the demand for aid from all eligible students. In an effort to generate revenue to ensure continued future funding of need-based aid, the state has moved to create a new need-based scholarship program that is funded from voluntary individual and business donations.

Georgia not only has a state-sponsored student aid program that does not address the financial barriers that limit enrollment in degree-granting programs but also responded to recent revenue shortfalls by increasing the extent to which the program allocates resources to those who are already high-achieving. Since the early 1990s, Georgia has used revenues from a state lottery to fund its HOPE Scholarship and Grant Programs. The reliance on state lottery funds to finance this program reflects an economically regressive approach, since low-income individuals are both more likely to purchase lottery tickets and less likely to benefit from the lottery proceeds (because they are less likely to enroll in degree-granting programs).[28] Rather than provide available resources to reduce financial barriers that limit enrollment in and completion of degrees from degree-granting institutions, the HOPE Scholarship Program increases the resources available to individuals with the highest academic credentials, individuals who are disproportionately from middle- and upper-income families. The effects of the HOPE Scholarship on the stratification of higher education attainment in Georgia will likely only be magnified by changes implemented in response to recent shortfalls in lottery revenues that heighten the academic eligibility requirements.[29]

Because states vary in the availability of resources and other contextual forces, the specific policies that effectively improve performance within a given state will necessarily vary. But the cross-case analyses point to three broad guidelines for strategically using available fiscal resources that improve the affordability of college for students, families, and taxpayers:

1. Link state appropriations, tuition, and financial aid to create a more coherent fiscal strategy for higher education attainment.
2. Limit tuition increases to increases in family income.
3. Ensure the adequacy of need-based financial aid.

Of the five states studied, Maryland has made the greatest progress in implementing higher education finance policies that, together, help to ensure college affordability for students, families, and taxpayers. Chapter 6 describes the concerted efforts of state and institutional leaders to work together to link available higher education finance levers to achieve this goal. Yet even though Maryland has created linkages between appropriations and tuition, and between tuition and family income, it has done less well with regard to its investment in student financial aid. Despite an increase in state investment in student aid between 2005 and 2009, Maryland continues to rank below many other states in terms of the availability of need-based grant aid. Moreover, the state's financial aid dollars are spread over a large number of discrete student aid programs, including several non-need-based aid programs.

Texas provides an example of the negative consequences for college affordability that come with decoupled higher education finance policies. Texas has been providing state funding to cover a decreasing portion of instructional costs at community colleges, forcing these institutions to rely increasingly on their local tax base and tuition. Many community colleges have portions of their service areas that are outside of their taxing district. Counties within each service area must approve local taxes supporting the community colleges in order for students to receive in-district tuition rates. Tuition rates are higher for those who live in the service area but outside the taxing district, and in-district and out-of-district tuition vary from 20% to 50% across the state. The lack of alignment between the service area and the taxing district results in a tax base that is insufficient to meet the educational needs of those living in the service area. Locally elected community college boards in Texas have sought to increase revenue by expanding their tax districts while providing lower tuition for in-district students. Yet districts with high shares of low-income (often minority) residents are often unable to approve higher local taxes. Given the large role of community colleges in the state's higher education system, Texas will not achieve its attainment goals without improving the alignment of these policies.

Policies That Promote the Preparation and Movement of Students across Educational Sectors and Levels without Loss of Academic Progress or Credit

A primary strength of the U.S. higher education system is its diversity. Yet with a diverse system, and one that fundamentally values the autonomy of individual colleges and universities, also come challenges, especially with regard to the preparation and movement of students across educational levels (from high school into postsecondary education) and across educational sectors (from community colleges to four-year institutions). Failure to ensure smooth movement of students across these transition points too often results in loss of academic progress or credit for students and reduces the efficiency of a state's higher education system. Moreover, the failure to improve these transition points has a disproportionately negative impact on the higher education attainment of students who currently have the lowest attainment.

To improve higher education performance, states must ensure that students are prepared to enter and are able to traverse the nation's complex, multilevel and multisector educational system without loss of academic progress or credit. Our analyses reveal that states are losing too many students at critical junctures in the pipeline from K–12 education through college completion. To advance the preparation and movement of students across educational levels and sectors, policies must promote the academic transition from high school to college and enable the transfer of students across colleges and universities without the loss of academic credit.

State Policies that Promote the Academic Transition from High School to College A central barrier to the successful movement of students from high school to postsecondary education is inadequate academic preparation.[30] One cause of inadequate academic preparation is the continued lack of alignment between curricular requirements and expectations at the K–12 and higher education levels.[31] High schools are preparing students to receive a high school diploma, but high school graduation requirements are typically not coordinated with the academic requirements and expectations of colleges and universities.

In all five of the states studied, K–12 and higher education are collaborating to some extent to improve academic readiness for college through dual enrollment, early college high schools, and/or other school-college transition programs. All five states also have, or have once had, a formal P–20 structure designed to improve the cooperation between K–12 and higher education. Even with the presence of these boundary-spanning entities, however, none of the states has fully aligned curricula and assessments between K–12 and higher education. The conclusion that P–20 structures have played a limited role in these five states is consistent with the finding from earlier studies. For instance, although noting the possible benefits of "convening a commission and holding cross-system discussions," Andrea Venezia and colleagues also argue that such efforts "are not sufficient for creating meaningful and lasting K–16 reform." Instead, meaningful change "must be anchored in policy and finance reform."[32]

The continued disconnect between K–12 and higher education policies is also evident in the five states we studied. For instance, Illinois requires students to pass an exam in order to receive a regular high school diploma, but this test is not aligned with college readiness standards. Maryland now requires students to pass end-of-course exams in order to graduate from high school, but state and institutional leaders note the need to improve the alignment between these tests and college-readiness indicators. Despite the success of its Running Start and I-BEST programs, Washington has also made slow progress in systemically improving college readiness for all students; the state has also only recently revised its high school exit exam and begun to implement end-of-course exams. In Georgia we found that the longevity of P–16 efforts could be jeopardized by changes in gubernatorial leadership.

Of the five states studied, Texas has achieved the greatest progress in developing and implementing policies to increase college readiness. Even before formally establishing its P–16 Council in 2003, the state legislature designated the college preparatory curriculum as the default program for high school students. More recently, the Texas Education Agency and the Texas Higher Education Coordinating Board have cooperated to establish college readiness standards in language arts and math. The state is also implementing end-of-course tests to determine the college readiness of high school juniors and creating twelfth grade transition courses to improve readiness for those who have not achieved the required standards. These strategies hold promise for increasing college preparation in Texas. That said, however, even in Texas performance on indicators of college preparation continues to be low for all students, and even lower for Black and Hispanic students and students from low-income families.

Some states (e.g., Maryland) appear to be deferring further efforts to improve college readiness until the PARCC (Partnership for Assessment of Readiness for College and Careers) Consortium and the Smarter Balanced Assessment Consortium complete their work. PARCC has 24 member states (including the District of Columbia), whereas Smarter Balanced has 27 member states. Five states are members of both (Alabama, Colorado, North Dakota, Pennsylvania, and South Carolina). Both PARCC and Smarter Balanced are state-led consortia designed to develop assessments in English language arts/literacy and mathematics that are aligned with the Common Core State Standards (CCSS). Released in 2010 by the National Governors Association and Council of Chief State School Officers, the Common Core State Standards have been adopted by 45 states.[33] The U.S. Department of Education awarded grants to PARCC and Smarter Balanced to develop assessments aligned with the CCSS. Member states have agreed to implement the new assessments beginning in the 2014–15 academic year. Although states may also adopt state-specific standards, CCSS must represent at least 85% of a state's total standards.[34] Each state may determine its own approach to implementing the standards and must pay the associated costs. Whether these initiatives will effectively promote students' academic preparation for college is not yet clear. Certainly this is an area that warrants continued attention.

State Policies That Facilitate Transfer between Higher Education Institutions Many students begin postsecondary education at one higher education institution but then transfer to another. Prior to the creation of the National Student Clearinghouse in 1993, little information was available to document the movement of students across institutions throughout the United States. But with data provided by 96% of all colleges and universities (n = 3,400), the Clearinghouse's Research Center is a now an invaluable source of longitudinal data describing student outcomes.[35] These data reveal, for example, that the degree completion rates that individual colleges report (as required by the Federal Student Right to

Know Act) understate students' actual completion rates. For instance, only 48.6% of students who first enrolled at a public four-year college in fall 2006 completed a bachelor's degree from their starting institution within six years, but 60.6% of students in this cohort completed a degree from any college or university within six years; moreover, an additional 16% were still enrolled (at any institution).[36] Although revealing nothing about the proportion of students leaving their initial college or university (i.e., those who "drop out") intending to transfer but without accomplishing this goal, the longitudinal data from the National Clearinghouse signal the importance of transfer to educational attainment.

Many students begin their postsecondary education in a community college but have the goal of earning a bachelor's degree. As described in chapter 3, about a third of all undergraduates nationwide in fall 2010 were attending a community college. The percentage of community college students who aspire to earn a bachelor's degree is difficult to ascertain, given the diverse functions and roles of our nation's community colleges. Nonetheless, most first-time, first-year students attending a community college self-report aspirations to complete at least a bachelor's degree: 81% of first-time, first-year students attending a community college nationwide in 2003–4 indicated this educational goal.[37] Despite these high reported aspirations, however, only about a fifth of community college students nationwide actually transfer to a four-year college or university within five years of first enrolling.[38] Moreover, those who do transfer often lose credits. This loss of credits represents inefficiencies in the higher education system as a whole and imposes real costs in terms of both time and money for students and taxpayers.

Longitudinal data from the National Student Clearinghouse illustrate variations across states in the patterns and success of transfer. Consistent with the challenges to transfer that we found in the Washington study, only 5% of students who first enrolled full-time in a public two-year college in Washington in fall 2006 completed a degree from a four-year institution within six years. However, in Maryland 22% of first-time, full-time students entering community colleges completed a degree from a four-year institution, raising the overall completion rate for this cohort to 51%.[39] These data suggest far greater ease of transfer from community colleges to four-year institutions in Maryland.

Our five state studies shed light on how characteristics of a state's higher education system and other forces can create barriers to the smooth and efficient transfer of students across higher education institutions. The challenges for transfer resulting from the structural differences between the Technical College System of Georgia and the University System of Georgia are particularly noteworthy. In Georgia, students have historically experienced relatively few challenges transferring between institutions within the University System of Georgia but substantial difficulties transferring between institutions across systems. By changing from a quarter system to a semester system and seeking regional accreditation of its institutions, the Technical College System has recently acted to reduce two structural barriers to the movement of students between the two systems. However, more time is required to assess the effectiveness of these changes.

To reach higher education performance goals, all five states in our study must make greater progress in establishing policies that facilitate the movement of students across higher education institutions without loss of credit. In most states, the receiving institution (typically a four-year college or university) continues to have discretion over the courses it accepts for credit. Differences in the courses that are accepted for credit across institutions undoubtedly create challenges for students seeking to transfer credits and contribute to the loss of credit that many transfer students experience. Negotiating transfer agreements on an institution-by-institution basis is especially challenging in states as large and diverse as Texas.

Although transfer continues to largely depend on institution-by-institution agreements, our study points to some potentially promising approaches to facilitating transfer across institutions without loss of credit. For instance, the Illinois Articulation Initiative, although not without limitations, appears to facilitate transfer of general education courses for students attending participating institutions in that state. In Texas and Maryland, two-year and four-year colleges and universities have worked together—outside of the formal state policy arena—to develop articulated programs that transfer credits as a group rather than as individual courses. These efforts began with articulated programs in teaching and have moved to include articulated programs in engineering. In Maryland, a state law guarantees admission to a University System of Maryland institution of choice (although not necessarily to the program of choice) to students who complete at least 56 credits or an associate's degree with a grade point average of 2.0 or higher at a Maryland public institution. One unintended consequence of a policy that allows community college students to transfer before completing an associate's degree, however, may be to reduce completion rates for that sector (as calculated traditionally and without National Clearinghouse data).

Our analyses also illuminate the need for a state to consider the unintended consequences of transfer policies, especially for the cost of delivering education at four-year institutions. For instance, in Washington, community college students who complete the 90 quarter-credit direct-transfer associate degree program enter public and participating private four-year institutions in the state with junior-year status and all lower-division and general education requirements met. Nonetheless, although the state establishes transfer goals for each public four-year institution, the state and institutional leaders we interviewed described the financial disincentives associated with accepting transfer students. In short, providing (more expensive) upper-division courses to transfer students requires greater institutional resources than providing lower-division courses to first- and second-year "native" students and fewer institutional revenues than accepting out-of-state students.

Policies That Optimize the Availability of Higher Education Opportunities for State Residents

A third category of public policies for improving higher education performance pertains to the optimization of opportunities for state residents to enroll and complete higher education. Despite substantial variations in their higher education systems, all five states in our study need greater alignment of postsecondary education options with the geographic distribution and educational needs of its population. Georgia and Texas must consider the ways their higher education systems may best address regional needs while also accommodating growing populations. In Washington, the four public comprehensive institutions are designed to serve particular regions, but the number of these institutions is small, and one of the four (Washington State University) is in a relatively isolated area. As a result, these institutions do not provide sufficient access to baccalaureate institutions for much of the state's population, particularly those living in more sparsely populated areas of the state.

Our analyses reveal five potential strategies for maximizing the availability of postsecondary educational opportunities and improving the alignment of postsecondary educational options with the location and needs of the state population:

1. Authorize community colleges to award bachelor's degrees.
2. Create local options that are connected to existing higher education providers.
3. Create postsecondary educational options through distance education.
4. Incentivize enrollment in private not-for-profit higher education institutions.
5. Utilize the capacity of for-profit postsecondary educational institutions.

The use of so many different approaches reflects the value of adopting strategies that recognize the characteristics of the state context and the nature of the necessary improvements in higher education performance. As discussed below, these strategies are not without challenges and limitations, and the extent to which these strategies level the playing field for higher education opportunity varies.

Authorize Community Colleges to Award Bachelor's Degrees Several of our states have attempted to increase bachelor's degree production by permitting community colleges to award bachelor's degrees. Washington has permitted community colleges in the state to award bachelor's degrees in applied sciences since 2005, and Texas first authorized community college baccalaureate degrees in applied science and applied technology in 2003. The University System of Georgia has transformed all of its former two-year colleges into state colleges that offer a limited number of baccalaureate-degree programs. In 2010, 18 states had granted approval to at least one community college to offer a four-year degree, up from 11 states in 2004.[40]

Allowing community colleges to award applied bachelor's degrees may improve bachelor's degree attainment particularly among residents living in areas without easy geographic access to a four-year college or university. Nonetheless, in both Washington and Texas relatively few applied bachelor's degrees have been awarded to date, indicating the limited impact of these programs on improving higher education attainment. This strategy may also help a state meet employers' demands for skilled workers, although an evaluation of the Texas program raises questions about the effectiveness of these programs in achieving this goal.[41] These programs may also improve the transfer of credits.[42]

Nonetheless, this strategy may also produce unintended consequences. Particularly worrisome is the potential for this strategy to distort the mission of community colleges. Permitting community colleges to award bachelor's degrees may incentivize these institutions to become more like regional comprehensive institutions, shifting community colleges away from their traditional core mission, that is, serving as the "social safety net" for higher education. Although some argue that this strategy may improve the affordability of a bachelor's degree to students and reduce the costs of a four-year degree to taxpayers, adding upper-division courses to community colleges will likely create additional costs as institutions upgrade libraries and laboratories and hire additional and more expensive faculty.[43]

Create Local Options Connected to Existing Higher Education Providers Another potential strategy for increasing higher education opportunities is to create local options that are connected to existing higher education institutions in the state. In one example of this approach, Maryland created eight regional centers with the goal of promoting access to bachelor's and graduate degree programs in the state's underserved areas. Maryland's regional centers are typically configured as collaborations between community colleges and four-year universities. Washington created university centers with the goal of increasing access to bachelor's degree programs. Yet so far this strategy has not substantially increased the number of bachelor's degrees awarded. One reason may be that states have provided few incentives to institutions to engage in this collaboration and few incentives for students to enroll in these programs.

Washington has also attempted to increase production of bachelor's degrees in the state by establishing five branch campuses to the state's two public research universities. One disadvantage of this strategy is that the affiliation of branch campuses with the state's public research universities rather than with the less-expensive comprehensive institutions raises the cost of a bachelor's degree for the state as well as for students and families. To date, the branch campuses have had a limited effect on bachelor's degree production. At first, as a concession to community colleges, the branch campuses were limited to upper-division students. Although that restriction has been lifted, the branch campuses are still limited by a lack of diverse programming, and enrollments are far below initial expectations.

Create Postsecondary Educational Options through Distance Education A third potential strategy for increasing the availability of higher education options is online or distance education. At the time of our data collection, this strategy was only beginning to emerge in a few of our study states. As a result, the extent to which these recent initiatives will improve higher education attainment is unclear. Georgia offers a Virtual School to promote online access to Advanced Placement courses and exams, other advanced courses, SAT preparation, and credit recovery courses to students in the state. Initiated by the University System of Georgia in October 2007, Georgia ONmyLINE is designed to increase access to courses and programs at the undergraduate and graduate degree levels. Maryland has the University of Maryland University College (UMUC), a virtual university, and Maryland and Texas are experimenting with blended educational models in the community colleges as a potential mechanism for more effectively delivering remedial education. Washington appropriated about $1.1 million in fiscal year 2010 and again in 2011 to the community and technical colleges "to enhance online distance learning and open courseware technology."[44] In Washington and Texas, Western Governor's University (WGU) is a new postsecondary education option. An online, not-for-profit university, WGU was created to serve primarily adults, many of them first-generation or low-income students, and offers career-focused bachelor's and master's degrees. WGU is funded via tuition revenue. It does not receive state appropriations, and students attending WGU in these states are not eligible for state financial aid, although this issue is under review by the legislature in Washington.

Incentivize Enrollment in Private Not-for-Profit Higher Education Institutions A fourth approach to maximizing the availability of higher education is to adopt policies that encourage enrollment in a state's private not-for-profit higher education institutions. Encouraging enrollment in private colleges and universities may expand the capacity of a state's higher education system without investing in new public institutions.[45] In their five-state study, Richardson and Martinez conclude that such aspects of higher education performance as high school completion, chance for college, and low-income student participation are higher in states where the private higher education sector has a formal role in meeting state higher education needs.[46]

Some states provide direct appropriations to private colleges and universities in the state. Since 1973, Maryland has appropriated unrestricted operating funds to private not-for-profit colleges and universities through a formula that links appropriations to these institutions to appropriations for the state's public four-year institutions. Other states encourage enrollment in private colleges and universities through their state-funded financial aid programs. Students attending the state's private four-year colleges and universities are eligible for the state's need-based grant program in Georgia, Illinois, Texas, and Washington and for tuition equalization grants in Georgia and Texas.

In an economic downturn, the availability of state dollars to encourage enrollment in private not-for-profit colleges and universities may decline. Faced with state revenue shortfalls, Illinois and Georgia reduced funding that had encouraged private-sector enrollment. In Illinois, a state that has had above average enrollment in private not-for-profit colleges and universities, smaller shares of the state's need-based grant dollars and awards are now available to students attending the state's private not-for-profit institutions, and the Board of Higher Education has proposed restricting the grant to students attending public institutions. Georgia reduced its Tuition Equalization Grants as well as HOPE Scholarships to students attending eligible private institutions in response to funding constraints. These policy changes will likely reduce the use of the private college and university sector in these states.

Utilize the Capacity of For-Profit Postsecondary Educational Institutions An additional potential strategy for increasing postsecondary educational opportunities that was notably absent across the five states is taking advantage of the presence and growth of for-profit postsecondary education providers. The share of students enrolled in for-profit institutions varies across the five states studied, ranging (in fall 2010) from 5% or less in Maryland, Texas, and Washington to 10% in Illinois and 11% in Georgia; the national average was 10%.[47] Nationwide, the share of students (at any degree level) who were attending a for-profit institution increased steadily over the past decade, rising from 3% in fall 2001 to 10% in fall 2010.[48]

Certainly, many questions remain about the quality of education provided and other characteristics of for-profit postsecondary education.[49] Yet even with these questions and the considerable growth, we found few regulatory frameworks for addressing public concerns about this sector in the five states studied, despite the consumer-protection role that governments often play.

Beyond acknowledging the growth and the associated regulatory burden, we found little attention among state leaders to the potential role of this sector in meeting their state's educational attainment needs and closing gaps across groups within the state. Various indicators point to the potential contribution of these institutions. In particular, they tend to be located in a state's urban centers, areas that have high current and projected unmet demand for postsecondary education. Moreover, for-profit institutions disproportionately enroll students from groups that are generally less-well served by other sectors of higher education, namely, individuals from low-income families and racial/ethnic minority groups. In 2007–8, Blacks and Hispanics represented considerably higher shares of undergraduates enrolled at for-profit institutions (24.7% and 21.0%, respectively) than of undergraduates enrolled at public two-year colleges (14.3% and 14.8%) and public or private not-for-profit four-year institutions (11.5% and 11.8%). Half (50.6%) of dependent undergraduates enrolled at for-profit institutions in 2007–8 were in the lowest family income quartile, compared with 31% of undergraduates enrolled at community colleges and only 20% of undergraduates enrolled at public and private not-for-profit four-year institutions.[50]

5. Monitor Performance and Adjust State Policies Appropriately

The fifth and final tenet of our conceptual model is that improving higher education performance requires regularly assessing progress toward achieving performance goals and adjusting public policies to correct for deficiencies and to recognize additional changes in the state context. As depicted by the feedback loop in figure 1, improving higher education performance is not a one-time-only activity, but rather an evolving process that occurs over time and that must be adjusted based on regular evaluation and changes in state context. In their conceptual model, Richardson and Martinez also assume that feedback on performance informs state leaders' subsequent actions.[51]

In their five-state study of the relationship between public policy and higher education performance, Richardson and Martinez concluded that indicators of data and information did not differentiate between states with lower and higher levels of performance. Nonetheless, the availability and use of data determines how higher education performance is measured, the problems in performance that are identified, and the extent to which public policymakers and institutional leaders are held accountable for improvements in performance.

Monitoring progress toward achieving statewide goals and priorities requires both the availability and the use of data.[52] Some states (e.g., Illinois and Maryland) have mechanisms for providing regular feedback to high schools about their graduates' academic performance during college. Nonetheless, in all five of our study states, state leaders described limitations of existing data systems, particularly with regard to tracking students longitudinally from K–12 into higher education, across sectors of higher education, and into the workforce. With the support of the federal Race to the Top grant program and/or state appropriations, several study states (Georgia, Maryland, Texas) are investing resources to develop longitudinal data systems.

In addition to making investments that enhance the capacity of their data systems, states must also consider the use of data that are collected. Ratings from the Education Sector and the Data Quality Campaign indicate that Illinois needs improvement in effectively using data to improve public policy,[53] and Maryland must improve the use of data in the state's strategic planning process.[54] Although Georgia has developed scorecards for reporting and monitoring progress toward state goals, the Data Quality Campaign noted that the state's data and accountability systems fell short on several dimensions.[55] At the time of our data collection, Washington had taken only four of ten actions that the Data Quality Campaign specified as creating a culture of data use.[56]

Ratings from the Data Quality Campaign and Education Sector suggest that Texas has made greater progress than these other states in monitoring educational outcomes and using data to inform governance and strategic planning.[57]

The Texas Higher Education Coordinating Board not only develops and updates the state plan for higher education, *Closing the Gaps*, but also annually reports progress toward reaching benchmarks, interim targets, and overall goals. Noting insufficient progress toward some goals in its 2010 annual progress report, the coordinating board developed "an accelerated action plan" to address four areas where progress was slower than expected. The Texas Business Leadership Council is among the entities in the state that has encouraged the collection and reporting of higher education performance measures. In 2003, the legislature specified that institutional progress toward achieving the *Closing the Gaps* goals was "a condition of tuition deregulation."

Approaches to ensuring accountability for achieving statewide goals and priorities include performance reporting and performance funding. As in most U.S. states, states in our study allocate appropriations to colleges and universities using formula that emphasize enrollment and credit hours. But as described in the individual case studies, this approach incentivizes enrollment growth and does not encourage improvements in academic preparation, college affordability, or degree completion. Allocating funding based on enrollment and credit hours also does not encourage cost-restructuring or the use of innovative practices. This approach also delays compensation for enrollment growth, providing institutions with funding for enrollments that occurred one or two years in the past. Moreover, the reliance on enrollment to determine institutional appropriations creates challenges for institutions when the growth in state funding for higher education does not keep pace with growth in enrollment. Nationwide, state and local revenue per FTE student (in constant dollars) is now at its lowest point in 25 years, largely due to the high rate of enrollment growth.[58]

Several of the states in our study expressed some level of interest in performance funding. This attention is consistent with the prediction by Eckl and Pattison that, in the context of constrained fiscal resources, state officials will focus greater attention on accountability and the effective and efficient use of available funding.[59] Washington recently developed and implemented a performance-funding system for its community and technical colleges. Designed to promote accountability and provide financial incentives to improve performance, the system first distributed funds based on performance in 2008–9. The state has also taken steps toward implementing performance funding for the public four-year institutions, but fiscal challenges have slowed these efforts. Texas has also made some movement toward a performance-funding system in recent years. Established in 2007, the Higher Education Performance Incentive Initiative provides a very small amount of money (less than 1% of all funding for higher education in FY 2009) to public colleges and universities for performance in a limited number of areas. Both the governor and legislature have expressed interested in a more extensive performance funding system.

At the time of our data collection, state leaders in Illinois told us that implementation of a performance-funding system was unlikely in the context of fiscal constraints. Nonetheless, a December 2010 report from a legislatively created commission noted the absence of links between higher education funding and the state's educational attainment and other goals and recommended the implementation of a performance-funding system. A law passed in spring 2011 requires the Board of Higher Education to include in its budget recommendations, beginning in fiscal year 2013, allocations to community colleges and public universities based on "performance in achieving state goals related to student success and certificate and degree completion."[60]

Performance-funding systems have been implemented in the past with limited meaningful impact on higher education performance.[61] Past systems have historically involved relatively small amounts of funding, likely creating insufficient incentives for colleges and universities to respond to statewide goals and priorities, and have had uneven political support, particularly from higher education.[62] Other forces that may have contributed to the limited effectiveness of past performance funding efforts pertain to the challenges of identifying performance measures that apply across higher education sectors, instability in funding and funding formula, inadequate attention to differences in institutional capacity and resources, and insufficient attention to unintended consequences for enrollment, academic selectivity of admissions, mission, and compliance costs.[63]

Nonetheless, Complete College America, suggesting optimism about this new wave of performance funding (Performance Funding 2.0), encourages the use as one "essential step" for improving college completion and recommends that states implement funding models that link appropriations to completion, not enrollment. Complete College America highlights Washington's Student Achievement Initiative, as well as funding models in Indiana and Ohio, as exemplars of "well-designed funding approaches that hold promise for yielding significant gains in completion." Nonetheless, it is too early to assess the effects of these newer efforts on improving higher education attainment and closing gaps in attainment across groups.

Political Implications

Recognizing that improvements in higher education performance are needed is far easier than identifying and implementing the strategies (as adapted to the characteristics of the state context and higher education system) that will effectively achieve this goal. The relatively stagnant overall attainment rates, combined with the stubborn persistence of gaps in higher education attainment across groups, signal the magnitude of the related challenges. Nonetheless, overcoming these challenges is critical, given the importance of higher educational attainment to individual and societal prosperity.

State leaders must recognize the evolution in the needs and priorities that many state higher education systems were originally designed to address. Rather than simply promoting the expansion of higher education, state higher education systems must now also encourage the completion of degrees and the reduction of gaps across groups in higher education outcomes and must accomplish these goals in the context of an increasingly diverse population of students, constraints on state fiscal resources, and other evolving state-specific characteristics. Richardson and colleagues articulate the need for states to reconsider the ways that they are advancing statewide goals and priorities in a changed context: "States that uncritically preserve policies and systems that were created to respond to a different set of priorities may be indulging either the self-serving tendencies of institutions or the most immediate demands of the market at the expense of emerging needs of greater long-term consequence."[64]

Underlying many current approaches to raising the nation's educational attainment is an economic argument: the necessity of improved educational attainment to the economic productivity of the nation and the readiness of workers for current and future jobs. Many of the public policies that have been implemented to improve educational attainment also tend to be justified from the perspective of economics: increasing the affordability of higher education and improving academic readiness increases student demand for higher education, whereas maximizing the availability of higher education options increases the supply.

However, as shown by our case studies and resulting conceptual model, attention to economic policies, although necessary, is insufficient. Raising educational attainment and closing gaps in attainment also requires attention to the extent to which higher education systems and structures are oriented toward achieving societal goals and purposes and leveling the playing field for higher education.

The emphasis of our conceptual model on the political dimensions—that is, the role of state policy leadership and steering in advancing a cohesive public agenda for higher education (tenet 2)—as well as the types of public policies that will raise overall attainment (tenet 3) and close gaps in attainment across groups (tenet 4), has conceptual parallels to the conclusions about the roles of political leadership and public policy drawn by scholars who have examined problems different from, but related to, higher education attainment. For instance, Joseph Stiglitz stresses the contributions of both politics and policy to the recent dramatic growth in income inequality in this nation. Noting that the "government sets and enforces the rules of the game," Stiglitz argues, "Our political system has increasingly been working in ways that increase the inequality of outcomes and reduce equality of opportunity."[65]

In *Why Nations Fail,* Daron Acemoglu and James Robinson also emphasize the roles of political and economic institutions in explaining why some nations are economically prosperous while other nations—even those that are situated similarly geographically and serving the same racial and ethnic populations—experience persistent poverty and inequality. Their analyses convincingly demonstrate that differences in economic prosperity between the world's richest and poorest nations are attributable, not to geography (e.g., climate), culture (e.g., work ethic), or knowledge of effective policies, but rather to whether a nation has "inclusive" political and economic institutions. Inclusive political leadership, a fundamental characteristic of an inclusive and pluralist society, is characterized by the broad distribution of political power, rather than concentration of "power in the hands of a few," as well as by its support for inclusive economic institutions. Inclusive economic institutions "create a level playing field" by encouraging individuals to build their education and skills. The broad investment in education, skills, and other infrastructure, in turn, contributes to technological advancement and economic progress. In short, Acemoglu and Robinson conclude that what differentiates prosperous nations from poor nations is the extent to which political leaders use their political power not to further advantage the already powerful but to encourage the broader well-being of the nation.[66]

Differences in wealth and prosperity are certainly not as dramatic among or within U.S. states as they are between the United States and many Latin American countries, between North and South Korea, or between many of the other nations that Acemoglu and Robinson compare and contrast. Nonetheless, their conclusions about the contributions of politics and policies to national economic prosperity has parallels to our understanding of the forces that explain differences in higher education attainment across U.S. states. Higher education attainment is not higher in Maryland and Washington than in Georgia or improving in Texas and declining in Illinois because of differences in the geographic location of these states or the lack of educational aspirations among the populace.[67] Instead, differences in higher education attainment across states are attributable to the extent to which higher education systems and leaders are oriented toward advancing societal goals and priorities for higher education and the extent to which state policies are serving to promote overall higher education attainment and close gaps in attainment across groups.

Adopting public policies that level the playing field for higher education opportunity is often politically challenging because equalizing educational opportunity requires breaking a vicious cycle in which current policies favor the advantaged, which in turn serves to further increase the political power and economic advantages of those who are already advantaged. This type of vicious cycle explains the persisting poverty of many nations and is a primary driver of the recent growth in inequality in the United States.[68] As Stiglitz argues, in the United States, the most affluent have disproportionate political power and have used this power "to strengthen their economic and political positions." The use of political power "to limit the extent of redistribution" and "shape the rules of the game in their favor" is a primary explanation for the growing inequality in the United States.[69]

In their study of the forces that contribute to the economic prosperity of nations, Acemoglu and Robinson highlight the southern region of the United States for its success in breaking a vicious cycle that perpetuated the stratification of political power and economic opportunity. They note that with a shift away from policies that increased the advantages of the affluent toward policies that equalized opportunity came dramatic improvements in economic and social well-being. As Acemoglu and Robinson describe, slaves in the U.S. South had little political or economic power until the Civil War. Even following the Civil War, when Black men received the right to vote, Jim Crow laws, activities of the Ku Klux Klan, disenfranchisement of Black voters, segregation of schools, and other forces continued to restrict Blacks' political power, opportunity for high-quality education, and access to high-wage jobs. With the civil rights movement, however, policies that maintained or advanced "the power of the landed elite, plantation agriculture, and low-wage, low-education labor" began to disintegrate, and the economic well-being of the South improved.[70]

Certainly, the political and economic institutions in the southern and other regions of the United States today are far less oriented toward limiting opportunity for Blacks and further enhancing the advantages of the elite than in the years of slavery and Jim Crow laws. Nonetheless, our analyses reveal the need for renewed attention to the extent to which political systems and economic policies throughout the United States continue to benefit only a small and already affluent and powerful elite rather than create incentives that encourage all to invest in increasing their education and skills and thereby improve economic and social well-being more broadly.

Although understanding the historical patterns that have contributed to the current situation is critical, Acemoglu and Robinson argue, "history is not destiny." Breaking a vicious circle of exclusive political and economic institutions is not easy, but "a critical juncture, a major event or confluence of factors disrupting the existing economic and political balance in society" may "cause a sharp turn in the trajectory of a nation" and permit the creation of more inclusive policies.[71] The growing importance of higher education attainment to economic and social prosperity, the sizeable persisting gaps in attainment across groups, changing demographic characteristics of the population, and other forces described in chapter 1, all suggest that states are at a "critical juncture." In short, we are at a point in time when state leaders need to rethink their role in advancing a cohesive public agenda for higher education that furthers societal goals and priorities and that orients public policies toward leveling the playing field for higher education attainment.

Implications for Future Research

The results of our analyses demonstrate the benefits of case study methodology for producing an in-depth understanding of the ways that public policy influences higher education performance within a particular state context. The analyses also suggest the benefits of drawing on multiple theoretical and conceptual perspectives for producing a more comprehensive understanding of this relationship.

In addition, the analyses illustrate the utility of broadening the definition of equity in higher education to include attention to gaps in outcomes based not only on race/ethnicity and income—the dimensions that are most commonly considered by researchers and policymakers—but also on other dimensions, including geographic location within a state. This comprehensive definition of equity should be used to ensure that public policy is appropriately targeted and adapted to reflect the forces that limit and promote higher education attainment across different groups.[72]

Since the conceptual model proposed in this study is derived from data and analyses describing the relationship between public policy and higher education attainment in just five states, we conclude by identifying recommendations and directions for future research. Additional research is required to test the transferability of the conceptual framework that emerged from our case studies for explaining the relationship between public policy and higher education performance in other states.

The findings from our analyses also suggest several other productive areas for future inquiry. First, additional research is required to identify the intended and unintended consequences of the various emerging strategies that the five states are using to improve the alignment of available higher education opportunities with the educational needs of their states. A number of the identified policies, including the expansion of the mission of community colleges to award bachelor's degrees, creation of additional options connected to existing higher education providers (such as branch campuses), use of online providers, encouragement of enrollment in private not-for-profit higher education institutions, and use of for-profit higher education providers, appear to have both potential positive and negative implications for overall attainment and gaps in attainment across groups. Research examining these and other policy initiatives, as well as any recommendations about the use of reforms in other states must, of course, take into account the role of state contextual characteristics.

Second, future research should consider the ways that public policies that are typically conceptualized and established independently come together to positively and negatively influence higher education attainment. For instance, recent efforts by Maryland to link state appropriations to tuition increases and to link tuition increases to family income suggest the value of linking various higher education finance levers to improve college affordability. Research should further explore the potential for coordinating other finance levers to improve affordability as well as linking other levers to achieve other aspects of higher education performance, including college preparation, participation, and completion.

Additional research is also required to inform and understand the implications of innovative approaches to allocating available public resources across institutions and students. Such research should seek to identify, for example, the appropriate distribution of state appropriations to colleges and universities with different missions and how this distribution influences a state's overall attainment and equity in attainment across groups. Like other states, the five states in our study allocate more public resources per student to the institutions that educate the best-prepared students than to other institutions (with more resources to the public research universities than to public two-year colleges, for instance). Further research should also consider the implications of a statewide approach to other aspects of higher education, including, for example, the possibility that developmental education be offered only at some of a state's institutions.[73]

Greater understanding of how federal policy interacts with state policy to influence the relationship between public policy and performance is also required. Like Richardson and Martinez, we acknowledge that state policy may be influenced by federal policy but focus on understanding the role of state policy.[74] Yet identifying the ways that federal policies pertaining to student financial assistance and academic research—the primary areas of federal policy intervention in higher education (as described in chapter 1)—influence state policy may generate important insights for how to productively improve overall attainment and increase equity in attainment across groups. Moreover, as argued by others, coordination of federal and state policies may result in even greater improvements in higher education performance.[75]

In addition, although our findings point to the role of state leadership in improving higher education performance, we know little about how to effectively enhance the capacity and competencies of state leaders to provide the leadership that is required in the current higher education, fiscal, and political context. Higher education requires policy leadership and steering that advances the public benefits of higher education. The conceptual model that emerged from our study stresses the importance of a state's steering capacity, but it does not reveal how to most effectively provide such steering. Moreover, writings from an earlier era (such as those of Lyman Glenny and Burton Clark) may have limited applicability to today's state higher education systems, given the many changes in context. Today's higher education systems must be focused not only on improving higher education enrollment but also on raising attainment and closing gaps in attainment across groups. Renewed attention to the steering capacity as opposed to the coordination of higher education that occurred in an earlier era must also recognize the need to secure political support for a statewide perspective, particularly given that higher education systems are now typically characterized by at least one large, prestigious, and politically powerful research university.

Greater attention is needed to the mechanisms that promote effective state policy leadership and steering within particular state contexts. Our state studies demonstrate variations in the extent to which state systems and state leaders are poised to improve educational attainment and reduce gaps in opportunity. Especially important appears to be the capacity of leaders to build consensus among stakeholders with sometimes divergent goals and priorities as well as the ability to strategically use available resources to address societal needs and achieve societal purposes. Also necessary is the ability of state leaders to promote connections across educational sectors and to hold themselves and higher education institutions accountable for progress. Mechanisms that promote differentiation of institutional missions are also important. Developing leadership and steering capacity seems to require identifying ways to encourage productive interactions with governors and legislators, especially about institutional budgets and funding priorities, while also maintaining a buffer that limits the influence of political partisanship. Future research should more systematically explore the attributes and skills of effective state leaders, while also considering the context in which leadership capacity is developed and leadership is executed. For example, building trust and consensus is undoubtedly more difficult in a state like Illinois, where there is a recent history of political corruption, a culture of distrust, and high rates of turnover among state leaders, than in a state like Maryland, which has a record of stable respected political leaders who have personal, direct connections to education. Experimentation with new structures (e.g., Oregon Education Investment Board) may generate fruitful insights.

Concluding Note

The low levels of overall higher education attainment and the sizeable gaps in higher education that persist based on family income, race/ethnicity, and geographic location are the culmination of processes and outcomes that began far earlier than high school and college. Moreover, efforts to level the playing field for higher education opportunity will always face opposition, since those who have realized the greatest benefits are motivated to use their available resources to maintain their privilege.[76]

Nonetheless, for economic and social justice reasons, public policymakers and college and school leaders have an obligation to challenge this opposition and identify and eliminate the forces that serve to perpetuate and institutionalize differences in higher educational outcomes across groups. We share Acemoglu and Robinson's conclusion that improving national economic prosperity requires more than "hectoring" lower-performing governments "into adopting better policies and institutions." Instead, like Acemoglu and Robinson, we argue that improving overall higher education attainment and improving equity in attainment across groups requires fundamental change, including deeper attention to "why bad policies and institutions are there in the first place."[77] Both state higher education leadership and higher education policies need to be reconsidered and adapted to reflect the current challenges and context if states and the nation are to achieve the required levels of higher education attainment in their populations.

From the perspective of state leadership and public policy, the central question underlying the issues raised in this volume is: What kind of society do we want to live in? More specifically, do we want to live in a society (that is, a nation or state) that is economically prosperous? If so, then greater effort is required to raise overall higher education attainment and close gaps in attainment across groups. This book offers a starting point.

Notes

CHAPTER 1: **Improving Higher Education Attainment of All Students**

1. Analyses of data from the Organisation for Economic Co-operation and Development 2009, as published in Baum, Ma, and Payea, *Education Pays 2010.*

2. Kelly, "Projected Degree Gap."

3. Based on his review of data from the U.S. Bureau of Labor Statistics, McMahon, *Higher Learning, Greater Good,* concluded: "All thirty occupations growing fastest percentage-wise, except for home health care, medical, and pharmacy aides, require a community college or four-year college education or more. . . . And for the thirty occupations expected to account for over two-thirds of the numerical decline in jobs, 28 out of 30 are lower skilled, requiring only on-the-job training after high school" (76).

4. Carnevale, Smith, and Strohl, *Help Wanted.* See also Zumeta, "Does the U.S. Need More College Graduates to Remain a World-Class Economic Power?"

5. Demographers define a generation as "a group of people born over a relatively short and contiguous time period that is deeply influenced and bound together by the events of their formative years"; Geoffrey and Schewe, "The Power of Cohorts."

6. Anderson and Kennedy, "Baby Boomer Segmentation."

7. Vedder, "Why College Isn't for Everyone." Among those providing persuasive counter-arguments are Carnevale, Smith, and Strohl, *Help Wanted;* and McMahon, *Higher Learning, Greater Good.*

8. McMahon, *Higher Learning, Greater Good.*

9. Organisation for Economic Co-operation and Development, *Education at a Glance 2012,* 184.

10. Ibid.

11. Acemoglu and Robinson, *Why Nations Fail,* 78–79.

12. We adopt McMahon's distinction between inequality and equity: "Equity is a normative term that involves a value judgment. Inequality is not; it is simply a description of the facts about the degree of equality in a distribution" (*Higher Learning, Greater Good,* 216). Like McMahon, Salmi and Bassett ("Opportunities for All?"), and others, our interest is in equality of opportunity to participate in and benefit from higher education.

13. Organisation for Economic Co-operation and Development, *Going for Growth.* In contrast, in Sweden, the most equitable nation on this measure, only 4.5% of the total pre-tax income went to the top 1%.

14. Organisation for Economic Co-operation and Development, *Going for Growth;* Stiglitz, *Price of Inequality.*

15. Stiglitz, *Price of Inequality.*

16. Haskins, Isaacs, and Sawhill, *Getting Ahead or Losing Ground.*

17. Stiglitz, *Price of Inequality.*

18. Salmi and Bassett, "Opportunities for All?" Recent uprisings in Tunisia, Egypt, and other Middle Eastern and North African nations suggest the importance of higher education opportunity to political stability and civility.

19. Stiglitz, *Price of Inequality,* 116.

20. Data from the Panel Study of Income Dynamics, as reported in 2005, "Education and Economic Mobility."

21. Analyses of data from the National Center for Education Statistics, as published in Baum, Ma, and Payea, *Education Pays.*

22. Ibid.

23. Analyses of data from the 2007–11 American Community Survey show that median family incomes were $42,239 for Blacks and $43,374 for Hispanics, considerably lower than for Whites ($72,088) and Asians ($81,268).

24. National Center for Education Statistics, *Digest of Education Statistics 2011,* table 213.

25. Ibid., table 210.

26. Ibid., table 10.

27. Humes, Jones, and Ramirez, *Overview of Race and Hispanic Origin: 2010.*

28. Ibid.

29. Western Interstate Higher Education Commission, *Knocking at the College Door.*

30. Humes, Jones, and Ramirez, *Overview of Race and Hispanic Origin: 2010.*

31. Acemoglu and Robinson, *Why Nations Fail;* Salmi and Bassett, "Opportunities for All?"

32. Shapiro et al., "Completing College." The *Digest of Education Statistics* published annually by the National Center for Education Statistics shows the percentage of students who first enroll full-time who complete a degree from the institution in which they first enroll within 150% of the expected time to completion (e.g., six years for a bachelor's degree). Drawing on data from the National Student Clearinghouse, these completion rates reflect the percentage of students who first enroll full-time or part-time who complete a degree or certificate within six years from their starting institution or from a different institution.

33. Schneider and Yin, *High Cost of Low Graduation Rates.*

34. Salmi and Bassett, drawing from the work of philosophers John Rawls, Amartya Sen, Ronald Dworkin, and John Roemer, conclude that promoting equity in college access and completion "promotes justice as fairness" ("Opportunities for All?" 6).

35. Baum, Ma, and Payea, *Education Pays,* figure 1.2.

36. National Center for Education Statistics, *Digest of Education Statistics 2011,* table 395.

37. Analyses of data from the Bureau of Labor Statistics, in Baum, Ma, and Payea, *Education Pays.*

38. Grusky et al., *How Much Protection Does a College Degree Afford?*

39. Baum, Ma, and Payea, *Education Pays;* Carnevale, Smith, and Strohl, *Help Wanted.*

40. Autor, *Polarization of Job Opportunities in the U.S. Labor Market.*

41. Perna, "The Private Benefits of Higher Education"; Vedder, "Why College Isn't for Everyone."

42. Leslie and Brinkman, *Economic Value of Higher Education;* Perna, "The Private Benefits of Higher Education."

43. Autor, *Polarization of Job Opportunities in the U.S. Labor Market.*

44. Baum, Ma, & Payea, *Education Pays.* McMahon, *Higher Learning, Greater Good,* stresses that these benefits should be categorized as "market" and "non-market" benefits rather than "economic" benefits, since the benefits go well beyond increased earnings.

45. Mayer, *Union Membership Trends in the United States.*

46. Carnevale, Smith, and Strohl, *Help Wanted.*

47. The Pew Charitable Trusts, Economic Mobility Project, *Economic Mobility and the American Dream.*

48. Carnevale, Smith, and Strohl, *Help Wanted.* Lower-income class is defined as the lower three deciles of household income; upper-income class is defined as the upper three deciles of household income. The authors calculated the distributions using data from the March Current Population Survey (CPS).

49. Haskins, "Education and Economic Mobility." More specifically, 45% of adults (at age 40) whose parents were in the lowest-income quintile (when they were about age 40) and who did not earn a college degree were also in the lowest-income quintile, compared with only 16% of adults whose parents were also in the lowest-income quintile but who earned a college degree.

50. Ibid. "Poor" is defined as the lowest parental income quintile.

51. See the comprehensive documentation of these and other benefits in Baum, Ma, and Payea, *Education Pays;* and McMahon, *Higher Learning, Greater Good.*

52. Baum, Ma, and Payea, *Education Pays;* Haskins, "Education and Economic Mobility"; McMahon, *Higher Learning, Greater Good.*

53. McMahon, *Higher Learning, Greater Good;* Zumeta et al., *Financing American Higher Education in the Era of Globalization.*

54. College Board, *Trends in College Pricing.*

55. College Board, *Trends in Student Aid.* Borrowing rates are higher for those in the bottom three income quartiles than for those in the highest quartile (42% versus 33%), but the amount borrowed is lower for those in the lowest quartile of family income than for others. The lower average amount borrowed likely reflects the tendency of lower-income students to attend lower-cost institutions.

56. National Center for Education Statistics, *Trends in Financing of Undergraduate Education.*

57. McMahon, *Higher Learning, Greater Good.*

58. Based on his comprehensive review, Michael K. McLendon concluded that, although scholars disagree on "the precise nature and extent of state governmental control over public higher education in the three centuries preceding World War II," there is clear agreement that with the end of World War II came "a new chapter in the history of the campus-state relationship" ("State Governance Reform of Higher Education," 67).

59. Stiglitz, *Price of Inequality;* Zumeta et al., *Financing American Higher Education in the Era of Globalization.*

60. Ibid.

61. Stiglitz, *Price of Inequality.*

62. Ibid., 28.

63. According to 2011 polling data from the Pew Charitable Trusts' Economic Mobility Project, 83% of Americans agree that the government should provide opportunities for the poor and middle class "to improve their economic situations" or "prevent them from falling behind"; 80% agree that "the government does an ineffective job of helping poor and middle class Americans"; and 54% agree that government initiatives typically assist the "wrong people."

64. Pew Charitable Trusts, Economic Mobility Project, *Economic Mobility and the American Dream.*

65. Heck, *Studying Educational and Social Policy,* 35

66. National Center for Education Statistics, *Digest of Education Statistics 2011,* table 374.

67. College Board, *Trends in Student Aid 2012.*

68. Hearn, "The Paradox of Growth in Federal Aid for College Students, 1960–1990," 269.

69. Mundel, "What Do We Know about the Impact of Grants to College Students?"

70. Perna and Titus, "Understanding Differences in the Choice of College Attended."

71. Heller, "Student Price Response in Higher Education"; Mundel, "What Do We Know about the Impact of Grants to College Students?"

72. Heller, "The Impact of Student Loans on College Access."

73. Cunningham and Santiago, *Student Aversion to Borrowing;* Perna, "Understanding High School Students' Willingness to Borrow to Pay College Prices."

74. Callan, "Reframing Access and Opportunity."

75. In their examination of the relationship between public policy and higher education performance, Richardson and Martinez, *Policy and Performance in American Higher Education,* focus on the role of state policy but assume that state policy is informed by federal policy and that state policy, in turn, is informed by institutional action.

76. McLendon, "State Governance Reform of Higher Education," 64–65.

77. For a listing of land-grant institutions, refer to the Association of Public and Land-Grant Universities, founded in 1887 and formerly known as the National Association of State Universities and Land-Grant Universities.

78. Heller, "The Changing Nature of Financial Aid."

79. U.S. Department of Education, *Leveraging Educational Assistance Partnership (LEAP) Program: Funding Status.*

80. U.S. Department of Education, Institute of Education Sciences, *National Assessment of Educational Progress.*

81. Perna and Thomas, "Barriers to College Opportunity."

82. Heck, *Studying Educational and Social Policy.*

83. National Center for Education Statistics, *Digest of Education Statistics 2011,* table 199.

84. National Center for Education Statistics, *Digest of Education Statistics 2011.*

85. Ibid., table 224.

86. In fall 2010, public two-year colleges enrolled 61% of all students enrolled in

degree-granting institutions in Wyoming, 58% in California, and 53% in New Mexico. National Center for Education Statistics, *Digest of Education Statistics 2011*, table 224.

87. Dougherty and Kienzl, "It's Not Enough to Get through the Open Door."

88. Desrochers, Lenihan, and Wellman, *Trends in College Spending 1998–2008*, figure 10.

89. Ibid., figure 13.

90. State Higher Education Executive Officers, *State Higher Education Finance, FY 2012*, table 7.

91. Kelly, "Projected Degree Gap."

92. Eckl and Pattison, "A New Funding Paradigm for Higher Education."

93. Hovey, *State Spending for Higher Education in the Next Decade*; Delaney and Doyle, "The Role of Higher Education in State Budgets."

94. State Higher Education Executive Officers, *State Higher Education Finance, FY 2012*. State and local support excludes appropriations for research, agricultural extension, and medical education.

95. Eckl and Pattison, "A New Funding Paradigm for Higher Education"; State Higher Education Executive Officers, *State Higher Education Finance, FY 2012*.

96. Boyd, *Projected State and Local Budget Surplus as a Percent of Revenues, 2016*.

97. Eckl and Pattison, "A New Funding Paradigm for Higher Education," 7.

98. For instance, in their case studies of seven states, Richardson et al., *Designing State Higher Education Systems for a New Century*, measured the performance of higher education using indicators of cost (i.e., state appropriations per FTE student), participation (i.e., the share of high school graduates enrolled in college), "equity" (i.e., retention of minority students relative to White students); affordability (e.g., tuition relative to household income), and retention of first-time freshmen.

99. See McMahon, *Higher Learning, Greater Good*, for an examination of the social returns to investment in research.

100. Ibid., 285. Based on his review of available data and research, McMahon concludes that, particularly for states (or nations) "that are farther from the technological frontier," as signaled by their lower per capita income, "the investment found to have the greatest growth payoff is in two- and four-year college degree programs" (21).

101. National Governors Association, *Complete to Compete*.

102. Institute for a Competitive Workforce, *Leaders and Laggards*.

103. Acemoglu and Robinson, *Why Nations Fail*, 448.

104. Ibid., 450.

CHAPTER 2: **Understanding the Relationship between Public Policy and Higher Education Performance**

1. For instance, a primary focus of the case studies conducted by Richardson et al., *Designing State Higher Education Systems for a New Century*, was to identify the system designs and the state policy "roles" that are associated with the performance of higher education in seven states.

2. Paulsen, "The Economics of the Public Sector," provides a useful discussion of the rationale for the role of public policy in the higher education market.

3. Richardson et al., *Designing State Higher Education Systems*, 2. For a comprehensive

review of the historical origins and development of autonomy and accountability in the U.S., see McLendon, "State Governance Reform of Higher Education."

4. Berdahl, *Statewide Coordination of Higher Education.*

5. E.g., Bloland, *Creating the Council for Higher Education Accreditation.*

6. Clark, *Higher Education System,* 121.

7. Berdahl, *Statewide Coordination of Higher Education,* 4.

8. Glenny, *Autonomy of Public Colleges.*

9. Richardson et al., *Designing State Higher Education Systems.*

10. Clark, *Higher Education System,* 129.

11. In his literature review, McLendon, "State Governance Reform of Higher Education," identifies a number of forces that contributed to the increased role of the state in higher education that occurred following World War II.

12. Richardson et al., *Designing State Higher Education Systems,* 6.

13. Clark, *Higher Education System,* 130.

14. Richardson et al., *Designing State Higher Education Systems.*

15. Clark, *Higher Education System.*

16. Ibid., 138, 203.

17. Ibid., 139.

18. Richardson et al., *Designing State Higher Education Systems,* 14.

19. Ibid., 172. They define a federal system as one with a state agency that "acts as an interface between state government and institutions." A unified system has one governing board for all degree-granting higher education institutions. In a segmented system most higher education institutions have their own governing boards.

20. Ibid., 15.

21. Richardson and Martinez, *Policy and Performance in American Higher Education.*

22. In her institutional analysis and development (IAD) framework, Ostrom defines an "institution" not as an organizational entity but as "the shared concepts used by humans in repetitive situations organized by rules, norms, and strategies" and focuses on the ways that rules, norms, and strategies influence the choices made by "actors" who are embedded in particular "action areas" ("Institutional Rational Choice," 37).

23. Richardson and Martinez, *Policy and Performance in American Higher Education.*

24. Consistent with a qualitative case study research methodology, Richardson and Martinez, *Policy and Performance,* also allow their conclusions about the "rules in use" that influence higher education performance to emerge from their case study analyses. Their exploratory approach sheds light on various dimensions of the complex relationship between public policy and higher education performance but also raises questions about the transferability of findings to other states. Richardson and Martinez organize the rules that emerged from their analyses into six groups, two of which are arguably part of the definition of performance (i.e., the dependent variable) rather than predictors of performance: access and achievement, and research and development. In addition, while Richardson and Martinez delineate the components of each of the six rule categories, they do not offer a theoretical or conceptual rationale that explains why rules pertaining to these particular categories (system design, state leadership, information, access and achievement, fiscal policies, and research and development) should be related to performance.

25. Richardson et al., *Designing State Higher Education Systems;* Richardson and Martinez, *Policy and Performance.*

26. Richardson et al., *Designing State Higher Education.*

27. Ibid.

28. Paulsen, "The Economics of Human Capital and Investment in Higher Education."

29. Becker, *Human Capital;* and Paulsen, "The Economics of Human Capital and Investment in Higher Education."

30. Baum, Ma, and Payea, *Education Pays 2010.*

31. Becker, *Human Capital.*

32. DesJardins and Toutkoushian, "Are Students Really Rational?"

33. McMahon, *Higher Learning, Greater Good,* 180, estimated that the private nonmarket benefits represent 122% of the private benefits of higher education.

34. Clark, *Higher Education System;* McMahon, *Higher Learning, Greater Good;* Paulsen, "The Economics of Human Capital and Investment in Higher Education"; Perna, Steele et al., "State Public Policies and the Racial/Ethnic Stratification of College Access and Choice in the State of Maryland"; and Stiglitz, *Price of Inequality.*

35. McMahon, *Higher Learning, Greater Good,* 44.

36. Stiglitz, *Price of Inequality.*

37. McMahon, *Higher Learning, Greater Good,* 51.

38. Paulsen, "The Economics of Human Capital and Investment in Higher Education"; McMahon, *Higher Learning, Greater Good.*

39. Stiglitz, *Price of Inequality,* 34.

40. Paulsen, "The Economics of the Public Sector."

41. The Institute of Education Sciences of the U.S. Department of Education established the What Works Clearinghouse in 2002 with the goal of determining the effectiveness, based on "scientific evidence," of various educational practices.

42. Heller, "The Impact of Student Loans on College Access."

43. Perna and Titus, "Understanding Differences in the Choice of College Attended."

44. Bettinger et al., *The Role of Simplification and Information in College Decisions.*

45. For a recent comprehensive review of the policies and practices that promote many outcomes on the path from college preparation to college enrollment, transfer, and degree completion, see Perna and Jones, *The State of College Access and Completion.*

46. Stiglitz, *Price of Inequality,* 28.

47. McLendon, "State Governance Reform of Higher Education."

48. Ness, "The Politics of Determining Merit Aid Eligibility Criteria"; Ness and Mistetta, "Merit Aid in North Carolina."

49. Doyle, McLendon, and Hearn, "The Adoption of Prepaid Tuition and Savings Plans in the American States."

50. McLendon, Hearn, and Mokher, "Partisans, Professionals, and Power."

51. Analyses by Venezia, Callan et al., *The Governance Divide,* reveal four categories of state policy levers that promote high school students' academic readiness for college: alignment of courses and assessments, finance strategies, data systems, and accountability. Their analyses suggest that, in order to effectively promote college readiness, policies and programs in all four areas must span K–12 and higher education.

52. Richardson et al., *Designing State Higher Education Systems.*

53. Richardson and Martinez, *Policy and Performance.*

CHAPTER 3: **Examining the Relationship between Public Policy and Performance in Five States**

The research reported here was supported in part by the Institute of Education Sciences, U.S. Department of Education, through Grant #R305B090015 to the University of Pennsylvania. The opinions expressed are those of the authors and do not represent the views of the Institute or the U.S. Department of Education.

1. Kelly, "Projected Degree Gap."

2. National Center for Higher Education Management Systems, "ACS Educational Attainment by Degree-Level and Age-Group (American Community Survey)."

3. Steurle et al., *Lost Generations?* Using longitudinal data from the Survey of Consumer Finances, this report shows that, after controlling for inflation, average net worth is lower for younger generations than for older generations, and that, unlike older cohorts, average net worth of younger generations is not increasing over time. These declines began before the Great Recession. Other explanations for these trends include fewer job prospects and a lower employment rate.

4. Kelly, "Projected Degree Gap."

5. Council for Adult and Experiential Learning, *Adult Learning in Focus.*

6. Preparation is measured by the percentage of high school students taking at least one upper-level science course, the shares of eighth graders scoring at least proficient on the National Assessment of Educational Progress (NAEP) test in math and science, the percentage of low-income eighth graders scoring at least proficient on the NAEP math test, the number of SAT/ACT scores (per 1,000 high school graduates) in the top quintile, and the number of scores per 1,000 high school juniors and seniors of 3 or higher on an Advanced Placement subject test. Measures of participation include the percentages of 18- to 24-year olds and 25- to 29-year olds enrolled in college and the chance of college enrollment for high school freshmen. Measures of completion include degree completions per 100 students, six-year bachelor's degree completion rates for first-time full-time students, and the number of certificates and degrees awarded per 1,000 state residents. Affordability is measured by the percentage of income required to pay college expenses (less financial aid) and state investment in need-based financial aid relative to the federal investment (National Center for Public Policy and Higher Education, *Measuring Up 2008*).

7. U.S. Census Bureau, "Table B1: The Total Population by Selected Age Groups."

8. They comprised 60.2 million of the nation's 308.7 million total population (19.5%). U.S. Census Bureau, "Table SF1:P5: Hispanic or Latino Origin by Race."

9. Georgia is home to Atlanta, 40th largest city in 2010, with a population of 420,000. Chicago, Illinois, is the nation's third-largest city, with a population of 2.695 million. Maryland is home to Baltimore, the 24th largest city, with a population of 620,000. In Texas, Houston has 2.099 million residents (4th largest city), San Antonio has 1.327 million (7th largest city), Dallas has 1.198 million residents (9th largest city), Austin has 790,000 residents (13th largest city), Fort Worth has 790,390 residents (16th largest city),

and El Paso has 649,000 residents (19th largest city). Seattle, Washington, is the nation's 22nd largest city, with a population of 609,000. U.S. Census Bureau, "City and Town Totals: Vintage 2011."

10. Calculation from Western Interstate Higher Education Commission, *Knocking at the College Door, Projections of High School Graduates.*

11. Western Interstate Higher Education Commission, *Knocking at the College Door, Projections of High School Graduates.*

12. Ibid.

13. Ibid.

14. Boyd, *Projected State and Local Budget Surplus as a Percent of Revenues, 2016.*

15. Ibid.

16. State Higher Education Executive Officers, *State Higher Education Finance, FY 2012.*

17. According to "Tax Facts" from the Tax Policy Center of the Urban Institute and Brookings Institution, 14 states required legislative supermajorities for all tax increases in 2010. Three of these states (Colorado, Missouri, and Washington) also required voter approval of tax increases in some situations. In Washington, the legislature temporarily reduced the two-thirds requirement to a simple majority between April 2005 and June 30, 2007, and then again in 2010 through June 30, 2011.

18. State Higher Education Executive Officers, *State Higher Education Finance, FY 2012.*

19. National Center for Higher Education Management Systems, "Per Capita Personal Income, 2011."

20. Analyses of Integrated Public Use Microdata Series Version 5.0 Machine-readable Database.

21. Ibid.

22. Carnevale, Smith, and Strohl, *Help Wanted.*

23. Ibid.

24. National Center for Education Statistics, *Digest of Education Statistics 2011.*

25. Ibid.

26. Ibid.

27. For more information on the coordinating and governing agencies in all 50 states, refer to the October 2007 compilation prepared by the Education Commission of the States: *State-Level Coordinating and/or Governing Agency,* http://ecs.force.com/mbdata/mbquestU?Rep=PSG01&SID=a0i70000009vZI&Q=Q0667.

28. When the state reorganized its higher education system in 1988, these two institutions opted out. Berdahl and MacTaggart, *Charter Colleges: Balancing Freedom and Accountability,* iv, highlighted St. Mary's College of Maryland as a "successful example of the charter college idea" applied to higher education.

29. According to the National Center for Education Statistics, *Digest of Education Statistics 2011,* table 280, Georgia was home to 40 public two-year colleges in 2010–11. However, as described in the chapter on Georgia, over the past few years the state has created changes in its community colleges and merged the administration (but not altered the campus locations) of several technical colleges. In June 2013 the Technical College System of Georgia reported 25 technical colleges. For a list, see: https://tcsg.edu/college_campuses.php.

30. Yin, *Applications of Case Study Research,* 2nd ed.

31. See, e.g., Richardson and Martinez, *Policy and Performance in American Higher Education.*

32. Yin, *Applications of Case Study Research,* 2nd ed.

33. Our preliminary review of public policies focused in particular on identifying the "rules in use" in each state, as defined by Richardson and Martinez (2009), as well as other potential policy levers identified from other reports published by the National Center for Public Policy and Higher Education, the Southern Educational Regional Board, and other organizations.

34. In most instances we divided our team into two groups with two to four researchers each during these visits in order to maximize the reach of our data collection. We conducted a small number of interviews by telephone before each visit to help identify the most appropriate ways to structure our visits and to gain preliminary insights. We conducted additional interviews after these visits with individuals who were unavailable at the time of our visit and to follow up on issues raised during the visits.

35. Richardson and Martinez, *Policy and Performance in American Higher Education.*

36. In Georgia (the first state that we visited), members of the research team took detailed notes, including verbatim quotes, during the interviews. In the four other states, nearly all interviews were audiotaped and then transcribed. The interviews lasted between 30 and 120 minutes but averaged one hour. Many informants provided us with additional relevant supporting documents. We incorporated these documents into our data analyses.

37. Following the guidelines identified by Yin in *Case Study Research, Design and Methods,* 3rd ed., the database includes transcriptions from the interviews, the state specific documents, and media reports, as well as the quantitative data describing the economic, demographic, and other aspects of the state context and the state's higher education performance.

38. Initial codes included categories of higher education performance (i.e., preparation, participation, completion, and affordability); dimensions of the state economic, demographic, political, and historical context; and types of public policies and strategies designed to improve aspects of performance (e.g., policies aimed at improving academic readiness for college, financial aid policies, etc.). We employed HyperResearch software to assist in the coding and compiling of data into categories.

39. The use of a common protocol and case study database also helps to ensure credibility and trustworthiness; Yin, *Case Study Research.*

CHAPTER 4: **Perpetuating Disparity**

The research reported here was supported in part by the Institute of Education Sciences, U.S. Department of Education, through Grant #R305B090015 to the University of Pennsylvania. The opinions expressed are those of the authors and do not represent the views of the Institute or the U.S. Department of Education.

1. This report focuses on higher education performance and policy through 2010. The research team conducted interviews with state and institutional leaders in spring 2010.

2. Carnevale, Smith, and Strohl, *Help Wanted.*

3. Kelly, "Projected Degree Gap."

4. Jones, *A Public Agenda for Higher Education.*

5. National Center for Higher Education Management Systems, "Percent of Adults with an Associate Degree or Higher."

6. U.S. Census Bureau, "Table SF1:P5: Hispanic or Latino Origin by Race."

7. Western Interstate Higher Education Commission, *Knocking at the College Door Georgia Report.*

8. U.S. Bureau of Economic Analysis, "Personal Income and Per Capita Personal Income by State and Region, 2006–2010."

9. U.S. Bureau of Economic Analysis, "Local Area Personal Income, 1969–2008."

10. State Higher Education Executive Officers, *State Higher Education Finance, FY 2012.*

11. State Higher Education Executive Officers, "All States Wave Chart."

12. Southern Regional Education Board, *Legislative Report.*

13. Georgia State Lottery Corporation, *2009 Annual Report.*

14. Georgia State Lottery Corporation, "Georgia Lottery Corporation Management's Discussion and Analysis for the Years Ended June 30, 2011 and 2010."

15. Nathan Deal, "Governor's State-of-the-State Speech, 2011."

16. Lenard and Lord, *Gaining Ground on High School Graduation Rates in SREB States.* Data are from 2006. The Cumulative Promotion Index (CPI) is used by Editorial Projects in Education Research Center, in *Diplomas Count, 2010: Graduation by the Numbers,* to calculate high school graduation rates for American public schools. This approach allows the research center to compute the percentage of public high school students who graduate on time with a diploma. The CPI method represents the high school experience as a process rather than an event, capturing the four key steps a student must take in order to graduate: three grade-to-grade promotions (9 to 10, 10 to 11, and 11 to 12) and ultimately earning a diploma (grade 12 to graduation). Each of these individual components corresponds to a grade-promotion ratio. Multiplying these four grade-specific promotion ratios together produces the graduation rate. See Editorial Project in Education Research Center, "Indicators."

17. National Center for Education Statistics, *Nation's Report Card: NAEP Data Explorer;* National Center for Public Policy and Higher Education, *Measuring Up 2008.*

18. College Board, *Georgia AP Supplement 2011.*

19. National Center for Higher Education Management Systems, "Percent of 18 to 24 Year Olds Enrolled in College."

20. Mortenson, *Chance for College by Age 19 by State, 1986 to 2008.*

21. National Center for Higher Education Management Systems, "Six-year Graduation Rates of Bachelor's Students."

22. National Center for Higher Education Management Systems, "Three-year Graduation Rates for Associate Students."

23. Ewell and Kelly, *State-level Completion and Transfer Rates.*

24. Ibid.

25. National Center for Public Policy and Higher Education, *Measuring Up 2008.*

26. These include certificates of less than one year, those equal to one year but less than two years, and those equal to two years but less than four years.

27. State Higher Education Executive Officers, *Certificate Production and the Race Toward Higher Degree Attainment.*

28. National Center for Public Policy and Higher Education, *Measuring Up 2008.*

29. National Center for Public Policy and Higher Education, *Affordability and Transfer.*

30. National Center for Education Statistics, *Nation's Report Card: NAEP Data Explorer;* and National Center for Public Policy and Higher Education, *Measuring Up 2008.*

31. Editorial Projects in Education Research Center, "Indicators."

32. Georgia Department of Education, "Testing Brief."

33. College Board, *Georgia AP Supplement.*

34. National Center for Higher Education Management Systems, "2005 ACS PUMS—Education Attainment by Age by Race by State."

35. Integrated Postsecondary Education Data System, "2008 Graduation Rates Survey"; IPEDS, "2008 Institutional Characteristics Survey."

36. National Center for Higher Education Management Systems, "Percent of Adults with an Associate Degree or Higher."

37. Integrated Postsecondary Education Data System, "2008 Enrollment Survey," and "2008 Institutional Characteristics Survey."

38. University System of Georgia, "USG Institutions by Group."

39. University System of Georgia, "USG Facts."

40. University System of Georgia, "Regents Approve Campus Consolidation Plan."

41. Technical College System of Georgia (TCSG), *2009–2010 Fact Sheet and College Directory.*

42. Integrated Postsecondary Education Data System, "2009 Completions Survey"; Integrated Postsecondary Education Data System, "2009 Institutional Characteristics Survey."

43. "TCSG State Board Approves Decision to Merge Heart of Georgia Technical College and Sandersville Technical College," Atlanta: 2010. https://tcsg.edu/press_detail.php?press_id=172.

44. *The New Georgia Encyclopedia;* Perna, Milem et al., "The Status of Equity for Black Undergraduates in Public Higher Education in the South."

45. University System of Georgia, *Strategic Plan FY 2009.*

46. Perna, Milem et al., "The Status of Equity for Black Undergraduates in Public Higher Education in the South."

47. Integrated Postsecondary Education Data System, "2008 Enrollment" and "2008 Institutional Characteristics Survey."

48. Georgia Research Alliance, "Origins."

49. Georgia Research Alliance, "About us."

50. Ibid.

51. National Center for Higher Education Management Systems, "Total Research and Development Expenditures per $1,000 of Gross State Product."

52. Jones and Kelly, "A New Look at the Institutional Component of Higher Education Finance."

53. Governor's Office of Planning and Budget, "Governor's Budget Reports: 2013–2004."

54. Technical College System of Georgia, *2008 Annual Report.*

55. Georgia Student Finance Commission, "HOPE Grant Program Regulations, 2009–2010." To be eligible, students must be Georgia residents, have no drug convictions, and meet other eligibility requirements. To apply, students must complete either the Free Application for Federal Student Aid (FAFSA) or the Georgia Student Finance's GSFAPPS electronic application.

56. Technical College System of Georgia, "HOPE Legislation Fact Sheet."

57. Technical College System of Georgia, "HOPE and Pell Recipients by Race, FY 2001 to FY 2010," email communication, April 4, 2012.

58. University System of Georgia, "Number of Pell Grant Recipients: Fall 2008."

59. Hispanics represented small shares of students in both sectors (2.4% and 3.5%, respectively). Integrated Postsecondary Education Data System, "2008 Enrollment," and "2008 Institutional Characteristics Survey."

60. Venezia, Callan, et al., *Governance Divide.*

61. Ibid.

62. Georgia Department of Education, "The Alliance of Education Agency Heads."

63. Georgia Department of Education, "Strategy Map."

64. University System of Georgia, *Strategic Plan,* 8; and Technical College System of Georgia, "Mission, Vision, and Goals and Strategies."

65. Perna and Armijo, "The Persistence of Unaligned K12 and Higher Education Systems."

66. Governor's Office of Student Achievement, "About the Scoreboard," www.gaosa.org/scoreinfo.aspx. Accessed April 16, 2012.

67. Georgia Department of Education, "Strategy Map."

68. Data Quality Campaign, *Data for Action 2010: Georgia DQC State Analysis.*

69. Education Sector, "Georgia Score Card," June 30, 2009.

70. Georgia Office of Student Achievement, "Race to the Top."

71. Twenty-six local school districts signed on to partner with the state in implementing Georgia's Race to the Top plan. These districts make up 41% of the public school students in Georgia, including 46% of students in poverty, 53% of African American students, 48% of Hispanics and 68% of the state's lowest achieving schools. Badertscher and McWhirter, "Race to the Top Win Means $400 Million for GA."

72. University System of Georgia, "General Education in the University System of Georgia."

73. State of Georgia, *Tough Choices or Tough Times.*

74. University System of Georgia, "Regents Approve 17 General Education Courses for Transfer to Support Complete College Goals."

75. University System of Georgia, "Regents Take Action to Help Students Transfer College Credits."

76. University System of Georgia, *Strategic Plan FY2009,* 8.

77. Mackun and Wilson, "Population Distribution and Change: 2000 to 2010."

78. University System of Georgia, "USG Facts."

79. University System of Georgia, "USG Tuition Strategy."

80. Ibid.

81. Delta Cost Project, "Trends in College Spending Online."

82. University System of Georgia, *Formula Funding in Georgia.*

83. University System of Georgia, "Chancellor's State of the System Address 2010."

84. National Association of State Student Grant & Aid Programs, *40th Annual Survey Report on State-sponsored Student Financial Aid.*

85. Georgia State Lottery Corporation, *2009 Annual Report.*

86. Georgia Student Finance Commission, "HOPE Grant Program Regulations, 2009–2010."

87. GAcollege411, "Georgia's HOPE Scholarship Program Overview."

88. Integrated Postsecondary Education Data System, "2008 Enrollments Survey" and "2008 Institutional Characteristics Survey"; University System of Georgia, "Number of Pell Grant Recipients: Fall 2008."

89. University System of Georgia, *Keeping the HOPE Scholarship throughout College.*

90. Students must be enrolled at least half-time to be eligible for LEAP and may attend a public or private college or university or a technical college. In order to receive LEAP, students must apply for and be eligible to receive the Federal Pell Grant. State of Georgia, *The Governor's Budget Report, Amended Fiscal Year 2011.*

91. L. Diamond, "State Begins Low-interest College Loan Program," *Atlanta-Journal Constitution,* June 15, 2011. www.ajc.com/news/georgia-politics-elections/state-begins-low-interest-977323.html.

92. Georgia Student Finance Commission, "Scholarship and Grant Award History."

93. Students graduating from high school after May 1, 2016, must take three (rather than two) advanced courses. Students graduating after May 1, 2017, must take four advanced courses. Southern Regional Education Board, *Legislative Report no. 4.*

94. Technical College System of Georgia, "HOPE Legislation Fact Sheet."

95. Perna and Steele, "The Role of Context in Understanding the Contributions of Financial Aid to College Opportunity."

CHAPTER 5: **A Story of Decline**

The research reported here was supported in part by the Institute of Education Sciences, U.S. Department of Education, through Grant #R305B090015 to the University of Pennsylvania. The opinions expressed are those of the authors and do not represent the views of the Institute or the U.S. Department of Education.

1. This report focuses on higher education performance and policy through 2010. The research team conducted interviews with state and institutional leaders in spring 2010.

2. Carnevale, Smith, and Strohl, *Help Wanted.*

3. Kelly, "Projected Degree Gap."

4. U.S. Census Bureau, Table C03002, "Hispanic or Latino Origin by Race."

5. Ibid., and U.S. Census Bureau, table P4, "Hispanic or Latino, and Not Hispanic or Latino by Race [73]."

6. Western Interstate Higher Education Commission, *Knocking at the College Door.*

7. National Center for Public Policy and Higher Education, *Measuring Up 2008.*

8. U.S. Census Bureau, *United States: ACS Demographic and Housing Estimates: 2005–2009.*

9. Ibid. Data are for 2009.

10. U.S. Census Bureau, "Chicago City, Illinois: Selected Economic Characteristics: 2005–2009."

11. Governor's Office of Management and Budget, "General Funds Appropriations 2006–2011."

12. Pew Center on the States, *Beyond California.*

13. National Conference of State Legislatures, *State Budget Update: November 2010.*

14. Governor's Office of Management and Budget, *FY 2011 Budget by Agency.*

15. Eric Kelderman, Chronicle of Higher Education, July 16, 2010.

16. Illinois Office of the Governor, "Senate Bill 2505—Economic Recovery and Budget Reform."

17. National Conference of State Legislatures, *State Budget Update: November 2010.*

18. National Center for Public Policy and Higher Education, *Measuring Up 2000.*

19. As measured using the Cumulative Promotion Index (defined in chapter 4, note 16), high school graduation rates increased from 71.3% in 1996–97 to 78.8% in 2007–8, as per Editorial Projects in Education Research Center, *Diplomas Count 2010.* The Illinois State Board of Education reported that, between 2002 and 2010, high school graduation rates increased from 85.2% to 87.8%, http://webprod.isbe.net/ereportcard/publicsite/getSearchCriteria.aspx.

20. The percentage scoring at or above proficient levels on NAEP math increased from 29% in 2003 to 33% in 2009, as per the National Center for Education Statistics, *The Nation's Report Card: Mathematics 2009.* However, the percentage scoring at or above proficient levels in NAEP reading declined from 34% in 2003 to 32% in 2009, as per NCES, *The Nation's Report Card: Reading 2009.*

21. Mortenson, *Postsecondary Education Opportunity.*

22. National Center for Higher Education Management Systems, "Percent of 18 to 24 Year Olds Enrolled in College."

23. National Center for Higher Education Management Systems, "Enrollment of 25 to 49 Year Olds as a Percent of 25 to 49 Year Olds with No Bachelor's Degree or Higher."

24. National Center for Public Policy and Higher Education, *Measuring Up 2000.*

25. National Center for Higher Education Management Systems, "Six-Year Graduation Rates of Bachelor's Students" and "Three-Year Graduation Rates for Associate Students."

26. National Center for Education Statistics, *Digest of Education Statistics, 2009.*

27. National Center for Public Policy and Higher Education, *Measuring Up 2008.*

28. National Center for Public Policy and Higher Education, *Affordability and Transfer.*

29. National Center for Public Policy and Higher Education, *Measuring Up 2000.*

30. National Association of State Student Grant & Aid Programs, *40th Annual Survey Report* and *31st Annual Survey Report.*

31. Illinois Board of Higher Education, *The Illinois Public Agenda for College and Career Success.*

32. Ibid.

33. Illinois Board of Higher Education, *Report to the Governor and General Assembly on Underrepresented Groups in Illinois Higher Education,* 1.

34. National Center for Public Policy and Higher Education, *Measuring Up 2008.*

35. National Center for Education Statistics, table 11, "First-time, Full-time Undergraduate Enrollment in Title IV Institutions," Fall 2006.

36. Integrated Postsecondary Education Data System, "2009 Graduation Rates Survey" and "2009 Institutional Characteristics Survey."

37. National Center for Education Statistics, *Digest of Education Statistics, 2011.*

38. Ibid., table 224.

39. Delta Cost Project, "Illinois State Data."

40. Illinois Board of Higher Education, *Databook on Illinois Higher Education.*

41. Richardson, *State Structures for the Governance of Higher Education.*

42. Ibid., and Van der Slik, "Reconsidering the Restructure of Higher Education," 27.

43. Richardson, *State Structures.*

44. Glenny, *A Master Plan,* 56–57.

45. Ibid.

46. Ibid.

47. Richardson, *State Structures,* 9.

48. Ibid., and Van der Slik, "Reconsidering the Restructure."

49. Van der Slik, "Reconsidering the Restructure."

50. Richardson, *State Structures,* 32.

51. Burns, Peltason, and Cronin, *State and Local Politics.*

52. Illinois State Board of Elections, *Ballots Cast, General Primary 2/2/2010, Governor,* 2011. www.elections.il.gov/ElectionInformation/VoteTotalsList.aspx?ElectionType=GP&ElectionID=28&SearchType=OfficeSearch&OfficeID=5064&QueryType=Office&.

53. Richardson, *State Structures.*

54. Van der Slik, "Reconsidering the Restructure," 28.

55. Ballot Pedia, "Illinois House of Representatives Elections 2010" and "Illinois State Senate Elections 2010."

56. J. S. Cohen, S. St. Clair, and T. Malone, "University of Illinois President B. Joseph White Resigns." *Chicago Tribune News,* September 24, 2009, www.chicagotribune.com/news/chi-u-of-i-white-resign-24-sep24,0,161068.story.

57. Illinois Board of Higher Education, *Report to the Governor and General Assembly on Underrepresented Groups in Illinois Higher Education.*

58. Illinois General Assembly, "Bill status of HB 4906, 96th General Assembly."

59. Education Sector, "Higher Ed Accountability Report: Illinois."

60. Ibid.

61. Data Quality Campaign, *Data for Action: Illinois DQC State Analysis.* The state had met four of the ten characteristics: "create stable, sustained support for robust state longitudinal data systems; develop governance structures to guide data collection, sharing and use; create reports that include longitudinal statistics on school systems and groups of students to guide school-, district-, and state-level improvement efforts; and develop a purposeful research agenda and collaborate with universities, researchers, and intermediary groups to explore the data for useful information." But it had not taken the other six actions: "link state K–12 data systems with early learning, postsecondary education, workforce, social services, and other critical agencies; build state data repositories that integrate student, staff, financial, and facility data; implement systems to provide timely

access to information; create progress reports with individual student data that provide information educators, parents, and students can use to improve student performance; implement policies and promote practices, including professional development and credentialing, to ensure educators know how to access, analyze, and use data appropriately; and promote strategies to raise awareness of available data and ensure that all key stakeholders . . . know how to access, analyze, and use the information."

62. Ewell and Kelly, *State-level Completion and Transfer Rates.*

63. Illinois Board of Higher Education, *FY 2011 Higher Education Budget Recommendations,* 10.

64. Kelly and Lach, *Evaluation of the Illinois Articulation Initiative.*

65. Illinois Student Assistance Commission, *2010 Data Book.*

66. The expected family contribution is a measure of the family's ability to pay college costs as calculated by formula from data collected from the application for federal student financial aid.

67. Illinois Student Assistance Commission, *Monetary Award Program Evaluation.*

68. These figures are estimates. National Association of State Student Grant Aid Programs, *40th Annual Survey Report.*

69. Illinois Board of Higher Education, *Report on the Efficiency and Sustainability of the Monetary Award Program.*

70. Thompson, "Behind the Eight Ball."

71. Illinois Student Assistance Commission, *Monetary Award Program Evaluation.*

72. Data are as of March 2011. Illinois Board of Higher Education, *Databook on Illinois Higher Education.* In FY 2012, 45.3% of MAP recipients had a family income below $20,000, and 9.2% had a family income above $60,000 (Personal communication, Susan Kleeman, April 5, 2013). The slight reduction between FY2008 and FY2012 in the share of MAP recipients from the lowest-income families (and simultaneous increase over this period in the share of MAP recipients from higher-income families) may be caused by the increasingly earlier suspension of MAP funds each year. This shift disproportionately disadvantages those who apply later, a group that includes high shares of independent students and students from the lower income levels.

73. Illinois Board of Higher Education, *FY 2011 Higher Education Budget Recommendations.*

74. In its *Report on the Efficiency and Sustainability,* Illinois Board of Higher Education identified nine potential options that "may target MAP funds more effectively to achieve student access and success goals."

75. Illinois Board of Higher Education, *Report to the Governor and General Assembly.*

76. Illinois Board of Higher Education, *Report on the Efficiency and Sustainability.*

77. Illinois Student Assistance Commission, "The Future of MAP Grants and Other State Grant Programs."

78. Illinois Board of Higher Education, *Report on the Efficiency and Sustainability,* 6.

79. Delta Cost Project, "Illinois State Data."

80. Illinois Board of Higher Education, *Report on the Efficiency and Sustainability.*

81. National Association of State Budget Officers, *State Expenditure Report: Fiscal Year 2008.*

82. Illinois Board of Higher Education, *State Matching Grant Program: Fiscal Year 2007 Grant Allocation.*

83. Villa-Komaroff et al., "Executive Summary."

84. Castro et al., "How Illinois' College and Career Readiness (CCR) Pilot Sites Address Five Key Goals."

85. Illinois Board of Higher Education, *FY 2011 Higher Education Budget Recommendations*, 7

86. Richardson, *State Structures.*

87. Illinois Board of Higher Education, *Higher Education Budget Recommendations*, v.

88. The commission was set up during the data-gathering phase, but the final report was delivered after interviews were completed.

89. Higher Education Finance Study Commission, *Report to the Governor, the Honorable Pat Quinn and Members of the Illinois General Assembly*, 1.

90. Ibid., 3–4.

91. Illinois General Assembly, "Bill Status of HB1503, 97th General Assembly."

CHAPTER 6: **Much Accomplished, Much at Stake**

The research reported here was supported in part by the Institute of Education Sciences, U.S. Department of Education, through Grant #R305B090015 to the University of Pennsylvania. The opinions expressed are those of the authors and do not represent the views of the Institute or the U.S. Department of Education.

1. This report focuses on higher education performance and policy through 2010, although some references are made to important developments in 2011. The research team conducted interviews with state and institutional leaders in the state in fall 2010.

2. National Center for Higher Education Management System, "ACS Educational Attainment by Degree-Level and Age-Group."

3. Maryland Higher Education Commission, *2009 Maryland State Plan for Postsecondary Education.*

4. Kelly, "Projected Degree Gap." The total projected increase includes both public and private institutions.

5. Jones, "A Public Agenda for Higher Education."

6. Carnevale, Smith, and Strohl, *Help Wanted.*

7. McCaffrey, "BRAC Plan Expected to Bring 22,000 Homeowners." Base Realignment and Closure (BRAC) is a process created by Congress to facilitate the complex and politically charged process of closing and realigning domestic military installations. Also employed in 1989, 1991, 1993, and 1995, the BRAC process in 2005 resulted in the decision to close some facilities and realign others, including a realignment at Fort Meade, Maryland. The realignment includes the transfer of some activities from other locations to Fort Meade. Required by law to be completed by 2011, the realignment was projected to produce 5,700 additional jobs at Fort Meade as well as create additional jobs in related local businesses.

8. Maryland Higher Education Commission, *2009 Maryland State Plan.*

9. Maryland Higher Education Commission, *Commission to Develop the Maryland Model for Funding Higher Education, Final Report.*

10. University System of Maryland, *Powering Maryland Forward*, 6.

11. U.S. Census Bureau, "State and County QuickFacts."

12. Ibid.

13. Western Interstate Higher Education Commission, *Knocking at the College Door.*

14. National Center for Higher Education Management Systems, "2005 ACS PUMS—Education by Age, by Race, by State"; and National Center for Higher Education Management Systems, "Educational Attainment by State, Age, Race and Gender, 1990–2000."

15. U.S. Census Bureau, table 20, "Large Metropolitan Statistical Areas—Population."

16. U.S. Census Bureau, "Baltimore City, Maryland QuickFacts."

17. U.S. Census Bureau, "Baltimore City, Maryland: Selected Social Characteristics in the United States: 2005–2009."

18. U.S. Census Bureau, "Baltimore City, Maryland: Selected Social Characteristics in the United States: 2005–2009"; and U.S. Census Bureau, "Maryland: Selected Social Characteristics in the United States: 2005–2009."

19. U.S. Census Bureau, "Baltimore City, Maryland QuickFacts."

20. Maryland Higher Education Commission, *Maryland State Plan for Postsecondary Education.*

21. Maryland General Assembly, "Spending Affordability Committee, 2009 Interim Report" and "Spending Affordability Committee, 2010 Interim Report."

22. Southern Regional Education Board, *Legislative Report.*

23. O'Malley, "State of the State."

24. University System of Maryland, *Powering Maryland Forward*, 5–6.

25. Editorial Projects in Education Research Center, "Indicators."

26. National Center for Education Statistics, *Nation's Report Card—NAEP Data Explorer.*

27. National Center for Higher Education Management System, "Percent of 18 to 24 Year Olds Enrolled in College."

28. Mortenson, "Chance for College by Age 19 by State, 1986 to 2008."

29. National Center for Higher Education Management System, "Six-year Graduation Rates of Bachelor's Students, 2009."

30. Ewell and Kelly, *State-Level Completion and Transfer Rates: Harnessing a New National Resource.*

31. Ibid.

32. National Center for Public Policy and Higher Education, *Measuring Up 2008.*

33. Integrated Postsecondary Education Data System, *2009 Institutional Characteristics Survey.*

34. National Center for Education Statistics, *Nation's Report Card.*

35. Editorial Projects in Education Research Center, "Indicators."

36. National Center for Higher Education Management System, "2005 ACS PUMS—Education by Age, by Race, by State."

37. Integrated Postsecondary Education Data System, *2008 Graduation Rates Survey* and *2008 Institutional Characteristics Survey.*

38. National Center for Education Statistics, *Digest of Education Statistics 2011*, table 280.

39. Ibid., table 224.
40. Maryland Higher Education Commission, "Commission Responsibilities."
41. Maryland State Archives, "Maryland Higher Education Commission."
42. University of Maryland University College, *Fiscal Year 2010 Fact Book.*
43. Van de Water, *Meeting Maryland's Postsecondary Challenges.*
44. Maryland State Archives, *Regional Higher Education Centers.*
45. 2+2 degree programs typically guarantee transfer with junior-year status into a four-year degree program for students who have successfully completed an approved program at a community college.
46. Maryland Higher Education Commission, *Regional Higher Education Centers Enrollment: FY 2006 to 2011.*
47. Van de Water, "Meeting Maryland's Postsecondary Challenges."
48. P–20 education refers to prekindergarten through graduate studies.
49. Southern Regional Education Board, *State College and Career Readiness Initiative,* 36.
50. Maryland State Department of Education, "Divisions: The Governor's P–20 Leadership Council of Maryland."
51. Maryland State Department of Education, "Testing."
52. Southern Regional Education Board, *State College and Career Readiness Initiative.*
53. Partnership for Assessment of Readiness for College and Careers, "About PARCC."
54. Maryland Office of the Secretary of State, *Code of Maryland Regulations.* 13B.02.03.02.
55. Maryland Higher Education Commission, "Interagency Initiatives."
56. Maryland Higher Education Commission, *Managing for Results Report for FY 2009,* 41.
57. Maryland Office of the Secretary of State, *Code of Maryland Regulations,* 13B.06.01.02-1; University System of Maryland Board of Regents, "III-4.00 Policy on Undergraduate Admissions," 3.
58. Maryland Higher Education Commission, *2008 Community College Graduates Follow-Up Survey Report.*
59. Maryland Higher Education Commission, *2009 Maryland State Plan,* 1.
60. Education Sector, "Maryland Score Card."
61. Maryland Higher Education Commission, *2009 Maryland State Plan,* 39.
62. Maryland Higher Education Commission, *Commission to Develop the Maryland Model for Funding Higher Education Final Report.*
63. Maryland Higher Education Commission, *Maryland's Report and the Partnership between the State of Maryland and the U.S. Department of Education, Office for Civil Rights.*
64. Maryland Higher Education Commission, "Partnership Agreement between the State of Maryland and the Office for Civil Rights." Letter dated June 19, 2006.
65. Ibid., 9.
66. Maryland Higher Education Commission, "Table 1: Comparison of State Annual Appropriations to Historically Black Institutions and Projections Based on the Share of Full-Time Equivalent Students, Four-Year Public Institutions, University of Maryland, College Park Not Included, 1990–2010"; and "Table 2: Comparison of State Annual Appropriations to Historically Black Institutions and Projections Based on the Share of Full-Time Equivalent Students, Four-Year Public Institutions, University of Maryland, College

Park, 1990–2010." When the University of Maryland at College Park is excluded (table 1), actual state appropriations to HBIs exceeded the appropriations that would have been expected each year since 1999.

67. Maryland Higher Education Commission, *Commission to Develop the Maryland Model for Funding Higher Education Final Report*, 23–24.

68. Ibid.

69. Ibid., 43.

70. Ehrlich, Jr., *Letter to the Honorable Thomas V. "Mike" Miller Jr.*

71. Maryland General Assembly, House Bill 506, 2008; and Maryland General Assembly, House Bill 900, 2009.

72. John L. Bohanan Jr. was appointed to the State House of Delegates in 1999 to fill a vacant seat. Since then, he has served as a member of the Appropriations Committee and chair of the Subcommittee on Education and Economic Development. In 2007, Delegate Bohanan was appointed chair of the Funding Commission.

73. Maryland Higher Education Commission, *2009 Maryland State Plan*, 8.

74. Maryland Higher Education Commission, *Commission to Develop the Maryland Model for Funding Higher Education Final Report*, xxi.

75. Maryland General Assembly, Chapter 193, "Higher Education Investment Fund—Tuition Stabilization and Funding."

76. Maryland Higher Education Commission, *2009 Maryland State Plan*, 8.

77. Maryland Higher Education Commission, *Commission to Develop the Maryland Model for Funding Higher Education Final Report*, 19.

78. Ibid., 15.

79. University System of Maryland, *Powering Maryland Forward*, 1.

80. Maryland General Assembly, Chapter 192, Senate Bill 283, 2010.

81. Maryland Higher Education Commission, *Commission to Develop the Maryland Model for Funding Higher Education, Final Report*, 18.

82. Maryland General Assembly, HB 470, 4.

83. Maryland General Assembly, Chapter 193, "Higher Education Investment Fund—Tuition Stabilization and Funding."

84. See, for example, St. Mary's College of Maryland, "Fiscal Year 2010 Budget Testimony." Appropriations for St. Mary's College are a "block" or "general" grant that is not determined by enrollment but an inflation-adjusted increment to the prior year's appropriation.

85. Maryland Higher Education Commission, *Commission to Develop the Maryland Model for Funding Higher Education Final Report*, 19.

86. However, for Baltimore County Community College, the state pays about two-thirds of the costs rather than one-third.

87. Maryland Independent College and University Association, Mission and History.

88. Maryland Independent College and University Association, Fast Facts.

89. Maryland Higher Education Commission, *Commission to Develop the Maryland Model for Funding Higher Education Final Report*, 7.

90. Ibid., 17.

91. Ibid.

92. Maryland Independent College and University Association, The Joseph A. Sellinger State Aid Program.

93. Maryland Higher Education Commission, *2009 Maryland State Plan,* 8.

94. Maryland Higher Education Commission, *Commission to Develop the Maryland Model for Funding Higher Education Final Report,* 16.

95. Maryland Higher Education Commission, *2009 Maryland State Plan,* 4.

96. National Association of State Student Grant & Aid Programs, *35th Annual Survey Report;* National Association of State Student Grant & Aid Programs, *40th Annual Survey Report.*

97. National Association of State Student Grant & Aid Programs, *40th Annual Survey Report.*

98. Maryland Higher Education Commission, *Commission to Develop the Maryland Model for Funding Higher Education Final Report,* 13.

99. Maryland Higher Education Commission, *2009 Maryland State Plan,* 18.

100. Maryland Higher Education Commission, *Commission to Develop the Maryland Model for Funding Higher Education Final Report.*

101. Ibid., 31.

102. Ibid., 22.

103. The statute is Maryland Annotated Code, section 10-209. University System of Maryland, *2009 USM Managing for Results Accountability Report.*

104. Maryland Higher Education Commission, *Commission to Develop the Maryland Model for Funding Higher Education,* "Some Discussion Points," 18.

CHAPTER 7: **Hard Choices Ahead**

The research reported here was supported in part by the Institute of Education Sciences, U.S. Department of Education, through Grant #R305B090015 to the University of Pennsylvania. The opinions expressed are those of the authors and do not represent the views of the Institute or the U.S. Department of Education.

1. This report focuses on higher education performance and policy through 2010. The research team conducted interviews with state and institutional leaders in fall 2010.

2. U.S. Census Bureau, table C15002, "Sex by Educational Attainment for the Population 25 Years and Over."

3. Carnevale, Smith, and Strohl, *Help Wanted.*

4. Kelly, "Projected Degree Gap."

5. Jones, *A Public Agenda for Higher Education.* To achieve this goal, Texas can seek to increase degree attainment of those residents who have some college experience but who have not yet earned a degree. In 2009, 28.7% of residents between the ages of 25 to 44 had "some college" but no degree.

6. Governor's Business Council, *Leading the Way,* 8.

7. National Center for Higher Education Management Systems, "2005 ACS PUMS—Education by Age, by Race, by State."

8. U.S. Census Bureau, table C03002, "Hispanic or Latino Origin by Race."

9. U.S. Census Bureau, "State & County QuickFacts."

10. Other than California, Texas has the largest estimated population of unauthor-

ized immigrants of any state. Pew Hispanic Center, *Unauthorized Immigrant Population: National and State Trends, 2010* (Washington, D.C.: 2011).

11. Legislative Budget Board, *Financing Higher Education in Texas: Legislative Primer*, 5th edition, 1. Total funding includes general revenues, general revenue-dedicated sources, other funds, and federal funds.

12. State Higher Education Executive Officers, *State Higher Education Finance, FY 2012;* National Center for Higher Education Management Systems, "State and Local Public Higher Education Support Per Full-Time Equivalent Student."

13. Southern Regional Education Board, *Governors' Legislative and Budget Proposals*, 4.

14. Bureau of Economic Analysis, "Table CA1-3: Personal Income, Population, Per Capita Personal Income, 2009."

15. The Cumulative Promotion Index (CPI) is defined in note 16 in chapter 4. Editorial Projects in Education Research Center, "Indicators."

16. Texas Education Agency, "Secondary School Completion and Dropouts in Texas Public Schools 2009–10." Texas calculates its graduation rate as follows: Divide the number of students who graduate, complete, or drop out by the end of grade 12 by the total number of students in the original seventh- or ninth-grade class.

17. National Center for Education Statistics, *Nation's Report Card.*

18. Mortenson, "Chance for College by Age 19 by State, 1986 to 2008."

19. Ibid.

20. National Center for Higher Education Management Systems, "Percent of 18 to 24 Year Olds Enrolled in College."

21. National Center for Higher Education Management Systems, "Enrollment of 25 to 49 Year Olds as a Percent of 25 to 49 Year Olds with No Bachelor's Degree or Higher."

22. National Center for Higher Education Management Systems, "Six-Year Graduation Rates of Bachelor's Students."

23. National Center for Higher Education Management Systems, "Three-Year Graduation Rates for Associate Students."

24. Ewell and Kelly, *State-Level Completion and Transfer Rates: Harnessing a New National Resource.*

25. National Center for Public Policy and Higher Education, *Measuring Up 2008.*

26. National Center for Public Policy and Higher Education, *Affordability and Transfer.*

27. Editorial Projects in Education Research Center, "Indicators."

28. National Center for Education Statistics, *Nation's Report Card.*

29. Texas Education Agency, *2009–10 State Performance Report.*

30. Texas Higher Education Coordinating Board, *Closing the Gaps Progress Report 2010*, 5–7.

31. Ibid, vi. For Hispanics and Blacks, the original target for 2015 was set at 5.7%, which requires a larger gain for Hispanics than for Blacks, given their baseline rates in 2000. In addition, the Hispanic population is much larger than the Black population in Texas, which makes increases more challenging to achieve. For Whites, the enrollment rate increased from 5.1% in 2000 to 5.8% in 2009.

32. Integrated Postsecondary Education Data System, "2009 Graduation Rates Survey" and "2009 Institutional Characteristics Survey."

33. National Center for Education Statistics, *Nation's Report Card.*

34. Texas Higher Education Coordinating Board, *Closing the Gaps Progress Report 2010.*

35. National Center for Education Statistics, *Digest of Education Statistics 2011,* table 280.

36. Ibid., table 216.

37. Ibid., table 224.

38. Delta Cost Project, "Texas State Data," 2011.

39. Combs, *Texas Works 2008.*

40. Education Commission of the States, "Texas: Postsecondary Governance Structures." The Texas Higher Education Coordinating Board is composed of 18 members representing the general public, appointed for six-year staggered terms by the governor, with senate confirmation.

41. Education Commission of the States, "Texas: Postsecondary Governance Structures"; California Higher Education Policy Center, "Characteristics of the Texas Higher Education System."

42. Dallas–Fort Worth–Arlington, also referred to as the "Metroplex," is 4th largest in the U.S.; Houston–Sugar Land–Baytown is 5th; San Antonio is 25th; Austin-Round Rock is 35th; El Paso is 66th; and McAllen-Edinburg-Mission is 68th. Brookings Institution, "State of Metropolitan America Indicator Map."

43. FSG Social Impact Consultants, *Texas Regional Action Plan for Postsecondary Completion.* The report was prepared for the Greater Texas Foundation, the Communities Foundation of Texas, the Houston Endowment Inc., and the Meadows Foundation. The five regions are the Metroplex (Dallas / Fort Worth); the Gulf Coast (Greater Houston); Central Texas (Waco, Temple, and Travis/Williamson/Hays counties); South Texas (San Antonio, Laredo, McAllen, Brownsville), and the Upper Rio Grande (El Paso).

44. Ibid., and Governor's Business Council, *Leading the Way.*

45. FSG Social Impact Consultants, *Texas Regional Action Plan.*

46. Beyle, "The Powers of the Governor in North Carolina," 27–45.

47. Office of the Lieutenant Governor, "Duties." www.ltgov.state.tx.us/duties.php.

48. Texas Higher Education Coordinating Board, *Closing the Gaps: The Texas Higher Education Plan,* 1–3,

49. Texas Higher Education Coordinating Board, *Closing the Gaps: Goals and Target Summaries,* 1.

50. Texas Higher Education Coordinating Board, *Closing the Gaps Progress Report, 2010.*

51. Texas Association of Business, "Education and Workforce."

52. Governor's Business Council, "About Us." www.texasgbc.org/about%20us.htm. Accessed February 19, 2011.

53. Governor's Business Council, *Leading the Way,* 10–12.

54. Texas Higher Education Coordinating Board, *Accountability System History.*

55. Data Quality Campaign, *Texas: 2011 DQC State Analysis.*

56. Alderman and Carey, "Texas Score Card."

57. Texas Higher Education Coordinating Board, "Texas Higher Education Coordinating Board Releases 2011 Texas Public Higher Education Almanac."

58. Texas P–16 Public Education Information Resource, "About Us."

59. Governor's Business Council, *Leading the Way*, 14.

60. Texas State Senate, "Permanent University Fund (PUF) and Higher Education Assistance Fund (HEAF) Overview," 1.

61. Ibid.

62. Block, "Permanent University Fund."

63. Texas Higher Education Coordinating Board, *Sources and Uses of Funds*, 3.

64. Ibid.

65. Ibid.

66. Lederman, "Colleges Win on Election Night."

67. Texas Higher Education Coordinating Board, "University Funding for Excellence in Specific Programs and Fields."

68. Texas Higher Education Coordinating Board, "Texas Research Incentive Program, 2009."

69. Governor's Business Council, *Leading the Way*.

70. Texas State Legislature, "Texas Legislature Online," Legislative Session 77(R), History for HB 1144.

71. Texas Education Agency, "Student Graduate Reports."

72. Texas Higher Education Coordinating Board, "Overview: Texas College and Career Readiness Standards," 1.

73. Texas Education Agency, "End-of-Course Assessment Plan College Readiness and Advanced-Course Readiness," 2.

74. Texas Education Agency, "End-of-Course (EOC) Assessments."

75. Texas Education Agency, "P–16 Council."

76. Texas Higher Education Coordinating Board, "P–16 Texas." Regional P–16 councils are made up of "local and regional K–12, higher education, and business leaders" and are charged with advancing achievement of the *Closing the Gaps* goals at the local level.

77. Texas Higher Education Coordinating Board, "Dual Credit Overview"; and Texas Education Agency, "Enrollment in Public School, 2010–2011," tables 9 and 11.

78. Texas Higher Education Coordinating Board, "Dual Credit Overview," 1–2.

79. Texas Education Agency, "Early College High School."

80. Texas Higher Education Coordinating Board, "Texas Course Redesign Project."

81. Southern Regional Education Board, *Clearing Paths to College Degrees*.

82. Texas Higher Education Coordinating Board, *Strategic Plan for Texas Public Community Colleges, 2009–2013*.

83. Texas Higher Education Coordinating Board, *Closing the Gaps: The Texas Higher Education Plan*, 2.

84. Texas Higher Education Coordinating Board, *Strategic Plan for Texas Public Community Colleges*, 7. The coordinating board approved these degrees in July 2004.

85. Texas Higher Education Coordinating Board. "Higher Education Accountability System."

86. Texas Higher Education Coordinating Board, *Closing the Gaps Progress Report, 2010*, 20.

87. Texas Higher Education Coordinating Board, *Feasibility of Expanding Texas' Community College Baccalaureate Programs*.

88. Davis, "Applied Baccalaureate Degrees in Texas."

89. Texas Higher Education Coordinating Board, *Feasibility of Expanding Texas' Community College Baccalaureate Programs,* 71.

90. Snell, *Annual and Biennial Budgeting.*

91. Texas Higher Education Coordinating Board, "Tuition Deregulation Overview."

92. Legislative Budget Board, *Financing Higher Education in Texas,* 13.

93. Texas Higher Education Coordinating Board, *An Overview of Article III House Bill 1, 80th Texas Legislature.*

94. Governor's Business Council, *Leading the Way,* 17.

95. The conditions are that the prospective students must have: (1) resided in Texas with a parent or guardian while attending high school in Texas, (2) graduated from a public or private high school or received a GED in Texas, (3) resided in Texas for the three years leading to graduation or receipt of a GED, and (4) provided their institutions a signed affidavit indicating an intent to apply for permanent resident status as soon as able to do so. Texas Higher Education Coordinating Board, "Residency and In-State tuition."

96. Delta Cost Project, "Texas State Data."

97. Ibid. Between 2003 and 2008, the share of average education and related expenses covered by tuition and fees increased from 43% to 56% at public research universities, from 36% to 46% at public institutions that offer up to a master's degree, from 43% to 55% at public institutions that offer up to a bachelor's degree, and from 24% to 28% at community colleges. Over the same period, the share covered by state subsidies declined from 57% to 44% at public research universities, from 64% to 54% at public master's institutions, from 57% to 45% at public baccalaureate institutions, and from 76% to 72% at community colleges.

98. Texas Higher Education Coordinating Board, "Tuition Deregulation Overview."

99. Ibid.

100. Higher Education Insight Associates, *Feasibility Study for Restructuring Texas Student Financial Aid Programs.*

101. Texas Higher Education Coordinating Board, "Tuition Set-Asides," 1.

102. Integrated Postsecondary Education Data System, "2009 Student Financial Aid Survey" and "2009 Institutional Characteristics Survey."

103. National Association of State Student Grant & Aid Programs, *40th Annual Survey Report on State-Sponsored Student Financial Aid* and *31st Annual Survey Report on State-Sponsored Student Financial Aid.*

104. National Association of State Student Grant & Aid Programs, *40th Annual Survey Report.*

105. State Higher Education Executive Officers, *State Higher Education Finance.* Figures adjusted for inflation.

106. Texas Higher Education Coordinating Board, "TEXAS Grant Overview," 1–2.

107. Higher Education Insight Associates, *Feasibility Study for Restructuring Texas Student Financial Aid Programs.*

108. Texas Higher Education Coordinating Board, "Financial Aid in Texas Overview."

109. Higher Education Insight Associates, *Feasibility Study for Restructuring Texas Student Financial Aid Programs,* 1.

110. Governor's Business Council, *Leading the Way,* 10.

111. Texas State Legislature, "Texas Legislature Online: History," 82nd session, SB 28.

112. Texas Higher Education Coordinating Board, "Financial Aid in Texas Overview."

113. Texas Higher Education Coordinating Board, *House (Enrolled), Senate (Enrolled) and Conference Committee Report on HB 1 Compared to 2010–11 Base.*

114. Texas Higher Education Coordinating Board, "Texas Educational Opportunity Grant," 1.

115. Ibid., 2.

116. Higher Education Insight Associates, *Feasibility Study for Restructuring Texas Student Financial Aid Programs.*

117. Legislative Budget Board, *Financing Higher Education in Texas,* 22.

118. Texas Higher Education Coordinating Board, *Strategic Plan for Texas Public Community Colleges,* 14.

119. Combs, *Texas Works 2008.*

120. Ibid.

121. Texas Association of Community Colleges, *Spring 2011 Tuition and Fees.*

122. Texas Higher Education Coordinating Board, *Strategic plan for Texas Public Community Colleges,* 26.

CHAPTER 8: **State Policy Leadership Vacuum**

The research reported here was supported in part by the Institute of Education Sciences, U.S. Department of Education, through Grant #R305B090015 to the University of Pennsylvania. The opinions expressed are those of the authors and do not represent the views of the Institute or the U.S. Department of Education.

1. This report focuses on higher education performance and policy through 2010, although some references are made to important developments early in 2011. The research team conducted interviews with state and institutional leaders in the state in spring 2010.

2. See above, chapter 1, table 1. National Center for Higher Education Management System, "ACS Educational Attainment by Degree-Level and Age-Group."

3. Ewing Marion Kauffman Foundation, *United States Must Address Fundamental Economic Competitiveness to Thrive in the New Economy.*

4. Carnevale, Smith, and Strohl, *Help Wanted.*

5. Ibid.

6. Washington Workforce Training & Education Coordinating Board, *High Skills, High Wages,* 24–25.

7. Washington Higher Education Coordinating Board, *2008 Strategic Master Plan for Higher Education in Washington.* After data for this case study were collected and analyzed in May 2011, the legislature passed a bill (E2SSB 5182) abolishing the Higher Education Coordinating Board, effective July 1, 2012. The governor signed the bill on June 6, 2011 (with a veto of unclear language about the date of the transfer).

8. Kelly, "Projected Degree Gap."

9. Washington Higher Education Coordinating Board, *2008 Strategic Master Plan,* 6.

10. National Center for Higher Education Management Systems, "2005 ACS PUMS—Education by Age by Race by State."

11. See chapter 3, table 6, for indicators of wealth relative to other states.

12. Zumeta, "Public Higher Education in Washington State," 275–303.

13. State of Washington, Office of Financial Management, *Washington State Budget Process.*

14. Zumeta, "Public Higher Education in Washington State."

15. Washington Higher Education Coordinating Board, *2011–2013 Higher Education Budget.*

16. State of Washington, Office of the Governor, *Proposed 2012 Supplemental Budget Highlights.*

17. The Cumulative Promotion Index is defined in chapter 4, note 16. Editorial Projects in Education Research Center, "Indicators."

18. Washington Higher Education Coordinating Board, *2008 Strategic Master Plan*, 4.

19. Washington Higher Education Coordinating Board, *2008 Strategic Master Plan.* Participation in higher education has remained virtually unchanged in Washington since the early 1990s: 28.2% of 18- to 24-year-olds were enrolled in college in 1991, compared with 29.6% in 2009, as per National Center for Higher Education Management Systems, "Percent of 18- to 24-Year-Olds Enrolled in College." At 50.7%, the college-going rate of high school graduates in Washington was fifth lowest in the nation in 2008, substantially lower than the national average of 63.3% and the median of the five top-performing states (74.2%), as per Mortenson, *Chance for College by Age 19 by State.* The "chance for college" understates the performance of Washington relative to other states, however. Unlike in other states, Washington's State Board for Community and Technical Colleges excludes from their calculations of first-time students recent high school graduates who earned college credit during high school. As such, the Washington HECB cites only the state's high school enrollment and graduation data.

20. National Center for Higher Education Management Systems, "Percent of 18- to 24-Year-Olds Enrolled in College."

21. National Center for Higher Education Management Systems, "Enrollment of 25- to 49-Year-Olds as a Percent of 25- to 49-Year-Olds with No Bachelor's Degree or Higher"; and National Center for Public Policy and Higher Education, *Measuring Up 2008.*

22. National Center for Higher Education Management Systems, "Six-Year Graduation Rates of Bachelor's Students."

23. Washington Higher Education Coordinating Board, *Key Facts 2011*, 54.

24. Ewell and Kelly, *State-Level Completion and Transfer Rates.*

25. National Center for Public Policy and Higher Education, *Measuring Up 2008.*

26. National Center for Public Policy and Higher Education, *Affordability and Transfer.*

27. Editorial Projects in Education Research Center, "Indicators."

28. Office of Superintendent of Public Instruction, "Washington State Report Card, Statewide Assessment Trend."

29. National Center for Education Statistics, *Nation's Report Card.*

30. Washington Higher Education Coordinating Board, *Key Facts about Higher Education in Washington, 2010*, 46.

31. Integrated Postsecondary Education Data System, "2008 Graduation Rates Survey" and "2008 Institutional Characteristics Survey."

32. Washington State Board for Community and Technical Colleges, *Academic Year Report*, 39–40.

33. National Center for Education Statistics, *Digest of Education Statistics*, 2011, table 280.

34. Ibid., table 224.

35. Delta Cost Project, *Washington State Data*.

36. Washington is also characterized by high performance on research, but this performance is driven largely by institutional success in attracting federal funding rather than by state policy.

37. Washington Office of the Governor, "Higher Education Funding Task Force," 3.

38. Washington Learns, *Washington Learns: World-class, Learner-focused, Seamless Education*.

39. Ibid. These initiatives appear to have persisted even with the constraints on state revenues caused by the Great Recession. For more information about these initiatives, see the following sources: the Department of Early Learning, www.del.wa.gov/about/what.aspx; Navigation 101; www.k12.wa.us/SecondaryEducation/CareerCollegeReadiness/default.aspxlpre-apprenticeships; www.lni.wa.gov/TradesLicensing/Apprenticeship/About/IntroProg/default.asp; the Transitions Mathematics Project, www.transitionmathproject.org; and the state's longitudinal data project, www.erdc.wa.gov/arraslds2009/reports/status.

40. Washington Learns released an interim report on November 15, 2005: *Washington Learns, 2005 Interim Report*.

41. Washington Learns, *Washington Learns*.

42. Washington Higher Education Coordinating Board, *2008 Strategic Master Plan*, ii.

43. Ibid., 14.

44. Ibid., 11.

45. Office of the Governor, "Governor Gregoire Creates P–20 Council to Hold State Government Accountable for Education Goals," news release, May 21, 2007, http://votesmart.org/public-statement/264161/governor-gregoire-creates-p-20-council-to-hold-state-government-accountable-for-education-goals#.UUXmZFsWlfU.

46. Office of the Governor, "Accelerating the Learning Curve by Building a Student-Centered Education System." Policy brief. www.digitalarchives.wa.gov/GovernorGregoire/priorities/budget/p20_system.pdf.

47. Chris Grygiel, "Gregoire: Put K–12, Higher ed. Under One Dept. to Save $," *Seattle Post-Intelligencer*, January 4, 2011. www.seattlepi.com/local/432807_education05.html?source=mypi.

48. Council of Presidents. "About Us." 2010. www.councilofpresidents.org.

49. Washington Higher Education Coordinating Board, *Key Facts about Higher Education in Washington 2010*, 112.

50. Washington Student Achievement Council, "About the Council."

51. The configuration of the new Council on Higher Education had not yet been determined at the time of our study. A local policy expert speculated that the new entity would have strong representation from higher education institutions and a very small staff. The Council of Presidents will continue to exist after the elimination of coordinating board.

One state policy expert said that the Council of Presidents would likely play some, as yet undetermined, role in the new Council on Higher Education.

52. Effective July 1, 2012, the Washington Student Achievement Council, a cabinet-level state agency, is responsible for "strategic planning, oversight, and advocacy to support increased student success and higher levels of educational attainment in Washington." One of the Council's responsibilities is "ensuring the quality of state financial aid programs and services." See Washington State Achievement Council, "About the Council."

53. State of Washington, "Engrossed Second Substitute Senate Bill 5182."

54. Washington State Legislature, "Definitions, 26B.76.020."

55. Washington State Board of Community and Technical Colleges, *Running Start: 2009–10 Annual Progress Report.*

56. Courses at community and technical colleges are funded through legislative appropriations and tuition (i.e., "state-supported"), agreements with external organizations (i.e., "contract-supported"), and tuition and fees only (i.e., student-funded). www.sbctc.ctc.edu/general/_n-frequentlyasked.aspx.

57. Washington State Board of Community and Technical Colleges, *I-BEST: A Program Integrating Adult Basic Education Workforce Training,* 1.

58. Washington Learns, *Washington Learns,* 35.

59. Washington Higher Education Coordinating Board, *Minimum College Admissions Standards for Students Entering College or University Summer or Fall 2012.*

60. Washington Higher Education Coordinating Board, *Minimum College Admissions Standards: College Academic Distribution Requirements—Guidelines for Educators,* 2.

61. Washington State Board of Education, "Washington State Board of Education Resolution to Approve Washington State Graduation Requirements."

62. Washington Higher Education Coordinating Board, *The System Design Plan,* 6.

63. Washington Higher Education Coordinating Board, *Regional Analysis Report 2011,* 7.

64. State of Washington, "Engrossed Substitute House Bill 1244."

65. Zumeta, "Public Higher Education in Washington State," 6.

66. Ibid., 9–10.

67. State of Washington, "Senate Bill 5774."

68. Washington Higher Education Coordinating Board, *Key Facts about Higher Education 2010,* 3.

69. Ibid., 31.

70. Ibid., 29.

71. Washington Higher Education Coordinating Board, 1990. *Designing for the 21st Century.*

72. Washington Higher Education Coordinating Board, *Key Facts about Higher Education 2010.*

73. Washington Higher Education Coordinating Board, *2011 Transfer Report.*

74. The transfer figures in this section exclude Running Start students. Washington Higher Education Coordinating Board, *2011 Transfer Report.*

75. Washington Higher Education Coordinating Board, *Policy on Intercollege Transfer and Articulation.*

76. Washington State Board for Community and Technical Colleges, *Student Progress and Success.*

77. Washington Higher Education Coordinating Board, *2011 Transfer Report.*

78. Ibid., 18.

79. Washington Higher Education Coordinating Board, *Regional Needs Analysis Report.*

80. University of Washington, *Transfer Admission and Planning.*

81. Ibid.

82. Washington State Board for Community and Technical Colleges, *Academic Year Report: 2009–10.*

83. Washington Higher Education Coordinating Board, *Key Facts,* 57.

84. Washington Office of the Governor *Higher Education Funding Task Force,* 3.

85. Ibid., 8.

86. Delta Cost Project, Washington State Data.

87. Washington Higher Education Coordinating Board, *Key Facts about Higher Education 2011.*

88. "In the 2007–9 operating budget approved May 2007, the legislature appropriated a total of $1.765 billion to the six public four-year institutions and $1.448 billion to the community and technical colleges." State of Washington, "Substitute House Bill 1128," 212. In the 2011 supplemental budget approved December 11, 2010, the legislature appropriated a total of $1.3 billion to the six public four-year institutions and $1.356 billion to the community and technical colleges. Washington State Legislative Budget Notes, 2010.

89. Washington Office of the Governor, "Higher Education Funding Task Force: Finance," 1.

90. Washington Learns, *Washington Learns,* 42.

91. State of Washington, "Engrossed Substitute House Bill 1244."

92. Washington State Budget and Policy Center, "Undermining Prosperity."

93. Washington Office of the Governor, "Higher Education Funding Task Force," 5.

94. State of Washington, "Engrossed Second Substitute House Bill 1795," 5.

95. Washington State House of Representatives, "Final Bill Report, E2SHB 1795."

96. See National Association of State Student Grant & Aid Programs, *41st Annual Survey Report; 40th Annual Survey Report; 39th Annual Survey Report;* and *38th Annual Survey Report: State-sponsored Student Financial Aid.*

97. Washington Higher Education Coordinating Board, *Keeping College Affordable,* 4.

98. Ibid., 19, 27, 29.

99. Ibid., 4.

100. Washington Higher Education Coordinating Board, *Regional Needs Analysis Report.*

101. Washington Higher Education Coordinating Board, *Keeping College Affordable.*

102. State of Washington, "Engrossed Substitute House Bill 1244, Chapter 564."

103. Washington Higher Education Coordinating Board, *Keeping College Affordable,* 5, 30.

104. Office of the Governor, *Higher Education Funding Task Force: Finance;* and Independent Colleges of Washington, *2010 Proposals Affecting Higher Education.*

105. Washington State Budget and Policy Center, "Undermining Prosperity," 1.

106. Washington Office of the Governor, *Higher Education Funding Task Force: Finance*, 3.

107. "Boeing and Microsoft pledge $50 million to New Scholarship Fund," www.microsoft.com/Presspass/press/2011/jun11/06–06MSBoeingEndowmentPR.mspx.

108. Washington State Board of Community and Technical Colleges, *Student Achievement Initiative*, 3.

109. Washington State Board of Community and Technical Colleges, *Student Achievement Initiative*, 2.

110. Shulock and Jenkins, *Performance Incentives to Improve Community College Completion.*

111. Washington Office of the Governor, "Higher Education Funding Task Force: Accountability and Performance," 2.

112. Ibid.

113. Washington Office of the Governor, "Governor Gregoire Proposes Strategies to Create a Seamless Early Learning to Career Education System." News release, January 5, 2011. http://earlylearning.org/news/gov-gregoire-proposes-strategies-to-create-a-seamless-early-learning-to-career-education-system.

114. State of Washington, "Engrossed Second Substitute House Bill 1795," 6.

115. Education Sector, *Washington Score Card.*

116. These four actions were: (1) linking data systems, (2) creating stable and sustained support, (3) developing governance structures, and (4) developing a P–20 workforce research agenda.

117. Data Quality Campaign, *Data for Action 2010.*

118. Office of Superintendent of Public Instruction, "The Smarter Balanced Assessment Consortium."

CHAPTER 9: **Lessons Learned**

1. Stiglitz, *Price of Inequality*, 267.
2. Kelly, "Projected Degree Gap." See table 1 in chapter 3 for further detail.
3. Organisation for Economic Co-operation and Development, *Going for Growth.*
4. Acemoglu and Robinson, *Why Nations Fail*, 429.
5. Western Interstate Higher Education Commission, *Knocking at the College Door.*
6. Perna, Milem et al., "The Status of Equity for Black Undergraduates in Public Higher Education in the South."
7. Richardson et al., *Designing State Higher Education Systems for a New Century.*
8. Acemoglu and Robinson, *Why Nations Fail*; Stiglitz, *Price of Inequality.*
9. Richardson et al., *Designing State Higher Education Systems*, 17.
10. Richardson and Martinez, *Policy and Performance in American Higher Education.*
11. Ibid., 232.
12. Richardson et al., *Designing State Higher Education Systems.*
13. National Center for Public Policy and Higher Education, *Measuring Up 2000.*
14. Richardson et al., *Designing State Higher Education Systems*, 179
15. Richardson and Martinez, *Policy and Performance*, 235.
16. McLendon, "State Governance Reform of Higher Education."

17. Berdahl, Altbach, and Gumport, "The Contexts of American Higher Education."

18. Stiglitz, *Price of Inequality*, 70

19. Heller, "Student Price Response in Higher Education."

20. Perna, "The Key to College Access: A College Preparatory Curriculum," provides a comprehensive review and synthesis of research establishing the importance of academic preparation and achievement to students' college enrollment and the gaps across groups in these measures.

21. McMahon, *Higher Learning, Greater Good.*

22. Perna, "Studying College Choice: A Proposed Conceptual Model."

23. McMahon, *Higher Learning, Greater Good*, 217.

24. Perna, "Studying College Choice."

25. Perna, "Toward a More Complete Understanding of the Role of Financial Aid in Promoting College Enrollment."

26. Illinois Board of Higher Education, *The Illinois Public Agenda for College and Career Success*, 2.

27. Western Interstate Higher Education Commission, *Knocking at the College Door.*

28. Cornwell and Mustard, "Race and the Effects of Georgia's HOPE Scholarship."

29. For a comprehensive review and synthesis on the history of HOPE and research examining the effects of the HOPE Scholarship and Grant program in its first 10 years, see Hamrick and McBee, *HOPE Scholarship: Joint Commission Report.*

30. Perna, "The Key to College Access" and "Studying College Choice."

31. Kirst and Usdan, "The Historical Context of the Divide between K–12 and Higher Education"; Venezia, Kirst, and Antonio, *Betraying the College Dream.*

32. Venezia et al., *Governance Divide*, xi.

33. Center for K–12 Assessment and Performance Management, *Coming Together to Raise Achievement.*

34. Ibid.

35. National Student Clearinghouse, *Who We Are.*

36. About 3% of all those who first enrolled in a public four-year institution in fall 2006 completed a degree at a two-year institution within six years of first enrolling. See Shapiro et al., "Completing College: A National View of Student Attainment Rates."

37. National Center for Education Statistics, *Community College Student Outcomes: 1994–2009.*

38. Of first-year students who enrolled for the first time in a community college in 2003–4, 21% transferred to a four-year institution within five years of first enrolling. National Center for Education Statistics, *Community College Student Outcomes.*

39. Shapiro et al., "Completing College."

40. Russell, "Update on the Community College Baccalaureate."

41. Texas Higher Education Coordinating Board, *The Feasibility of Expanding Texas' Community College Baccalaureate Programs.*

42. Bragg and Ruud, "Information and Advice Regarding Applied Baccalaureate Degree Programs."

43. Russell, "Update on the Community College Baccalaureate."

44. State of Washington, "Engrossed Substitute House Bill 1244," Chapter 564, Laws of

2009, May 19, 2009. http://apps.leg.wa.gov/documents/billdocs/2009-10/Pdf/Bills/House%20Bills/1244-S.E.pdf.

45. Zumeta, "State Policies and Private Higher Education."

46. Richardson and Martinez, *Policy and Performance*, specify that improvements in these aspects occur when at least 19% of students are enrolled in private colleges and universities. Given variations in state context and higher education systems, we do not attempt to identify a threshold that applies across states.

47. For more information on the distribution of undergraduates by sector, see the information provided in chapter 3 or the source from which those data were drawn: National Center for Education Statistics, *Digest of Education Statistics 2011*.

48. National Center for Education Statistics, *Digest of Education Statistics 2011*.

49. For a comprehensive review of important questions pertaining to for-profit higher education providers, see Tierney and Hentschke, *New Players, Different Game*.

50. National Center for Education Statistics, *Students Attending For-Profit Postsecondary Institutions*.

51. Richardson and Martinez, *Policy and Performance*.

52. See Perna and Jones, *The State of College Access and Completion*, for further discussion of the importance of data availability and use for improving college access, persistence, and completion.

53. Data Quality Campaign, *Data for Action 2010: Illinois DQC State Analysis*.

54. Data Quality Campaign, *Data for Action 2010: Maryland DQC State Analysis*.

55. Data Quality Campaign, *Data for Action 2010: Georgia DQC State Analysis*.

56. Data Quality Campaign, *Data for Action 2010: Washington DQC State Analysis*.

57. Data Quality Campaign, *Data for Action 2010: Texas DQC State Analysis*.

58. Per FTE student, educational appropriations from state and local governments for general higher education operations were $5,906 in 2012. See State Higher Education Executive Officers, *State Higher Education Finance, FY 2012*.

59. Eckl and Pattison, "A New Funding Paradigm for Higher Education."

60. Illinois General Assembly, "Bill status of HB1503, 97th General Assembly."

61. For example, in their exploration of the effects of accountability systems in six states, Dougherty and Hong, "Performance Accountability as Imperfect Panacea," concluded that performance-funding and performance-budgeting systems are only weakly related, at best, to such outcomes as community college remediation, retention, graduation and transfer.

62. Complete College America, *Essential Steps for States*. Dougherty and Hong, "Performance Accountability as Imperfect Panacea," noted that the performance-funding system involved just 0.2% of community colleges' total revenues in Illinois and 5% in Florida at the time of their data collection.

63. Dougherty and Hong, "Performance Accountability as Imperfect Panacea"; Hearn et al., "Access, Persistence, and Completion in the State Context."

64. Richardson et al., *Designing State Higher Education Systems*, 195.

65. Stiglitz, *Price of Inequality*, 30–31.

66. Acemoglu and Robinson, *Why Nations Fail*, 429–30.

67. Data from national polling show that, while the share of adults who agree that "a college education is necessary for a person to be successful in today's work world" increased between 2000 and 2008, the share agreeing that "the vast majority of qualified, motivated students have the opportunity to attend college" declined (Immerwahr and Johnson, *Squeeze Play 2010*, 4).

68. Acemoglu and Robinson, *Why Nations Fail*; Stiglitz, *Price of Inequality.*

69. Stiglitz, *Price of Inequality*, 31–32.

70. Acemoglu and Robinson, *Why Nations Fail*, 357.

71. Ibid., 101.

72. For a recent comprehensive review of the obstacles that limit higher education attainment of adult students, see Bragg "Pathways to College for Underserved and Nontraditional Students."

73. Long and Boatman, "The Role of Remedial and Developmental Courses in Access and Persistence."

74. Richardson and Martinez, *Policy and Performance.*

75. This point is argued in several of the chapters in the volume edited by Perna and Jones, *The State of College Access and Completion.*

76. This conclusion is consistent with the notion of the "vicious cycle" discussed by Acemoglu and Robinson, *Why Nations Fail*, and the role of political forces in exacerbating income inequality discussed by Stiglitz, *Price of Inequality*, as well as the conclusions by Oakes et al., "The Social Construction of College Access," about the forces that limit academic "detracking."

77. Acemoglu and Robinson, *Why Nations Fail*, 447.

References

Acemoglu, Daron, and James A. Robinson. *Why Nations Fail: The Origins of Power, Prosperity, and Poverty.* New York: Crown Publishing Group, 2012.

Alderman, C., and Kevin Carey. 2009. "Texas Score Card." Washington, DC: Education Sector, 2009. www.educationsector.org/publications/texas-score-card.

Anderson, Doug A., and Laurel Kennedy. "Baby Boomer Segmentation: Eight Is Enough." *Consumer Insight* 8 (2006): 4–11.

Autor, David. *The Polarization of Job Opportunities in the U.S. Labor Market: Implications for Employment and Earnings.* Washington, DC: Center for American Progress, April 2010.

Badertscher, Nancy, and Cameron McWhirter. "Race to the Top Win Means $400 Million for GA." *Atlanta Journal Constitution,* August 24, 2010. www.ajc.com/news/race-to-the-top-598171.html?printArticle=y.

Ballot Pedia. *Illinois House of Representatives Elections, 2010.* http://ballotpedia.org/wiki/index.php/Illinois_House_of_Representatives_elections,_2010

———. *Illinois State Senate elections, 2010.* http://ballotpedia.org/wiki/index.php/Illinois_State_Senate_elections,_2010.

Baum, Sandra, Jennifer Ma, and Kathleen Payea. *Education Pays 2010.* Washington, DC: College Board, 2010. http://trends.collegeboard.org/education-pays.

Becker, Gary. *Human Capital: A Theoretical and Empirical Analysis, With Special Reference to Education.* 3rd edition. Chicago: University of Chicago Press, 1993.

Berdahl, Robert O. *Statewide Coordination of Higher Education.* Washington, DC: American Council on Education, 1971.

Berdahl, Robert O., Philip G. Altbach, and Patricia J. Gumport. "The Contexts of American Higher Education." In *American Higher Education in the Twenty-first Century,* 2nd ed., edited by Philip G. Altbach, Robert O. Berdahl, and Patricia Gumport, 1–14. Baltimore: Johns Hopkins University Press, 2005.

Bettinger, Eric, Bridget T. Long, Philip Oreopoulous, and Lisa Sanbonmatsu. *The Role of Simplification and Information in College Decisions: Results from the H&R Block FAFSA Experiment.* NBER Working Paper No. 15361, 2009. www.nber.org/papers/w15361.

Beyle, T. L. "The Powers of the Governor in North Carolina: Where the Weak Grow Strong—Except for the Governor." *North Carolina Insight* (1990): 27–45.

Block, L. "Permanent University Fund: Investing in the Future of Texas." UT-Austin, 2011. http://txtell.lib.utexas.edu/stories/p0002-full.html.

Bloland, Harland G. *Creating the Council for Higher Education Accreditation.* Phoenix, AZ: American Council on Education and Oryx Press, 2001.

Boyd, Donald. *Projected State and Local Budget Surplus as a Percent of Revenues, 2016*. Rockefeller Institute of Government: Unpublished manuscript, 2009.

Bragg, Debra. "Pathways to College for Underserved and Nontraditional Students: Lessons from Research, Policy, and Practice." In *The State of College Access and Completion: Improving College Success for Students from Underrepresented Groups*, edited by Laura W. Perna and Anthony Jones, 34–56. New York: Routledge, 2013.

Bragg, Debra, and Collin Ruud. "Information and Advice Regarding Applied Baccalaureate Degree Programs." Oregon State Board of Higher Education, November 23, 2009. http://former.ous.edu/state_board/meeting/dockets/ddoc091123-UEE1.pdf.

Brookings Institution. "State of Metropolitan America Indicator Map." Washington, DC: 2012.www.brookings.edu/metro/StateOfMetroAmerica/Map.aspx#/?subject=7&ind=70&dist=0&data=Number&year=2010&geo=metro&zoom=0&x=0&y=0.

Bureau of Economic Analysis. "Table CA1–3: Personal Income, Population, Per Capita Personal Income, 2009." 2010. www.bea.gov/regional/reis/default.cfm?selTable=CA1-3§ion=2.

Burns, J. M., J. W. Peltason, and T. E. Cronin. *State and Local Politics*. Englewood Cliffs, NJ: Prentice-Hall, 1984.

California Higher Education Policy Center. "Characteristics of the Texas Higher Education System." 2011. www.capolicycenter.org/texas/texas3.html.

Callan, Patrick M. "Reframing Access and Opportunity: Public Policy Dimensions." In *The States and Public Higher Education Policy: Affordability, Access, and Accountability*, edited by Donald E. Heller, 87–105. Baltimore: Johns Hopkins University Press, 2011.

Callan, Patrick M., Peter T. Ewell, Joni E. Finney, and Dennis P. Jones. *Good Policy, Good Practice: Improving Outcomes and Productivity in Higher Education, A Guide for Policymakers*. San Jose, CA: National Center for Public Policy and Higher Education, 2007.

Carnevale, Anthony, Nicole Smith, and Jeffrey Strohl. *Help Wanted: Projections of Jobs and Education Requirements through 2018*. Washington, DC: Georgetown Center on Education and the Workforce, 2010. www.georgetown.edu/grad/gppi/hpi/cew/pdfs/FullReport.pdf.

Castro, E. L., D. D. Bragg, S. Khan, L. D. Baber, L.D., and B. H. Common. "How Illinois' College and Career Readiness (CCR) Pilot Sites Address Five Key Goals." *In Brief*, June 2010. http://occrl.illinois.edu/files/InBrief/Brief-CCR-2010.pdf.

Center for K–12 Assessment & Performance Management. *Coming Together to Raise Achievement: New Assessments for the Common Core State Standards*. Princeton, NJ: Education Testing Service, 2012. www.k12center.org/rsc/pdf/Coming_Together_April_2012_Final.pdf.

Clark, Burton R. *The Higher Education System: Academic Organization in Cross-National Perspective*. Berkeley: University of California Press, 1983.

College Board, *Georgia AP Supplement 2011*. New York, 2011.

———. *Trends in College Pricing 2012*. Washington, DC, 2012a. http://trends.collegeboard.org/college-pricing.

———. *Trends in Student Aid 2012*. Washington, DC, 2012b. http://trends.collegeboard.org/student-aid.

Combs, S. 2008. *Texas Works 2008: Training and Education for All Texans*. Austin: Texas

Comptroller of Public Accounts, 2008. www.window.state.tx.us/specialrpt/workforce/career.php#exhibit3-5.

Complete College America. *Essential Steps for States: Shift to Performance Funding.* www.completecollege.org/path_forward/essentialsteps.

Cornwell, Christopher, and David Mustard. "Race and The Effects of Georgia's HOPE Scholarship." In *Who Should We Help? The Negative Social Consequences of Merit Scholarships*, edited by Donald E. Heller and Patricia Marin, 57–92. Cambridge, MA: The Civil Rights Project, Harvard University, 2002.

Council for Adult and Experiential Learning. *Adult Learning in Focus: National and State-By-State Data*, 2008. www.cael.org/pdf/publication_pdf/State_Indicators_Monograph.pdf

Cunningham, Alisa F., and Deborah A. Santiago. *Student Aversion to Borrowing: Who Borrows and Who Doesn't.* Washington, DC: Institute for Higher Education Policy, 2008.

Data Quality Campaign. *Data for Action 2010: Georgia DQC State Analysis*, Washington, DC: 2010.

———. *Data for Action 2010: Illinois DQC State Analysis.* Washington, DC: 2010.

———. *Data for Action 2010: Maryland DQC State Analysis.* Washington, DC: 2010.

———. *Data for Action 2010: Texas DQC State Analysis.* Washington, DC: 2010.

———. *Data for Action 2010: Washington DQC State Analysis.* Washington, DC: 2010.

Davis, Vanessa. "Applied Baccalaureate Degrees in Texas." N.d. www.ous.edu/sites/default/files/dept/indaffairs/AB/Davis.pdf.

Deal, Nathan. "Governor's State-of-the-State Speech, 2011." WAGT, Channel 26, NBC News. (transcript). www2.wagt.com/member-center/share-this/print/?content=ar1334007.

Delaney, Jennifer, and William Doyle. "The Role of Higher Education in State Budgets." In *The Challenges of Comparative State-Level Higher Education Policy Research*, edited by K. M. Shaw and D. E. Heller, 55–76. Sterling, VA: Stylus, 2007.

Delta Cost Project. "Illinois State Data." Accessed Oct. 12, 2010. http://deltacostproject.org/data/state/pdf/il.pdf.

———. "Texas State Data." Accessed October 12, 2011. http://deltacostproject.org/data/state/pdf/tx.pdf.

———. "Trends in College Spending Online." Accessed Nov. 1, 2011. www.tcs-online.org.

———. "Washington State Data." Accessed October 12, 2010. http://deltacostproject.org/data/state/pdf/wa.pdf.

DesJardins, Stephen L., and Robert K. Toutkoushian. "Are Students Really Rational? The Development of Rational Thought and Its Application to Student Choice." In *Higher Education: Handbook of Theory and Research*, Vol. 20, edited by J. C. Smart, 191–240. Dordrecht, The Netherlands: Kluwer Academic Publishers, 2005.

Desrochers, Donna M., Colleen M. Lenihan, and Jane V. Wellman. *Trends in College Spending 1998–2008: Where Does the Money Come From? Where Does It Go? What Does It Buy?* Washington, DC: Delta Cost Project, 2010. www.deltacostproject.org/resources/pdf/Trends-in-College-Spending-98–08.pdf.

Dougherty, Kevin J., and Esther Hong. "Performance Accountability as Imperfect Panacea: The Community College Experience." In *Defending the Community College Equity Agenda*, edited by T. Bailey and V. S. Morest, 51–81. Baltimore: Johns Hopkins University Press, 2006.

Dougherty, Kevin J., and Gregory S. Kienzl. "It's Not Enough to Get Through The Open Door: Inequalities by Social Background in Transfer From Community Colleges to Four-Year Colleges." *Teachers College Record* 108 (2006): 452–87.

Doyle, William R., Michael K. McLendon, and James C. Hearn. "The Adoption of Prepaid Tuition and Savings Plans in the American States: An Event History Analysis." *Research in Higher Education* 51 (2010): 69–86.

Eckl, Corina, and Scott Pattison. "A New Funding Paradigm for Higher Education." Paper presented at Raising the Bar for Higher Education in a Time of Fiscal Constraints, sponsored by the Miller Center of Public Affairs, Association of Governing Boards of Universities and Colleges, National Conference of State Legislatures, and National Governors Association, Charlottesville, VA, 2010.

Editorial Projects in Education Research Center. *Diplomas Count 2010: Graduation by the Numbers.* Bethesda, MD: Education Week, 2010.

———. "Indicators." Accessed June 28, 2013. www.edcounts.org/createtable/step1.php.

Education Commission of the States. *State-Level Coordinating and/or Governing Agency.* Denver, CO: Author, October 2007. http://ecs.force.com/mbdata/mbquestU?Rep=PSG01&SID=a0i70000009vZI&Q=Q0667.

———. *System/Institutional Governing Boards.* Denver, CO: Author, October 2007. http://ecs.force.com/mbdata/mbquestU?Rep=PSG02&SID=a0i70000009vZI&Q=Q0668.

———. "Texas: Postsecondary Governance Structures." Denver, CO: 2011. http://mb2.ecs.org/reports/Report.aspx?id=221.

Education Sector. "Georgia Score Card." June 30, 2009. www.educationsector.org/publications/georgia-score-card.

———. *Higher Ed Accountability Report: Illinois.* 2010. www.educationsector.org/usr_doc/Illinois.pdf.

———. "Maryland Score Card." 2009. www.educationsector.org/sites/default/files/publications/Maryland.pdf.

———. "Washington Score Card." Washington, DC: 2009. www.educationsector.org/publications/washington-score-card.

Ehrlich, Robert L. *Letter to the Honorable Thomas V. "Mike" Miller, Jr., President of the Senate,* May 26, 2006. http://mgaleg.maryland.gov/2006rs/veto_letters/sb0998.pdf.

Ewell, Peter, and Patrick Kelly. *State-Level Completion and Transfer Rates: Harnessing a New National Resources.* Boulder, CO: National Center for Higher Education Management Systems, 2009.

Ewing Marion Kauffman Foundation. *United States Must Address Fundamental Economic Competitiveness to Thrive in the New Economy.* www.kauffman.org/newsroom/2010-ranking-of-new-economy-states-highlights-leaders-and-laggers.aspx.

FSG Social Impact Consultants. *Texas Regional Action Plan for Postsecondary Completion.* 2011. http://greatertexasfoundation.org/wp-content/uploads/2011/03/Texas-Regional-Action-Plan-2-18-11.pdf.

GAcollege411. "Georgia's HOPE Scholarship Program Overview." www.gacollege411.org/Financial_Aid_Planning/HOPE_Program/Georgia_s_HOPE_Scholarship_Program_Overview.aspx.

Geoffrey, Meredith, and Charles Schewe. "The Power of Cohorts." *American Demographics* 12 (December 1994): 22–27.

Georgia Department of Education. "The Alliance of Education Agency Heads." www.aypf.org/tripreports/2011/documents/Georgia's%20Alliance%20of%20Education%20Agency%20Heads%202011.pdf.

———. "Strategy Map." http://publicuat.doe.k12.ga.us/strategicPlan.aspx?&PageReq=Strategy.

———. "Testing Brief." Atlanta: GADOE, 2010.

Georgia Office of Student Achievement. "Race to the Top." www.gaosa.org/highlights.aspx.

Georgia Research Alliance. "About Us." www.gra.org/AboutGRA.aspx.

———. "Origins." www.gra.org/AboutGRA/Origins.aspx.

Georgia State Lottery Corporation. *2009 Annual Report.* Atlanta: Georgia State Lottery Corporation, 2009.

———. "Georgia Lottery Corporation Management's Discussion and Analysis for the Years Ended June 30, 2011 and 2010." Atlanta: Georgia State Lottery Corporation, 2011.

Georgia Student Finance Commission. "HOPE Grant Program Regulations, 2009–2010." www.gsfc.org/main/publishing/pdf/2009/hope_grant_regs.pdf.

———. "Scholarship and Grant Award History." www.gsfc.org/gsfcnew/SANDG_FACTS.CFM?sec=3

Glenny, Lyman. *Autonomy of Public Colleges: The Challenge of Coordination.* New York: McGraw-Hill, 1959.

———. *A Master Plan for Higher Education in Illinois—Phase II.* Springfield, IL: Illinois State Board of Higher Education, 1966.

Governor's Business Council. *Leading the Way: An Action Plan for Making Texas Higher Education Globally Competitive* Austin, TX: 2007. www.texasgbc.org/pdfs/leading%20the%20Way.pdf.

Governor's Office of Management and Budget. *FY 2011 Budget by Agency.* July 10, 2010. www2.illinois.gov/gov/budget/Documents/Budget%20Book/FY%202011/FY2011%20Budget%20By%20Agency%2008021o.pdf.

———. *General Funds Appropriations 2006–2011.* July 1, 2010. www.illinois.gov/public includes/statehome/gov/documents/Historical%20Approp%20Master.pdf.

Governor's Office of Planning and Budget. *Governor's Budget Reports: 2013—2004.* Atlanta: Office of the Governor, 2013. http://opb.georgia.gov/governors-budget-reports.

Grusky, David B., Beth Red Bird, Natassia Rodriguez, and Christopher Wimer. *How Much Protection Does a College Degree Afford? The Impact of the Recession on Recent College Graduates.* Washington, DC: The Pew Charitable Trusts, Economic Mobility Project, January 2013.

Hamrick, Bill, and Louise McBee. *HOPE Scholarship: Joint Commission Report.* Atlanta, GA: Carl Vinson Institute of Government, 2003.

Haskins, Ron. "Education and Economic Mobility." In *Getting Ahead or Losing Ground: Economic Mobility in America,* edited by Isabel V. Sawhill, 91–104. Washington, DC: Brookings Institution, 2008.

Haskins, Ron, Julia B. Isaacs, and Isabel V. Sawhill. *Getting Ahead or Losing Ground: Economic Mobility in America.* Washington, DC: Brookings Institution, February 2008.

Hearn, James C. "The Paradox of Growth in Federal Aid for College Students, 1960–1990." In *The Finance of Higher Education, Theory, Research, Policy, and Practice,* edited by Michael B. Paulsen and John C. Smart, 267–320. New York: Agathon Press.

Hearn, James C., Anthony P. Jones, and Elizabeth R. Kurban. "Access, Persistence, and Completion in the State Context." In *The State of College Access and Completion: Improving College Success for Students from Underrepresented Groups*, edited by Laura W. Perna and Anthony Jones, 166–89. New York: Routledge, 2013.

Heck, Ronald H. *Studying Educational and Social Policy: Theoretical Concepts and Research Methods.* Mahwah, NJ: Lawrence Erlbaum Associates, 2004.

Heller, Donald E. "The Changing Nature of Financial Aid." *Academe* (2004): 36–38. www.aaup.org/AAUP/pubsres/academe/2004/JA/Feat/hell.htm.

———. "The Impact of Student Loans on College Access." In *The Effectiveness of Student Aid Policies: What the Research Tells Us*, edited by S. Baum, M. McPherson, and P. Steele, 39–68. Washington, DC: College Board, 2008.

———. "Student Price Response in Higher Education: An Update to Leslie and Brinkman." *Journal of Higher Education* 68 (1997): 624–59.

Higher Education Finance Study Commission. *Report to the Governor, the Honorable Pat Quinn, and members of the Illinois General Assembly.* Springfield, IL: Author, November 2010.

Higher Education Insight Associates. *Feasibility Study for Restructuring Texas Student Financial Aid Programs.* Report submitted to the Texas Higher Education Coordinating Board, 2008.

Hovey, Harold. *State Spending for Higher Education in the Next Decade: The Battle to Sustain Current Support.* San Jose, CA: California State Policy Research, Inc., 1999.

Humes, Karen R., Nicholas A. Jones, and Roberto R. Ramirez. *Overview of Race and Hispanic Origin: 2010.* Washington, DC: U.S. Census Bureau, C2010-BR-02, March 2011. www.census.gov/prod/cen2010/briefs/c2010br-02.pdf.

Illinois Board of Higher Education. *Databook on Illinois Higher Education.* Springfield, IL: Author, 2010.

———. *FY 2011 Higher Education Budget Recommendations.* Springfield, IL: Author, 2010.

———.*The Illinois Public Agenda for College and Career Success.* Springfield, IL: Author, 2008.

———. *A Report on the Efficiency and Sustainability of the Monetary Award Program.* Springfield, IL: Author, 2010.

———. *Report to the Governor and General Assembly on Underrepresented Groups in Illinois Higher Education.* Springfield, IL: Author, 2013.

———. *State Matching Grant Program: Fiscal Year 2007 Grant Allocation.* Springfield, IL: Author, 2006.

Illinois General Assembly. "Bill Status of HB4906, 96th General Assembly." www.ilga.gov/legislation/BillStatus.asp?DocTypeID=HB&DocNum=4906&GAID=10&SessionID=76&LegID=49387.

———. "Bill Status of HB1503, 97th General Assembly." www.ilga.gov/legislation/BillStatus.asp?DocNum=1503&GAID=11&DocTypeID=HB&LegID=58527&SessionID=84&GA=97.

Illinois Office of the Governor. *Senate Bill 250—Economic Recovery and Budget Reform.* www2.illinois.gov/gov/Documents/Press%20Releases/SB%202505%20one-Pager.pdf.

Illinois Student Assistance Commission. *2010 Data Book*. Springfield, IL: 2010. www.isac.org/rppa/data-book/2010-data-book.html.

———. *The Future of MAP Grants and Other State Grant Programs*. 2010. Presentation to the 2010 Illinois Association of Student Financial Aid Administrators conference.

———. *Monetary Award Program Evaluation*. 2009. www.collegezone.com/media/map_eval_09_elec.pdf.

Immerwahr, John, and Jean Johnson. *Squeeze Play 2010: Continued Public Anxiety on Cost, Harsher Judgments on How Colleges are Run*. San Jose, CA: A joint project of Public Agenda and the National Center for Public Policy and Higher Education, February 2010.

Independent Colleges of Washington. *2010 Proposals Affecting Higher Education*. Olympia, WA: 2010. www.icwashington.org/budget10.html.

Institute for a Competitive Workforce. *Leaders & Laggards: State by State Report Card on Public Postsecondary Education*. Washington, DC: U.S. Chamber of Commerce, 2012.

Integrated Postsecondary Education Data System. "2008 Enrollment Survey." http://nces.ed.gov/ipeds/datacenter/login.aspx.

———. "2008 Graduation Rates Survey." http://nces.ed.gov/ipeds/datacenter/login.aspx.

———. "2008 Institutional Characteristics Survey." http://nces.ed.gov/ipeds/datacenter/login.aspx.

———. "2009 Completions Survey." http://nces.ed.gov/ipeds/datacenter/login.aspx.

———. "2009 Graduation Rates Survey." http://nces.ed.gov/ipeds/datacenter/login.aspx.

———. "2009 Institutional Characteristics Survey." http://nces.ed.gov/ipeds/datacenter/login.aspx.

———. "2009 Student Financial Aid Survey." http://nces.ed.gov/ipeds/datacenter/login.aspx.

Integrated Public Use Microdata Series Version 5.0 Machine-readable database. Minneapolis: University of Minnesota, 2013.

Jones, Dennis. *A Public Agenda for Higher Education: What Is It? Do We Have One?* Boulder, CO: National Center for Higher Education Management Systems, 2009.

Jones, Dennis, and Patrick Kelly. *A New Look at the Institutional Component of Higher Education Finance: A Guide for Evaluating Performance Relative to Financial Resource*. Boulder, CO: NCHEMS, 2007.

Kelly, K. F., and Lach, I. J. *Evaluation of the Illinois Articulation Initiative: Report and Recommendations*. www.ibhe.state.il.us/Board/agendas/2006/April/Item11Report.pdf.

Kelly, Patrick. "Projected Degree Gap: Percent of 25 to 64 Year Olds with Associate Degrees or Higher." Unpublished table. Boulder, CO: NCHEMS, 2010.

Kirst, Michael W., and Michael D. Usdan. "The Historical Context of the Divide between K–12 and Higher Education." In *States, Schools, and Colleges: Policies to Improve Student Readiness for College and Strengthen Coordination Between Schools and Colleges*, 5–22. San Jose, CA: National Center for Public Policy and Higher Education, 2009.

Lederman, D. 2011. "Colleges Win on Election Night." *Inside Higher Ed*, Nov. 4, 2009. www.insidehighered.com/news/2009/11/04/elect.

Legislative Budget Board. 2011. *Financing Higher Education in Texas: Legislative Primer*, 5th edition. Austin, TX: 2011. www.lbb.state.tx.us/Higher_Education/HigherEd_Financing Primer.pdf.

Lenard, Matthew A., and Joan M. Lord. *Gaining Ground on High School Graduation Rates in SREB States: Milestones and Guideposts.* Atlanta: SREB, 2009.

Leslie, Larry, and Paul Brinkman. *The Economic Value of Higher Education.* Phoenix, AZ: American Council on Education and Oryx Press, 1988.

Long, Bridget T., and Angela Boatman. "The Role of Remedial and Developmental Courses in Access and Persistence." In *The State of College Access and Completion: Improving College Success for Students from Underrepresented Groups,* edited by L. W. Perna and A. P. Jones, 77–95. New York: Routledge, 2013.

Mackun, Paul, and Steven Wilson. "Population Distribution and Change: 2000 to 2010." Washington DC: U.S. Census Bureau, 2011. www.census.gov/prod/cen2010/briefs/c2010br-01.pdf.

Maryland General Assembly. Chapter 192, Senate Bill 283. 2010. http://mgaleg.maryland.gov/2010rs/chapters_noln/Ch_192_sb0283E.pdf.

———. Chapter 193, "Higher Education Investment Fund—Tuition Stabilization and Funding." 2010. http://mgaleg.maryland.gov/2010rs/chapters_noln/Ch_193_hb0470T.pdf.

———. House Bill 506. 2008. http://mgaleg.maryland.gov/2008rs/bills/hb/hb0506f.pdf.

———. House Bill 900. 2009. http://mgaleg.maryland.gov/2009rs/bills/hb/hb0900f.pdf.

———. Spending Affordability Committee, 2009 Interim Report. http://167.102.242.144/search?client=mgaleg_default&proxystylesheet=mgaleg_default&output=xml_no_dtd&getfields=author.title.keywords&filter=0&entqr=3&ie=latin1&oe=UTF-8&num=100&q=spending%20affordability%20committee&site=all.

———. Spending Affordability Committee, 2010 Interim Report. http://167.102.242.144/search?client=mgaleg_default&proxystylesheet=mgaleg_default&output=xml_no_dtd&getfields=author.title.keywords&filter=0&entqr=3&ie=latin1&oe=UTF-8&num=100&q=spending%20affordability%20committee&site=all.

Maryland Higher Education Commission. *2008 Community College Graduates Follow-Up Survey Report.* Annapolis, MD: Author, 2009. www.mhec.state.md.us/higherED/about/Meetings/CommissionMeetings/3-24-10/2008CCGraduatesFollow-UpSurveyReport+Memo.pdf.

———. *2009 Maryland State Plan for Postsecondary Education.* www.mhec.state.md.us/higherEd/2004Plan/JUNE_2009_FinalEdited.pdf.

———. *Commission to Develop the Maryland Model for Funding Higher Education Final Report.* Baltimore, MD: 2008. http://dls.state.md.us/data/polanasubare/polanasubare_edu/Commission-to-Study-the-Maryland-Model-for-Funding-Higher-Education.pdf.

———. Commission Responsibilities. 2010. www.mhec.state.md.us/higherEd/about/commissi.asp.

———. Interagency Initiatives. 2011. http://mhec.maryland.gov/highered/interagency initiatives.asp.

———. *Managing for Results Report for FY 2009.* http://mhec.maryland.gov/publications/research/annualreports/mfrfy2009.pdf.

———. *Maryland's Report and the Partnership between the State of Maryland and the U.S. Department of Education, Office for Civil Rights (OCR).* 2006. www.mhec.state.md.us/highered/ocrplan/#partnership.

———. Partnership Agreement between the State of Maryland and the Office for Civil Rights. Letter dated June 19, 2006. www.mhec.state.md.us/higherEd/ocrplan/OCR Letterandattachments.pdf.

———. *Regional Higher Education Centers Enrollment: FY 2006 to 2011.* N.d. Unpublished table produced from 2014 budget requests. Annapolis, MD.

———. "Table 1: Comparison of State Annual Appropriations to Historically Black Institutions and Projections Based on The Share Of Full-Time Equivalent Students, Four-Year Public Institutions, Four-Year Public Institutions, University of Maryland, College Park Not Included, 1990–2010." Annapolis, MD: 2011.

———. "Table 2: Comparison of State Annual Appropriations to Historically Black Institutions And Projections Based on the Share of Full-Time Equivalent Students, Four-Year Public Institutions, Four-Year Public Institutions, University of Maryland, College Park, 1990–2010." Annapolis, MD: 2011.

Maryland Independent College and University Association. Fast Facts. 2010. www.micua .org/fast-facts.

———. The Joseph A. Sellinger Program. www.micua.org/eSellinger.pdf.

———. Mission and History. 2010. www.micua.org/about-micua/mission-history.

Maryland Office of the Secretary of State. Code of Maryland Regulations, 13B.02.03.02. N.d. www.dsd.state.md.us/comar/comarhtml/13b/13b.02.03.02.htm.

———. Code of Maryland Regulations, 13B.06.01.02-1. N.d. www.dsd.state.md.us/comar/comarhtml/13b/13b.06.01.02-1.htm.

Maryland State Archives. Maryland Higher Education Commission: Origin and Functions. 2010. www.msa.md.gov/msa/mdmanual/25ind/highered/html/43highf.html.

———. *Regional Higher Education Centers.* 2011. www.msa.md.gov/msa/mdmanual/01glance/html/edregion.html.

Maryland State Department of Education. Divisions: The Governor's P–20 Leadership Council of Maryland. 2010. www.marylandpublicschools.org/MSDE/divisions/leader ship/programs/P-20_Partnership.

———. "Testing." 2013. www.marylandpublicschools.org/NR/rdonlyres/4BE0DBA0-5159 -4E9D-823F-6BADD8A4CECF/3390/StudentQA.pdf.

Mayer, Gerald. *Union Membership Trends in the United States.* CRS Report for Congress. Washington, DC: Congressional Research Service, August 31, 2004.

McCaffrey, R. "BRAC Plan Expected to Bring 22,000 Homeowners." *Washington Post,* October 25, 2007. www.washingtonpost.com/wp-dyn/content/article/2007/10/23/AR 2007102302621.html.

McLendon, Michael K. "State Governance Reform of Higher Education: Patterns, Trends and Theories of the Public Policy Process." In *Higher Education: Handbook of Theory and Research,* Vol. 18, edited by J. C. Smart, 57–144. Norwell, MA: Kluwer Academic Publishers, 2003.

McLendon, Michael K., James C. Hearn, and Christine G. Mokher. "Partisans, Professionals, and Power: The Role of Political Factors in State Higher Education Funding." *Journal of Higher Education* 80 (2009): 686–713.

McLendon, Michael K., Donald Heller, and Stephanie Lee. "High School to College Transition Policy in the American States." *Educational Policy* 23 (2009): 385–418.

McMahon, Walter W. *Higher Learning, Greater Good: The Private and Social Benefits of Higher Education.* Baltimore, MD: Johns Hopkins University Press, 2009.

Microsoft. "Boeing and Microsoft pledge $50 million to New Scholarship Fund." 2011. www.microsoft.com/Presspass/press/2011/jun11/06-06MSBoeingEndowmentPR.mspx.

Mortenson, Tom G. *Chance for College by Age 19 by State, 1986 to 2008.* Oskaloosa, IA: Postsecondary Education Opportunity, 2010.

———. *Postsecondary Education Opportunity.* August 2010. www.postsecondary.org/statereportslist.asp?subcat2=IL.

Mundel, David. "What Do We Know About the Impact of Grants to College Students?" In *The Effectiveness of Student Aid Policies: What the Research Tells Us,* edited by S. Baum, M. McPherson, and P. Steele, 9–38. Washington, DC: College Board, 2008.

National Association of State Budget Officers. *State Expenditure Report: Fiscal Year 2008.* Washington, DC: 2009.

National Association of State Student Grant & Aid Programs. *31st Annual Survey Report on State-Sponsored Student Financial Aid.* Washington, DC: 2001. www.nassgap.org/viewrepository.aspx?categoryID=3.

———. *35th Annual Survey Report on State-Sponsored Student Financial Aid.* Washington, DC: 2005. www.nassgap.org/viewrepository.aspx?categoryID=3#.

———. *38th Annual Survey Report: State-Sponsored Student Financial Aid.* Washington, DC, 2008. www.nassgap.org/viewrepository.aspx?categoryID=3#.

———. *39th Annual Survey Report: State-Sponsored Student Financial Aid.* Washington, DC, 2009. www.nassgap.org/viewrepository.aspx?categoryID=3#.

———. *40th Annual Survey Report: State-Sponsored Student Financial Aid.* Washington, DC, 2010. www.nassgap.org/viewrepository.aspx?categoryID=3#.

———. *41st Annual Survey Report: State-Sponsored Student Financial Aid.* Washington, DC, 2011. www.nassgap.org/viewrepository.aspx?categoryID=3#.

National Center for Education Statistics. *Community College Student Outcomes: 1994–2009.* Washington, DC: U.S. Department of Education, 2012. http://nces.ed.gov/pubsearch/pubsinfo.asp?pubid=2012253.

———. *Digest of Education Statistics 2009.* http://nces.ed.gov/pubs2010/2010013.pdf.

———. *Digest of Education Statistics 2011.* Washington, DC: U.S. Department of Education, 2012.

———. *The Nation's Report Card: Mathematics 2009.* Snapshot State Report. http://nces.ed.gov/nationsreportcard/pdf/stt2009/2010454IL8.pdf.

———. *Nation's Report Card—NAEP Data Explorer.* Washington, DC: 2010. http://nces.ed.gov/nationsreportcard/naepdata/dataset.aspx.

———. *The Nation's Report Card: Reading 2009.* Snapshot State Report. http://nces.ed.gov/nationsreportcard/pdf/stt2009/2010460IL8.pdf.

———. *Students Attending For-Profit Postsecondary Institutions: Demographics, Enrollment, Characteristics, and 6-Year Outcomes.* NCES 2012-173. Washington, DC: U.S. Department of Education, December 2011.

———. "Table 11: First-time, Full-time, Undergraduate Enrollment in Title IV Institutions, by Race/Ethnicity and State: Fall 2006." Table files: IPEDS state tables 2006. http://nces.ed.gov/das/library/tables_listings/state2006_enrollment.asp.

———. *Trends in Financing of Undergraduate Education: Selected Years 1995–96 to 2007–08.* NCES 2011-218. Washington, DC: U.S. Department of Education, 2011. http://nces.ed.gov/pubsearch/pubsinfo.asp?pubid=2011218.

National Center for Higher Education Management Systems. "2005 ACS PUMS—Education Attainment by Age by Race by State." Revised September 2007. www.higheredinfo.org/analyses.

———. "ACS Educational Attainment by Degree-Level and Age-Group (American Community Survey)." Boulder, CO: 2007. www.higheredinfo.org/dbrowser/index.php?measure=93.

———. "Enrollment of 25 to 49 Year Olds as a Percent of 25 to 49 Year Olds with No Bachelor's Degree or Higher." 2009. www.higheredinfo.org/dbrowser/index.php?measure=105.

———. "Per Capita Personal Income, 2011." www.higheredinfo.org/dbrowser/index.php?submeasure=103&year=2011&level=nation&mode=data&state=0.

———. "Percent of 18 to 24 Year Olds Enrolled in College." Boulder, CO: 2011. www.higheredinfo.org/dbrowser/index.php?measure=104.

———. "Percent of Adults with an Associate Degree or Higher: Gaps between Whites and Minorities." Boulder, CO: 2007. www.higheredinfo.org/dbrowser/index.php?submeasure=352&year=2007&level=nation&mode=data&state=0.

———. "Six-Year Graduation Rates of Bachelor's Students." Boulder, CO: 2011. www.higheredinfo.org/dbrowser/?level=&mode=definitions&state=0&submeasure=27.

———. "State and Local Public Higher Education Support Per Full-Time Equivalent Student." www.higheredinfo.org/dbrowser/index.php?measure=36.

———. "Three-Year Graduation Rates for Associate Students." 2011. www.higheredinfo.org/dbrowser/index.php?submeasure=24&year=2009&level=nation&mode=data&state=0.

———. "Total Research and Development Expenditures per $1,000 of Gross State Product." Boulder, CO: 2009. www.higheredinfo.org/dbrowser/?level=nation&mode=map&state=0&submeasure=199.

National Center for Public Policy and Higher Education. *Affordability and Transfer: Critical to Increasing Baccalaureate Degree Completion.* San Jose, CA: 2011.

———. *Measuring Up 2000: The State by State Report Card on Higher Education.* http://measuringup.highereducation.org/2000/reporthome.htm.

———. *Measuring Up 2008: The National Report Card on Higher Education.* San Jose, CA: 2008. http://measuringup2008.highereducation.org.

National Conference of State Legislatures. *State Budget Update: November 2010.* www.ncsl.org/documents/fiscal/november2010sbu_free.pdf.

National Governors Association. *Complete to Compete: Briefing Paper.* Washington, DC: 2010. www.nga.org/Files/pdf/C2CBriefingPaperAttainmentGoalsAndMeasures.pdf.

National Student Clearinghouse. *Who We Are.* www.studentclearinghouse.org/about.

Ness, Erik C. "The Politics of Determining Merit Aid Eligibility Criteria: An Analysis of the Policy Process." *Journal of Higher Education* 81 (2010): 33–60.

Ness, Erik C., and Molly A. Mistretta. "Merit Aid in North Carolina: A Case Study of a 'Nonevent.'" *Educational Policy* 24 (2009): 703–34.

The New Georgia Encyclopedia. Atlanta: Georgia Humanities Council, 2010. www.georgiaencyclopedia.org/nge/Home.jsp.

Oakes, Jeannie, John Rogers, Martin Lipton, and Ernest Morrell. "The Social Construction of College Access: Confronting the Technical, Cultural, and Political barriers to Low-Income Students of Color." In *Increasing Access to College: Extending Possibilities for All Students,* edited by W. G. Tierney and L. S. Hagedorn, 105–21. Albany: State University of New York Press, 2002.

Office of Superintendent of Public Instruction. "The Smarter Balanced Assessment Consortium." Olympia, WA: 2011. www.k12.wa.us/smarter.

———. "Washington State Report Card, Statewide Assessment Trend." Olympia, WA: 2011. http://reportcard.ospi.k12.wa.us/waslTrend.aspx?year=2008-09&gradeLevelId=10&waslCategory=6&chartType=1.

O'Malley, Martin. "State of the State." Annapolis, MD: 2010. www.governor.maryland.gov/speeches/sos2010.pdf.

Organisation for Economic Co-operation and Development. *Education at a Glance 2012: OECD Indicators.* OECD Publishing.

———. *Going for Growth: Economic Policy Reforms 2012.* www.oecd.org/eco/labour/49421421.pdf.

Ostrom, Elinor. "Institutional Rational Choice: An Assessment of the Institutional Analysis and Development Framework." In *Theories of the Policy Process: Theoretical Lenses on Public Policy,* edited by P. A. Sabatier, 35–72. Boulder, CO: Westview Press, 1999.

Partnership for Assessment of Readiness for College and Careers. "About PARCC." www.parcconline.org/about-parcc.

Paulsen, Michael B. "The Economics of Human Capital and Investment in Higher Education." In *The Finance of Higher Education: Theory, Research, Policy, and Practice,* edited by M. B. Paulsen and J. C. Smart, 55–94. New York: Agathon Press, 2001.

———. "The Economics of the Public Sector: The Nature and Role of Public Policy in the Finance of Higher Education." In *The Finance of Higher Education: Theory, Research, Policy, and Practice,* edited by M. B. Paulsen and J. C. Smart, 95–132. New York: Agathon Press, 2001.

Perna, Laura W. "The Key to College Access: A College Preparatory Curriculum." In *Preparing for College: Nine Elements of Effective Outreach,* edited by W. G. Tierney, Z. B. Corwin, and J. E. Colyar, 113–34. Albany: State University of New York Press, 2005.

———. "The Private Benefits of Higher Education: An Examination of the Earnings Premium." *Research in Higher Education* 44 (2003): 451–72.

———. "Studying College Choice: A Proposed Conceptual Model." In *Higher Education: Handbook of Theory and Research,* Vol. 21, edited by J. C. Smart, 99–157. New York: Springer: 2006.

———. "Toward a More Complete Understanding of the Role of Financial Aid in Promoting College Enrollment: The Importance of Context." In *Higher Education: Handbook of Theory and Research,* Vol. 25, edited by J. C. Smart, 129–80. New York: Springer, 2010.

———. "Understanding High School Students' Willingness to Borrow to Pay College Prices." *Research in Higher Education* 49 (2008): 589–606.

Perna, Laura W., and Michael Armijo. "The Persistence of Unaligned K–12 and Higher Education Systems: Why Have Statewide P–20 Councils Been Ineffective?" Paper presented at the Association for the Study of Higher Education (ASHE), Las Vegas, NV, November 2012.

Perna, Laura W., and Anthony Jones, eds. *The State of College Access and Completion: Improving College Success for Students from Underrepresented Groups.* New York: Routledge, 2013.

Perna, Laura W., Jeffrey Milem, Danette Gerald, Evan Baum, Heather Rowan, and Neal Hutchens. "The Status of Equity for Black Undergraduates in Public Higher Education in the South: Still Separate and Unequal." *Research in Higher Education* 47 (2006): 197–228.

Perna, Laura W., and Patricia Steele, "The Role of Context in Understanding the Contributions of Financial Aid to College Opportunity." *Teachers College Record* 113 (2009): 895–933.

Perna, Laura W., Patricia Steele, Susan Woda, and Taifa Hibbert. "State Public Policies and the Racial/Ethnic Stratification of College Access and Choice in the State of Maryland." *Review of Higher Education* 28 (2005): 245–72.

Perna, Laura W., and Scott L. Thomas. "Barriers to College Opportunity: The Unintended Consequences of State-Mandated Tests." *Educational Policy* 23 (2009): 451–79.

Perna, Laura W., and Marvin Titus. "Understanding Differences in the Choice of College Attended: The Role of State Public Policies." *Review of Higher Education* 27 (2004): 501–25.

Pew Center on the States. *Beyond California: States in Fiscal Peril.* Washington, DC: 2009.

The Pew Charitable Trusts. "Income and Wealth in America across Generations: The Economic Mobility Project." www.pewstates.org/research/data-visualizations/income-and-wealth-in-america-across-generations-85899453568.

The Pew Charitable Trusts, Economic Mobility Project. *Economic Mobility and the American Dream: Where Do We Stand in the Wake of the Great Recession?* Washington, DC: 2011.

Pew Hispanic Center. *Unauthorized Immigrant Population: National and State Trends, 2010.* Washington, DC: 2011.

Richardson, Richard C. *State Structures for the Governance of Higher Education: Illinois Case Study Summary.* San Jose, CA: California Higher Education Policy Center, 1997.

Richardson, Richard C., Kathy R. Bracco, Patrick M. Callan, and Joni E. Finney. *Designing State Higher Education Systems for a New Century.* Phoenix, AZ: American Council on Education and Oryx Press, 1999.

Richardson, Richard C., and Mario Martinez. *Policy and Performance in American Higher Education: An Examination of Cases across State Systems.* Baltimore: Johns Hopkins University Press, 2009.

Russell, Alene. "Update on the Community College Baccalaureate: Evolving Trends and Issues." In *Policy Matters: A Higher Education Policy Brief* (October 2010). Washington, DC: American Association of State Colleges and Universities.

Salmi, Jamil, and Roberta Malee Bassett. "Opportunities for All? The Equity Challenge in Tertiary Education." Paper presented at the Salzburg Global Seminar, Salzburg, Austria, October 2012.

Schneider, Mark, and Lu Michelle Yin. *The High Cost of Low Graduation Rates: How Much Does Dropping Out of College Really Cost?* Washington, DC: American Institutes for Research, 2011. www.air.org/files/AIR_High_Cost_of_Low_Graduation_Aug2011.pdf.

Schultz, Theodore W. "Investment in Human Capital," *American Economic Review* 51 (1961): 1–17.

Shapiro, Doug, Afet Dundar, Jin Chen, Mary Ziskin, Eunkyoung Park, Vasti Torres, and Yi-Chen Chiang. "Completing College: A National View of Student Attainment Rates." Bloomington, IN: Project on Academic Success and Indiana University and National Student Clearinghouse Research Center, November 2012.

———. "Completing College: A State-Level View of Student Attainment Rates." Washington, DC: National Student Clearinghouse Research Center. www.studentclearinghouse.info/signature/4state.

Shulock, Nancy, and Davis Jenkins. *Performance Incentives to Improve Community College Completion: Learning from Washington State's Student Achievement Initiative.* New York: Community College Research Center, 2011.

Snell, R. *Annual and Biennial Budgeting: The Experience of State Governments.* Washington, DC: National Conference of State Legislatures, 2011. www.ncsl.org/default.aspx?tabid=12658.

Southern Regional Education Board. *Clearing Paths to College Degrees: Transfer Policies in SREB States.* Atlanta, GA: 2007.

———. *Governors' Legislative and Budget Proposals.* Atlanta, GA: 2011. http://publications.sreb.org/2011/11S03_Leg_Rep_2.pdf.

———. *Legislative Report.* Report No. 4. Atlanta, GA: March 2011. http://publications.sreb.org/2011/11S05_Leg_Rep_4.pdf.

———. *State College and Career Readiness Initiative: Final Progress Reports.* Atlanta, GA: August 2011.

St. Mary's College of Maryland. *Fiscal Year 2010 Budget Testimony.* www.smcm.edu/govtrelations/pdfs/FY2010BudgetTestimony.pdf.

State Higher Education Executive Officers. "All States Wave Chart." Boulder, CO: 2012. www.sheeo.org/sites/default/files/publications/SHEF_All_States_Wavechart_2012.pdf.

———. *Certificate Production and the Race toward Higher Degree Attainment.* Boulder, CO: 2010.

———. *State Higher Education Finance, FY 2012.* Boulder, CO: 2013.

State of Georgia. "Engrossed Second Substitute Senate Bill 5182." Chapter 11, Laws of 2011, Aug. 24, 2011. http://apps.leg.wa.gov/documents/billdocs/2011-12/Pdf/Bills/Session%20Laws/Senate/5182-S2.SL.pdf.

———. "Engrossed Substitute House Bill 1244." Chapter 564, Laws of 2009, May 19, 2009. http://apps.leg.wa.gov/documents/billdocs/2009-10/Pdf/Bills/House%20Bills/1244-S.E.pdf.

———. "Engrossed Substitute House Bill 1244." Chapter 564, Laws of 2009, Operating Budget, May 20, 2009.

———. *The Governor's Budget Report, Amended Fiscal Year 2011.* Atlanta, GA: Governor's Office, 2011.

———. "Senate Bill 5774: An Act Relating to Consolidation of Cascadia Community College and Lake Washington Technical College." 62nd Legislature, 2011 regular session.

———. "Substitute House Bill 1128." Chapter 522, Laws of 2007, May 15, 2007. http://

apps.leg.wa.gov/documents/billdocs/2007-08/Pdf/Bills/House%20Passed%20Legislature/1128-S.PL.pdf.

———. *Tough Choices or Tough Times*. Atlanta, GA: Governor's Office, 2008. www.gaosa.org/toughtimes.aspx.

State of Washington. Office of Financial Management. Office of the Governor. *Proposed 2012 Supplemental Budget Highlights*. Olympia, WA. www.ofm.wa.gov/budget12/highlights/highlights.pdf.

———. *Washington State Budget Process*. Olympia, WA: 2011. www.ofm.wa.gov/reports/budgetprocess.pdf.

Steurle, Eugene, Signe-Mary McKernan, Caroline Ratcliffe, and Sisi Zhang. *Lost Generations? Wealth Building among Americans*. Washington, DC: Urban Institute, March 2013.

Stiglitz, Joseph E. *The Price of Inequality: How Today's Divided Society Endangers Our Future*. New York: W.W. Norton, 2012.

Tax Policy Center of the Urban Institute and Brookings Institution. *Tax Facts*. www.taxpolicycenter.org/taxfacts/displayafact.cfm?DocID=494&Topic2id=90&Topic3id=91.

Technical College System of Georgia, *2008 Annual Report*. Atlanta: 2009. www.tcsg.edu/all_documents/2009_Directory%28web%29.pdf.

———. *2009–2010 Fact Sheet and College Directory*, Atlanta: 2010.

Texas Association of Business. "Education and Workforce." Austin, TX: 2011. www.txbiz.org/issues/education_and_workforce.

Texas Association of Community Colleges. *Spring 2011 Tuition and Fees: Texas Public Community Colleges*. Austin, TX: 2011. www.tacc.org/documents/Sp11tuition_000.pdf.

Texas Education Agency. *2009–10 State Performance Report*. 2011. http://ritter.tea.state.tx.us/perfreport/aeis/2010/state.html.

———. "Early College High School." 2011. www.tea.state.tx.us/index3.aspx?id=4464.

———. "End-of-Course Assessment Plan College Readiness and Advanced-Course Readiness." www.tea.state.tx.us/student.assessment/eoc/AssessmentPlan.pdf.

———. "End-of-Course (EOC) Assessments." 2011. www.tea.state.tx.us/student.assessment/eoc.

———. "Enrollment in Public School, 2010–2011," tables 9 and 11.

———. "P–16 Council." 2011. www.tea.state.tx.us/index3.aspx?id=4767.

———. "Secondary School Completion and Dropouts in Texas Public Schools 2009–10." Austin, TX: Division of Accountability Research, Department of Assessment, Accountability and Data Quality. www.tea.state.tx.us/acctres/DropComp_2009-10.pdf.

———. "Student Graduate Reports." 2011. http://ritter.tea.state.tx.us/adhocrpt/adstg.html.

Texas Higher Education Coordinating Board. *Accountability System History*. Austin, TX: 2004. www.txhighereddata.org/Interactive/Accountability/accountability-history.docx.

———. *Closing the Gaps: Goals and Target Summaries*. Austin, TX: 2006. www.thecb.state.tx.us/reports/PDF/1724.PDF?CFID=15740677&CFTOKEN=94113072.

———. *Closing the Gaps Progress Report 2010*. Austin, TX: 2010. www.thecb.state.tx.us/reports/PDF/2045.PDF?CFID=15740677&CFTOKEN=94113072.

———. *Closing the Gaps: The Texas Higher Education Plan*. Austin, TX: 2000. www.thecb.state.tx.us/reports/PDF/0379.PDF?CFID=25046458&CFTOKEN=64560304.

———. "Dual Credit Overview." 2011. www.thecb.state.tx.us/download.cfm?download

file=037484CD-A613-8B1E-3AFD8EC2E8CC4D56&typename=dmFile&fieldname=filename.

———. *The Feasibility of Expanding Texas' Community College Baccalaureate Programs.* Austin, TX: 2010.

———. "Financial Aid in Texas Overview." 2010. www.thecb.state.tx.us/reports/pdf/1552.pdf.

———. "Higher Education Accountability System." www.txhighereddata.org/Interactive/Accountability/UNIV_Success.cfm?FICE=445566&CFID=42864612&CFTOKEN=34258241.

———. *House (Enrolled), Senate (Enrolled) and Conference Committee Report on HB 1 Compared to 2010–11 Base.* Austin, TX: 2011. www.thecb.state.tx.us/download.cfm?downloadfile=31E4E484-B55A-CE94-454A2AC7C4855000&typename=dmFile&fieldname=filename.

———. *An Overview of Article III House Bill 1, 80th Texas Legislature, General Appropriations Act, agencies of public higher education.* April 2008. www.thecb.state.tx.us/index.cfm?objectid=503AE0CA-E26B-77E7-989C9C76FB7AC934.

———. "Overview: Texas College and Career Readiness Standards. Austin, TX: 2009. www.thecb.state.tx.us/reports/PDF/1513.PDF?CFID=12248181&CFTOKEN=59932212.

———. "P–16 Texas." 2011. www.p16texas.org/index.cfm?objectid=22901A11-EA09-4EDB-6513705565A2A93B.

———. "Residency and In-State Tuition." 2011. www.thecb.state.tx.us/reports/PDF/1528.pdf.

———. *Sources and Uses of Funds: Universities, Health-Related Institutions, Lamar State Colleges and Texas State Technical Colleges, FY 2010.* Austin, TX: 2011. www.thecb.state.tx.us/reports/PDF/2106.pdf.

———. *Strategic Plan for Texas Public Community Colleges, 2009–2013.* Austin, TX: 2008. www.thecb.state.tx.us/reports/PDF/1581.PDF?CFID=11740735&CFTOKEN=44734399.

———. "Texas Course Redesign Project." 2011. www.thecb.state.tx.us/index.cfm?ObjectID=13ABB072-E2BC-CB37-6F66D82A6A528BED.

———. "Texas Educational Opportunity Grant." 2010. www.thecb.state.tx.us/index.cfm?objectid=7D014C29-BE66-0063-3E7B104B8BC5DF3E.

———. "TEXAS Grant Overview." 2010. www.thecb.state.tx.us/index.cfm?objectid=7D014C29-BE66-0063-3E7B104B8BC5DF3E.

———. "Texas Higher Education Coordinating Board Releases 2011 Texas Public Higher Education Almanac." News release. April 14, 2011. www.thecb.state.tx.us/index.cfm?objectid=26AEABDA-D2CC-4D37-5AB48345339DFCE1.

———. "Texas Research Incentive Program, 2009." 2011. http://info.sos.state.tx.us/pls/pub/readtac$ext.TacPage?sl=R&app=9&p_dir=&p_rloc=&p_tloc=&p_ploc=&pg=1&p_tac=&ti=19&pt=1&ch=15&rl=10.

———. "Tuition Deregulation Overview." 2011. www.thecb.state.tx.us/Reports/PDF/2010.pdf.

———. "Tuition Set-asides." House Bill 3015, 78th Texas Legislature. 2011. www.thecb.state.tx.us/download.cfm?downloadfile=0367B5CF-0F3B-89E2-0759EB2B190A3757&typename=dmFile&fieldname=filename.

———. "University Funding for Excellence in Specific Programs and Fields." 2011. www.thecb.state.tx.us/index.cfm?objectid=3AEE7B8C-C9A0-F730-737CF4D01A404487#University%20Funding%20for%20Excellence%20in%20Specific%20Programs%20and%20Fields.

Texas P–16 Public Education Information Resource. "About us." 2013. www.texaseducationinfo.org/tea.tpeir.web/aboutus.aspx.

Texas State Legislature. "Texas Legislature Online: History," 82nd session, SB 28. 2011. www.legis.state.tx.us/BillLookup/History.aspx?LegSess=82R&Bill=SB28.

———. "Texas Legislature Online: Legislative Session 77(R), History for HB 1144." 2011. www.legis.state.tx.us/BillLookup/History.aspx?LegSess=77R&Bill=HB1144.

Texas State Senate. "Permanent University Fund (PUF) and Higher Education Assistance Fund (HEAF) Overview." 2011. www.senate.state.tx.us/75r/senate/commit/c535/20080625/062508_THECB_HEAF_PUF_Overview.pdf.

Thompson, S. C. "Behind the Eight Ball: Illinois Resorts to Budgetary Sleight-of-Hand and One-Time Fixes to Maintain Higher Education Funding." *National CrossTalk* 17, no. 2 (2009). www.highereducation.org/crosstalk/ct1209/news1209-illinois. html.

Tierney, William G., and Guilbert C. Hentschke. *New Players, Different Game: Understanding the Rise of For-Profit Colleges and Universities.* Baltimore: Johns Hopkins University Press, 2007.

U.S. Bureau of Economic Analysis. "Local Area Personal Income, 1969–2008." Washington, DC: 2010. www.bea.gov/regional/reis/default.cfm?selTable=CA1–3§ion=2.

———. "Personal Income and Per Capita Personal Income by State and Region, 2006–2010." Washington, DC: 2010. www.bea.gov/newsreleases/regional/spi/spi_newsrelease.html.

U.S. Census Bureau. "ACS Demographic and Housing Estimates: 2005–2009."

———. "Baltimore City, Maryland: Selected Social Characteristics in the United States: 2005–2009." 2011. http://factfinder2.census.gov/faces/tableservices/jsf/pages/productview.xhtml?pid=ACS_09_5YR_DP5YR2&prodType=table.

———. "Baltimore City, Maryland QuickFacts." 2011. http://quickfacts.census.gov/qfd/states/24/24510.html.

———. "Chicago City, Illinois: Selected Economic Characteristics: 2005–2009." 2011. http://factfinder.census.gov/servlet/ADPTable?_bm=y&-qr_name=ACS_2009_5YR_G00_DP5YR3&-geo_id=16000US1714000&-ds_name=&-_lang=en&-redoLog=false.

———. "City and Town Totals: Vintage 2011." *All Incorporated Places: 2010 to 2011.* www.census.gov/popest/data/cities/totals/2011/index.html.

———. "Hispanic or Latino Origin by Race." American Community Survey, Social explorer tables, 2007–2011 5-year estimates. Washington, DC: 2013.

———. "Maryland: Selected Social Characteristics in the United States: 2005–2009." 2011. http://factfinder2.census.gov/faces/tableservices/jsf/pages/productview.xhtml?pid=ACS_09_5YR_DP5YR2&prodType=table.

———. "State & County QuickFacts." 2011. http://quickfacts.census.gov/qfd/states/24000.html.

———. "Table 20: Large Metropolitan Statistical Areas—Population." In *The 2012 Statistical Abstract.* 2011. www.census.gov/compendia/statab/cats/population/estimates_and_projections—states_metropolitan_areas_cities.html.

———. "Table B1: The total population by selected age groups." Summary Tables of Projections. Washington, DC: 2005. www.census.gov/population/projections/data/state/projectionsagesex.html.

———. "Table C03002: Hispanic or Latino Origin by Race—Universe, Total Population." Data set: 2009 American Community Survey. Washington, DC: 2010. http://factfinder.census.gov.

———. "Table C15002: Sex by Educational Attainment for the Population 25 Years and Over—2009." American Community Survey. Washington, DC: 2010. http://factfinder2.census.gov/faces/tableservices/jsf/pages/productview.xhtml?pid=ACS_09_1YR_C15002&prodType=table.

———. "Table SF1:P5: Hispanic or Latino Origin by Race." Summary file 1, Social explorer tables. Washington, DC: 2010.

———. *United States: ACS Demographic and Housing Estimates: 2005–2009*. 2011. http://factfinder.census.gov/servlet/ADPTable?_bm=y&-qr_name=ACS_2009_5YR_G00_DP5YR5&-geo_id=01000US&-ds_name=ACS_2009_5YR_G00_&-_lang=en&-_caller=geoselect&-redoLog=false&-format=.

U.S. Department of Education. *Leveraging Educational Assistance Partnership (LEAP) Program: Funding Status*. 2013. www2.ed.gov/programs/leap/funding.html.

University of Maryland University College. *Fiscal Year 2010 Fact Book*. www.umuc.edu/visitors/about/ipra/upload/UMUCFY10FactBook.pdf.

University of Washington. *Transfer Admission and Planning*. Seattle, WA: Office of Admissions, 2011–12. http://admit.washington.edu/files/PDFs/TAP_2010-2011.pdf.

University System of Georgia. "Chancellor's State of the System Address 2010." www.usg.edu/chancellor/speeches/chancellors_state_of_the_system_address_2010/.

———. *Formula Funding in Georgia: Present and Future*. 2005. http://turing.gcsu.edu/~aaccd/Formula%20Presentation_Revised%20Jo.pdf.

———. "General Education in the University System of Georgia." 2008. www.usg.edu/academic_programs/information/transferring_core_curriculum_credit_-_faq.

———. *Keeping the HOPE Scholarship throughout College: The Status of Fall 2003 First-time Freshmen Six Years Later*. Atlanta, GA: USG, 2009.

———. "Number of Pell Grant Recipients: Fall 2008." 2009. www.usg.edu/research/documents/finaid/pell_ftf_fall_08.pdf.

———. "Regents Approve 17 General Education Courses for Transfer to Support Complete College Goals." News release, March 14, 2012. www.usg.edu/news/release/regents_approve_17_general_education_courses_for_transfer_to_support_comple.

———. "Regents Approve Campus Consolidation Plan." January 24, 2012. www.usg.edu/system_supplement/regents_approve_campus_consolidation_plan.

———. "Regents Take Action to Help Students Transfer College Credits." News release, June 7, 2011. www.usg.edu/news/release/regents_take_action_to_help_students_transfer_college_credits.

———. *Strategic Plan, FY 2009*.

———. *USG Facts*. www.usg.edu/news/usgfacts.

———. "USG Institutions by Group." 2011. www.usg.edu/inst/group.

———. "USG Tuition Strategy." www.usg.edu/student_affairs/high_school/tuition_and_financial_aid/usg_tuition_strategy.

University System of Maryland. *2009 USM Managing for Results Accountability Report.* College Park, MD: 2009. www.usmd.edu/usm/adminfinance/accountability.

———. *Powering Maryland Forward: USM's 2020 Plan for More Degrees, a Stronger Innovation Economy, a Higher Quality of Life.* College Park, MD: 2010. www.usmd.edu/10yrplan/index.html.

University System of Maryland Board of Regents. "III-4.00 Policy on Undergraduate Admissions." In *USM Bylaws, Policies and Procedures of the Board of Regents.* Adelphi, MD: 2011.

Van de Water, S. *Meeting Maryland's Postsecondary Challenges: A Model to Guide Maryland's Public Investments in Postsecondary Education in the Coming Decades.* Report prepared for the Maryland Higher Education Commission, 2006. www.vandewaterconsulting.org.

Van Der Slik, J. R. "Reconsidering the Restructure of Higher Education." *Illinois Issues* 36, no. 9 (September 2010): 27.

Vedder, Richard. "Why College Isn't for Everyone." *Bloomberg Business Week*, April 9, 2012. www.businessweek.com/articles/2012-04-09/why-college-isnt-for-everyone.

Venezia, Andrea, Patrick M. Callan, Michael Kirst, and Michael Usdan. *The Governance Divide: The Case Study for Georgia.* San Jose, CA: National Center for Public Policy and Higher Education, 2006.

Venezia, Andrea, Joni E. Finney, Michael W. Kirst, and Michael D. Usdan. *The Governance Divide: A Report on a Four-State Study on Improving College Readiness and Success.* San Jose, CA: The Institute for Educational Leadership, National Center for Public Policy and Higher Education, and The Stanford Institute for Higher Education Research, 2005.

Venezia, Andrea, Michael W. Kirst, and Anthony L. Antonio. *Betraying the College Dream: How Disconnected K–12 and Postsecondary Education Systems Undermine Student Aspirations.* Stanford, CA: The Bridge Project, 2003.

Villa-Komaroff, L., M. Brenner, E. Cota-Robles, and C. Maziar. *Evaluation of the Illinois State Matching Grant Program for fiscal year 2000: Executive Summary.* 2002. Unpublished report: Northwestern University, Evanston, IL.

Washington Higher Education Coordinating Board. *2008 Strategic Master Plan for Higher Education in Washington: Moving the Blue Arrow Pathways to Educational Opportunity.* Olympia, WA: 2008. www.wsac.wa.gov/sites/default/files/2008MasterPlan-fromPRT.pdf.

———. *2011–2013 Higher Education Budget.* Olympia, WA: 2011. www.wsac.wa.gov/sites/default/files/TAB3.2011-13HigherEdBudget-final_0.pdf.

———. *2011 Transfer Report.* Olympia, WA: 2011. www.hecb.wa.gov/sites/default/files/TransferReport2011.pdf.

———. *Designing for the 21st Century: Expanding Higher Education Opportunity in Washington.* Olympia, WA: 1990. www.wsac.wa.gov/sites/default/files/1990MP7-1990.pdf.

———. *Keeping College Affordable: Annual Report on Student Financial Aid Programs.* Olympia, WA: 2011.

———. *Key Facts about Higher Education in Washington 2010.* Olympia, WA: 2010. www.wsac.wa.gov/sites/default/files/KeyFacts2009-10.pdf.

———. *Key Facts about Higher Education in Washington 2011*. Olympia, WA: 2011. www.wsac.wa.gov/KeyFacts2011.

———. *Minimum College Admissions Standards: College Academic Distribution Requirements—Guidelines for Educators*. Olympia, WA: 2009. http://olympia.osd.wednet.edu/media/olympia/ccenter/college_and_career_plan/college/revisedmcascadrguidelines-booklet-cs-1.pdf.

———. *Minimum College Admissions Standards for Students Entering College or University Summer or Fall 2012*. Olympia, WA: 2010. www.wsac.wa.gov/sites/default/files/MCASMarch2011Revised.pdf.

———. *Policy on Intercollege Transfer and Articulation among Washington Public Colleges and Universities*. Olympia, WA: 1986. www.wsac.wa.gov/sites/default/files/PolicyonIntercollegeTransferandArticulation-UmbrellaPolicy1986.pdf.

———. *Regional Needs Analysis Report 2011*. Olympia, WA: 2011. www.wsac.wa.gov/sites/default/files/RegNeedsAnalysis-Binder.pdf.

———. *The System Design Plan: A Statewide Plan for Moving the Blue Arrow*, 2009. www.hecb.wa.gov/research/issues/documents/ReportSystemDesign-FINAL2010.pdf.

Washington Learns. *Washington Learns, 2005 Interim Report*. www.washingtonlearns.wa.gov/report/Interim2005_report.pdf.

———. *Washington Learns: World-class, Learner-focused, Seamless Education*. Olympia, WA: 2006. www.washingtonlearns.wa.gov/report/FinalReport.pdf.

Washington Office of the Governor. *Higher Education Funding Task Force*. 2013. www.psrc.org/assets/5470/HETF-Proposal.pdf.

———. "Higher Education Funding Task Force: Accountability and Performance." Unpublished manuscript. 2010.

———. "Higher Education Funding Task Force: Finance." Unpublished manuscript. 2010.

Washington State Board for Community and Technical Colleges. *Academic Year Report: 2009–10*. Olympia, WA: 2010. www.sbctc.ctc.edu/college/studentsvcs/4prog_0910.3.pdf.

———. *I-BEST: A Program Integrating Adult Basic Education Workforce Training*. Olympia, WA: 2005. www.sbctc.ctc.edu/docs/data/research_reports/resh_05–2_i-best.pdf.

———. *Running Start: 2009–10 Annual Progress Report*. Olympia, WA: 2011. www.sbctc.ctc.edu/college/_d-high-school-reports.aspx.

———. *Student Achievement Initiative*. Olympia, WA: 2010. www.sbctc.edu/college/education/student_achieve_summary_nov2010.pdf.

———. *Student Progress and Success*. Olympia, WA: 2011. www.sbctc.edu/college/studentsvcs/4prog_0910.3.pdf.

Washington State Board of Education. "Washington State Board of Education Resolution to Approve Washington State Graduation Requirements: Career and College Ready." Olympia, WA: 2010. www.sbe.wa.gov/documents/2010.11.10%20Grad%20Req%20Resolution.pdf.

Washington State Budget and Policy Center. "Undermining Prosperity: Higher Education Cuts Weaken Access, Affordability, and Quality." *Sound Research, Bold Solutions*. Policy brief. 2011. http://budgetandpolicy.org/reports/undermining-prosperity-higher-education-cuts-weaken-access-affordability-and-quality/pdf_version.

Washington State House of Representatives. "Final Bill Report, E2SHB 1795." http://apps.leg.wa.gov/documents/billdocs/2011-12/Pdf/Bill%20Reports/House/1795-S2.E%20HBR%20FBR%2011%20E1.pdf.

Washington State Legislature. "Definitions, 26B.76.020." Revised Code of Washington, Chapter 28B.76, Office of Student Financial Assistance (formerly Higher Education Coordinating Board). http://apps.leg.wa.gov/rcw/default.aspx?cite=28B.76&full=true.

———. "Legislative Budget Notes." 2010. http://leap.leg.wa.gov/leap/budget/lbns/2010he.pdf.

Washington Student Achievement Council. "About the Council." 2013. www.wsac.wa.gov/AboutTheCouncil.

Washington Workforce Training and Education Coordinating Board. *High Skills, High Wages*. Olympia, WA: 2009. www.wtb.wa.gov/Activities_HighSkills.asp, 24–25.

Western Interstate Higher Education Commission. *Knocking at the College Door, Projections of High School Graduates*. Boulder, CO: 2012. http://wiche.edu/knocking-8th.

Yin, Robert K. *Applications of Case Study Research*, 2nd edition. Applied Social Research Methods Series, Vol. 34. Thousand Oaks, CA: Sage Publications, 2003.

———. *Case Study Research: Design and Methods*, 3rd edition. Applied Social Research Methods Series, Vol. 5. Thousand Oaks, CA: Sage Publications, 2003.

Zumeta, William. "Does the U.S. Need More College Graduates to Remain a World-Class Economic Power?" Paper prepared for National Discussion and Debate Series, Miller Center of Public Affairs, University of Virginia, 2010.

———. "Public Higher Education in Washington State: Aspirations Are Misaligned with Fiscal Structure and Politics." In *What's Happening to Public Higher Education?* edited by R. G. Ehrenberg, 275–303. Baltimore: Johns Hopkins University Press, 2006.

———. "State Policies and Private Higher Education: Policies, Correlates and Linkages." *Journal of Higher Education* 63 (1992): 363–417.

Zumeta, William, David W. Breneman, Patrick M. Callan, and Joni E. Finney. *Financing American Higher Education in the Era of Globalization*. Cambridge, MA: Harvard Education Press, 2012.

Index

About the Authors

Laura W. Perna is the director of the Alliance for Higher Education and Democracy (AHEAD) and a professor in the Graduate School of Education at the University of Pennsylvania and is editor and co-author of several books, including *Preparing Today's Students for Tomorrows Jobs in Metropolitan America: The Policy, Practice, and Research Issues* and *The State of College Access and Completion: Improving College Success for Students from Underrepresented Groups.*

Joni E. Finney is a practice professor of education and the director of the Institute for Research on Higher Education (IRHE) at the University of Pennsylvania. She was the principal author of *Measuring Up*, the first state report cards for higher education, and is co-author or editor of several books, including *Financing American Higher Education in the Era of Globalization.*

Michael Armijo is a doctoral candidate and an Institute of Education Sciences Predoctoral Fellow in the Graduate School of Education at the University of Pennsylvania.

Awilda Rodriguez is a Research Fellow at the American Enterprise Institute Center on Higher Education Reform.

Jamey Rorison is a doctoral candidate and an Institute of Education Sciences Predoctoral Fellow in the Graduate School of Education at the University of Pennsylvania.